Trade Unions
in Communist States

Trade Unions
in Communist States

Edited by

Alex Pravda and Blair A. Ruble

Boston
ALLEN & UNWIN, INC.
London   **Sydney**

Allen & Unwin, Inc.,
8 Winchester Place, Winchester, Mass. 01890, USA

Allen & Unwin (Publishers) Ltd,
40 Museum Street, London WC1A 1LU, UK

Allen & Unwin (Publishers) Ltd,
Park Lane, Hemel Hempstead, Herts HP2 4TE, UK

Allen & Unwin (Australia) Ltd,
8 Napier Street, North Sydney, NSW 2060, Australia

First published in 1986

Library of Congress Cataloging-in-Publication Data
Main entry under title:

Trade unions in communist states.

  Includes index.
  1. Trade-unions and communism—Case studies.
2. Trade-unions—Communist countries—Case studies.
I. Pravda, Alex, 1947–   II. Ruble, Blair A.,
1949–
HX544.T68   1986   322'.2'091717   85–30717
ISBN 0–04–331108–3 (alk. paper)

British Library Cataloguing in Publication Data

Trade unions in communist states.

1. Trade-unions—Communist countries.
2. Trade unions and communism.
I. Pravda, Alex.   II. Ruble, Blair A.
331.88'09171'7   HX544

ISBN 0–04–331108–3

To Imogen and Sally

Contents

Preface

Comparative surveys of trade unionism scarcely take account of unions in communist states, treating them as insignificant and idiosyncratic organizations that have nothing in common with their Western namesakes. Such a position ignores the potential importance of the unions which, after all, remain the largest organizations in communist states. While not seeking to advance extravagant claims for such unions as institutions of first-rank importance, we feel that they deserve closer and more systematic study than they have received to date on at least three counts.

In the first place, the very great differences separating communist from capitalist unions should not preclude comparison. While communist unions clearly mobilize rather than defend labor they still have a notional dual role of protecting the interests of their members and promoting those of production. Inherent in this dualism are elements of the role many unions are called upon to play in Western socialist polities. Moreover, some of the welfare and protectionist functions which communist unions perform bear comparison with those carried out by their Western namesakes.

A second and perhaps more important reason for paying closer attention to communist unions is that they are far from uniform; indeed, they differ significantly. Behind apparent organizational uniformity lies a surprisingly wide variation in operation, style, and performance. How union officers respond to shop-floor demands, whether they protect basic rights such as job security, all this varies by enterprise, sector, and most importantly by country. As this volume shows, unions in Romania conform to the worst stereotype of labor mobilization organizations while those in the GDR play a far more effective protectionist and welfare role than is commonly supposed. Less surprisingly, economic, political, and cultural factors make Hungarian, Yugoslav, and Chinese unions particularly distinctive.

Just as there is considerable variation between unions in different communist states, so one finds important shifts over time. The last ten to fifteen years have seen changing conditions undermine the efficacy of traditional mobilizing unions. Dwindling supplies of cheap materials have made higher labor productivity vital, while the growing numbers of educated and less tractable workers have made it more difficult to achieve by mobilization techniques. Managing industrial relations and discontent is fast becoming a major problem for communist states. Solidarity was an extreme example of what can happen if leaders fail to respond in time and to adapt organizations to changing conditions and demands. In the years since Solidarity Communist Party leaders have laid greater emphasis on the need for trade unions to upgrade their representative role and mediate far more effectively between party, management, and labor. The greater prominence given to unions and the likelihood of their developing increasingly in the direction of mediating organizations, albeit still under party control, is the third and last reason for examining them more thoroughly and systematically. This volume attempts to take a first step towards this goal. In form it is a thick sandwich; analytical and comparative chapters enclose a solid corpus of country chapters which contain basic information as well as analysis on particular union movements. The introductory chapter outlines the Leninist model of dual functioning unions, traces its subsequent modifications, discusses its two most important variants, and assesses the factors shaping current union movements. The nine country chapters which follow examine trade unions in a broad range of communist states—the Soviet Union, the GDR, Czechoslovakia, Romania, Poland, Hungary, Yugoslavia, and China—and show how different economic, political, and cultural settings and factors affect union operation, style, and performance. While the editors made no attempt to impose any Procrustean framework on chapters dealing with such a varied range of states, all the contributors have sought to cover basic themes including historical background; institutional arrangements; relations with party and management; union roles; union rights; and performance within the enterprise and at higher levels. The concluding chapter sets communist unionism within a broader comparative context.

Needless to say, in the process of producing this volume we became keenly aware of how much work still needs to be done in this area. We hope that this first effort at a broad-ranging examination of communist trade unions will stimulate further research and help us progress toward a better understanding of the role these organizations play in the industrial relations and politics of communist states.

Alex Pravda
Blair Ruble

Acknowledgments

We would like to take this opportunity to express our gratitude to the Ford Foundation for providing financial support for this project. A subgrant from Ford Foundation funds, administered by the Joint Research and Development Committee of the British Universities Association of Slavists and the British National Association of Soviet and East European Studies, made possible a working conference, held at Park House, University of Reading, June 21– 23, 1983. Organization of the conference was facilitated by financial and institutional support from the Graduate School of European and International Studies at Reading University.

All the chapters in this volume, with one exception, originated as papers presented at the conference. They were revised in the light of incisive and helpful comments from those who acted as discussants. Thanks are due here to George Kolankiewicz, John Sandford, George Schopflin, Janet Schwartz and especially to David Lane and Craig Littler. Particular thanks are due to Craig Littler and Gill Palmer for readily taking on the daunting task of writing a concluding chapter comparing communist with capitalist unions. Finally, our thanks to Marjorie McNamara and the secretarial staff of the Politics Department at the University of Reading for their unstinting assistance.

Alex Pravda
Blair Ruble

1

Communist Trade Unions:
Varieties of Dualism

Alex Pravda
Blair A. Ruble

At first sight communist trade unions appear to be very similar. In structure, organization, and function they all seem to adhere closely to the Leninist model which emerged from the debates on Soviet trade unions in the 1920s. On closer inspection such uniformity gives way to a picture of varying styles and performance. Heirs to different union traditions and operating in a wide range of social, economic, cultural, and political settings, communist unions present an interesting spectrum of variations on the Leninist proto-type. In this chapter we attempt to map the contours of the Leninist model—Classic Dualism, sketch the historical settings in which communist unions have evolved, briefly outline the types of adjustment and reform which have produced variations on the Leninist theme, and finally, consider some of the major factors shaping the development of trade unionism in communist states. Comparisons between communist and non-communist trade union-ism are explored by Craig Littler and Gill Palmer in the last chapter of the book.

Classic Dualism: The Leninist Model of
Dual Functioning Trade Unions

The Leninist doctrine of dual functioning unions emerged from a political compromise struck at the Tenth Soviet Communist Party Congress in 1921 (Kommunisticheskaia partiia, 1963:337−401). Faced with compet-

Alex Pravda, Department of Political Science, Stanford University, Stanford, California 94305.

Blair A. Ruble, Social Science Research Council, 605 Third Avenue, New York, New York 10158.

ing proposals—one subordinating unions to the state, the other placing the economy under union control—Lenin and his supporters successfully pushed through a resolution which accomplished neither objective by seeking to achieve both. Conceding that trade unions in socialist societies should encourage labor productivity, Lenin's Group of Ten accepted that unions should also protect workers from harsh treatment by managers supposedly working for the same economic and political ends. As will be discussed in greater detail in Chapter 2, they thus established a model of trade unionism that reflected the fundamental ambivalence of a system where labor was no longer pitted against capital yet remained under managerial control in an effort to further the economic growth of what was only notionally a worker's state.

Formulated as a temporary compromise appropriate for a transitional stage of socialist development, the Leninist dual functioning model when implemented embodied all the ambivalence of that stage. Institutional practice under Stalin eliminated much of the ambivalence inherent in the dualism of promoting production and protecting labor. While Lenin stressed the need for unions that defended workers' interests precisely because these would continue to differ in some respects from management (Lenin, 1971), Stalin saw no reason for such a defense role in a socialist society that had to combat rather than sustain deviation. The building of a command economy based on strong management and mobilization meant the virtual elimination of any protective role for trade unions. Increasingly Lenin's theoretical balance between production and protection gave way under Stalin to unions with an almost wholly production and labor mobilization orientation. Furthermore, what Lenin envisaged largely as political leadership of unions by the Communist Party changed into total organizational domination by party and state. Thus the Leninist model evolved into a new orthodoxy which we shall call Classic Dualism.

With the coming into power of communist parties throughout Eastern Europe and eventually in China after the end of World War II, all trade unions in those societies were quickly transformed into dual functioning labor organizations closely modeled on their Soviet counterparts (Lowit, 1972: 30−4). In the years following Stalin's death the Soviet Classic Dualism underwent some limited change; the overwhelming functional bias to production was partially redressed and some of the ambivalence of Lenin's original scheme reappeared. Several East European leaders followed Khrushchev in placing greater stress on the need for unions to protect workers' legal rights. State dominance over unions declined but party control remained firm. By and large unions in communist states still conform to the basics of Classic Dualism in as much as they adhere to the guiding principle that trade unions must seek both increased productivity and labor protection, in that order of priorities. And where variations have developed they are best understood as adaptations of the dual functioning model rather than departures from it. Yet, it is precisely such variations, limited though they at first may appear from afar, that will differentiate this particular comparative volume from previous studies focusing exclusively upon the Soviet experience.

Before moving on to explore variations in communist unionism we shall briefly consider union functions, organization, and relations with management, government, and the Communist Party which are characteristic of archetypical Classic Dualism.

One may conceive of the dual role in terms of two sets of functions: the first concerned with the mobilization of labor production, the second, with the protection of members' rights and interests. Under the "production" heading come tasks that amount to union management of labor. These include the maintenance of discipline, the mobilization of members to higher productivity, and their education in the spheres of production, management, and ideology. This educational dimension of the unions' role is summarized in the oft-cited Leninist description of unions as schools of administration, management, and communism. Two interrelated yet distinct functions make up the unions' "protective " role: the guardianship of member's legal rights against managerial arbitrariness; and the defense of labor interests. The notion of dualism implies parity between the two sets of functions, yet production tasks effectively take precedence over those associated with the guardianship function. Inherent within the model is a bias toward labor management and against the defense and representation, let alone promotion, of workers' interests as such interests are understood in the West. Of all the protective functions, guardianship of legal rights possesses by far the greatest legitimacy.

This functional bias stems directly from the concept of interests that underlies Classic Dualism. Since no "antagonistic" social conflicts exist within socialist society, so the theory goes, neither can any fundamental cleavages of interests divide the working population as employees from the state as employer. Short-term differences in priorities and preferences may persist and produce some interest dissonance, yet by definition this is of minor importance (Prokhorov, 1982). Trade unions must help resolve any discord and ensure it does not disturb the overriding harmony of relations between labor, management, party, and government. The unions should seek to blend any discordant individual or group interests with the overall national interest embodied in the policies of party and state. In effect, unions must subordinate the protection of their members' interests to the promotion of party and government policy which, axiomatically in a workers' state, best serves the "true" long-term interests of all trade unionists. This entire theoretical edifice rests, of course, on the assumption that socialist interest consensus already exists.

The notion of unitary socialist interest finds reflection in the two basic organizational tenets on which Classic Dualist trade unions are based: the production principle and the principle of democratic centralism (Iampol'skaia, 1973). According to the production principle, all those employed in a given sector of the economy are eligible for membership in the same union, regardless of whether they are workers or managers. Communist trade unions are thus industrial unions, lacking provision for sections catering to different professional groups. Democratic centralism claims to combine the benefits of democratic discussion in the formulation of policies with the advantages of central control and discipline in execution. In practice democratic centralism sustains a highly centralized system of bureaucratic decision-making and authority in which local union officials are subject to the intertwined hierarchies of industrial union and inter-union bodies (see Table 1.1) Directives and communications generally flow vertically downward, all contact between union locals being channeled through higher bodies. Buttressing this hierarchical structure of power is a system of appointment— the *nomenklatura*—which ensures that all positions are filled by executive selection.

Not only is power within the union movement thus highly centralized, it also becomes subject to outside control by the Communist Party at all levels. Key union positions come within the party, as opposed to trade union, *nomenklatura* and party executives get all important union appointments. This system secures majority presence of communists in all union executives, even within factory committees where party members are typically over-represented by a factor of two or more (Witałec,1978). All communist-unionists form party groups which caucus to make sure that union decisions comply with party policy. After all, unions are conceived as "transmission belts" between party and masses, conveying party policy to labor (and theoretically also sending information from the shop-floor to the party hierarchy) (Sorenson, 1969: 122−3). Thus, trade unions remain closely subordinated to the party yet organizationally distinct from it. This distinction affords a degree of administrative latitude but excludes policy neutrality, let alone union autonomy.

No comparable organizational and policy subordination ties union to government. Notionally, trade unions may formulate policy lines quite independently of government and may criticize government performance. However, the close policy interaction between government and party ensures that all government measures have a party imprimatur that makes them binding upon the unions.

Only at the enterprise level do unions, even in theory, possess anything

Table 1.1
Dual Functioning Union Organization Structure

Level	Inter-Union Agencies	Intra-Union Agencies
National	Central trade union council (presidium) (secretariat)	Branch trade union central committee (presidium) (secretariat)
Republican"	Republican trade union council (presidium) (secretariat)	Branch trade union republican committee (presidium) (secretariat)
Regional	Regional trade union council (presidium) (secretariat)	Branch trade union regional committee (presidium) (secretariat)
City	City trade union council (presidium) (secretariat)	Branch trade union city committee (presidium) (secretariat)
District	District trade union council (presidium)	Branch trade union district committee (presidium)
Enterprise		Enterprise trade union committee (presidium)
Shop		Shop trade union groups and committees

"Found in the federal state systems of the USSR, Czechoslovakia, and Yugoslavia.

approaching autonomy. Close collaboration between management and party officials within the enterprise nonetheless severely limits independent union activity. The influence management exercises over the filling of local union posts further circumscribes union autonomy, a diminution of authority sustained by the fact that most union officers below the union chairman remain off the enterprise payroll.

The restrictions placed on the resources and methods unions may ultimately deploy in carrying out their functions further underscore the subordinate position of trade unions vis-à-vis management, government, and party. Within the enterprise unions seek to achieve their ends through collaboration not confrontation. Where management infringes on members' trade unionists' rights, the unions may protest and refer the matter to high authorities for arbitration. Such managerial use of pressure is seen as illegitimate within the context of socialist industrial relations. Yet, there remains no room here for industrial action, strikes being viewed as symptoms of union failure rather than legitimate union weapons. Differences with management must be settled through amicable negotiation, not by adversarial collective bargaining. Indeed, as the arena for labor—management disagreement is confined to minor specific issues, little scope for such bargaining exists. The same line of reasoning strictly limits union action at the national level. Since there can be no serious policy conflicts with government, let alone party, all differences can be settled by means of consultation. Such consultation involves the union providing government and party officers with information, advice, and consent.

To sum up, Classic Dualism assumes a community of interest within socialist society so broad as to remove the very possibility of systemic industrial conflict, leaving only the most isolated, specific grievances open to debate and dispute. Trade unions "serve" their members' interests by protecting selected rights but chiefly by promoting their involvement in production, thus subordinating any short-term group preferences to the overriding national interest of economic growth. Organized along industrial and democratic centralist lines, unions are strictly subordinated to the Communist Party and obliged to collaborate with government and management. Dual functioning unions, then, may protect workers against specific management abuse; they cannot and may not defend the same union members against official government and party policies that may well be more damaging.

While no national trade union organization precisely conforms to the model of Classic Dualism, most trade unions in communist states remain easily identifiable as dual functioning unions operating within the Classic Dualistic framework. Soviet unions perhaps offer the closest empirical approximation to the model as union traditions and national values are most consonant with the Leninist model; indeed, they helped to mould its contours. Elsewhere, from Prague to Peking, labor traditions and political cultures are less compatible with Classic Dualism and have left distinctive imprints upon trade union movements throughout the communist world. To understand how such national variations on the Classic Dualist model have evolved we must briefly consider the question of historical and cultural context.

National Traditions and Contemporary Union Activity

First, we must take into account the general histories of national prerevolutionary union traditions. The political and organizational frailty of Russian unions, for example, undermined their ability to initiate and chart a distinctive course of action during the collapse of political authority in 1905 and again in 1917 (Deutscher, 1950). Their previous experience of policy surveillance and harassment did little to prepare union organizers for the vicissitudes of industrial negotiations and political struggle in a period of revolutionary upheaval. Indeed, as discussed in Chapter 2, Russia's unions had little independent stature or authority in an environment increasingly dominated by proletarian political parties. Unions invariably subordinated themselves to political authority. Within the Bolshevik Party union leaders played only a very secondary role during and after the revolution. Had the unions' pre-revolutionary record been different, would the subsequent activities of dual functioning Leninist unions also have been different? To what extent have historical and cultural continuities made a difference in the eventual form and function of communist trade unions? To answer such questions requires a comparison of pre- and post-communist patterns of union behavior elsewhere.

Pre-communist union movements in several of the East European states under examination experienced strikingly different political, economic, and even cultural pressure during their development from those experienced by their Russian counterparts. Prior to the rise of Hitler, German unions had long represented a powerful force to be reckoned with in their own right (see Chapter 3). Hungarian, Czechoslovak, and, to a lesser degree, Polish and Yugoslav unions remained active and assertive throughout lengthy periods of the interwar years. Pre-communist unions in these societies differed significantly, then, in national strength and cohesion as well as in their political allegiance. Both size and political affiliation, whether to socialist or to communist parties, influenced their subsequent adaptation to dualism. Yet the directions of that influence appear to be far from straightforward. Large, well-organized union movements aligned as much with social democrats as with communists, or even closer to the former, as was the case in Czechoslovakia and to some extent in Germany, tended to maintain nondualist traditions for a longer period than their smaller and more politically fragmented counterparts in Poland or Hungary. The active role they played in union reform in 1968 suggests that social democratic influences lingered within the Czech trade union movement despite the purges of the early 1950s. The size and political contribution of organized labor to communist victory may also have had some bearing on post-revolutionary developments. One might attribute the relatively egalitarian wage policies followed by East German and Czechoslovak party leaders, especially through the 1950s and 1960s, in large part to the strength of longstanding union and what may be called "laborist" traditions.

The sheer weight of industrial workers within societies also varies markedly among the nations under examination in this volume. Social structure must be considered as an important factor of the laborist tradition shaping adaptation in Classic Dualism. In predominately agrarian societies such as Romania and Bulgaria trade union traditions were clearly weak, and post-revolutionary unions tended to act *inter alia* as agents of modernization and as vehicles for the induction of first-generation workers into industrial production. On the one hand, this role enhanced their production mobilization function, thus strengthening the functional bias of Classic Dualism. On the other hand, problems besetting modernization generated tension between workers and unions. In the end, some hard-pressed unions were even content to incorporate traditional structures of authority such as the gang-boss system in China (Lockett and Littler, 1985). In the more developed societies, however, trade unions have faced fewer problems of industrial mobilization and education. Instead, unionists in such countries as East Germany and Czechoslovakia have been forced to cope with higher expectations of union representation and protection. It is hardly surprising, therefore, that East German union officials place greater emphasis upon their protective functions within the framework of Classic Dualism than do their Soviet or Chinese counterparts. Similarly,the apparent acquiescence of Romanian union officials to their powerlessness in the face of repressive dictatorship may reflect the behavior of pre-communist labor organizations rather than mere adherence to Leninist norms.

In addition to the factors just identified, more general variation in national culture and values has also served to modify further patterns of union behavior across the communist world. Given the absence of possibilities for field research investigating attitudes and values, we can only surmise the possible impact such variables may have had upon union performance. Given that fact, it nonetheless remains apparent that in its willingness to accept the persistence of fundamental societal conflict even in martial law Poland stands in sharp contrast to official Soviet denials of the existence of "antagonistic" relationships in the USSR. Concern among Hungarian officials over the absence of perceived union independence contrasts with the all too apparent disregard of worker sentiment and opinion among Romanian union leaders. Finally, Soviet preoccupation with legalism—as opposed to legality—in labor law regulation and enforcement differs sharply from a near-total absence of written and publicized labor codes in China. In each instance, these differences in public pronouncements and official actions suggest underlying differences in behavior and values which reflect and point up variations in political culture. While it is difficult to assess the weight of such differences, they are significant insofar as they occur despite formal and structural adherence to the Leninist concept of dual functioning trade unionism. Such departures from Classic Dualism model are best clarified through a comparison of contemporary unions not only with their pre-communist predecessors but also with each other.

Similarities and Differences among Communist Unions

Perhaps the first conclusion one reaches in any attempt to compare and contrast trade unions in communist states is that through nearly four decades of development within markedly different cultural and historical national contexts, the Leninist model of Classic Dualism has maintained itself remarkably well. A highly centralized union hierarchy organized around economic sectors operating on the basis of an assumed unity of interest between labor, management, government, and Communist Party typically continues to prevail. Only in Hungary and Yugoslavia have trade unions sustained development along significantly distinctive lines, and even here the departures from Classic Dualism have been partial, and well within the basic principles of dual functioning unions.

Overall, four kinds or levels of adjustment to Classic Dualism have emerged.

1. The first level of fine-tuning in response to national traditions as well as to the changes in social, political, and economic environments we discuss more fully below under the section of this chapter examining "Dynamics." Such adjustment includes partial correction of the heavy functional bias to production, with unions being urged by politicians to protect members' rights more vigorously though still within the strict limits set by national interest priority and party control.

2. A more significant level of modification in trade union organization through change in conduct typically coincides with or follows periods of regime change and popular ferment as in Yugoslavia (1984–1950), in Hungary and Poland (1956–1958), and in Czechoslovakia (1966–1969) (Lowit, 1972: 269, 311). These modifications develop from efforts to defuse tensions by adjusting union structures and operations to take greater account of national tradition, cultural norms, and shop-floor pressure. Usually such change militates in favor of more defensive unionism. Efforts to establish a more balanced relationship between the unions' dual roles may be accompanied by measured decentralization of union structures and some reduction in the intensity of direct administration of party control over union appointments and operations. Nevertheless, there is no attempt to reverse basic subordination of unions to party. The unions remain subordinated generally to the national interest as defined by the party. Since adjustment in each case

departs from pure Classic Dualism without violating the fundamental principles of dual function and subordination to the Communist Party, we label the unionism they produce Culturally Modified Dualism.

3. Modifications resulting from general systemic crises can be propelled far beyond the limits of Classic Dualism. Typically, as in Hungary in 1956 and in Poland in 1956 and 1980–1981, advocates of radical reforms press for defensive, independent, and adversarial trade unionism. They reverse the functional bias of Classic Dualism, placing protection and promotion of membership interests at the head of union priorities. This shift is justified insofar as members' interests are seen as having as much validity as the national interest, indeed, as defining that interest. To defend members' interests effectively, reformers argue, the unions must be independent of employers. Indeed, union organizations must be free to deploy whatever means they see fit in their advocacy of workers' rights, including the strike which they affirm as a basic labor right. Union independence of management frequently extends to independence of government and Communist Party as well. Since such radical reforms break with Classic Dualism and reject the fundamental principles underlying the Leninist model, we group these short-lived union movements under the heading of Adversarial Non-Dualism.

4. Less radical yet longer lasting and therefore perhaps more significant are shifts which combine elements of cultural modification with some of the reforms that lead to distinctive variants of dualism. In Yugoslavia and Hungary union developments of this kind, conditioned by major changes in the political economy, have broken with the notion of unitary interest while adhering to functional dualism and subordination to the Communist Party.

Evolving definitions of the place of group interest in society have led in these two instances to distinct variants of dual functioning unionism. Yugoslav and particularly Hungarian party and union leaders explicitly acknowledge the existence in their societies of a *multiplicity* of competing and even conflicting interests. In Yugoslavia such realism has undoubtedly been promoted by ethnic cleavage; in Hungary it forms part of a more general strategy that sees the recognition of certain conflicts as a necessary preliminary to their resolution. In both cases the party has encouraged union efforts to establish a more even balance between their production and protection roles and to use a wide range of resources to safeguard their members' interests. In Yugoslavia legitimate union resources include industrial action where the circumstances warrant such drastic steps. To preempt conflict, unions are allowed greater leeway in influencing and even challenging employers' decisions. In Hungary this is evident particularly in relation to the national government; in Yugoslavia union influence is more obvious at the enterprise level, where unions are supposed to coordinate action closely with workers' councils. In neither case is there any change in the subordination of trade union to party so that there is no question of union independence or neutrality. As the Hungarian and Yugoslav departures from standard Leninist norms and practices have now been sustained for considerable periods, these variations deserve particular attention in any survey of the differences among communist unions.

Yugoslav and Hungarian Variants

Yugoslav trade unions began to demonstrate greater assertiveness in their participation in managerial decision-making affecting workers almost immediately after the Tito−Stalin split of 1948 (Hunnius, 1973). This tendency toward vigorous union behavior continued as the party and state formulated new institutional arrangements designed to facilitate workers' participation in management, so that the period 1948−1950 may generally be regarded as one of Culturally Modified Dualism in Yugoslav trade union development. Beginning in 1950, the state established a system of workers' councils as the basic component of a general system of worker self-management. Those councils consist of elected representatives of enterprise employees and have become the cornerstone of a more thorough going decentralization of the entire Yugoslav economic and political system enshrined in the 1963 Constitution. Workers' councils, representing Basic Organizations of Associated Labor, quickly assumed broad authority in their relations with factory management, consulting on such important operational issues as performance evaluation standards and investment policy. While general managers and factory directors retained administrative authority over their plants, the workers' councils eventually established operational control over many aspects of personnel policy and procedure. Trade union operations remained largely confined to administering social welfare funds and policies. Concern with sluggish union performance and loss of shop-floor confidence eventually led to further reforms in the unions' structure and role in the 1970s, the role of basic union organizations growing at the cost of national union bureaucracy.

More clearly than before, then, the union role has become defined in terms of guardianship of self-management rights vis-à-vis professional management. At communal and higher administrative levels where workers' councils do not exist, unions seek to coordinate self-management activity and act as political spokesmen for labor. Union may still use industrial action against management where all other means have failed. Strikes are not illegal, though infrequent and very rarely supported by union organizations. But the thrust of the unions' activity now supports worker self-management so that protection becomes possible within a dominant framework of participation. Given that unions remain subordinated to the Yugoslav Communist League, the broad principles of dual functioning unionism continue to be preserved. In this sense the Yugoslav unions should be considered a variant of rather than a departure from, the Leninist model. On the other hand, they operate within a highly decentralized economic system and have ties with powerful workers' councils. Indeed, Bernard Carter sees the role of helping and guiding self-management, even if it is often poorly preformed, and an additional basic function of Yugoslav trade unions (see Chapter 9). Hence we identify trade unionism as if is developing in Yugoslav as Participatory Dualism.

Just as the general environment in which Yugoslav unions operate defines their dualism as participatory, so the development of the Hungarian political economy over the last twenty years has moved trade unions there in a corporatist direction.

Given the broad use made of the term "corporatism," it is worth briefly specifying the type of corporatism we see as relevant in the Hungarian context. Our basic understanding of the concept derives from Schmitter's definition of corporatism as a system of interest intermediation which has, as its primary objective, the achievement of unity of interests that breaks down class divisions by means of a system of "singular, compulsory, noncompetitive, hierarchically ordered and functionally differentiated" sectoral organizations (Schmitter, 1974). Schmitter distinguishes clearly between societal corporatism, which contains relatively autonomous competitive and ideologically varied subunits, and state corporatism, which tends to be associated with centralized, one-party, ideologically exclusive state systems (Schmitter, 1977). Other scholars have explored the relevance of state corporatism of the analysis of established one-party communist systems, particularly that of the Soviet Union (Bunce and Echols, 1980; Bunce, 1983; Ruble, 1983). Yet much work needs to be done to refine the concept in the context of communist politics. Clearly one needs to take particular account of the ways in which the leading role of the Communist Party conditions corporatist relationships. The presence of the party as the dominant agency distinguishes state corporatism in communist systems. One needs also to recognize that communist states may exhibit corporatist traits without being fully fledged corporatist system.

We would argue that the style of government and especially the system of national policymaking and interest intermediation in Hungary for the last twenty years has exhibited features which have a close affinity with state corporatism. These have varied in salience and strength over time, perhaps peaking in the early years of the New Economic Mechanism. As a system, Hungarian corporatism remains based on personal links and conventions rather than on institutionalized procedures. Most important, corporatist arrangements remain dominated by a strong, authoritarian statist agency—

the Communist Party (the Hungarian Socialist Workers' Party). It is the somewhat less directive way, by communist standards, in which it exercises its leading role that creates the scope for corporatist politics. Such qualifications notwithstanding, elements of corporatism have been sufficiently strong in Hungary to color the role and nature of major agencies, notably the trade unions.

Predictably such corporatist elements are less in evidence at local than at regional and national level. Enterprise unions emerge as potential rather than actual corporatist actors.

Within the enterprise, Hungarian unions enjoy considerably more scope for negotiation with management and more extensive veto rights (Weltner, 1970) than do their counterparts in other communist states, with the exception of Yugoslavia. Yet union locals seem to have done little to take advantage of the situation. As István Kemény points out in Chapter 8, bargaining in enterprises is typically undertaken by informal groups of workers operating within a framework of custom and practice. Union officers have generally been timid in using their powers—hence the widespread shop-floor skepticism about the effectiveness of trade unions as representatives of workers' interests. This clearly undermines their effectiveness as intermediary organizations forming part of a state corporatist system.

The situation may be changing, however, given the greater assertiveness of shop stewards recently in advancing union rights (*Nepszava,* January 28, 1984; Noti, 1985: 4–7). Stewards now play a more active part than before in personnel appointments, vetting wage rates, and distributing bonus payments. Such closer involvement in pay and personnel is part of an overall increase in their participatory role in management. Just how this will affect the nature of union activities within the factory is still unclear. In the meantime Hungarian enterprise unionism remains within the bounds of a Culturally Modified Dualism which displays growing participatory features.

At higher administrative levels Hungarian unionism is more distinctive and its nature best captured by the term corporatist dualism.

Branch and national union bodies certainly have greater opportunity that other communist unions, with the possible exception of the Yugoslav, to exercise influence over policy through consultative channels and by taking public stands that differ from those of ministries and central government. The extent to which Hungarian unions have exercised such influence and behaved like corporatist actors at national level has varied. During the early years of the New Economic Mechanism (1968–1974) national union officials adopted stances visibly critical of government policy. Union pressure helped to modify and even reverse measures on such major issues as labor redeployment and income differentials (Toma and Volgyes, 1977: 34–5). With the toning down of economic reform and the onset of recession in the mid-1970s, union assertiveness declined (Pravda, 1983: 255−6). The revival of the reform caused in the early 1980s prompted renewed union criticism of aspects of official policy, especially those seen to fuel inflation (*Magyar Hirlap,* October 6, 1984; Noti, 1985: 12−17).

These shifts in policy stance reflect the close alignment between conservatives in the top union leadership and the party which Kemeny stresses in Chapter 8. Older national leaders—notably Gáspár who has long been effective trade union head and a member of the Politburo—have certainly furthered the interest of conservative union hierarchy rather than of the membership as a whole. However politically motivated their criticism of some of the aspects of economic reform, these leaders do echo the opinions of certain groups of older industrial workers. And when one turns from national to branch union the link between membership interests and leaders' policy positions becomes far closer. What is important for purposes of defining the nature of Hungarian unionism is the very fact that union leaders have repeatedly criticized government measures and exercised some real policy influence through a combination of political deals and consultation at ministry and central executive level. This suggests that Hungarian unions often operate as actors within corporatist system, even if this remains far from firmly established.

The part the unions play here, and indeed the nature of the system itself, depend of course on the way in which the party exercises its leading role. The unions still accept their political subordination to the party; there is no question of union independence. On the other hand, the Hungarian union hierarchy has fewer professional party officials and many more experienced union men than is typically the case in communist unions. And the party has generally afforded the unions greater leeway to voice policy disagreement than is usual in communist states.

All this makes the unions more like members of a corporatist system than the politically powerless labor management adjuncts of Classic Dualism. We therefore identify the Hungarian variant of the Leninist model as emergent Corporatist Dualism.

Dynamics of Development

It is far simpler to map out a typology of communist trade unions than to suggest a framework within which to analyze their dynamics. The following is meant neither as a full etiology of communist unionism nor as an attempt to list all the factors involved in its development; many of these are discussed in the individual chapters of this volume. Rather, we are concerned here with identifying some of the major trends and variables associated with movements away from Classic Dualism toward modification and beyond.

Over the last twenty years, and particularly over the last ten, a number of changes in the environment in which trade unions operate have placed increasing strains on Classic Dualism: changes in the composition of the workforce leading to more demanding memberships, shifts in the economic context shaping labor relations, and a deteriorating economic climate. We will discuss each of these changes separately.

1.   The emergence of a more critical and demanding union membership stems from changes in the social and educational profile of many of the societies under examination in this volume. An overall slowdown in social mobility coincident with the end of large-scale structural change in these societies has resulted in a growing proportion of hereditary workers within the labor force. Since many of these workers aspire to white-collar/ intelligentsia status, their presence on the shop-floor affects trade unions indirectly and directly: indirectly inasmuch as higher expectations increase pressures on management and thereby on the unions control tasks; directly insofar as workers tend to be more critical of union performance. Too much time and energy, the majority of workers in many of these societies contend, is spent on production and labor management; not enough on defending member rights and promoting their interests. In many of the nations under review a general lack of confidence in trade unions as labor organizations seems to stem not so much from perceived union failure to register members' complaints as from their apparent inability to act upon them and influence management and government policy. True, such views of union performance and their proper role have been widespread for decades. Over the last ten to fifteen years, however, they have become more deeply embedded, particularly among strategic groups of skilled, higher-paid workers. Whether these are informal opinion group leaders or members of the union *aktiv*, they effectively control the intensity and pace of labor effort. Therefore, it is significant that they are becoming increasingly critical of Classic Dualism and more interested in defense-oriented unions.

2.   This sharper focus on unions as defensive and representative labor organizations links up with changing labor-management relations within the enterprise. Under traditional command economies, the stranglehold of central authorities over all aspects of enterprise development left very little decision-making in the hands of factory management. This condition afforded markedly limited, if any, scope for formal negotiations within the factory. With the relaxation of this command grip over the last twenty years—slight and fitful though this process has been—management discretion has in-

creased in areas such as pay, conditions, and social welfare. Issues of importance to the shop-floor—payment for special conditions or the distribution of factory social funds—fall within the collective agreements supposedly negotiated between management and union. Since collective agreements are typically agreed to by unions without any negotiation, let alone bargaining, their increased potential focuses rank-and-file criticism on union co-responsibility for poor conditions and pay.

Wider management discretion and union passivity do not automatically produce grass-roots pressure for more adversarial unionism. After all, labor and management may well be able to reach mutual accommodation without institutionalized negotiating machinery. Indeed, the relative stability of industrial relations in these societies has long been due at least in part to extensive informal bargaining between lower management and solidary workgroups. For Classic Dualist unions this makes life easier insofar as it reduces pressure coming from the most vocal and best organized groups in the factory. On the other hand, the operation of informal bargaining further reduces confidence in the unions. From a managerial standpoint informal bargaining is also a mixed blessing. True, the fragmentation and differentiation it produces among workgroups within the labor force makes it easier to divide and control. Yet informal bargaining of this kind can increase tension and is both difficult to control and costly in terms of labor productivity. What is more, the resources available for management use in such informal bargaining have been squeezed by economic developments. In a command economy and under conditions of extensive growth, formal management discretion may be small but its scope for indulgence is considerable. Management frequently tolerates overmanning, slack work pace, absenteeism, and general indiscipline for the sake of good relations which ensure that workers will cooperate in the sudden bursts of activity (i.e. storming) regularly needed to achieve plan targets. So long as quantitative production targets are met, few superiors trouble overmuch about the efficiency with which this is done. With the shift from extensive to intensive stages of economic development, heralded since the 1960s and actively promoted over the last decade, such indulgence has become increasingly expensive. Party and state pronouncements now urge managers to be efficiency-conscious, to extract more and higher-quality production from dwindling resources including labor. Such demands distinguish more sharply between management and labor interests and increase the likelihood of friction between them. As the scope for indulgence narrows so does the room for informal accommodation. The stress on efficiency and the larger formal discretion given to management combine to raise the need for improved formal negotiation between management and institutional representatives of the whole workforce. Faced with constant demands to improve labor productivity, directors have more need of unions that can articulate as well as moderate workers' claims, negotiate on their members' behalf, and make agreements hold. Classic dual functioning unions have neither the personnel nor the popular support and confidence to do any of these things effectively. Hence perhaps the recent attempts in the GDR, Czechoslovakia, Hungary, and even the Soviet Union to enlist small group leaders as shop stewards and thus incorporate informal networks into a stronger institutionalized framework built around more effective, representative trade unions.

Aware of the dangers inherent in encouraging more effective defense and representation of members' interests, the authorities seem to favor steering union activation into participatory channels. Giving unions a larger role in organizing and coordinating worker participation has several potential benefits. It could help to raise the union stock on the shop-floor. It may also stem tendencies toward adversarial unionism by combining more credible unions with maintenance of control. Most generally, moves towards Participatory Dualism, even though the participation involved hardly measures up to Yugoslav standards, may help to assuage the growing calls for a greater labor "voice." The need for labor "voice" is likely to increase as educational levels rise further among a workforce whose "exit" options—absenteeism and changing jobs—are becoming more constrained. In a sense, then, Participatory Dualism may come to function as a substitute for both self-management and more defensive unionism.

3.   Changes in economic climate also affect trade unions as national organizations. Austerity measures, necessitated by falling economic growth, focus the critical attention of politicians on the performance of unions as mediators between labor and regime, as managers of expectations and discontent, and, as all too frequently intransigent guardians of tenure rights. The declining effectiveness of disciplinary sanctions and material incentives lends union mediation and management roles added importance. Responsiveness to shop-floor opinion is fast becoming the key to the successful management of relations between authority and labor. Here again trade unions have a critical part to play. Yet Classic Dualist unions measure up very inadequately to such tasks. Even where they have been able to assert themselves, as with the issue of dismissal in the Soviet Union, union officers frequently appear overbearing and unsophisticated. In the broader context of labor relations, they have proven themselves poor conveyors of information from the shop-floor: accurate reports from stewards are often distorted or blocked at the middle and upper echelons of the union hierarchy. Even the conveyance of official information downwards remains ineffective as the unions' ability to persuade members to accept unpopular measures is severely handicapped by a general lack of credibility. One way to improve unions' credibility and enhance their usefulness as intermediaries between labor and regime is to

boost their image as actors in the national policy arena. Efforts to involve trade unions more prominently in policy-making would take unionism in a corporatist direction.

To sum up, then, social and economic changes are making Classic Dualism less cost-effective for these regimes. The same considerations make more popular and representative unions, mediating between labor on the one hand and state and management on the other, increasingly attractive. In short, there are strong tendencies militating for a move away from Classic Dualism in many of the societies under examination.

Whether such moves get under way and how far they go does not depend solely on such tendencies. It depends also on a complex of additional factors, including the images decision-makers have of union performance; the costs of change; and general political and environmental conditions.

Before party leaders will consider taking action they must be convinced that poor productivity and morale are really serious problems and that their resolution is linked with union performance. This linkage has to become part of the prism through which they view trade union development. Tradition-ally that prism has highlighted union administrative and social policing roles. And these are the roles which many older union officials presumably under-line as strengths when pointing out to politicians the advantages of the status quo. The vested interests and inertial force of the huge trade union apparatus should not be underestimated as obstacles to union reform. Still, the strength of such conservative forces is far from immutable. As younger, better quali-fied officials assume power within the trade union hierarchies, so resistance to change may become less stubborn. Far more important, views are also changing within the party elite. Official recognition that interests differ and may even conflict in developed socialism, long confined to Hungary and Yugoslavia, is emerging within the Soviet Union. So is leaders' awareness of the need to resolve such differences through more effective representative mediating institutions. Gorbachev, for instance, has shown particular con-cern about these issues as well as a keen awareness of the linkage between poor morale and low productivity (Gorbachev, 1984). All this suggests a possible shift in attitudes that could incline party leaders to see the costs of maintaining Classic Dualism as greater than those of change.

The outcome of any such cost-benefit calculation hinges on the kind of changes involved. What is clearly most probable in the immediate term is further fine-tuning and modification of Classic Dualism. Such measures may alleviate some problems at what seems to be low political cost. The higher quality and energy of many East German enterprise union officials in protect-ing members' rights apparently helps to maintain more productive workgroups in the GDR (see Chapter 3). Soviet evidence suggests that better industrial relations depend not just on able union officers but also on responsive management. Improving managers' labor relations skills and recruiting more vigorous, better trained union officers may be ways of enhancing union performance without major institutional reform. Not that such measures offer any security against reform. More vigorous and able trade unionists may well press for greater union powers.

Another way to upgrade the unions' public image at little apparent political cost is to encourage national union leaders publicly to criticize unpopular economic measures. This presumably is the rationale for permitting the official post-Solidarity unions in Poland to object to, and appear to help moderate, large price increases. But while such union "objections" may well start as a cosmetic public relations exercise, they could pave the way to moves in the direction of Corporatist Dualism.

Whether moves away from Classic Dualism go beyond fine-tuning and modification depends not just on the factors outlined but also on economic and political settings. Different variants of unionism emerge under different economic and political circumstances and are driven by different motors of change. The vested interests and inertial force of the huge trade union apparatus should not be underestimated as obstacles to union reform, as can be seen in the often overly jealous protection of job rights in the USSR and elsewhere.

Drives toward Adversarial Non-Dualism have usually come from grass-roots pressure to radicalize modifications proposed by party and union leaders. Campaigns for adversarial unionism tend to come to fruition within the context of broader radical movements that ultimately challenge the whole system of Communist Party rule. By contrast, Corporatist Dualism is typically sponsored from above by union and party officials aware of the need for more effective policymaking and control. Participatory Dualism finds favor among two opinion groups. It attracts the support of union officials, technicians, skilled workers, and those managers, economists and party officials who wish to further economic reform. It is also advocated by those aware of the need for greater shop-floor involvement to improve productivity, yet anxious to curb any tendencies toward a self-management movement with national political ambitions.

Union development in Yugoslavia and Hungary points up two developments as critical in taking change beyond Culturally Modified Dualism: decentralizing and marketizing economic reform, and more flexible and indirect party control and leadership. Both, of course, are important factors in broader processes of change in communist states. They seem to be necessary enabling conditions for significant union change.

Of particular importance in economic reform is the wider discretion possessed by enterprise directors over work conditions as well as the greater commercial pressures under which management has to operate. Market-type pressures reduce the scope for overmanning and general management indulgence. They thus tend to drive a larger wedge between labor and management—as Hungarian export firms have found—and increase the need for effective mediating unions. At the same time, decentralizing reforms tend to produce moves toward self-management. Since politicians generally see self-management as a threat to central control, they seek to constrain such moves by involving unions more closely in guiding and controlling participation at the enterprise level. Union officials favor such moves since self-management undermines their influence. From a party leader's standpoint, a non-Yugoslav version of Participative Dualism (without real self-management) combines more responsive but controllable enterprise unions with the benefits of manageable participation. Recent moves in the USSR, China, Hungary, and even to some extent Romania to upgrade union involvement in enhanced participation frameworks testify to the attraction of Participative Dualism for politicians wishing to see changes at enterprise level.

Economic reform also affects what happens to unionism at national level. The higher income differentials and prices often associated with reform attract criticism from union leaders. How far such union outspokenness goes and what impact it makes on policy, however, hinges on shifts in the way in which the party exercises its leading role. The enabling condition for Corporatist Dualism, for instance, is a shift from direct comprehensive party control over the unions to more indirect steering. Needless to say, this shift does not allow trade unions anything resembling independence. It may afford them greater latitude in selecting their officials and a greater measure of policy influence. Certain issues previously decided unilaterally by the party without any real input from the unions become subjects for real consultation and even negotiation between unions and government with the party sometimes acting as arbiter.

Taken together, the complex of factors we have discussed as shaping the dynamics of unionism points to change, gradual and perhaps uneven, but change nonetheless. The incidence and timing of such change depend on decision-makers recognizing that the growing costs of Classic Dualism outweigh its practical benefits as well as the political expense of implementing change. Ultimately union reform hinges, to use Gustafson's terms (1981), on party leaders deciding that it is worth changing *traditional* structures and methods of control in order to increase *effective* power.

The growing pressures for higher productivity, coupled with changing social conditions and leadership perceptions, make likely an intensified modification of Classic Dualism. We see such developments leading to the spread within communist trade unions of both Participative and Corporatist Dualism in *complementary* fashion. Within enterprises unions will become more involved in participatory bodies, while at higher and especially national levels they will take on a more corporatist role. With this transition from Classic to Participatory and Corporatist Dualism trade unions will come to play a more prominent role in communist states.

References

Bunce, Valerie (1983), "The Political Economy of the Brezhnev Era: The Rise and Fall of Corporatism," *British Journal of Political Science,* vol. 13, pp. 129−58.

Bunce, Valerie, and Echols, John M., III (1980), "Soviet Politics in the Brezhnev Era: 'Pluralism' or 'Corporatism'?," in Donald R. Kelley (ed.), *Soviet Politics in the Brezhnev Era* (New York: Praeger), pp. 1−26.

Deutscher, I. (1950), *Soviet Trade Unions* (New York: Oxford University Press).

Gorbachev, M. S. (1984), "Zhivoe tvorchestvo naroda," *Pravda,* December 11.

Gustafson, T. (1981), *Reform in Soviet Politics. Lessons of Recent Policies on Land and Water* (New York and London: Cambridge University Press).

Hunnius, G. (1973), "Workers' Self Management in Yugoslavia," in G. Hunnius, G. D. Garsov, and J. Case (eds.), *Workers' Control: A Reader on Labor and Social Change* (New York: Vintage Books), pp. 268−321.

Iampol'kaia, Ts. A. (1973), "O sisteme profsoiuzov SSSR," in Ts. A. Iampol'skaia, and A. I. Tsepin (eds.), *Pravovye aspekty deiatel'nosti profsoiuzov SSSR* (Moscow: Nauka), pp. 41−93.

Kommunisticheskaia partiia (1963), Sovetskogo soiuza, *X s" ezd RKP (b): Stenograficheskii otchet* (Moscow: KPSS Partiizdat).

Lenin, V.I. (1971), "The Role and Function of the Trade Unions under New Economic Policy," in V.I. Lenin, *Selected Works in Three Volumes* (London: Lawrence & Wishart), pp. 656−66.

Lockett, M., and Littler, C. (1985), *Industry and Management in China* (London: Heinemann).

Lowit, T. (1972), *Le Syndicalisme de type soviétique* (Paris: A. Colin).

Noti, S. (1985), "The Shifting Position of the Hungarian Trade Unions in the Midst of Social and Economic Reforms" (mimeo paper).

Pravda, A. (1983), "Trade Unions in East European Communist Systems: Toward Corporatism?," *International Political Science Review,* vol. 4 no. 2, pp. 241−60.

Prokhorov, V. (1982), "Profsoiuzy—vliiatel'naia sila nashego obshchestva," *Partiinia zhizn',* no. 14, pp. 27-34.

Ruble, Blair A. (1983), "The Applicability of Corporatist Models to the Study of Soviet Politics: The Case of Trade Unions," *The Carl Beck Papers in Russian and East European Studies* (Pittsburgh, Pa: University of Pittsburgh Russian and East European Studies Program:, p. 35.

Schmitter, P. (1974),"Still the Century of Corporatism?," in F. B. Pike and T. Stritch (eds.), *Social-Political Studies in the Iberian World. The New Corporatism* (Notre Dame, Ind.: Notre Dame University Press), pp. 85−131.

Schmitter, P. (1977), "Models of Interest Intermediation and Models of Societal Change in Western Europe," *Comparative Political Studies,* vol. 10, no. 1, pp. 7−38.

Sorenson, J. B. (1969), *The Life and Death of Soviet Trade Unionism 1917−28* (New York: Atherton Press).

Toma, Pj, and Volgyes, I. (1977), *Politics in Hungary* (San Francisco: Freeman).

Weltner, A. (1970), *Fundamental Traits of Socialist Labour Law* (Budapest: Akedémiai Kiádo).

Witałec, A. (1978), "Organizacja partyjna pomocnikem i inspiratorem związkowego działania," *Przegląd Związkowy,* no. 12, pp. 21−22.

2
Industrial Trade Unions in the USSR

Blair A. Ruble

The summer and autumn of 1917 were the best of times and the worst of times for Russian trade unionism. Freed from the government harassment that had been their lot under the *ancien régime*, independent unions quickly reformed their ranks and reemerged on the scene with significant force for one of the few times since the revolution of 1905. Despite new life and new members, however, the role of the unions in the collapse of political author-ity in 1917—just as in 1905—was marginal at best (Grinevich, 1923; Turin, 1935; Gordon, 1941; Anweiler, 1973). Weakened by years of police surveil-lance and political repression, the unions remained isolated from the main-stream of working-class life. The informal social life of the Russian worker continued to revolve around localized self-help associations such as mutual aid societies and funds (Balabanov, 1925; Dogadov, 1927); the revolutionary political parties dominated proletarian political life. Hindered by unskilled leadership and a paucity of comprehensive policy proposals, the unions remained more a screen for political activism than a power base for political advocacy. Not surprisingly, spontaneously generated worker councils, the soviets, emerged as the central focus of labor politics (Anweiler, 1973; Sirianni, 1982: 11–62).

Yet the unions offered the political parties one resource the soviets could not: nationally oriented institutional structures with rapidly growing memberships. The unions, in short, could quickly mobilize thousands of workers in a given industry (ILO, 1924; Dewar, 1956; Carr, 1966: II, 200–224). Thus the very nature of the union movement in 1917—vast but

Blair A. Ruble, Social Science Research Council, 605 Third Avenue, New York, New York 10158.

amorphous—determined that the unions would be treated seriously by Lenin's government but not on the unions' own terms. The state–union relationship could not be political for one side and economic for the other. The unions under the Bolshevik regime would perforce be subjugated to the power of the Communist Party.

As noted in Chapter 1, the pressure of the civil war and the demands of war-communism only exacerbated a tendency toward union submission to political authority. As the final communist military victory became inevitable, however, remnants of a working-class leadership stemming from informal pre-revolutionary labor organizations came to question the necessity of the harsh labor policies previously justified by the demands of civil war. Increasingly, labor-oriented members of the party began to challenge the prevailing understanding of the role to be played by the unions in the fledgling Soviet state. The emerging Workers' Opposition of A. Shlyapnikov and A. Kollontai demanded that the unions function as something more than simply another arm of the Bolshevik administration. The resulting trade union debate of 1920–1921 ended with the ratification of a new, distinctly Soviet approach to trade unionism, the concept of dual functioning trade unions.

The discussion of the trade union question reached its conclusion at the Tenth Party Congress in March 1921, at which time three contending resolutions concerning the unions were proposed (Kollontai, 1921; Dewar, 1956; KPSS, 1963: 377–401; Kaplan, 1968; Anweiler, 1973: 244–53; Sirianni, 1982: 230–9; Leonova and Savinchenko, 1982). The first, put forth by the Workers' Opposition, emphasized trade union independence from party and state supervision. This proposal entailed a syndicalist arrangement under which the unions would manage major sectors of the economy. Directly contradicting this position, the second proposal, put forth by Leon Trotsky and Nikolai Bukharin, urged the subjugation of the unions to the party and state. According to Trotsky and Bukharin, the unions would continue to manage compulsory labor programs, improve productivity, and enforce labor discipline as they had under war-communism. Finally, a compromise proposition, put forth by Lenin, trade union leader Mikhail Tomsky, and the so-called Group of Ten, offered a solution which foresaw limited union independence within the strict confines of broader party and government policies. This third proposal carried the day, offering, as it did, an alternative to Lenin's opponents on both the left and right without alienating (or truly satisfying) either. Like many political compromises, of course, the proposal lacked internal consistency. Lenin conceded that the unions should help raise productivity but with the proviso that they also guarantee workers' rights against exploitation by management. The two competing elements form the basis of the doctrine of dual functioning trade unionism.

The essential ambiguity of such a theory is a central concern of this chapter, for it is this ambiguity that both defines the position of labor in the USSR and prescribes certain alternative courses to ameliorate it. Industrial unions generally cannot promote higher labor productivity and improve the lot of the laborer at the same time without compromising either or both of these goals. Yet they must try, as a matter of policy, to do both in the Soviet Union.

It is hardly surprising, then, that despite unwavering rhetorical obeisance to the dual functioning principle, the history of Soviet trade unionism has been marked in practice by the selection of policy options and preferences within the context of the concept of dual functioning trade unionism which, at times, favor the production element of that management approach at the expense of worker welfare and, at other times, uphold a more balanced formulation of union obligations. For example, during the 1930s and 1940s Soviet trade union organizations participated in the elimination of collective agreements, arbitration mechanisms, and safety inspectorates while simultaneously endorsing and enforcing harsh criminal sanctions against truancy, a dramatic decrease in worker's real incomes, and the linkage of social welfare payments to job performance (Schwarz, 1952). By contrast, the 1950s witnessed union cooperation with party institutions in efforts to reestablish union authority over factory personnel policies (including the development of plant-level union veto authority over managerial decisions to dismiss workers); while the 1970s were a time of union support for an emergent "human relations" approach to labor relations, stressing the need to increase labor productivity through the creation of a "healthier socio-psychological climate" at the workplace (Shibaev, 1981). The precise nature of such balances among the various elements of dual functioning trade unionism has varied over time so that no single image of trade union activities is satisfactory for the entire Soviet period. Rather, union and party officials have constantly altered labor policies in various ways—large and small—in attempts to resolve the unresolvable tension inherent within the concept of dual functioning trade unionism itself. This reactive process still continues today.

E. H. Carr once observed that the Russian unions' lack of prerevolutionary organization combined with their failure to join the revolutionary movement on their own terms to ensure that trade union survival would be based upon and subordinated to state and party policies. "The organs of the workers," Carr wrote, "and the organs of the workers' state could not go their separate ways" (Carr, 1978). As the discussion thus far suggests, the precise definition of what constitutes "going a separate way" on the union side has changed with time. This chapter will concentrate on the course taken by the Soviet Union's industrial trade unions in most recent times, that of the General Secretaryships of Leonid Brezhnev, Yuri Andropov, and Konstantin Chernenko (that is, largely prior to the elevation of Mikhail Gorbachev as Communist Party General Secretary in March 1985).

Workers' Legitimate Interests, Soviet Style

As already discussed in Chapter 1, the concept of dual functioning trade unionism rests upon the assumption that workers and the workers' state share certain common interests (Prokhorov, 1982). As state policies are, by mutually accepted definition, in the interest of the working class, union leaders can only legitimately oppose those violations of individual rights which might occur. Classical industrial conflict becomes illegitimate, a condition reinforced by a system of centralized economic planning which places a premium upon bureaucratic maneuvering rather than on the rough and tumble conflict and competition of the marketplace. The resulting conceptual framework reduces detrimental managerial actions from a whole "genre" of social problems to the realm of mere isolated and exceptional occurrences. The institutional arena for labor – management discord thus becomes severely constricted.

This definitional trivialization of labor grievances often obscures broad policy concerns which are reflected only obliquely in specific complaints and labor law violations. In the case of female industrial workers one finds that women tend to be segregated by function and by industry (Lapidus, 1979; Moses, 1983). Female-dominated shops, plants, and industries are less frequently recipients of capital investment, just as traditionally female occupations are less well compensated, as a rule, than are male-dominated professions. This discriminatory pattern is not the result of overt state and party favoritism. A Soviet woman working at the same job in the same industry as a man receives the same salary. Rather, the pattern derives from various social and cultural definitions of female roles which seemingly inadvertently but nonetheless effectively reduce employment opportunities for women. To official eyes, no discrimination exists; therefore, women have no grounds for complaint except in specific inequitable circumstances.

In late January 1983 then General Secretary Andropov visited the Moscow Machine Tool Plant (Andropov, 1983b). After a tour of the plant's facilities, the General Secretary addressed a factory meeting. At that meeting T. A. Komarova, a foreman from the factory's decoration shop, observed that men never worked very long in the shop, moving onward as soon as possible, while women stayed behind. This pattern resulted in a permanently female workforce. The shop's workers had an exemplary disciplinary record, some problems with family-connected absenteeism notwithstanding. The work was tedious, relying primarily upon the hand application of lacquer to various tool parts. The shop, therefore, could benefit greatly from automation. Indeed, Komarova indicated that the introduction of some new machines had already increased productivity substantially.

Here was a case in which capital investment and technological innovation could dramatically improve both the shop's productivity record and the working conditions of the shop's employees at the same time. During the entire discussion, however, neither Komarova nor, more to the point, Andropov suggested that there might be broader policy issues at stake beyond the immediate difficulties at the decoration shop of the Moscow Machine Tool Plant.

When such case-specific individuation of industrial shortcomings takes place, the effectiveness of Soviet trade union organizations becomes severely limited. Such practices all but eliminate the need for union officials to communicate with one another concerning managerial indiscretions as every managerial failure becomes, by definition, unique. At that point Soviet trade unions lose their ability to defend the same worker against overarching (and perhaps more deleterious) policies approved by the party and state. Instead they can only protect lone workers against case-specific abuses by individual managers. This phenomenon led East German dissident and former Communist Party member Rudolf Bahro to observe that unions in socialist systems are even more powerless in institutional terms than before socialist political and economic forms were established, as workers are now atomized even within associations which are organized for them rather than by them (Bahro, 1981: 24).

The obverse of the assumed mutuality of interest on the part of the workers and the workers' state is also true; union efforts to support Party and state policies are legitimated. In March 1981, the then AUCCTU Chairman Aleksei Shibaev defined the role of the trade unions in a socialist society for an Communist Party's Central Committee (Shibaev, 1981). Shibaev attacked the notion that trade unions in socialist societies could genuinely fail to acknowledge and support the leadership of the Communist Party. Such ideas were generated, he suggested, by "opponents of socialism" who frequently sought to "free" the unions from Party influence. The proponents of such views, Shibaev continued, did not understand the fundamental differences between the functions of trade unions under capitalism and under socialism. In the former, laborers struggle against monopolies and the power of the bourgeois exploitive state, while in the latter the workers themselves, as owners of the means of production and participants in rational economic planning, are masters of their destiny and captains of their fate.

Shibaev's article represents but one more restatement of the theoretical justifications for union cooperation with management and Party officials in the common efforts to increase labor productivity. The interests of the worker and the workers' state are held to be identical on paper and in reality, even at the mundane level of daily factory life. If workers produce more, they themselves will benefit more. Andropov put this oft-repeated Soviet maxim in particularly stark terms when he told the workers at the Moscow Machine Tool Plant in January 1983 that, "miracles, as it is said, do not happen on earth. You yourselves understand that the state can give only those goods which have been produced" (Andropov, 1983b).

The identification of worker and state interests serves also to justify the principle that the trade unions must be led by the Communist Party, since the Party, as the leading agency of proletarian authority, must coordinate and guide all elements within the socialist state system. In turn, this leadership provides general direction to union policy and activities. As noted in a textbook for Party activists:

> Free from petty tutelage over the relationship of state agencies with economic agencies, free from direct interference in the industrial-managerial responsibilities of those agencies, Party organizations and their senior officials have the ability to concentrate their undivided attention upon those fundamental and principal issues which have a decisive impact upon the development of the economy. (Petrovichev, 1976: 346–7)

To reiterate, dual functioning trade unions assume a community of interest as broad as to remove classic industrial conflict as an issue, frequently leaving only the most isolated and, some might argue the most trivial grievances open for analysis and debate. Moreover, a system of centralized planning reinforces this outlook as it largely precludes relationships between economic partners predicated on conflict. Unions consult with managers and ministers, advise Party and state officials, participate in the centralized planning process, and identify and oppose specific managerial actions; they do not challenge the basic principles and policies of the Soviet state and the Communist Party.

The Union as Bureaucracy

In order to fulfill their dual function, Soviet trade unions organize themselves on the basis of the so-called production principle as well as the principle of democratic centralism (Alekseev and Ivanov, 1968; Iampol'skaia, 1973). According to the first, all employees in a given sector of the economy are eligible to become members of the same union, regardless of profession. During the early 1980s there were thirty-two such unions with over 130 million members, approximately 98 percent of the Soviet workforce (Table

2.1). According to the principle of democratic centralism, policies are viewed as being democratically conceived: rank-and-file union members may suggest policy alternatives. It is defined as centrist insofar as central institutions dictate policy direction once priorities have been established (Smoliarchuk, 1973: 5–11; Pavlova and Protopopov, 1979: 13; Kisturga, 1982: 110–112). These two organizational principles combine to create an organizational double-helix of sectoral intraunion committees and regional interunion councils rendering local union officials subject both to branch unions and to regional inter-union councils. The trade union chairman at a local enterprise such as Leningrad's Bus Depot No. 4 would therefore report to superior officials at the Vasili Island Auto-Transport and Highway Workers District Trade Union Committee as well as to the Vasili Island Trade Union District Council and, through those bodies, to the Leningrad Auto-Transport and Highway Worker Regional Committee and the Leningrad Trade Union Regional Council and eventually to the Auto-Transport and Highway Workers Trade Union Central Committee and the All-Union Central Council of Trade Unions and their departments (Krivolopov and Martuseivich, 1975; Martiushev, 1975). (See Table 1.1, page 5 above.)

In practice, four institutions dominate this system of union sectoral committees and regional councils: the All-Union Central Council of Trade Unions (AUCCTU); thirty-two branch trade union central committees; more than a hundred regional trade union councils; and thousands of factory trade union committees (Table 2.2).

The AUCCTU, elected by trade union congresses convened every five years, serves as the Soviet Union's supreme trade union institution (Smoliarchuk, 1971). It elects a presidium and secretariat which are charged with the supervision of union administration, the establishment of broad union policies, and the implementation of policy directives. The secretariat consists of some ten members and, in turn, supervises the work of fifteen departments

Table 2.1
Membership of Soviet Trade Unions, 1976–1982 (millions, on January 1)

	1976	1980	1982
Total Membership	109.6	127.3	131.2
Blue- and white-collar workers	98.3	106.6	110.2
Collective farmers	3.2	11.7	11.9
Students in institutions of higher and specialized secondary education	5.4	5.8	5.8
Students in professional-technical schools	2.7	3.2	3.3

Source: Tsentral'noe statisticheskoe upravlenie SSSR, *Narodonoe khoziaistvo SSR: 1922–1982* (Moscow: Finansy i Statistika, 1982), p. 50.

Table 2.2
Total Number of Elected Officials in Trade Union Agencies, 1982

Level of Organization	Membership
All-Union Central Council of Trade Unions	590
Central committees of branch unions and auditing commissions	5,357
Republican, *krai,* and *oblast* (regional) councils and auditing commissions	23,245
Republican, *krai,* and *oblast* (regional) councils and territorial committees and auditing commissions	186,460
District and city committees and auditing commissions	688,178
Primary committees, auditing commissions and organizers	7,044,395

Source: Tsentral'noe statisticheskoe upravlenie SSSR, *Narodnoe khoziaistvo SSSR: 1922–1982* (Moscow: Finansy i Statistika, 1982), p. 50.

covering every aspect of daily union administration, such as those of labor protection, social insurance, and legal affairs (Beliarov, 1975; Dzhelomanov, 1975; Kositsyn, 1975).

The branch trade union central committees retain responsibility for the implementation of all national policies and labor legislation as they apply to specific industries. Both the elected members of a union central committee and that body's employed staff meet regularly with representatives of the appropriate industrial ministries to resolve conflicts over interpretations of industry-wide rules and regulations. A majority of a central committee's membership, usually upwards of 150 unionists, is drawn from the ranks of the industry's "outstanding workers" and those who have been involved in union administration at the local and regional level (Slovinskii, 1979). Most members participate in the work of the committee's commissions and work closely with appropriate ministerial offficials.

The regional trade union councils include representatives of each trade union operation in a given region. A council is usually subdivided into commissions (chaired by council members and staffed by volunteer union activists, the *aktiv*), and departments (staffed by professional administators and specialists). During the 1970s for example, the Leningrad Trade Union Regional Council was organized into eleven departments (Bulov, 1975; Kliuev, 1975; Vinogradova, 1975). One typical department, that for social insurance, employed fourteen full-time staff workers during the mid-1970s to administer a program with a budget of more than 95 million rubles (Vinogradova, 1975). Department official supervised factory medical facilities and operated vacation and health care facilities throughout the Leningrad region.

Finally at the lowest level of the union hierarchy there are thousands of factory trade union committees. While no single factory union committee may be said to be typical, the structure of the committee at Moscow Watch Factory No. 2 is representative of the size and scope of many (Riabkova, 1975). In 1975 that factory's union chairman presided over a committee of thirty-five members, each elected for a one-year term. The committee (80 percent of which came from blue-collar professions) met once a month; its twelve-member presidium, or executive board, met every other week to discuss pressing concerns. In the interim, the daily work of the unions within the plant became the responsibility of some thirteen commissions staffed by volunteer activists and chaired by a full member of the full committee. These institutional arrangements combined with the sheer scale of union organization to create a bureaucracy sufficiently centralized to grant considerable authority to key coordination institutions (i.e. the AUCCTU, branch central committees, and regional councils). Nevertheless, those coordinating institutions remain sufficiently weak to emphasize the importance of informal, extra-bureaucratic relationships. Both patterns are reinforced by an internal union personnel system, the *nomenklatura*, which assigns full-time officials to specific union agencies according to the relative importance of both (Hough, 1969: 149–77; Morrell, 1965: 174–90). Under intricate election rules (which grant effective authority over appointments to senior union agencies), a union's central committee selects officials at an enterprise of national significance prior to formal election, while a union's regional committee similarly selects union officers at an enterprise of regional significance. Such preselection occurs through a system of auditing commissions drawn up to include leading union party officials who establish a list of candidates created in accordance with the *nomenklatura* and offer it to the workers for approval (Spravochnik..., 1974: 21–9). Then, after discussion at a general factory meeting, an open voice vote accepts the list of candidates in its entirety. During the subsequent secret ballot workers have an opportunity to vote "for "or "against" the individual candidates on the list. Nominees receiving a simple majority affirmative vote are elected to the union committee. Should a candidate fail to gain such approval (an infrequent but not unknown occurrence) the meeting immediately nominates a new candidate for that position. After such an election meeting, the newly elected committee convenes to select its officers.

The system of auditing commissions combines with the unions' *nomenklatura* system to make even the lowliest factory union chairman accountable to higher union institutions. A factory union chairman's career hinges upon a positive or negative evaluation by an organizational superior rather than upon the goodwill of the worker who (nominally) elected him in the first place. The end result is an integrated organizational matrix designed to maximize the subordination of factory officers to regional, and eventually national, officials while minimizing inter- and intra-enterprise union ties.

The Trade Unions and Factory Management

The concept of dual functioning trade unions assumes union participation in economic management. At the national level this activity includes permanent liaison activities between the AUCCTU and both the USSR State Planning Committee (Gosplan) and the State Committee on Labor and Social Question (established by the USSR Council of Ministers in 1955 to coordinate Soviet wage policies) (Hough, 1979). Trade union officials also maintain direct contact with several Communist Party Central Committee departments (e.g. the Heavy Industry Department) which are charged with various aspects of the economic and labor management. Moreover, the AUCCTU has a right of legislative initiative by which the USSR Supreme Soviet and its legislative commissions are obliged to review and consider legislative proposals forwarded by the unions (Tsepin and Shchiglik, 1979: 78--80). Finally, as discussed above, the thirty-two branch trade union central committees work closely with their corresponding ministries. In sum, then, the AUCCTU and its constituent agencies and committees function as fully integrated components of a broader system of state economic management.

At the local level, union officials participate in the factory decision-making process. The factory trade union chairman shares responsibility for the management of the labor force with the factory director, who oversees a large and complex administrative pyramid within the plant. While the director exercises immediate authority over plant operations under the managerial principle of one-man rule (*edinonachalie*), union approval is required for managerial action in some seventy administrative areas (Bokarev, 1979). In addition, the party organization at the enterprise has the right to validate the work of management and to enforce laws and plant norms under the principle of the Communist Party's right to control. Irresolvable disputes among these potentially conflicting principles are resolved by higher-ranking party agencies (Hough, 1979).

The dynamic of the triangular relationship of plant director, party chairman, and union chairman doubtless varies from enterprise to enterprise. In general, party and managerial officials share responsibility for planning; the unions and management, for productivity and working conditions; and the unions and the Party, for general educational, cultural, and ideological work. Factory trade union organizations claim to foster union and worker participation in management through a series of mechanisms, including forums for joint worker–management decision-making, and support for worker collectives (Aleksandrov, 1972; Tsepin and Shchiglik, 1979: 148–82; Ziegler, 1983).

Current regulations governing labor disputes mediation specify that labor–management disputes should be given two hearings within a given plant; in most cases, an initial examination by a shop disputes commission consisting of equal union and management representation, as well as a second review by the shop trade union committee (Ushkov, 1976). Both workers and management may appeal shop-level decisions to a factorywide commission on labor disputes as well as to the factory trade union committee. Beyond the individual enterprise, decisions may be appealed to the next highest union agency and eventually to local procurators and the courts (M. McAuley, 1969). Regional union and ministerial officials prefer to resolve disputes through informal channels between union, ministerial, and party officials rather than turning the conflict over to the judicial system. For example, Leningrad regional union officers frequently call up their counterpart at the city party committee and city soviet to suggest mutually agreeable solutions to lingering disputes (Kliuev, 1975).

Another device for worker participation under union supervision—the production conference—emerged during the 1920s. Lenin originally endorsed the concept of joint managerial–worker production councils as an important vehicle for involving blue-collar and white-collar workers in industrial decision-making. Although the conferences have existed ever since, more authoritarian forms of industrial management nearly brought them to extinction during the 1930s. Official support for the conferences recommenced in the late 1950s and they acquired their "permanent" legal status in 1958 at a time when worker self-management mechanisms were emerging in Yugoslavia. According to 1973 statutes governing the operation of the conferences, all industrial establishments employing more than 300 persons are required to organize a conference of elected deputies, representing 10–15 percent of the total workforce (Spravochnik..., 1974: 66–71). In 1983 approximately 142,000 factory and shop production conferences with some 6.2 million delegates were functioning throughout the Soviet Union (Torkanovskii, 1983). The size of any single conference can be rather cumbersome; production conferences in Kazakhstan averaged 40 percent participants each during the late 1940s and early 1980s (Turysov, 1982; the Kalinin Chemical Combine alone operates twelve shop and one combinewide conferences with more than 800 delegates in all (Bokarev, 1979). Such unwieldly numbers combine with inadequate leadership and a lack of enforcement authority to undermine the potentially serious role such bodies could play in the managerial process. Conference failings are forthrightly reported in letters to the union monthly *Sovetskie profsoiuzy* which portray production conferences as inexperienced, insufficiently staffed, charged with ill-defined duties, and generally ineffectual (Dumachev, 1979; Ivanovskii, 1977; Khaitovich, 1977; "PDPS...", 1977, "Proizvodstvennoe soveshchanie...", 1977). Finally, administrators frequently ignore conference decisions or withhold necessary production data required to formulate sensible recommendations for managerial action (Torkanovskii, 1983: 38–39).

The organization of socialist competition, a third official participatory mechanism, allows brigades of workers to compete with one another for various forms of bonus (Tsepin and Shchiglik, 1979: 163–176). Soviet union leaders portray these contests as vehicles for worker participation in the managerial decision-making process as target norms are (theoretically) established by workers themselves and distributed within worker brigades on the basis of peer review. In the 1974 Kamsk Cable Factory Agreement (Kamskii kabel'nyi zavod, 1974) production goals projected total annual output of various categories of cable according to completion dates established in consultation with workers ranging from September 1 to December 20. Assuming such targets were achieved, additional production would be in excess of centrally planned norms with profits from their production being divided up among labor and management by the workers themselves. Despite such claims to the contrary, the weight of the available evidence suggests that the joint elaboration of socialist obligations functions primarily as a contrived substitute for piece-rate wage scales. It does provide, however, a potentially significant mechanism for integrating new workers into the factory workforce.

Soviet trade unions also supervise a series of forums for worker–management joint decision-making, the most successful of which are a nationwide network of technical societies established during the late 1950s: the Scientific-Technical Societies (NTO) and the All-Union Society of Innovators and Rationalizers (VOIR) (Lee, 1979; Kisturga, 1982: 152–172). Both societies are subdivided into twenty-four sectoral agencies (Torkanovskii, 1983: 42). At the factory level, such groups mobilize support for innovation among workers, defend inventor rights, and attempt to eliminate bureaucratic barriers to innovation. Of all the formal participatory mechanisms sponsored by the unions, the technical societies have had the most significant impact on industrial decision-making. During the five-year period 1976–1980 both societies were credited with facilitating more than 29 billion rubles in technological innovations (Torkanovskii, 1983: 42).

In recent years, several small-scale experiments with more direct forms of worker participation have been conducted, including the election of on-line managerial and brigade personnel by workers (Kisturga, 1982: 164–67). While such experiments have not, in and of themselves, achieved large-scale results, they have created a sense of movement toward greater participation; a tendency reinforced by a series of major party decisions encouraging worker involvement in management (Torkanovskii, 1983: 36). This ill-defined official perception of increased worker participation has been amplified following the enactment of a new law on the labor collective in June 1983 ("Zakon . . .", 1983).

The June 1983 law on the labor collective brought about little significant institutional change in the daily operation of the Soviet factory. Rather, the Act represented a benchmark in the development of Soviet participatory institutions. For the first time Soviet law recognized the labor collective as an integral component of enterprise organization, thereby providing a juridical basis for participatory mechanisms beyond the control of the trade unions (Torkanovskii, 1983: 37; Aliev, 1983; Slider, 1983). The symbolic value attached to the act by official commentators stressed ever-increasing worker participation in management, a theme harkening back to the ideological pronouncements of the Nikita Khrushchev period more than to the more pragmatic industrial policies expounded during Leonid Brezhnev's tenure as Communist Party General Secretary.

During the Brezhnev period (1964–1982) Soviet industrial decision-makers abandoned various instruments fostering direct worker participation in factory administration in favor of mechanisms granting union officials more authority within plant administration. One former union officer explained during a 1974 conversation that the factory union chairman sits in an office down the hall from those of the factory director and Communist Party and Young Communist League chairmen. These officials meet frequently on the way to and from their desks and, more often than not, get together each morning to resolve the day's problems. Meanwhile, production-line workers are spatially and socially removed from such informal ties with management.

In addition to a dearth of informal communication channels from workers to managers, the skills demanded of factory administrators and union officials have become sufficiently complex so as to remove both groups from the experiences of the shop-floor. In a 1975 interview I. Riabkova, the deputy union chairman of Moscow Watch Factory No. 2, listed a dozen primary areas of responsibility demanding that she be administrator and teacher, counselor and housing superintendent, engineer and bookkeeper (Riabkova, 1975). These obligations require skills which differentiate Riabkova from the plant's workforce as well as taking up sufficient time to prevent her from remaining familiar with the stresses of the production-line. This state of affairs can only exacerbate already existing tensions between professional *nomenklatura* union officials and rank-and-file union members.

During the mid-1970s Leningrad sociologists questioned 1,468 workers in the city's machine construction industry, 90 percent of whom were men, and 1,324 workers in local light industry and food production, 90 percent of whom were women, concerning their attitudes toward social organizations and worker participation (Alekseev and Nazimova, 1981). The researchers found fairly high quantitative levels of participation in social organizations of some form (59.3 percent of workers in machine construction and 50.2 percent in light industry and food production). Nevertheless,

qualitative indices offered a far less glowing picture of local worker participation. Only 14.7 percent of respondents in machine construction and 19.1
percent in light industry and food production were permanently engaged in
such activities; 48 percent of the respondents in machine construction and
82.1 percent in light industry and food production had not put forward
suggestions concerning improvements in labor organization and factory
management. While it is dangerous to formulate general conclusions on the
basis of this single survey, it nonetheless suggests that the quality and quantity
of worker participation in Soviet factories may fall short of officially proclaimed expectations.

Unions, Workers, and Factory Management: An Evaluation

The legacy of Communist Party and trade union policies on worker
participation during the Brezhnev period was one of encouragement for
union involvement in the managerial process and discouragement of direct
worker participation in plant administration. Overall, Soviet policies during
the 1970s supported mechanisms facilitating the active integration of union
officials—but not necessarily workers—into factory managerial operations.
This pattern emerged in part as a response to concern over the inability of
many assembly-line workers to satisfy the increasingly complex demands of
modern management.

Such a policy failed to recognize the emergence of a large, skilled, and
increasingly well educated cohort of younger workers moving into techno-
logically advanced positions (Institut filosofii AN SSSR *et al.*, 1981; Parol',
1982: 161–3; Pravda, 1982). These new workers are likely to make increasing demands on factory union representatives and managers alike so that the
renewed official interest in participation may, in part, anticipate their arrival
on the factory scene. The 1983 law on the labor collective marked a possible
break with policies of the 1970s and may have represented the initiation of
efforts under subsequent regimes to increase the quantity and quality of
worker (as opposed to union) participation in management (Slider, 1983).
Those most likely to benefit from such a policy direction would not have
been the traditional, unskilled, ill-disciplined peasant-workers of old but a
new skilled working middle class now emerging from within older worker
groups. The future of such policies remains murky. Nevertheless, one may
choose to speculate on the basis of the past record that any new pattern of
policy implementation will be inchoate at best.

That Soviet factory trade union institutions—participatory and nonpar-
ticipatory—fail in fulfilling their two opposing obligations is to be expected.
The tension deriving from the unions' dual role is likewise natural, a conse-

quence of normal human responses to a dilemma with no apparent resolution. The question of moment is not whether such tension exists (Soviet theories notwithstanding) but rather what pattern, if any, has emerged from the ensuing conflicts. An examination of Soviet trade union behavior reveals two general sets of variables which have some predictive value: union officials in heavy industry appear most likely to fulfill their duties to both the party and the Soviet state as well as to the workers themselves; union officials in metropolitan areas similarly appear to be most likely to fulfill their multifaceted duties (Ruble, 1981: 104—18).

For the past half-century Soviet investment priorities have favored heavy industry over light. As a result considerable variation exists in the quality and quantity of resources available to diverse forms of economic production. Not surprisingly, such discrepancies adversely affect both the quality and quantity of benefits available to workers in less well funded industries. Indeed, in this regard, the inequalities in the distribution of wealth between heavy and light industry (and between light industry and nonindustrial sectors of the Soviet economy) are every bit as acute as any disparities deriving from professional, occupational, and sex differences.

In addition to differentiation by industrial sector, one can discern a geographic pattern of distribution of effective union performance. Party policies, state laws, and union decrees charge each primary union cell with what seems an infinite number of duties, ranging from labor protection to organizing folk dance competitions. Factory trade union committees must drawn upon a vast array of talent in order to fulfill even the most pressing of their obligations. Since Moscow, Leningrad, and a handful of other metropolitan centers support an affluence not found elsewhere in the Soviet Union (Nechemias, 1980), the competition for employment in these areas is intense. The factories of these major centers attract the best workers nationwide and channel many of them into union work. Moreover, the *nomenklatura* personnel system and salary structures reward successful union, party, and managerial officials in other regions by relocating them in one of these centers. The superior performance of union organizations in established centers compared to that of unions in recently industrialized regions is therefore readily understandable; the best people do the best work.

The performance of the trade union committees at two disparate factories—Leningrad's Kirov (formerly Putilov) Metal Works and Bukhara's Ten Years of October Silk Factory—effectively illustrate just how wide a variation may exist in union effectiveness. Few factories in the Soviet Union are more important or have a more prestigious past than the Kirov Works in Leningrad (Zinov'ev, 1975). Work on the assembly-line at the Kirov offers substantial material reward by Soviet standards. The success of the plant in socialist competition ensures a worker regular bonus payments. The union

Table 2.3
General Population Characteristics, 1980 (on January 1)

	Millions	Percentage of Total
Total Population	266.6	
Urban	168.9	63.0
Rural	97.7	37.0
Male	124.5	46.7
Female	142.1	53.5
Workforce		
Male		49.0
Female		51.0

Source: Tsentral'noe statisticheskoe upravlenie SSSR, *Narodnoe khoziaistvo SSSR: 1980g.* (Moscow: Finansy i Statistika, 1981), pp. 7, 8, 361.

committee and factory administration operate some of the best housing, medical, and recreational facilities in the Soviet Union. The plant's vacation center on the Black Sea as well as its cultural programs in Leningrad are among the most extensive in the country. In short, Kirov union leaders and managers have created a work environment and a trade union organization that fits the optimal dual functioning model as closely as any in the Soviet Union today.

By contrast, a 1975 visit to Bukhara's Ten Years of October Factory revealed skilled seamstresses using antiquated looms and sewing machines to produce exquisitely embroidered cloth. Seemingly ancient machines dating from a Dickensian epoch of industrial development emit an ear-shattering din. Despite dangerously high noise levels, the plant's management has taken few—if any—precautions to deaden the sound or to improve working conditions. As the guide noted openly, the problem was simply that "machines make noise."

In summary, union efforts to protect workers from managerial injury and to encourage worker participation in management appear to be most successful in priority enterprises (e.g. major heavy industrial plants) in priority cities (e.g. Moscow and Leningrad) where administrators face only minimal human and financial constraints. Once compromise among competing ends becomes necessary, union performance begins to fall short of legally established norms. Finally, in light industrial plants in nonmetropolitan areas, where both adequate financial and human resources are frequently wanting, the ability of enterprise union agencies to protect even the most basic social and legal rights suffers considerably. Such difficulties, one must assume, increase proportionately—in any location—with a decrease of resources, a fact which may raise serious dilemmas for both union leaders and state planners, as the Soviet economy enters a period of increasingly constrained economic development.

Soviet Trade Unions in a Period
of Economic Constraint

Until fairly recently it was impossible to discuss the Soviet political system without mentioning the working class. This was true, for one thing, because many credulous observers long accepted the notion that the ideological underpinnings of the Soviet state essentially served the Soviet worker's interests. In addition, another more agnostic segment of Soviet watchers regularly linked the topics of state and worker in questioning the government's ability to maintain working-class support in the face of centrally imposed deprivations (Barton, 1962). By the late 1960s, however, it had become difficult to find any serious observer of the Soviet system who still recognized the lowly *rabochii* as a pivotal actor on the Soviet scene.

The precipitous decline in the interest afforded the Soviet working class occurred at a time when labor issues within the Soviet system had become depoliticized. Crucial decisions and policies determining the fate of millions had been made but had not even caught the attention of many Western Soviet specialists. Western analysts cannot be blamed for this lacuna in their scholarship, however, as the Soviet political and cultural leadership itself appeared to turn its attention away from the proletariat. Even in literature, as Vera Dunham has reported, the once ubiquitous theme of the "worker-hero" virtually dropped from sight (Dunham, 1979).

Labor, of course, did not cease to be a major concern of the Soviet state. But its political importance most certainly declined dramatically. This diminution resulted from the emergence among party, state, and union officials of a broad consensus regarding labor policies during the late 1950s (Hough, 1979). This consensus served three ends: it assured greater authority for the trade unions as an institution; it permitted the emergence of a new "human relations" approach to labor relations; and it encouraged a general levelling-off of monetary wage differentials (Ruble, 1981).

New economic exigencies dating from the late 1970s eroded this consensus of two decades in many crucial respects. The seemingly absolute necessity of increasing industrial productivity to sustain even the most modest levels of economic growth led to heightened interest in technological innovation—to the point where even the job security of many Soviet workers (one of the system's most vaunted values) is now threatened by Gorbachev's drive to increase productivity. As will be discussed further in a moment, this threat, in turn, increased concern over labor discipline and wage differentials. The apparently pro-worker policies of the Khrushchev and early Brezhnev periods were replaced by approaches to labor relations which, at first blush, appear to be less supportive of worker interests. If nothing else, the issue of who will bear the burden of constrained economic development has become salient once again.

The policies of the Andropov and Gorbachev regimes were designed to push the labor issue to the political center-stage. Much-publicized discipline campaigns of late have heightened attention to material labor incentives, rekindled interest in worker participation, and the sustained attack on malfeasance in the service sector have all pointed to an increased seriousness in Soviet labor policies. The growing prominence of the labor question was seen first and foremost in party and state policies on the labor discipline issue.

Discipline, Inequality, and the Unions

Since the late 1950s, when criminal sanctions against truancy and absenteeism were lifted (ILO, 1959: 130−1), Soviet managers have been confronted with the problem of how best to motivate workers with two positive incentives: material and spiritual rewards. The problem has been exacerbated by the prolonged failure of the Soviet economy to produce the former in qualities and quantities sufficient to spur higher levels of productivity and by the sheer impossibility of making inroads on the latter front in an era of chronic indifference to stimuli based on ideology. The end result has been the increasingly visible exercise of the "freedom not to work too hard" rather than the hoped-for dramatic increase in labor productivity rates. It is hardly surprising, then, that Andropov launched an attack on labor indiscipline as soon as he assumed the party's highest office. What Western commentators frequently overlooked, however, was the startling degree to which Andropov defined the labor discipline problem as one of managerial failure rather than of worker inefficiency, incompetence, and/or sloth. Here Gorbachev has followed in Andropov's footsteps.

The designation of labor indiscipline as a managerial problem did not represent a startling break from the pronouncements of the Brezhnev era. Indeed, it was only the logical culmination of a two-decade-long process in which social scientists and union leaders drew attention to the need to seek increased productivity by creating a "healthy moral-psychological climate" for the worker rather than by simply increasing the size of the manager's stick ("Vliiatel'naia sila . . . ," 1978). The most important policy statement on labor indiscipline during the late Brezhnev era—the 1979 joint decree of the Central Committee of the CPSU, the Presidium of the USSR Supreme Soviet, the USSR Council of Ministers, and the AUCCTU "On the further Strengthening of Labor Discipline and the Reduction of Labor Turnover in the National Economy"—focused far more upon rewards for good performance than upon punishment for bad ("V VTsSPS . . . ," 1980; "Krepit' . . . ," 1980). Moreover, the decree chided economic managers, party and union officials, as well as municipal governments—and not workers—for contributing to the inadequate labor productivity of recent years.

This determination of blame for labor indiscipline is readily apparent in the speeches of the leaders of the new regime during the months immediately following Andropov's accession to the General Secretaryship. After ten days in office, Andropov reported to the Party's Central Committee on the draft economic plan for 1983 (Andropov, 1982). In his address the new General Secretary identified labor productivity as the major indicator of economic efficiency and observed that productivity must rise above current levels. He then advocated improvement of "all spheres of economic leadership— management, planning, and economic mechanization." In doing so Andropov clearly implied that the inability of economic leaders to make the most rational use of those material and labor resources available to them represented the primary problem confronting the Soviet economy at that time. Increased labor productivity could only result, it followed, from more intelligent and effective management—not from from the introduction of harsher sanctions against workers.

A week later AUCCTU Chairman S. A. Shalaev similarly identified low labor productivity as the central problem of the Soviet economy (Shalaev, 1982). Like Andropov, Shalaev stressed the need for organizational improvements and technological innovation rather than harsher punishments for indiscipline. The union chief praised various attempts to link wages to production performance and closed by noting that union administration should become more businesslike. The same night that Shalaev addressed the AUCCTU, the then Leningrad Regional Party First Secretary Grigorii Romanov (who also happened to be a full member of the Politburo and was subsequently elevated to the Central Committee's Secretariat) stressed identical themes in a report to the Leningrad Regional Party Committee covering the same draft economic plan for 1983 (Romanov, 1982). Indeed, Romanov may have gone even further than either Andropov or Shalaev in his enthusiasm for technological innovation as a solution to economic inertia. At the close of his speech, Romanov in turn singled out corruption rather than traditional labor indiscretions as the primary cause for alarm. Romanov's colleague, Leningrad City Party Committee First Secretary Yu. F. Solov'ev, echoed this view most succinctly of all in his report to the Leningrad City Party Committee on March 29, 1983, when he observed that "contemporary production places high demands on workers of all levels. But special responsibility lies with leaders" ("V ukreplenii . . . ," 1983).

Beyond the remarks of leading regime spokesmen, the Central Committee, the Council of Ministers, and the AUCCTU issued a new decree on labor discipline in August, 1983 which explicitly drew upon the December 1979 Central Committee, Council of Ministers, Supreme Soviet, and AUCCTU labor discipline decree ("V TsK KPSS . . . ," 1983). The August 1983 decree on labor discipline emphasized the efficacy of peer pressure in dealing with labor discipline violators. The August 1983 decree also echoed the call of the

December 1979 decree for the maintenance of a balance between sanctions and incentives, improved economic management, upgraded public and housing services as well as expanded media coverage of model workers ("V VTsSPS...", 1980; Ruble, 1981: 74−75). However, unlike the previous policy statement, the August 1983 decree specified a number of sanctions to be applied by factory union, party, and managerial officials against chronic discipline violators, including:

(*a*)   the reduction of vacation time by one day for every day lost at work;

(*b*)   the demotion of shirkers to lower-paid positions and the summary dismissal of workers found drunk on the job;

(*c*)   the establishment of a six-month probationary period with half the normal monthly bonuses for dismissed workers who obtain new positions (a sanction which can be reduced to three months by factory administrators and trade union officials); and

(*d*)   the deduction of up to one-third of a worker's salary for payments to cover lost or damaged products, with full payment of the damaged or lost value being required of workers who incurred the production loss while in a state of drunkenness ("V TsK KPSS...," 1983).

In addition to these sanctions, the decree specified a number of regressive procedural changes, including:

(*a*)   the extension of the period of written notice required of a worker wishing to leave a job from one month to two (prior to December, 1979, the requisite waiting period had been only two weeks);

(*b*)   the establishment of a maximum three-week break in tenure to remain eligible for benefits accrued to workers with uninterrupted work service;

(*c*)   the provision that more than three hours' absence on any given day shall constitute a full day lost from work; and

(*d*)   the reduction of paper work required for the hiring and dismissal of workers ("V TsK KPSS . . . ," 1983).

These measures operationalize many of the hard-line pronouncements on discipline questions made by Andropov and other senior Soviet political leaders during the early months of 1983. Such severe sanctions—the toughest imposed upon workers in nearly three decades— reflected a seriousness of purpose on the discipline issue altogether lacking before the last years of the Brezhnev era. Nevertheless, it is important to note that the decree's specific sanctions imposed most hardship upon unskilled workers who reputedly had developed a lifestyle predicted upon the easy transfer from job to job and factory to factory. Productive skilled workers with long-term commitment to a given employer were not affected by the new policies nearly as seriously.

Andropov, Shalaev, Romanov, Solov'ev, and other high-level Soviet officials as well as the Communist Party's Central Committee all left little doubt that labor discipline and labor productivity must improve. As noted above, they stated on several occasions that labor indiscipline could not be tolerated. Yet, they directed their attention in their remarks and declarations as much to managers as to workers. Moreover, the specific solutions they proposed (e.g. improved organization of the factory workforce and increased technological innovation) stood to reward a highly skilled and already productive and well-paid working middle class (Pravda, 1982). This favoritism was more apparent when one examines fluctuations in industrial wage scales.

Wage inequality (as opposed to total income inequality) decreased in the Soviet Union as the result of major wage reforms in 1956 and 1968 (Chapman, 1970; Kirsch, 1972; Chapman, 1979; A. McAuley, 1979). The Soviet minimum wage, for example, rose by nearly 150 percent (from a pre-1956 level of 27 rubles per month to a 1978 level of 70 rubles per month). This increase in base pay occurred while upper-level salaries remained stable; a director of a coal mining trust earned the same 450 rubles per month in the years 1960 and 1975. That salary represented eleven times the industrywide wage in 1960, but only 6.5 times the 1975 minimum. In addition, wage differentials between economic sectors decreased during the same period. The lowest average earnings of workers and salaried employees (paid in the garment industry) were only 38.6 percent of those paid in the highest (coal mining) in 1955, and 38.9 percent in 1966; by 1975, that figure had risen to 42 percent (see Tables 2.4 and 2.5).

By the 1980s contradictory statistical evidence emerged which suggested that the post-Stalin decline in income inequality may have been reversed as early as 1968 (Rabkina and Rimashevskaia, 1978; Ellman, 1980; Nove, 1982; A. McAuley, 1982). Close examination of the available data suggests one likely explanation for this trend may be found in the sizable increase paid to already well-compensated industrial workers—the working middle class.

Acknowledging that the data for the late 1970s are not of sufficient quality to identify any single trend with certainty, the perception that wage inequality had increased in recent years may have become widespread among at least some Soviet workers. For example, a survey of workers at the Sigma and El'fa Production Association in the Latvian capital of Riga by

Table 2.4
Employment and Average Wage by Economic Sector, 1980 (millions of employees and rubles per month, on January 1)

Economic Branch	Number of Employees	Average Monthly Wage
Entire Economy	112.5	168.9
Industry	36.9	185.4
Agriculture	11.7	149.2
Forestry	0.5	—
Transport	10.3	199.9
Communication	1.6	145.8
Construction	11.2	202.3
Trade	9.7	138.2
Municipal and consumer services	4.5	133.2
Health, physical culture and social insurance	6.2	126.8
Education	9.1	135.9
Culture	1.3	111.3
Science and science services	4.4	179.5
Credit and state insurance	0.6	162.2
State, cooperative, and bureaucratic apparatus	2.5	156.4
Other	2.0	—

[a]To which is added, on average, 63.9 rubles per month in social benefits in the form of transfer payments and subsidized services.

Source: Tsentral'noe statisticheskoe upravlenie SSSR, *Narodnoe khoziaistvo SSSR v 1980* (Moscow: Finansy i Statistika, 1982), p. 50.

sociologists from the neighboring Lithuanian Academy of Sciences Institute of Philosophy, Sociology, and Law in 1970, 1974, and again in 1977 discerned heightened concern on wage questions across time as workers found the increases in their wages to be diminishing (Tamotsiunene, 1981). More important for the present discussion, a belief in the existence of benefit to be derived from increased wage inequality was evident in the remarks of Andropov at the June 1983 Central Committee Plenum (Andropov, 1983a). Such pronouncements indicated a revised party policy on the wage question even though the actual wage data still reflected a far more complex pattern in workers' real earnings. The party leadership under Andropov and Gorbachev remains acutely concerned about improving labor productivity across the board, and, as Soviet economist L. S. Sbytova bluntly wrote in 1982: "Differentiation of wages is a powerful means for developing the national economy" (Sbytova, 1982: 20).

Andropov's two major labor policy initiatives—a crackdown on labor indiscipline and support for increased wage differentials—were welcome and unwelcome respectively to Soviet trade unions. The first conformed to

Table 2.5
Average Earnings of Workers and Salaried Employees by Selected Branches of Industry, USSR, 1955–1975[a]

	Rubles per Month		
	1955	*1966*	*1975*
All Industry	78.3	106.8	162.2
Electric energy	85.0	113.2	167.3
Coal mining	126.8	195.3	274.9
Ferrous metallurgy	102.0	129.0	188.0
Chemicals	83.7	110.0	165.2
Machinery	84.0	106.5	164.1
Wood and paper	73.6	105.3	169.3
Timber	79.4	117.4	241.2
Wood working	64.7	93.8	155.3
Cellulose and paper	85.2	106.2	163.8
Construction materials	69.1	104.3	165.4
Light industries	57.6	81.3	124.6
Textiles	62.2	83.8	129.7
Garments	49.0	76.1	115.5
Shoes	56.7	85.1	131.9
Food industries	61.0	92.7	145.9
Milling	—	—	129.2
Bread	—	—	126.5
Beverages	—	—	122.9
Meat[b]	58.1	86.6	134.6
Sugar	52.0	81.1	—
Tobacco	—	—	136.3
Fish	109.2	181.2	—
Other food[c]	—	—	165.9
Lowest as a percentage of highest	38.6%	38.9%	42.0%

[a]The figures for 1975 include all bonuses from the bonus fund and other sources. The figures for 1955 and 1966 include bonuses from the bonus fund only for those enterprises which had transferred to the reformed system. This may mean also that bonuses from the former "enterprise fund" are excluded.

[b]Meat and milk for 1975.

[c]Refers to all of food industry for which figures are not shown above.

Source: 1955–1966: Tsentral'noe statisticheskoe upravlenie pri Sovete Ministrov SSSR, *Trud v SSSR* (Moscow: Statistika, 1968), pp. 140–4; 1970 and 1975: *Vestnik statistiki*, 1972, no. 11, p. 93 and 1976, no. 8, p. 90, as published in J. C. Chapman, "Recent Trends in the Soviet Industrial Wage Structure," in A. Kahan and B. Ruble (eds.), *Industrial Labor in the USSR* (Elmsford, N.Y.: Pergamon, 1979), p. 170.

longstanding union positions while the second contradicted similarly entrenched union percepts. On the question of labor discipline, one finds that investigations into the motivation underlying compliance and noncompliance with labor discipline conducted during the late 1960s by legal scholars utilizing sociological survey methods demonstrated that labor turnover, absenteeism, truancy, and alcoholism were not so much the result of worker malevolence as the natural product of the social and work environments in which workers function (Barabash, 1968; Abramova, 1969; Filatov and Turchenko, 1971; Nikitinskii, 1971; Smirnov, 1972; Yanowitch, 1979). This view gradually gained the acceptance of wider groups of political and trade union leaders; by the late 1970s AUCCTU decrees concerning labor discipline had incorporated the need for improvement in the "socio-living conditions" of workers rather than the imposition of tougher sanctions ("Vysokaia rol' . . . ," 1978). Discussions at a number of regional trade union conferences in January and February of 1982 similarly focused upon the need to upgrade working conditions (Mezhsoiuznye . . . , 1982; Kazakov, 1982; Pozdniakova, 1982). By the early 1980s union leaders were beginning to define labor indiscipline as managerial, not worker, inspired. The pronouncements of Andropov to the same effect—such as his rhetorical questioning at the June, 1983 Central Committee Plenum of the value of unions which did not raise their voice in defense of workers' interests (Andropov, 1983a: 2)— were thus in accordance with an established union position. On the other hand, union agreement with Andropov's and, subsequently Gorbachev's policies, evaporates when one examines the traditional union position against that of the new leadership on wage differentials.

Soviet trade unions exert influence over industrial wage policies at several different levels (Guliaev, 1976). Nationally, the central committees of individual unions meet on a regular basis with representatives from the corresponding ministries to discuss changes in wage rates. Moreover, the State Committee on Labor and Social Questions is legally bound to examine AUCCTU wage proposals. The AUCCTU also maintains a staff of liaison officers who lobby both the State Committee and the State Planning Committee (Gosplan) for changes in the wage structure. At the local level, wage commissions of the factory or shop union committees verify calculation of workers' wages. In addition, factory trade union committees administer a wide variety of cash transfer payments (including old age pensions, disability pensions, survivor pensions, and so on) as well as free or subsidized services (primarily in the areas of education, medical care, and housing)—all of which together can increase a worker's real income by as much as one-third (A. McAuley, 1981; Madison, 1979).

National, regional, and local union officials have almost uniformly supported attempts to reduce wage differentials. At the national level, several major union spokesmen advocated more equitable distribution of wages during the 1970s. For example, in November, 1978 AUCCTU Secretary Viktorov appeared before the USSR Supreme Soviet and boldly asserted that the social needs of Soviet citizens should not be ignored in an effort to

improve national economic performance (Viktorov, 1978). Chairman Shibaev, for his part, supported a national union program designed to improve
worker barracks and dormitories. Some regional union agencies, such as the
Leningrad Trade Union Regional Council, have attempted to eliminate the
most visible inequities in union social programs by pressing individual enterprise trade union organizations to share their jealously guarded services with
workers from neighboring and less advantaged factories (Vinogradova, 1975).

Conclusion

As one looks beyond Brezhnev, Andropov, and Chernenko to Gorbachev, one finds that, for the first time in Soviet history, industrial union
membership includes perhaps a majority whose parents worked at similar
jobs. Upward mobility is more likely to mean movement within the working
class than movement out of it (Kahan, 1979). Improving education levels
among workers will eventually lead to better-educated union cadres and
have already led to a better-educated General Secretary in Gorbachev. In
each of these ways, the Soviet scene has moved away from the pattern of a
modernizing society such as may still be found in communist states such as
China and Romania toward the industrial maturity found in the German
Democratic Republic, Hungary, and Czechoslovakia. All of these trends presage challenges to union institutions which are qualitatively different from
those presented by revolution, civil war, collectivization, and industrialization. Such developments will not undermine the Leninist framework of dual
functioning unionism; but they will, most likely, force Gorbachev and his
fellow party, state, and union officials to create a new range of labor policy
options within that broader context. The essential ambiguity of the dual
functioning theory of labor relations, one which designates industrial unions
as advocates both of higher productivity and of improved labor welfare, will
continue. Soviet industrial union leaders of the future, like those of the past
and present, will oppose individual violations of workers' rights as those
rights are defined by state law and party pronouncement. Industrial conflict
per se will remain illegitimate and the arena for labor−management discord
will remain severely confined by fundamental definitions and bureaucratic
obstacles inherent in centralized economic planning. Yet national labor
policies under Gorbachev as well as future leaders may come to favor a group
practically nonexistent during nearly any other period of Soviet history: a
stable urban industrial proletariat.

Acknowledgments

I would like to thank Mark H. Teeter and Murray Feshbach for their invaluable comments and assistance during the preparation of this chapter. In addition, I would like to take this opportunity to acknowledge my deep personal and unequaled intellectual debt to Jerry Hough, whose encouragement and advice have stimulated my research on Soviet trade unions ever since my first days in graduate school.

References

Abramova, A.A. (1969), *Distsiplina truda v SSSR* (Moscow: Iuridicheskaia literatura).

Aleksandrov, N. G. (1972), "Prava profsoiuzov v oblasti uchastiia v upravlenii proizvodstvom," in N. G. Aleksandrov (ed.), *Sovetskoe trudovoe pravo* (Moscow: Iuridicheskaia literatura, pp. 196–201.

Alekseev, A. N., and Nazimova, A. K. (1981), "Obshchestvannaia aktivnost' Sovetskikh rabochikh (sotsiologicheskie aspekty problemy)," in L. A. Gordon, E. V. Klopov and A. K. Nazimova (eds.), *Rabochii klass na rubezhe 80-x godov* (Moscow: IMRD AN SSSR), pp. 127–45.

Alekseev, G., and Ivanov, E. (1968), *Profsoiuzy v period stroitel'stva kommunizma* (Moscow: Profizdat).

Aliev, G. A. (1983), "O proekte zakona SSSR o trudovykh kollektivakh i povyshenii ikh roli v upravlenii predpriiatiiami, uchrezhdeniiami, organizatsiiami. Doklad pervogo zamestitelia predsedatelia deputata G. A. Alieva," *Leningradskaia pravda*, June 18, p. 2.

Andropov, Iu. V. (1982), "Rech' General'nogo Sekretaria TsK KPSS Iu. V. Andropova," *Leningradskaia pravda*, November 23, pp. 1–2.

Andropov, Iu. V. (1983a), "Rech' General'nogo Sekretaria Tsentral'nogo komiteta KPSS tovarishcha Iu. V. Andropova na plenume TsK KPSS 15 iiuniia 1983 goda," *Pravda*, June 16, pp. 1–2.

Andropov, Iu. V. (1983b), "Vstrecha Iu. V. Andropova s Moskovskimi stankostroitel'iami," *Pravda*, February 1, pp. 1–2.

Anweiler, O. (1973) *The Soviets, The Russian Workers', Peasants' and Soldiers' Councils: 1905–1921*,Trans. R. Hein (New York: Random House Pantheon).

Bahro, Rudolf (1981), *The Alternative in Eastern Europe*, Trans. David Fernbach (London: New Left Books Verso).

Balabanov, M. (1925), *Istoriia rabochei kooperatsii v Rossii* (Moscow: Ekonomicheskaia zhizn').

Barabash, A. T. (1968), "Ob izuchenii effektivnosti distsiplinarnogo i obshchestvennogo vozdeistviia," *Sovetskoe gosudarstvo i pravo*, no. 11, pp. 104–8.

Barton, Paul (1962), "The Current Status of the Soviet Workers," in Abraham Brumberg (ed.), *Russia under Khrushchev* (New York: Praeger), pp. 263–79.

Beliarov, Iu. A. (1975), Administrator, Technical Inspection Section of the Labor Protection Department, All-Union Central Council of Trade Unions, interview, Moscow, February 21.

Bokarev, N. N. (1979), "Vozrastnie roli obshchestvennykh organizatsii v upravlenii proizvodstvom," in N. N. Kokarev and A. A. Beliakov (eds.), *Voprosy sovershenstvovaniia deiatel'nosti obshchestvennykh organizatsii* (Moscow: ISI/SSA AN SSSR), pp. 7–46.

improve national economic performance (Viktorov, 1978). Chairman Shibaev, for his part, supported a national union program designed to improve worker barracks and dormitories. Some regional union agencies, such as the Leningrad Trade Union Regional Council, have attempted to eliminate the most visible inequities in union social programs by pressing individual enterprise trade union organizations to share their jealously guarded services with workers from neighboring and less advantaged factories (Vinogradova, 1975).

Conclusion

As one looks beyond Brezhnev, Andropov, and Chernenko to Gorbachev, one finds that, for the first time in Soviet history, industrial union membership includes perhaps a majority whose parents worked at similar jobs. Upward mobility is more likely to mean movement within the working class than movement out of it (Kahan, 1979). Improving education levels among workers will eventually lead to better-educated union cadres and have already led to a better-educated General Secretary in Gorbachev. In each of these ways, the Soviet scene has moved away from the pattern of a modernizing society such as may still be found in communist states such as China and Romania toward the industrial maturity found in the German Democratic Republic, Hungary, and Czechoslovakia. All of these trends presage challenges to union institutions which are qualitatively different from those presented by revolution, civil war, collectivization, and industrialization. Such developments will not undermine the Leninist framework of dual functioning unionism; but they will, most likely, force Gorbachev and his fellow party, state, and union officials to create a new range of labor policy options within that broader context. The essential ambiguity of the dual functioning theory of labor relations, one which designates industrial unions as advocates both of higher productivity and of improved labor welfare, will continue. Soviet industrial union leaders of the future, like those of the past and present, will oppose individual violations of workers' rights as those rights are defined by state law and party pronouncement. Industrial conflict per se will remain illegitimate and the arena for labor–management discord will remain severely confined by fundamental definitions and bureaucratic obstacles inherent in centralized economic planning. Yet national labor policies under Gorbachev as well as future leaders may come to favor a group practically nonexistent during nearly any other period of Soviet history: a stable urban industrial proletariat.

Acknowledgments

I would like to thank Mark H. Teeter and Murray Feshbach for their invaluable comments and assistance during the preparation of this chapter. In addition, I would like to take this opportunity to acknowledge my deep personal and unequaled intellectual debt to Jerry Hough, whose encouragement and advice have stimulated my research on Soviet trade unions ever since my first days in graduate school.

References

Abramova, A.A. (1969), *Distsiplina truda v SSSR* (Moscow: Iuridicheskaia literatura).

Aleksandrov, N. G. (1972), "Prava profsoiuzov v oblasti uchastiia v upravlenii proizvodstvom," in N. G. Aleksandrov (ed.), *Sovetskoe trudovoe pravo* (Moscow: Iuridicheskaia literatura, pp. 196 – 201.

Alekseev, A. N., and Nazimova, A. K. (1981), "Obshchestvannaia aktivnost' Sovetskikh rabochikh (sotsiologicheskie aspekty problemy)," in L. A. Gordon, E. V. Klopov and A. K. Nazimova (eds.), *Rabochii klass na rubezhe 80-x godov* (Moscow: IMRD AN SSSR), pp. 127 – 45.

Alekseev, G., and Ivanov, E. (1968), *Profsoiuzy v period stroitel'stva kommunizma* (Moscow: Profizdat).

Aliev, G. A. (1983), "O proekte zakona SSSR o trudovykh kollektivakh i povyshenii ikh roli v upravlenii predpriiatiiami, uchrezhdeniiami, organizatsiiami. Doklad pervogo zamestitelia predsedatelia deputata G. A. Alieva," *Leningradskaia pravda*, June 18, p. 2.

Andropov, Iu. V. (1982), "Rech' General'nogo Sekretaria TsK KPSS Iu. V. Andropova," *Leningradskaia pravda*, November 23, pp. 1 – 2.

Andropov, Iu. V. (1983a), "Rech' General'nogo Sekretaria Tsentral'nogo komiteta KPSS tovarishcha Iu. V. Andropova na plenume TsK KPSS 15 iiuniia 1983 goda," *Pravda*, June 16, pp. 1 – 2.

Andropov, Iu. V. (1983b), "Vstrecha Iu. V. Andropova s Moskovskimi stankostroitel'iami," *Pravda*, February 1, pp. 1 – 2.

Anweiler, O. (1973) *The Soviets, The Russian Workers', Peasants' and Soldiers' Councils: 1905 – 1921*,Trans. R. Hein (New York: Random House Pantheon).

Bahro, Rudolf (1981), *The Alternative in Eastern Europe*, Trans. David Fernbach (London: New Left Books Verso).

Balabanov, M. (1925), *Istoriia rabochei kooperatsii v Rossii* (Moscow: Ekonomicheskaia zhizn').

Barabash, A. T. (1968), "Ob izuchenii effektivnosti distsiplinarnogo i obshchestvennogo vozdeistviia," *Sovetskoe gosudarstvo i pravo*, no. 11, pp. 104 – 8.

Barton, Paul (1962), "The Current Status of the Soviet Workers," in Abraham Brumberg (ed.), *Russia under Khrushchev* (New York: Praeger), pp. 263 – 79.

Beliarov, Iu. A. (1975), Administrator, Technical Inspection Section of the Labor Protection Department, All-Union Central Council of Trade Unions, interview, Moscow, February 21.

Bokarev, N. N. (1979), "Vozrastnie roli obshchestvennykh organizatsii v upravlenii proizvodstvom," in N. N. Kokarev and A. A. Beliakov (eds.), *Voprosy sovershenstvovaniia deiatel'nosti obshchestvennykh organizatsii* (Moscow: ISI/SSA AN SSSR), pp. 7 – 46.

Bulov, V. T. (1975), Chief, Production and Wage Department, Leningrad Regional Trade Union Council, interview, Leningrad, March 28.

Carr, E. H. (1966), *The Bolshevik Revolution* (Harmondsworth, Mddx: Penguin).

Carr, E. H. (1978), "Marriage of Inconvenience," *New York Review of Books*, May 18, pp. 42−3.

Chapman, Janet G. (1970), *Wage Variation in Soviet Industry: The Impact of the 1956−1960 Reform* (Santa Monica, Calif.: RAND Corporation).

Chapman, Janet G. (1979), "Recent Trends in the Soviet Industrial Wage Structure," in Arcadius Kahan and Blair Ruble (eds.), *Industrial Labor in the USSR* (Elmsford, N.Y.: Pergamon), pp. 151−83.

Dewar, Margaret (1956), *Labour Policy in the USSR* (London: Royal Institute of International Affairs).

Dogadov, A. (1927), *Sostoianie professional'nogo dvizheniia v SSSR (1924−1926gg.)* (Moscow: VTsSPS).

Dumachev, Ya (1977), "Kak povysit' rol' PDPS?," *Sovetskie profsoiuzy*, no. 6, pp. 16−17.

Dunham, Vera (1979), "The Waning Theme of the Worker as Hero in Recent Soviet Literature," in Arcadius Kahan and Blair Ruble (eds.), *Industrial Labor in the USSR* (Elmsford, N.Y.: Pergamon), pp. 379−412.

Dzhelomanov, V. (1975), Administrator, Organizational Department, All-Union Central Council of Trade Unions, interview, Moscow, February 4.

Ellman, Michael (1980), "A Note on the Distribution of Earnings in the USSR under Brezhnev," *Slavic Review*, vol. 29, no. 4 (December), pp. 669−71.

Filatov, N. A., and Turchenko, V. N. (1971), *Trud i distsiplina* (Moscow: Politicheskaia literatura).

Gordon, M. (1941), *Workers Before and After Lenin* (New York: Dutton).

Grinevich, V. (1923), *Professional'noe dvizhenie rabochikh v Rossii* (Moscow: Krasnaia nov').

Guliaev, G. I. (1976), "Pravovoe regulirovanie zarabotnoi platy," in A. A. Pashkov (ed.), *Sovetskoe trudovoe pravo* (Moscow: Iuridicheskaia literatura), pp. 349−404.

Hough, Jerry F. (1969), *The Soviet Prefects* (Cambridge, Mass.: Harvard University Press).

Hough, Jerry F. (1979), "Policy-Making and the Worker," in Arcadius Kahan and Blair Ruble (eds.), *Industrial Labor in the USSR* (Elmsford, N.Y.: Pergamon), pp. 367−96.

Iampol'skaia, Ts. A. (1973), "O sisteme profsoiuzov SSSR," in Ts. A. Iampol'skaia and A. I. Tsepin (eds.), *Pravovye aspekty deiatel'nosti profsoiuzov SSSR* (Moscow: Nauka), pp. 41−93.

Institut Filosofii AN SSSR, Institut Sotsiologicheskikh Issledovanii AN SSSR, Institut Istorii AN ESSR, NITS VKSH pri TSK VLKSM, Sovetskaia Sotsiologicheskaia Assotsiatsiia, Vsesoiuznoe Obshchestvo "Znanie" (1981), *Razvitie sotsial'noi struktury Sovetskogo obshchestva i sfera proizvodstvo: Preprinty dokladov Vsesoiuznoi nauchnoi konferentsii razvitie sotsial'noi struktury Sovetskogo obshchestva (dlia obsuzhdeniia)* (Moscow, 1981), vyp. 3.

(ILO) INTERNATIONAL LABOUR OFFICE (1924), *Industrial Life in Soviet Russia, Studies and Reports, Series B, No. 14* (Geneva: ILO).

(ILO) INTERNATIONAL LABOUR OFFICE (1959), *Trade Union Rights in the USSR, Studies and Reports, New Series, No. 49* (Geneva: ILO).

Ivanovskii, L. (1977), "Vyigryvaet proizvodstvo," *Sovetskie profsoiuzy*, no. 23, pp. 14−15.

Kahan, Arcadius (1979), "Some Problems of the Soviet Industrial Worker," in Arcadius Kahan and Blair Ruble (eds.), *Industrial Labor in the USSR* (Elmsford, N.Y.: Pergamon), pp. 283−312.

Kamskii, Kabel'nyi zavod im. 50-letita sssr (1974), *Kollektivnyi dogovor na 1974 god* (Kudymkar: Kudymkarskaia tipografiia).

Kaplan, F. (1968), *Bolshevik Ideology and the Ethics of Labor* (New York: Philosophical Library).

Kazakov, Iu. (1982), "Saratovskaia oblastnaia mezhsoiuznaia konferentsiia," *Trud*, February 3, p. 2.

Khaitovich, B. (1977), "S uchetom spetsifiki," *Sovetskie profsoiuzy*, no. 23, p. 14.

Kirsch, L. J. (1972), *Soviet Wages, Changes in Structure and Administration Since 1956* (Cambridge, Mass.: MIT Press).

Kisturga, M. G. (1982), *Profsoiuzy—shkola narodnogo samoupravleniia* (Kishinev: Shtinitsa).

Kliuev, A. A. (1975), Chief Legal Department, Leningrad Regional Council of Trade Unions, interview, Leningrad, January 13.

Kollontai, Alexandra (1921), *The Workers' Opposition in Russia* (Chicago: Industrial Workers of the World).

KPSS (Kommunisticheskaia partiia sovetskogo soiuza) (1963), *X s"ed RKP(b): Stenograficheskii otchet* (Moscow: KPSS/Partiizdat).

Kositsyn, I. (1975), Chief, Comrades' Courts and Labor Disputes Section, All- Union Central Council of Trade Unions, interview, Moscow, February 7.

"Krepit' distisipliny truda" (1980), *Trud*, January 13, p. 1.

Krivolopov, A. I., and Martuseivich, I. P. (1975), Director, Leningrad Bus Depot No. 4, and Chairman, Factory Trade Union Committee, Leningrad Bus Depot No. 4, interview, Leningrad, May 28.

Lapidus, Gail W. (1979), "The Female Industrial Labor Force: Dilemmas, Reassessments, and Options," in Arcadius Kahan and Blair Ruble (eds.), *Industrial Labor in the USSR* (Elmsford, N.Y.: Pergamon), pp. 232−79.

Lee, Rensselaer W., III (1979), "The Factory Trade Union Committee and Technological Innovation," in Arcadius Kahan and Blair Ruble (eds.), *Industrial Labor in the USSR* (Elmsford, N.Y.: Pergamon), pp. 116−34.

Leonova, L. S., and Savinchenko, N. V. (1982), "X s"ezd RKP(b) i ego istoricheskoe znachenie," *Vestnik Moskovskogo universiteta, seriia 8, istotiia*, no. 1, pp. 3−14.

Madison, Bernice (1979), "Trade Unions and Social Welfare," in Arcadius Kahan and Blair Ruble (eds.), *Industrial Labor in the USSR* (Elmsford, N.Y.: Pergamon), pp. 85−115.

Martiushev, A. S. (1975), Chairman, Leningrad Regional Committee of the Trade Union of Auto Transport and Highway Workers, interview, Leningrad, May 8.

McAuley, Alastair (1979), *Economic Welfare in the Soviet Union* (Madison, Wisc.: University of Wisconsin Press).

McAuley, Alastair (1981), "Welfare and Social Security," in Leonard Schapiro and Joseph Godson (eds.), *The Soviet Worker: Illusions and Realities* (New York: St. Martin's Press), pp. 194−230.

McAuley, Alastair (1982), "Sources of Earnings Inequality: A Comment on Alec Nove's Note on Income Distribution in the USSR," *Soviet Studies*, vol. 24, no. 3 (July), pp. 443−7.

McAuley, Mary (1969), *Labour Disputes in Soviet Russia, 1957−1965* (Oxford: Clarendon).

"Mezhsoiuznye konferentsii profsoiuzov" (1982), *Trud*, January 6, p. 1.

Morrell, E. (1965), "Communist Unionism: Organized Labor and the Soviet State," PhD dissertation, Harvard University.

Moses, Joel C. (1983), *The Politics of Women and Work in the Soviet Union and the United States* (Berkeley, Calif.: University of California/Institute of International Studies).

Nechemias, Carol (1980), "Regional Differentiation of Living Standards in the RSFSR: The Issue of Inequality," *Soviet Studies*, vol. 32, no. 3 (July), pp. 366−378.

Nikitinskii, V. I. (1971), *Effektivnost' norm trudovogo prava* (Moscow: Iuridicheskaia literatura).

Nove, Alec (1982), "Income Distribution in the USSR: A Possible Explanation of Some Recent Data," *Soviet Studies*, vol. 24, no. 2 (April), pp. 286−8.

Parol', V. I., *Sotsialisticheskii gorod* (Tallin: Valgus).

Pavlova, L. M., and Protopopov, A. S. (1979), "Profsoiuznoe dvizhenie v SSSR na etape razvitogo sotsializma," *Istoriia SSSR*, no. 4, p. 13.

"PDPS: koordinaty effektivnosti" (1977), *Sovetskie profsoiuzy*, no. 23, pp. 14−15.

Petrovichev, N. A., (1976), *Partiinoe stroitel'stvo* (Moscow: Isdatel'stvo politicheskoi literaturu).

Pozdniakova, O. (1982), "Volgogradskaia oblastnaia mezhsoiuznaia konferentsiia," *Trud*, January 31, p. 2.

Pravda, Alex (1982), "Is There a Soviet Working Class?", *Problems of Communism*, vol. 31, no. 6 (November/December), pp. 1−24.

"Proizvodstvennoe soveshchanie ili rabochei sobranie?" (1977), *Sovetskie profsoiuzy*, no. 12, pp. 16−17.

Prokhorov, V. (1982), "Profsoiuzy—vliiatel'naia sila nashego obshchestva," *Partiinaia zhizn'*, no. 14, pp. 27−34.

Rabkina, N. E., and Rimashevskaia, N. M. (1978), "Raspredelitel'nye otnosheniia i sotsial'noe razvitie," *Eko*, no. 5, p. 20.

Riabkova, Iu. I. (1975), Deputy Factory Trade Union Chairman, Moscow Watch Factory No. 2, interview, Moscow, February 13.

Romanov, G. V. (1982), "Leninskim kurson k novym sversheniiam. Iz doklada G. V. Romanova," *Leningradskaia pravda*, December 4, pp. 1−3.

Ruble, Blair A. (1981), *Soviet Trade Unions: Their Development in the 1970s* (Cambridge: Cambridge University Press).

Sbytova, L. S. (1982), *Struktura zaniatosti i effektivnost'proizvodstva* (Moscow: Nauka).

Schwarz, Solomon (1952), *Labor in the Soviet Union* (New York: Praeger).

Shalaev, S. A. (1982), "Rech'," *Trud*, December 4, pp. 1−2.

Shibaev, A. (1981), "Samaia massovaia organizatsiia trudiashchikhsia," *Kommunist*, no. 4, pp. 72−83.

Sirianni, Carmen (1982), *Workers Control and Socialist Democracy: The Soviet Experience* (London: Verso).

Slider, Darrell (1983), "Reforming the Workplace: The 1983 Soviet Law on Labor Collectives," unpublished paper presented at Southern Conference on Slavic Studies, Atlanta, Georgia, October 7.

Slovinskii, I. (1979), "Doverie obviatyvaet," *Sovetskie profsoiuzy*, no. 11, pp. 22−3.

Smirnov, V. N. (1972), *Distsiplina truda v SSSR* (Leningrad: LGU).

Smoliarchuk, V. I. (1971), "Vsesoiuznyi tsentral'nyi sovet professional'nykh soiuzov," *Bol'shaia sovetskaia entsiklopediia*, 3rd edn. (Moscow: Sov. Ents.) Vol. 5, pp. 473−4.

Smoliarchuk, V. I. (1973), *Prava profsoiuzov v regulirovanii trudovykh otnoshenii rabochikh i sluzhiashchikh* (Moscow: Profizdat).

Spravochnik profsoiuznogo rabotnika (1974) (Moscow: Profizdat).

Tamotsiunene, R. (1981), "Regional'nyi aspekt razvitiia professional'noi aktivnosti rabochikh," in Institute filosofii, sotsiologii i prava AN Lit SSR, Pribaltiskoe otdelenie Sovetskoi sotsiologicheskoi assotsiatsii, *Gorod kak sreda zhiznediatel'nosti cheloveka* (Vil'nius, 1981), Vol. 1, pp. 99−102.

Torkanovskii, E. (1983), "Razvitie demokraticheski!:h nachal v upravlenii proizvodstvom," *Kommunist*, no. 8, pp. 36−46.

Tsepin, A., and Shchiglik, A. (1979), *Gosudarstvo i profsoiuzy v razvitom sotsialisticheskom obshchestve* (Moscow: Profizdat).

Turin, S. P. (1935), *From Peter the Great to Lenin* (London: Frank Cass).

Turysov, K. T. (1982), "Rech'," *Kazakhstanskaia pravda*, February 19, p. 2.

Ushkov, B. I. (1976), "Poriadok rassmotreniia trudovykh sporov," in A. S. Pashkov (ed.), *Sovetskoe trudovoe pravo* (Moscow: Iuridicheskaia literatura), pp. 471−89.

"V TsK KPSS, Sovete Ministrov SSSR i VTsSPS rassmotren vopros ob usilenii rabotu po ukrepleniiu sotsialisticheskoi distsipliny truda i priniaty sootvetsvuiushchie postanovleniia," (1983), *Leningradskaia pravda*, August 7, pp. 1−2.

"V ukreplenii distsipliny, organizovannosti—zalog uspekha" (1983), *Leningradskaia pravda*, March 30, p. 1.

"V VTsSPS, Prezidiume Verkhovnogo Soveta SSSR, Sovete Ministrov SSSR i VTsSPS o dal'neishem ukreplenii trudovoi distsipliny i sokrashchenii tekuchesti kadrov v narodnom khozi-aistve" (1980), *Trud*, January 12, pp. 1–2.

Viktorov, A. (1978), "V interesakh liudei truda" (1978), *Trud*, December 1, p. 2.

Vinogradova, L. (1975), Chief, State Social Insurance Department, Leningrad Regional Council of Trade Unions, interview, Leningrad, March 24.

"Vliiatel'naia sila Sovetskogo obshchestva" (1978), *Trud*, June 10, p. 2.

"Vysokaia rol' trudovogo kollektiva" (1978), *Trud*, April 12, p. 2.

Yanowitch, Murray (ed.) (1979), *Soviet Work Attitudes* (White Plains, N.Y.: Sharpe).

"Zakon SSSR o trudovykh kollektivakh i povyshenii ikh roli v upravlenii predpriiatiami, uchrezh-deniiami, organizatsiiami" (1983), *Leningradskaia pravda*, June 19, pp. 1–2.

Ziegler, Charles E. (1983), "Worker Participation and Worker Discontent in the Soviet Union," *Political Science Quarterly*, vol. 98, no. 2 (Summer), pp. 235–53.

Zinov'ev, N. I. (1975), Chairman, Leningrad Regional Committee of the Trade Union of Machine Construction, interview, April 11, 1975, Leningrad.

3

Labor Unions in the German Democratic Republic

Marilyn Rueschemeyer
C. Bradley Scharf

Historical Development

The German labor movement is one of the oldest in Europe, but its history is scarcely an unbroken train of success. The first attempt to create a widespread workers' organization, inspired by Stephan Born, was virtually stillborn in the wake of the abortive 1848 revolution. Considerably greater success followed Ferdinand Lassalle in his founding of the General German Workers' Association in 1863, with its decidedly socialist orientation. But struggles among competing unions and aspiring working-class parties thwarted any significant progress until the formation of the Social Democratic Party in 1875. The Bismarck government quickly drove new fissures into the nascent labor movement by the twin tactics of "enlightened" social policies—state-mandated disability insurance and retirement pensions—and the prohibition of socialist political activity (1878–1890) (Grebing, 1969: 29–59).

Around the turn of the century, Carl Legien led a rapidly growing union movement into an influential partnership with the German Social Democrats and to a dominant role in the international labor movement. Yet tangible gains for German workers were few. And the few experiments with worker consultation in the factories were the product of progressive entrepreneurs, not of labor union pressure. Not until the specter of the Russian revolution and the collapse of the empire did German employers accede to the principle of collective bargaining and other long-sought reforms, in a Bismarck-like attempt to avert more radical changes (Braunthal, 1978: 22–3; Barthel and

Marilyn Rueschemeyer, Department of Sociology, Rhode Island School of Design, Providence, Rhode Island, and Department of Sociology, Brown University, Providence, Rhode Island.

C. Bradley Scharf, Department of Political Science, Seattle University, Seattle, Washington.

Dickau, 1980: 67−9). The Weimar Constitution prescribed the participation of worker representatives in enterprise councils and in economic councils at the county and national levels. The enterprise councils never developed a clear course of action in light of their dual task of preserving the interests of the workers on the one hand, and supporting enterprise management, protecting the firm from "disturbances," and promoting "good relations" between the employer and employees, on the other (Enterprise Council Law of January 18, 1920). The economic councils did not evolve beyond a form of hollow co-optation, as the political power of the labor unions was diverted to attempting to save the Republic from a right-wing takeover, fighting off the Communist challenge within the labor movement, and struggling to preserve working-class gains in the face of economic collapse. Larger aspirations of a more fundamental implementation of "economic democracy" never became more than high-sounding rhetoric. Even many of the more modest reforms never touched large segments of the working class (Braunthal, 1978: 32−62; Barthel and Dickau, 1980: 68−72). Disagreement over appropriate tactics paralyzed the labor federation before the challenge of National Socialism, and the leadership and structure of the movement was effectively destroyed in May, 1933.

Following World War II, entrepreneurs in the Western Zones revived the technique of granting large nominal concessions to the unions, in order to undermine support for socialism. The subsequent evolution of labor union power and its effect on both worker interests and the national economy of the Federal Republic are the subject of great controversy (Barthel and Dickau, 1980: 153−63). In the Eastern Zone the rapid introduction of state socialism and the transition to single-party government simplified the tasks of organized labor, while also depriving it of vital bargaining resources.

The creation of the FDGB (Freier Deutscher Gewerkschaftsbund— Free German Labor Union Federation) in the early years of the German Democratic Republic (GDR) was largely an effort to adapt a previous form of social organization to the requirements of a radically altered political and economic order. However, it is a mistake to draw too close an analogy between the functions of the FDGB and those of labor unions in the USSR and many of the other states under examination in this volume. For much of their history, Soviet labor unions had a primary purpose a "civilizing" function, the task of training nineteenth-century peasants to respond to the demands of the urban industrial life of the twentieth century. Following World War II, the Soviet Zone suffered from economic destruction and disorder, but it had a disciplined workforce. The FDGB, therefore, never had to devote an effort to instilling labor discipline that was in any sense comparable to most of the other unions discussed here.

Yet the FDGB did face discipline problems of another sort. The early union structure was permeated by Social Democratic influences which fostered expectations of worker democracy. The founding conference in February, 1946 brought together Communist, Social Democratic, and Christian unionists in support of a program of union democracy, economic nationalization, and a "total right of co-determination," a program thoroughly consistent with the 1928 German Labor Union Congress. The spontaneous revival of enterprise councils was legitimized in all zones by the Inter-Allied Control Council, their tasks to be carried out "in cooperation with the recognized labor unions." A Soviety Military Administration order of October, 1947 constituted a new labor law, which stipulated a number of progressive union goals concerning equitable pay and benefits, improved productivity, and better working and living conditions. Like the 1920 law on enterprise councils, this order explicitly assigned to worker organizations the obligation to assist the enterprise director in the fulfillment of his functions.

Despite faltering attempts to imitate Soviet practice (the "shock workers' movement," for example, was not especially successful), the FDGB avoided open conflict between its Soviet Democratic majority and its Communist minority until the collapse of the joint occupation regime in 1948. Hans Jendretzky, who would later be accused of promoting indsicriminate concessions during the 1953 workers' uprising, was replaced by Herbert Warnke as FDGB chairman. Warnke directed a purge of Social Democratic elements, which nearly decimated the ranks of union officials. By 1950 worker disenchantment with autocratic union leaders and with increasing signs of the permanence of Soviet predominance rendered the FDGB almost wholly illegitimate. It became common for union officials to be intimidated by their fellow factory workers. New contracts were greeted by strikes and slowdowns. The lack of FDGB authority was most obvious in June 1953 when Berlin construction workers precipitated an upheaval which encompassed over 350 separate public demonstrations throughout the nation. Only the deployment of Soviet tanks restored order.

In the uneasy ensuing truce, the FDGB began the protracted, painful process of recruitment to union posts. A limited experiment with workers' committees, undertaken possibly in response to workers' roles in the 1956 events in Hungary and Poland, was abandoned after only fourteen months, as Social Democratic influences resurfaced. FDGB acquisition of authority for administering labor safety rules and the social security system, as well as formal cooptation of union representatives into high-level economic bodies, were feeble attempts to create some measure of union legitimacy. Yet the alienation of the rank-and-file persisted.

The decade of the 1960s offers three milestones which together facilitated a noteworthy change in both the functions of the FDGB and its relations with the workers. First, the closure of the Berlin border made terribly plain the permanence of the SED (Sozialistische Einheitspartei: Deutschlands—Socialist Unity Party)—FDGB regime and gradually induced the East German citizenry to come to terms with prevailing political and economic realities. Second, the economic reforms of 1963 to 1966 introduced an element of decentralized authority and, with it, the potential for meaningful work participation in the factories. Third, the Seventh SED Congress (April 1967), which consolidated the economic reforms into a somewhat more centralized Economic System of Socialism, also envisioned an expanded scheme of "social control," by which "popular" organizations, especially the unions, would actively supplement the ruling party as monitors of economic activity (Scharf, 1976).

The Union Role

The present definition of the purposes of labor organizations in the GDR arises from two partially incompatible views of society. On the one hand, an organic perspective regards society as composed of functional elements, devoid of fundamental antagonisms, and harmoniously linked in a finely orchestrated pursuit of the common good. On the other hand, an egalitarian, anti-statist perspective regards concentrations of economic and political power as potentially subject to abuse and, therefore, in constant need of guidance and watchfulness in order to prevent the distorted application of power in violation of the public interest. Both perspectives are authentically Marxist-Leninist and typical of communist states. In the GDR, as elsewhere in the communist world, it is the overarching function of the ruling SED to reconcile these two views of reality, while presumably not falling victim itself to the temptation to exercise power in a self-serving manner—a presumption severely disputed by domestic and foreign observers.

In its idealized role as guardian of the public interest, the SED is nominally supported by an array of social organizations, most notably the FDGB, whose purposes differ from those of the SED only in that they are less authoritative and usually tailored to emphasize the needs of some social segment in the short run. In the absence of antagonistic class differences, (virtually everyone is a "worker" in some sense, i.e. not a capitalist), organized labor has a "constituency" as large as the citizenry itself. Since both the unions and the party exist as expressions of the "interests of all working people," it is difficult to avoid the conclusion that one of these institutions is superfluous, and it is equally difficult to deduce a rational division of functions between the two on strictly theoretical grounds. This anomaly present elsewhere in the communist world is at the root of Lenin's view of organized labor as "a very peculiar institution, which is set up under capitalism, which inevitably exists in the transition from capitalism to communism, and whose future is a question mark" (Lenin, 1921/1960). At the present time East Germany's labor unions express this ambiguity in their pro-statist and anti-statist functions and in their ostensible duplication of many SED roles.

The FDGB's pro-statist role is most evident in the relationship of central bodies to the central executive organs of government. The FDGB Federal Board directs several specialized departments, each with regular access to corresonding government agencies, especially the Office for Labor and Wages and the State Plan Commission. Official sources emphasize the continuous process of union–government consultation, for example, in the phased reform of the wage system (begun in 1977). Such collaboration would scarcely have been possible in earlier years; only since the early 1970s have the union departments disposed of sufficiently expert staffs to make substantive contributions to major policy discussions. These formal linkages are supplemented by the longstanding participation of union representatives in the National Assembly, where the FDGB permanently occupies 68 of the 500 seats. The National Assembly, for the most part, retains its modest role as a legitimating forum for previously agreed policy. A pro-statist role is further anchored in the customary assignment of the FDGB chairman (currently Harry Tisch) to a post in the Politburo, the chief party–state coordinating committee and collective executive.

The sum of these arrangments is a state–party–FDGB ruling triumvirate for many policy purposes at the national level. A formal recognition of this corporatist scheme occurred in 1972, when the FDGB was afforded joint status with the Council of Ministers as the initiator of legislation in the realm of incomes and social policy. Unlike worker–management relations in the enterprise, union–government relations are depicted as uniformly harmonious. "Reciprocal cooperation with the government and its organs has developed well. For that which we introduce from the standpoint of workers' concerns, for our union views and suggestions, we have always found in the Council of Ministers an accommodating and active partner" (Tisch, 1982: 38).

Additional union–government linkages occur in the regular consultations between the central boards of the branch unions for each economic sector and the corresponding economic ministries. Compared with information on the central FDGB and on enterprise union organization, relatively little is published about the branch-specific union structures. In general, their activity appears to be focused on negotiating those aspects of industrywide agreements directly related to remuneration, training, and safety. Because they necessarily operate within the parameters of planned increases in real income and projected ratios between productivity and worker compensation, the branch unions are necessarily concerned with measures to increase labor productivity (i.e. increased capital investments) and to ensure equitable pay for workers. Not surprisingly, the respective economic ministries are also interested in maximizing both capital investment and workers' pay. The logic of central economic planning, therefore, creates a natural alliance between each economic ministry and its corresponding branch union, as together they compete for increased allocation of resources before the State Plan Commission and the Presidium of the Council of Ministers. The ensuing political contest, then, does not take place between the state on one side and the union on the other, but rather pits one ministry – union alliance against another.

Table 3.1 illustrates one area of conflicting interests among union branches. Labor unions in the higher paid sectors have an interest in preserving income differentials, while unions in the lower paid sector seek significant redistribution of incomes. In their quest to attract more qualified workers, of course, the corresponding economic ministries share union perspectives. As is the case in evaluating wage structures in market economies, ambiguous evidence does not permit clear conclusions about the course of changes in the relative position of wages across sectors. The relative

Table 3.1
Average Income of Workers and Employees by Economic Sector as a Percentage of National GDR Average, 1970 and 1980

Sector	1970	Rank	1980	Rank
Energy, fuel	109.2	4	111.9	1
Metals	114.6	1	111.9	1
Railway	101.4	7	111.3	3
Chemicals	105.1	6	105.6	4
Machines, vehicles	105.5	5	103.9	5
Trucking	111.7	2	103.3	6
Electronics	101.2	9	102.0	7
Construction	109.3	3	101.1	8
Construction materials	101.4	7	100.1	9
Forestry	93.8	11	99.1	10
Food	93.0	12	95.3	11
State agriculture	88.7	14	93.9	12
Hydro-economy	94.0	10	91.3	13
Light industry	88.7	14	91.1	14
Post, communication	85.7	16	90.1	15
Textiles	81.1	18	87.7	16
Wholesale trade	93.0	12	86.1	17
Retail trade	83.3	17	83.9	18

Source: Calculated from *Statistiches Jahrbuch 1981 der Deutschen Demokratischen Republik* (Berlin: Staatsuerlag der DDR, 1981), pp. 109, 137, 152, 169, 217, 232.

gains or losses by sectors (energy and railway vs. trucking and wholesale trade) may be attributed to differential union effectiveness, to changing influence among economic ministries, or to shifts in the labor market.

Officially, the central FDGB, which is the nominal representative of *all* workers, asserts that changes in the wage structure reflect changes in relative working conditions and requisite skills. The FDGB claims credit (along with the party and the state) for the modest compression of income differentials, portrayed as evidence of further socialist development. The notion that conflicts of interest might exist among unions representing different economic sectors is rigorously excluded from all union discussions; the assertion of working-class unity is one of the most fervently guarded myths of the GDR.

As in many of the states under examination in this volume, both the central FDGB and the branch unions have territorial executive bodies at the county (*Bezirk*) and district (*Kreis*) levels. Union activity at the county level is highly variable. In general, the FDGB organs are active, but not very visible. Their functions are concentrated on developing union personnel, on training, guidance, and support for district FDGB organs, which represent the more important operative level. The activity of county branch unions varies from nonexistent, where there is no significant employment in the relevant sector, to extremely important where there is a high territorial concentration of a specific economic employment (e.g. mining). In the latter case, the county branch union assumes many of the functions of a branch union central board in dealing directly with the economic ministry.

Proceeding down the organizational hierarchy, a marked shift in union emphasis emerges at the level of district FDGB bodies. The primary institutional linkage is no longer with national and regional government executives, but with enterprise directors and combine general directors. And the object of concern is no longer the general interest of workers, but the rights of specific employees under very specific circumstances. In the last analysis, of course, truly significant worker representation, if it is to occur at all, must occur in the workplace. Yet enterprise union organizations are chronically unequal to this task, chiefly due to the shortage of union spokespersons who are both trained to deal competently with expert management and trusted by their fellow workers. The main function of district FDGB boards thus becomes the continuous supervision of enterprise unions, combined with occasional direct intervention, in order to transform local union leaders into legitimate worker representatives and viable negotiating partners with enterprise management.

It should be recalled that the 1950s featured many serious FDGB errors, as the unions moved to eliminate overt expression of antisocialist and anti-Soviet sentiments. The 1960s were a transition period, as the FDGB cultivated a new crop of officials accustomed to the prevailing order and worked

to develop positive responses to the problem of deep-seated worker alienation. The most recent decade is characterized by efforts to elicit and reward
a positive, critical engagement of workers in the twin tasks of economic
rationalization and advocacy of workers' rights. In the works of FDGB chairman Harry Tisch: "The active collaboration of workers and their union
interest representatives in all questions of work, wages, and living conditions
is a documented right. Consequently, when it comes to violations of socialist
democracy and legality, we expect that all union boards and leaders will
confront such manifestations promptly and without indulgence" (Tisch,
1982: 28). In short, the FDGB strives to be less an instrument of repression
than a vehicle of expression. In the present phase, the district FDGB organs
constitute the lynchpin in the process of transformation.

The foregoing discussion suggests rather clearly the extent to which
the unions have matured beyond the days of postwar reconstruction. At that
time the old Leninist formula of the unions as "transmission belts" from the
party and government elites to the workers was a fitting description. While
this basic communication function remains, it has been supplemented by
many more challenging tasks.

Unions and Party

Through this evolutionary change, subtle shifts have also occurred in
the relationship of the unions to the ruling SED. In the early days the FDGB
competed unsuccessfully with the party in the recruitment of competent
personnel. The consequent dependence upon former Social Democrats and
other pre-communist union leaders to occupy posts in enterprise and branch
unions led directly to the open conflicts which devastated the FDGB through
the 1950s. Such conflicts, in turn, justified the repeated intrusion of SED
officials into the personnel policies of the unions and further delayed the
creation of a coherent union structure. An important legacy of the 1960s
transition was the allocation of increased funding for training union officials,
combined with the gradual subsiding of frequent party intervention in to
FDGB organizational matters. As always, virtually all paid union officials, as
well as a great many volunteer union officials, are members of the SED. In
addition, the modes of interaction between union and party bodies are
extensive and formally specified. Yet this very formalism suggests the degree
of institutional separation, which now exists along with a rather intense
party–union collaboration. In principle, certain SED officials can still influence the selection of union leaders in specific cases, yet the costs of doing so
overtly will outweigh the better course of allowing the FDGB's own established personnel function to operate independently. The exclusion of anti-
socialists results not just from bald political proscription but also from the

awareness that effective union work can be performed only by leaders acceptable to those who control the prevailing political and economic system.

Today, the FDGB is more than a residual "mass organization" floating in the wake of the ruling party. It has become something of an active junior partner. Just as the SED is formally represented in union bodies, the unions are represented in party bodies. While it is clear that the unions may not publicly advocate significant policy changes without high-level SED authorization, there is nevertheless ample opportunity to present union perspectives without closed forums. Relative to unions in liberal democracies, of course, the force of FDGB initiatives is blunted by the inability to impose electoral sanctions or call for strikes against public employers.

The Union in the Enterprise:
The Economic and Social Context

Unlike some European and American unions, the FGB is organized not by trades, but by economic sector. Thus there are eight industrial unions, plus additional unions for food and retail trade, government and public services, state-owned agriculture, health, education, science, art, and civilian employees of the military. Only cooperative farmers, self-employed persons, and those in active military service are excluded. Total membership in 1981 was more than 9.1 million, roughly 97 percent of those eligible.

Despite the noteworthy growth of service sector employment, the industrial unions still account for the bulk of the membership (Table 3.2). Largely for this reason, industrial or production enterprises provide the setting for what GDR sources apparently regard as the paradigmatic union structure. An additional consideration is the fact that, apart from the national capital and the major cities, production enterprises frequently represent the focal point of urban and suburban communities; larger enterprises act as a hub around which revolve the economic, social, and political lives of employees and other nearby residents. Many dimensions of community welfare and development depend upon the viablity of dominant firms, their cooperation with local public officials, and their ability to provide financial support for community endeavors. Not only does this emphasis on production units accord with a Marxist value on economic roles, it also provides a marginal element of systemic decentralization, which is not always evident in formal characterizations of the GDR's centralized, unitary government and the integrative machinery of the ruling SED.

Making production and work central for the whole of social life is the fundamental rationale for the work collective, the lowest level of union organization in the enterprise. A formally organized structure within every

Table 3.2
Membership of FDGB Branch Unions, 1976

Union	Membership	Membership as percentage of total sector employees
Metals	1,643,128	97.7
Trade, food, entertainment	943,689	94.6
Construction, lumber	843,256	94.9
Transport, communications	707,850	97.9
Textiles, clothing	603,419	95.7
State employees and communal economy	541,338	96.4
Agriculture, forestry	539,909	91.0
Chemicals	514,141	97.7
Health	451,704	96.9
Education	422,907	98.3
Mining, energy	390,033	98.5
Printing and paper	151,129	97.0
Science	148,421	98.4
Arts	62,324	94.9
Bismuth/uranium		—
Civil employees of the military	192,273[a]	—
Total	8,155,521	

[a]Estimate.

Source: Günther Erbe, *et al., Politik, Wirtschaft und Gesellschaft in der DDR* (Opladen: Westdeutscher Verlag, 1979), p. 135.

factory, administration, or other work organization, the work collective is to establish work and the workgroup as a central reference point in people's lives. Work collectives vary in size and may be composed of just the few people one works with directly in the enterprise. In this chapter we concentrate on the normally somewhat larger union collective with an elected representative (*Vertrauensperson*) which is ideally, though not always, composed of twenty-five to thirty people. In a university collective, to take one example, the group may include all academic professionals, as well as secretaries and technical assistants in one field of research and teaching such as chemistry.

If we focus on questions of worker autonomy and control of work and on the related issues of antagonistic interests of management and workers, it appears that worker autonomy—conceptually distinguishable from union autonomy—is likely to increase as we go down the hierarchy of enterprise organization. This makes an examination of work collective crucial for our discussion. Union work collectives in manufacturing enterprises seem to differ from those in professional work organizations in the methods used to affect the worklife of their members and in their ability to command some autonomy. Similarly, union collectives of unskilled or semi skilled workers function differently from collectives of highly skilled workers. Recent development in the composition of the East German labor force make these consequences of occupational qualification significant indeed.

Economic growth and the full implementation of the "scientific-technological revolution" (*wissenschaftlich-technische revolution*) are paramount goals of the East German state. This has far-reaching consequences for the issues under discussion here. Several specific developments should be at least briefly indicated.

Some experimentation with enterprise autonomy and the increased use of specialized expertise at the local production level are two developments which have widened the room for independent decision-making within the enterprise itself. The fact that industrial mangement depends more than ever on skilled experts who can exert influence on enterprise decisions is bound to result in significant gains for the techical intelligentsia. However, the widening of the decision-making arena in the enterprise does not necessarily increase either worker input or worker autonomy; the interests of the workers may or may not be furthered by the new production arrangements (Zimmerman, 1970: 98−112).

The importance of cooperation of workers in implementing the scientific organization of work (*Wissenschaftliche Arbeitsorganisation*) has often been stressed by union and state officials. However, relatively little space in this literature has been devoted to group participation, although it was recognized that a good work collective reduces turnover (Kahl, 1981: 77−81; Heck *et al.,* 1975). Discussions of worker participation typically focus on the contribution of the individual. Political−ideological persuasion is used to encourage active participation. Ideally, discussion begins with union officials asking the workers for proposals. Essentially, however, union functionaries clearly define tasks which are then "implemented" in the collective. The goal is to improve the quantity and quality of work without letting groups of workers take over actual decision-making because such a situation would go against the tenets of "democratic centralism."

> The principle of individual management in the economy must be implemented just as consistently as the all-round democratic participation of the workers . . . The right to give instructions, on the one hand, and the duty to draw on the collective in the process of management and to enable them to ever greater participation in management functions, on the other, are inseparable. This unity implies the manager's duty to explain the tasks thoroughly and, while doing so, to develop the participation of the collective in working out their respective tasks. (Richter, 1977: 13−14)

The literature reflects a realistic awareness that the technological revolution has not done away with dull and repetitive tasks and that technological innovation may lead—in the assembly-line, for example—to psychic stress, reduction of social contact, and emptying work of content (Kahl, 1981; Schneider, 1981; Stollberg, 1978).

Concern with economic growth has led to tremendous pressure on workers to improve their productivity, to use their working time and materials effectively, to adapt to the use of new technological possibilities, and to participate actively in the "movement" for socialist competition and innovation. Despite these goals, labor productivity is one-third lower than in West Germany (Zimmerman, 1978: 25). There are persistent difficulties in coordinating economic production and distribution so that appropriate materials and tools are available when needed. This, as we shall see, is even reflected in worker complaints about their working conditions. Moreover, as in the United States and Great Britain, there has been less than adequate investment in new technology. Difficulties of staffing multiple shifts in the expensive electronic factories present an additional problem. Women are unwilling to work night shifts without compensatory pay and other amenities to accommodate their household and parenting roles. These factories operate well below their capacity. Finally, guaranteed job security in the GDR and a high demand for labor have led to an exploration of new ways of motivating workers, some of which will be quite familiar to Western readers.

Piece-rates as well as bonus wages tied to enterprise profit are used when possible. Bonuses are made dependent upon the result achieved by the enterprise as a whole and are financed from the enterprise's profit (Leptin and Melzer, 1978: 45–46). In 1976 additional wage reforms were introduced in some branches of industry with the goal of further relating income to performance (Zimmermann, 1978: 27).

Other related developments supplement a more individualized material incentive structure. In particular, increased union participation in enterprise decision-making and what skeptics might call a manipulative "human relations" approach to worker needs have emerged. Work safety is reported to have improved significantly (see Table 3.3). Other efforts, too, often focus on down-to-earth changes in the work environment, frequently reflecting physiological and psychological traditions of research on work. Interview

Table 3.3
Work Accidents That Have To Be
Reported per 1,000 Workers

1960	48.6
1971	40.4
1975	33.0
1980	29.0

Source: *Statistisches Jarbuch 1981 der DDR* (Berlin: Staatsverlag der DDR), 1981, p. 17.

Table 3.4
Level of Qualification of Labor Force (percent of total labor force)

Qualification Level	1945	1955	1969	1975	1977
Unskilled and semiskilled workers	76	70	46	29	25
Skilled workers and master craftsmen	21	25	45	57	58
Workers with advanced technical training and university education	3	5	9	14	17

Source: Schneider, 1981: 100.

respondents who studied improving work conditions in enterprises (Rueschemeyer, 1982/83: 27–47) emphasized the importance of physical improvements, of provision for exercise, of food served at the workplace, and of adequate transportation for shift workers. One particular design involved relocating doors and windows and the use of color for stimulating emotion.

Finally, in response to the demands of the "scientific-technological revolution," the regime has sought to improve the education of its workers, and this effort has been very successful, with a tremendous increase in the number of skilled workers being most noteworthy (see Table 3.4). While the proportion of unskilled and semiskilled workers declined from three quarters at the end of World War II to one quarter in 1977, the percentage of skilled workers and craftsmen more than doubled and has reached nearly 60 percent. This development went far beyond an older German tradition of strong occupational training, as it incorporated the new comprehensive polytechnical high school system (first to tenth grade). Despite such gains, a new problem now presents itself. Twenty percent of the workers are not employed at their proper levels and are working at jobs which do not make use of their skills; the scientific-technological employment and qualified work has not grown at the same speed as the educational expansion. Although present wage reform considers training or educational programs completed to be important criteria for higher wage brackets, there is nevertheless considerable discontent among these workers. Recognition of these problems has resulted, among other things, in the reduction of admissions to institutions of higher learning in general (from 44,000 in 1971 to 32,000 in 1976) and of admissions to correspondence courses in particular (in 1971, 9,711 people were admitted to these courses; in 1976, only 3,405; Zimmermann, 1978: 30). While this may have reduced educational expenditure and kept people in their places of work, it has disrupted one of the more attractive features of East German worklife: broad-based opportunity for continued education.

Underutilization of skills as well as other discontents are closely related to turnover in the workplace. Despite the absence of precise data on turnover, the matter greatly concerns management as well as central planners and researchers and is of critical importance to the issue of worker autonomy. Workers with valuable skills, acquired in formal training or on-the-job learning, and those willing to improve their qualifications, can express dissatisfaction with work conditions by leaving. This option remains contingent on their ability to find other jobs or study places. Side by side with an apparent oversupply of acquired skills and education exist pervasive indications of unfulfilled demand for qualified workers and chronic labor shortages. Sabel and Stark have argued that labor shortages are inherent in the basic structure of East European socialist economies (1982: 439–75). At the same time, policymakers and academic commentators insist that the overall educational expansion and the concept of lifelong education are crucial for the development of socialist society, relatively independent of the changing economic needs (Bohring, 1981: 244–53).

Thus far discussion has focused upon the political and socioeconomic context for the operation of unions in the GDR enterprises. However fragmentary and partial, it has identified some of the larger tensions which shape the relations between management and union and between the official organizational structure and workers. It also indicates bases and leverage points for worker autonomy vis-à-vis that structure, however limited. With these points in mind, it is now appropriate to direct attention toward the role of the union in the production enterprise.

The Union in the Enterprise: The Organizational Context

Over the years, enterprise union organizations have become larger and somewhat more differentiated. There also have been increased efforts to include larger proportions of the population in some dimension of "socialist democracy," as well as to afford worker representatives more direct access to enterprise decision processes. Because the enterprise union shares in the FDGB role as the "interest representative of all working people," its putative tasks are enormous. An *abbreviated* list includes the following: (1) to promote the broadest possible participation of all employees in improving production, reducing waste and inefficiency, and discovering new resources; (2) to familiarize all employees with the production plan and, through joint management–worker committees, to take part in the formation and evaluation of annual plans; (3) to lead work collectives in "socialist competition" to achieve higher levels of performance; (4) to assure adherence to wage and bonus regulations; (5) to guarantee management's attentive handling of workers' suggestions and the payment of appropriate financial rewards; (6) to assure employee observance of work rules and to prevent arbitrary management behavior, especially with regard to job assignments and dismissals; (7) to promote worker training and career advancement; (8) to enforce laws regarding labor safety; (9) to promote the special concerns of women and younger employees; (10) to recommend expenditures from the enterprise culture fund and social fund; (11) to advocate the housing and consumer needs of employees; and (12) to administer the social security system. Extramural responsibilities include facilitating cooperation with related enterprises, aiding school programs for socialization to the work environment, ensuring worker representation in the assemblies of local government, and supporting local activities of the National Front (*Protokoll des VII FDGB-Kongresses*, 1968). Today most enterprise unions have a full-time paid leader and as many as twelve unpaid commissions: agitation/propaganda, social policy, labor safety, union finance, social security, culture and education, youth questions, women's questions, socialist competition, worker's innovations, labor and wages, and the standing production council (Belwe, 1979: 111–19). More than 25 percent of the union members exercise at least nominal voluntary duties within the enterprise union (Tisch, 1982: 42; Table 3.5).

In principle, all officials of the enterprise union are elected by a membership assembly. But in practice continuity in office is high, and the infrequent replacements are designated by the remaining incumbents and submitted as part of an unopposed slate. The post of full-time enterprise union leader is subject to designation by the district FDGB board. Sometimes the designated union leader has never worked in the enterprise.

Table 3.5
Participation of FDGB Members in Volunteer Roles, 1980

Total FDGB Members	8,806,754
Shop stewards	229,589
Culture coordinators	281,468
Sport organizers	224,590
Social security recorders	280,754
Labor safety monitors	262,237
Women's commission members	80,385
Youth commission members	30,810
Members of central standing production councils	64,632
Members of innovators' circle	77,933
Members of conflict commission	229,829

Source: Statistisches Jahrbuch 1981 der Deutschen Demokratischen Republic (Berlin: Staatsuerlag der DDR, 1981), p. 395.

By way of contrast, greater worker initiative is evident in the selection of the shop steward (*Vertrauensmann*), culture coordinator, and social security recorder in each union group. The union group, usually including 20−35 members, is the lowest union subdivision within the enterprise. Here the designation of successors is mainly through consensus of the group members, although voting contests are not uncommon. The absence of explicit outside guidance ostensibly encourages the emergence of trusted spokespersons, who can forge a useful link to the more passive workers. At the same time, individuals who thus receive the endorsement of coworkers are an important source of subsequent recruitment to more responsible union posts.

After much experimentation with diverse nonunion forms of worker participation, the present practice is to incorporate all of these activities under the purview of the enterprise union leader. This change corresponds to the improved recruitment and training of union officials, as well as the general effort to upgrade the prestige of the FDGB. Thus, competition and innovation are now firmly under union leadership, and the standing production councils have emerged as a primary institution of union−management interaction (Belwe, 1979: 161−5).

This general movement to make more visible and distinctive the institutional face of the enterprise unions occurs within the context of extensive personnel interpenetration of the enterprise union, the enterprise management and staff, and the enterprise party organization. Because union membership is not divided by trades or occupations, all employees of a given enterprise—including management personnel—are encompassed by a single union. Thus, management and staff employees are entitled to a voice in labor union forums; as a practical matter, however, management personnel never hold leadership roles in the enterprise union and rarely even head union commissions. Similarly, the enterprise union leader (as well as, perhaps, a deputy) is entitled to sit as a consultative member at all meetings of enterprise officers. Accumulated amendments to relevant labor law clearly point away from a one-sided cooptation of union officials and toward a more balanced linkage for collaboration, exchange of information, and mutual watchfulness. The extent to which this situation approaches genuine reciprocity depends on a number of variables, of course, including the personalities of the individuals involved.

The SED is present in the enterprise in the form of both management and union officials. As a general rule, both the enterprise director and the union leader are party members. In addition, as many as one third of management and staff personnel and 10−20 percent of unpaid union officials, shop stewards, and commission members also hold SED membership. In larger enterprises the enterprise party secretary is a full-time paid official who, in reality, cannot be counted among either management or workers. Consequently, when the enterprise party organization convenes for its monthly discussion, it is composed of roughly equal proportions of management and union personnel. In fact, the party organization does little more than bring together management and union officials who ordinarily deal with one another in the routine exercise of their respective functions (Belwe, 1979: 101–117). This shared party membership requires management and union officials to acknowledge their common goals and responsibilities. It does not, however, preclude their having sharply different points of view on occasion. Conflicts unresolved in the context of union–management consultations will not be conveniently overcome simply because the setting has changed to an SED forum.

In principle, the enterprise party organization—more accurately, its secretary—retains the authority to render decisions in the event of deadlocks between union and management officials. However, the secretary is not likely to exercise this prerogative except in execution of an explicit directive from a higher party authority outside the enterprise, such as a city or district party secretary. Given the statutory limits on decision authority within which both management and union officials must operate, all enterprise participants in this process have a strong incentive to resolve conflicts by internal bargaining, rather than invite intrusion by outside powers and a further restriction of autonomy.

The broad spectrum of union—management conflicts can be comprehended under three central issues: (1) short-term production targets vs. specific workers' rights (e.g., safety, just remuneration, job training, living conditions, cultural and social amenities); (2) enterprise benefit vs. public benefit; and (3) managerial discretion vs. processes of worker participation.

General SED goals, FDGB guidelines, and a multitude of national economic and labor laws impose on management, union officials, and workers the simultaneous tasks of increasing production and improving working and living conditions. In the abstract, of course, these tasks are perfectly compatible. The current GDR slogan—"We can consume only that which we have first produced"—is a sound economic principle in all systems, as even labor unions in inflation-ridden capitalist economies are realizing anew (Tisch, 1982: 28). In specific cases, however, enterprise managers (and some workers as well) perceive a conflict of priorities. Changes in work rules and expenditures for protective equipment may improve worker safety, for example, but they may also impede the production process and divert scarce resources away from the acquisition of fixed capital and the accumulation of labor and material reserves. Although "legally" obliged to promote both production and safety, managers correctly perceive that their financial rewards and career mobility depend most directly on increased production and profitability. Thus, there is a strong temptation to defer indefinitely major investments in safety. Similar calculations apply to other "imperatives" to improve working and living conditions (Bundesvorstand des FDGB, 1969: 39–44).

To some extent, certain categories of workers may support the managerial priority of short-run production; this would apply to workers in capital-intensive units, whose incomes are more closely tied to production bonuses and who already enjoy relatively more workplace and residential amenities. Under such circumstances, the primary responsiblity of the enterprise union leaders is to introduce a longer-term perspective to production planning, arguing that healthier, happier, better-trained workers are a more certain source of increased productivity than are short-term production increments which jeopardize worker welfare (Manz and Winkler, 1979: 90–116). (This physical, psychological, and occupational development and renewal of human resources is comprehended by GDR labor sociologists as the "reproduction process.") At the same time, government statutes and FDGB directive also enjoin the local union to emphasize equity considerations in the distribution of benefits among categories of employees. This task is often difficult to achieve, because it is precisely the group of privileged better paid workers who are likely to become more involved in the work of union commissions. Moreover, as enterprise management perceives the positive collaboration of these privileged workers as vital for the short-run achievement of production targets, it becomes more likely to be attentive to their demands.

Union Performances

Enterprise union officials in pursuit of their function as worker representatives in an inclusive sense (i.e., regarding workers as wage-earners, consumers, and contributors to the national economic plan) have long relied on normative appeals to their management counterparts. Not surprisingly, abstract socialist ideals of improving the conditions of workers' lives often count for little in the eyes of managers whose careers are determined by the achievement of output targets. However, the gradual creation of an array of legal remedies has increased the potential for effective union defense of workers' rights, The elevation of the judicial status of the conflict commissions (for the resolution of labor disputes) and their closer linkage to the union structure represent key developments in this regard (Lieser-Triebnigg, 1977: 1286–89). Nevertheless, the effectiveness of union rights depends on the assertive exercise of those rights by determined union leaders. The assertiveness of union leaders, in turn, hinges upon appropriate processes of recruitment and training, as well as upon the tangible support of district FDGB boards and local party officials. The fact that such support is not always forthcoming may be attributed to inadequate personnel resources in territorial union and party organizations and, more important, to the absence of signals and rewards from national FDGB and SED bodies, indicating that attention to workers' rights is, indeed, a clear-cut priority.

The success of enterprise unions in defending a wide variety of workers' rights cannot be measured in absolute terms. But changes over time are discernible. Both aggregate data and copious specific examples indicate gradual but unmistakable progress in reducing accidents (Table 3.2), improving workers' health, raising job qualifications, expanding the supply of adequate housing, providing ample recreation and vacation facilities, among other achievements (Manz and Winkler, 1979: 92–100). Such improvements depend entirely or in part on enterprise funding and at least nominal participation by the enterprise union leadership. Whether these changes can be attributed to assertive unions, to altered SED priorities, or to enterprise competition for skilled labor is not evident. Within the organic conception of East German society, this question may not even be especially relevant. In pluralist democracies, efforts to demonstrate the differential effects of collective bargaining, political parties, and labor market forces on working-class benefits are also inconclusive (van de Vall, 1970: 53–85; Dahl and Lindblom, 1953: 141–4). With regard to protecting workers from arbitrary dismissal, assuring proper job assignments, and securing prompt payment of production and innovation bonuses, FDGB sources claim great progress, although job assignments and innovators' bonuses continue to be a frequently mentioned item of dispute.

The issue of enterprise benefits vs. public benefit has emerged as a second potential source of union–management conflict. This problem revolves around the fact that most elements in the central economic plan are tied to a reward system which encourages managers to maximize enterprise income and their own salaries at the cost of deficient integration with other sectors of the national economy, inefficient use of scarce raw materials, and other social externalities, such as pollution and unbalanced community development. Efforts to supplement the basic plan with legal mandates, penalties, and rewards designed to elicit more attention to macroeconomic and social needs have not proven entirely successful. Consequently, SED and FDGB directives attempt to enlist enterprise unions in the cause of monitoring enterprise management on behalf of a larger public interest. In this sense, the unions emerge as the "loyal supporters" and "tested collaborators of the SED." When enterprise unions promote worker initiatives to reduce waste, increase productivity, and increase enterprise support for community needs, the intended outcomes ostensibly provide greater benefit to the national welfare and to the general public than to the immediate workers. The fact that such initiatives occasionally bring forth individual monetary prizes theoretically demonstrates a natural harmony between the private good and the collective good (Felgentreu and Menzzer, 1976: 40−2). Although the FDGB press vigorously applauds incidents of such initiatives in the public interest, such activity has not become an obvious institutional priority for enterprise unions. Given what is known about the major incentive systems, in fact, it is far more likely that union leaders would take the side of management in adopting a shorter range, microeconomic perspective. In other words, it is unlikely that—FDGB pronouncements to the contrary—this issue has truly become a focus of union−management conflict.

As in other communist systems, a third union−management issue, managerial discretion vs. worker participation, is definitely a vigorous point of contention. East German labor sociologists portray active worker participation in the process of evaluating annual plans, in developing more rational organization of work, in incorporating technological change, and in numerous other enterprise decisions as the touchstones of evolving "socialist democracy" (Manz and Winkler, 1979: 430−3). The current comprehensive labor law stipulates a variety of mechanisms for worker−management consultation and accountability, with the decided emphasis on expanding the manager's obligations to his employees. The pivotal institution in this relationship is the standing production council, in effect a joint union−management group for periodic review of the annual plan and actual performance. The production council is supplemented by the work of several union commissions, which also include management representatives, and by periodic management reports to shop stewards and, in smaller enterprises, to assemblies of all employees.

Managers commonly resist accountability mechanisms, in part because they can consume extraordinary amounts of time. In addition, such mechanisms generally lead to specific commitments in response to worker suggestions and grievances, commitments which add a further layer of restrictions upon a management structure struggling to satisfy the requirements of the annual plan and accommodate amending instructions from superiors in the economic hierarchy. The increasing call for union participation in the quest for higher labor productivity is of particular concern here. In the GDR, as in all advanced industrial economies, the primary determinants of labor productivity are capital spending for technological change and the organization of work. Enterprise managers claim with some justification that union representatives lack sufficient expertise to deal with such complex issues. Moreover, worker participation in these two areas constitutes a serious intrusion into conventional managerial prerogatives.

As with all elements of the labor law, effective implementation depends upon assertive union leadership. A common complaint in the FDGB is the failure of mangement to reply promptly to workers' suggestions and to justify the refusal to adopt suggestions. Managers have also been criticized for withholding planning data until the time for thoughtful union participation has passed. Some managers have attempted to divert attention from central planning issues by assigning to union representatives the "less consequential" tasks of separately developing the enterprise culture and social plans, which—because they are not integrated with the production plan—have only a limited effect. Tolerance of such practices, of course, involves the complicity of enterprise union officials (Belwe, 1979: 187–200).

FDGB commentary implies an expectation of a degree of arbitrary management behavior in the absence of assured and highly qualified worker representatives. Ineffectual union participation merely reinforces managers' impatience and expectaion that workers have little substantive contribution to make. National FDGB officials repeatedly exhort enterprise union leaders to more demanding performance in the interest of worker participation. Former national chairman Herbert Warnke put the matter most emphatically: "The union officials are the stewards of the working class, *they are not the assistants of enterprise managers*" (Warnke, 1968: 27). A more recent statement notes the salutary effect of vigorous advocacy in setting the terms of "socialist competition" in the enterprise: "In this we naturally experience an occasional confrontation. If conflicts of opinion arise now and then among evaluators of competition plans or between economic officials and union leaders, they can only benefit the conduct of the campaign" (Tisch, 1982: 22). These themes recur in several other chapters in this volume.

FDGB theoreticians advocate broader and more effective use of the avenues of participation on two grounds (Menzzer, Winkler, *et al.*, 1968: 232–3 and *passim*; Diedrich and Kallabis, 1979: 188–90). First, they argue that participatory experience can be intrinsically valuable. Worker initiatives in innovation, rationalization, and plan discussion, if properly recognized and carried through with tangible results, are a vindication of workplace democracy, which is itself an expression of a larger "socialist democracy." Such an exercise of democracy should enhance the human quality of life in its original Marxist sense. Second, worker participation can be valued instrumentally, both as a means to better decisions (through the inclusion of broader sources of information) and as a means to enhance the proprietary interest of workers in the well-being of the enterprise. A heightened proprietary interest will presumably reduce labor turnover, absenteeism, and routine tolerance of waste in human and material resources—all of which have an important effect on labor productivity, economic growth, and the general standard of living.

In addition to these unresolved issues of conflict with management, the enterprise union leadership has problems dealing with its own members. Most of these problems emerge from the union–management issues outlined above. For example, despite the frequent unresponsiveness of management, union leaders must constantly elicit new forms of worker initiative. If they are so inclined, most managers possess sufficient resources effectively to extinguish all elements of spontaneity in the ranks of the workers. In fact, it requires an exceptionally adroit union leader and a perceptive and receptive manager to elicit and sustain meaningful worker initiative. Failing such fortuitous conditions, worker participation can easily become formalistic and contrived. As is the case in many of the other countries under examination here, official sources provide impressive figures on the total number of participants in worker initiatives, but such data convey nothing about the content of participation (Belwe, 1979: 111–19; for information on other volunteer roles, see Table 3.5).

Union leaders also encounter difficulty in mobilizing worker support for other tasks in which immediate tangible rewards are not evident. To be sure, many workers do become engaged in community development concerns, as well as in the defense of specific workers' rights. But except for the few who perceive public service activity as a key to personal career advancement, worker participation is likely to be limited to those who are personally affected by existing problems, for example, those unable to find adequate housing, or those immediately exposed to hazardous working conditions. To put it bluntly, GDR workers are no more likely than workers in nonsocialist countries to devote themselves to problems beyond the domain of immediate private benefit. The important distinction here is that union leaders in the FDGB are charged with conducting their affairs as if such a commitment to the public existed. All of this is not to say that East German workers are exclusively self-serving. Concern for, and interaction with, coworkers is a very important part of everyday life in the more immediate context of the work collective. Here, too, we find important bases for some measure of worker autonomy.

Work Collectives

The socialist work collective is different from the informal work group in the West, an institution which has been the object of much sociological and psychological attention. The collective is not an independent group developing apart from the formal organization and managerial leadership. As officially conceived, the collective is characterized by cooperation in the fulfillment of work tasks, a shared political and ideological world view which embraces the goals of socialist society, and a mutual readiness to help in personal matters and in the development of a socialist personality (Stollberg, 1978: 98). The socialist work collective has a critical mediating function, mediating not only between worker and enterprise but also between the world of work and personal life outside. The experiences in the collective affect a person's wider social relationships and the worker's identification with socialist society; here one practices how to be with other human beings.

The activities of work collectives ideally influence individual commitments and mobilize motivation through encouragement and critique. The potentially powerful influence of the collective rests on the satisfaction it gives its members. If successful, it integrates the organization and goals of the enterprise and its union with the informal personal interaction of its members. The collective combines within the same social context work planning, discussions of promotions and salary premiums, protection of employees' rights, social relations at work, shared leisure activities, and encouragement of mutual help, as well as access to certain privileges such as attractive vacation places.

In a work collective all are expected to perform social activities in addition to their particular work obligations. The work collectives encourage such *gesellschaftliche arbeit* and offer a variety of opportunities for union work in their own structure. In addition to the union representative, the *Vertrauensmann* or *Vertrauensfrau,* there are many members of the collective elected to deal with women's issues, social questions, cultural activities, and so on.

Social scientists in the GDR have conducted a number of studies on work collectives as well as on the responses of workers to their collectives and to their work situation in general. In fact, the sociology and social psychology of work has emerged as perhaps the leading area of empirical research in the social sciences in the GDR. However, only a few studies are published, and others are merely referred to in overview publications. The information on methods used tends to be limited, and often it is difficult to distinguish normative from factual arguments or causal conditions from mere correlates and the social consequences of good work collectives.

Despite all of the above, sufficient data remain available to examine the following important questions about the collective. What is the overall response of workers in the GDR to their work collectives? What are some specific criteria—often implied—for success and failure of a work collective? Which conditions are conducive to successful work collectives? Finally, do work collectives effectively protect worker interests and advance worker autonomy?

In 1973 the "Fritz Heckert" union academy conducted a study in which 43 percent of the respondents thought that they had an open atmosphere of cooperation in their work collective, 34 percent saw good beginnings for such a development of their collective, 13.5 percent considered cooperation in their group as not good, while 6 percent were unable to judge and 3 percent did not answer (Heck *et al.,* 1975: 7−8). In 1977 Rudhard Stollberg, the leading sociologist in this area of research, studied 745 production workers of different levels of qualification in one enterprise; he found that for four out of five workers the satisfaction derived from cooperation in the collective was an important motivation for good work. An earlier study of 732 workers in two chemical factories showed that collegial relations in the workplace ranked highest in judgments of work satisfaction, followed closely by work safety, technical guidance, and the behavior of supervisors, while dissatisfaction was stronger in regard to opportunities for using one's mind, wages (men complained here more than women), the organization of work, and in particular the quality of materials supplied and the technical equipment used (Stollberg, 1980: 1, and 1978: 153). Stollberg quotes the comment of the West German sociologist Erwin K. Scheuch that the most interesting result of an internationally comparative study of "time budgets" of people was that in the socialist countries of Eastern Europe personal friends are more often also colleagues at work than in the West. In his own study Stollberg found that one out of three workers had personal friends among their co-workers (Stollberg, 1978: 101, note 102).

What are some of the criteria by which a work collective is judged? This question has been explored elsewhere in some depth (Rueschemeyer, 1982: 155−63). Here it is sufficient to note that beyond comfortable relations between coworkers, issues of managerial control and authority and assertions of worker autonomy play a pervasive role. Workers question the use of speaking out in the collective when nothing of importance changes as a consequence; this is evident from the literature as well as from complaints about the lack of real participation published in *Die Tribune*, the GDR's union newspaper, and it emerged also in personal interviews conducted by M. Rueschemeyer (Rueschemeyer, 1982: 155−63). An indirect indication is found in the fact that an "open and frank" atmosphere is frequently stressed as important for the collective. In one study of 299 workers in a metallurgical *Kombinat,* an open and critical atmosphere correlated significantly with good relations among work colleagues (Krämer, 1976, cited in Stollberg, 1978: 104).

Conflicts with management may concern important material interests, in particular work norms and performance control. The report of a union district organization indicates that some workers believe that with scientific work organization "they'll get us back to the norms" (Heck *et al.,* 1975: 46). In turn, one official comment suggested that the planning of work standards for each individual prevents the work collective from hiding or covering a worker who is not doing his job properly. If the available evidence points to good relations with supervisors as normal, there are also some indications of tensions. A study of twenty-seven groups of students in technical training showed a tendency for the collectives' representatives for cultural and political work to be isolated (Hiebsch and Vorweg, 1976: 222–3). Another study, dealing with "advanced" work collectives of workers, yielded the following rank evaluation of the collectives' achievements which indicates reservations about "further improvement of directive work":

(1)   improved interpersonal relations,
(2)   mutual help developed,
(3)   clear (ideological) orientation of activities,
(4)   activation of all members,
(5)   better work organization,
(6)   stimulation of competition,
(7)   increase in qualifications,
(8)   further improvement of directive work. (Weidig, 1978, cited in Stollberg, 1978: 112–113)

Researchers in the GDR have attempted to identify those conditions under which good collective can develop (Stollberg, 1978: Hiebsch, 1977: 93–145). Such conditions include satisfaction with salaries and fringe benefits, the relation between the size of the smallest collaborating workgroup and that of the union collective, the degree of interdependence and collaboration as determined by the technical structure of work, the extent of independent decision-making by the workers, the quality of communication in the organization, the political-ideological development of the collective and the members' attitudes to collective work, the quality of personal relations existing in and between collectives, and the continuity of the collective's membership. The importance of the conditions of life outside of work is also discussed in the literature; most attention here is given to how difficulties with transportation, marketing, and nurseries for children affect general work attention and satisfaction.

Several researchers found that the success of the work collective and general participation are related to the qualification of the workers. The higher the level of qualification, the more importance attached to the collective and the greater the interest in the collective and in responsible work. Those less interested in their collectives have less than an average interest in social participation generally, in information and in qualification (Stollberg, 1978: 104; Bohring, 1981: 250). Winzer (1981: 242) suggests the better the quality of work and the greater the pride of the worker, the happier they are in their collective. The description of one work collective in a wire factory (Heck *et al.*, 1975: 8–12) shows that experienced skilled workers form the core of the collective and that they gain the trust and support of less qualified and younger workers because they are respected for their knowledge and technical ability as well as for other personal qualities.

Such findings demonstrate the relevance of the recent and dramatic upgrading of occupational qualifications for the improved functioning of the work collectives. An overview of relevant research by Gunther Bohring (1981: 250−2) suggests a positive answer, though he also points to "still existing contradictions," not the least of which are perhaps reflected in the dissatisfactions of workers employed below their level of qualification.

The objective character of the division and organization of labor also shapes the quality of the work collective. The more the nature of work and its actual organization require cooperation between interdependent workers, the better the conditions for a successful work collective. An academy collective studied by Rueschemeyer (1982/3: 27−47) was contrasted with two collectives in a dental clinic where work had a more parallel, "segmented" character. The latter had more problems which, however, also seemed related to a more conservative leadership style. Another study of scientists published in the German Democratic Republic shows that those whose work was more cooperative in nature valued "a well developed collective" higher as a factor in job satisfaction than those who worked more independently. In the group as a whole, this factor ranked second only to "appropriate salary and premiums" and above "normal relations to the leader" or good technical conditions" (Hiebsch, 1977: 93−145). This study indicated similar findings to Rueschemeyer's earliest interviews (1981a, 1981b); under favorable conditions, the work collective is a very important element in people's lives.

Does a successful work collective make a difference for substantial worker interests and for worker autonomy? Aside from the reporting of occasional complaints about useless participation, there has been little discussion in the East German writings on the work collective as an institution which could develop some autonomy, which modifies the impact of organizational demands, establishes norms of its own, negotiates, bargains, denies, changes. These characteristics have been studied in research on informal groups in the West. One GDR author, Alice Kahl (1981: 79) *warns* that collectives with more than thirty-five members may develop informal subgroups which then substitute for the formal collective and dominate in setting norms and sanctioning of behavior. Automation may lead to such informal groups because of separation and isolation in the factory.

Even though it is formally constitued, a well-functioning work collective is indeed an instrument of adapting the formal demands of the state and the work organization to the needs of its members; its formal design has typically undergone various adaptations due to pressure from its members (Rueschemeyer, 1982: 155−63). Indeed, the more influence workers are allowed to exercise, the more they participate; the less influence they are able to exert as a collective, the more they resort to less formal means of shaping their worklives. Although a set of union principles exists to promote internal democracy, there is evidence that these principles are widely violated. Such limitations of democracy are in part justified by referring to organizational priorities. At the lowest level of union organization, however, in the work collectives, the representatives are nominated and elected directly by the group.

A great deal of internal bargaining appears to take place in the collective among experienced skilled and semiskilled workers. An unsuccessful or an authoritarian collective can easily result in lack of initiative, passive negligence, absenteeism, cynicism, and turnover. Managers and work leaders are aware of these possibilities and try not to engage in unnecessary conflict with the workers. Similarly, the union representatives try to maintain smooth relations. If one assumes a rough harmony between supervisors and workers, evident in a close reading of the available research literature, as well as the existence of conflicting interests on the part of workers and management in the work collective, then it appears that workers have a significant degree of autonomy and influence at the lowest level of union and enterprise organization.

Sable and Stark (1982: 439–75) have demonstrated how a planned socialist economy creates the precondition for such shop-floor power: permanently tight labor markets. In order to meet centrally determined plans, Sabel and Stark argue, managers "hoard" workers even when they are not immediately needed. Workers can then threaten to leave for a better job if piece-rates and bonuses are not kept high and production goals low. Complaints by workers and outspoken criticism of work conditions and management are also not unusual in these circumstances. We do not suggest therefore that workers can reorganize production plans in their own interests, but we believe that managerial manipulation is limited because of the factory's need to keep its workers in order to meet production goals. This underlying pattern of countervailing worker power receives added strength, if it can be defined as a legitimate expression of the role of the working class in a socialist society and if it can be integrated with the anti-authoritarian strands in Marxism-Leninism.

The autonomy and influence of work collectives clearly varies with the occupational qualifications and occupational identifications of their members. While the finer nuances among production workers remain elusive, a look at professional work collectives beyond the narrow confines of groups made up exclusively or predominantly of workers with a higher education can be developed from the existing literature. As in the USSR, the experience of the GDR has demonstrated that the greater the need for highly trained technical experts and professionals, the greater the power of professional work collectives. The higher the regard for the work done—regard by others and by the workers themselves—the better the conditions for a successful work collective. For both of these reasons, it is likely that professional workgroups have a better chance of succeeding than others. Personal professional commitment and high mutual regard engenders *esprit de corps* and solidarity, and regard from others engenders self-respect. Workgroup autonomy is most likely when workers have to be trusted if they are to do their work efficiently and successfully. There is no piecework in professional work organizations and bonuses typically do not depend on profit as they do in the factory.

Professionals often work in circumstances which insulate them from the more immediate production pressures. In a revealing article on law in the Soviet workplace, Louise Shelley (1981/2: 429−54) shows that lawyers in social and cultural organizations adhered more to the law than in factories under pressure to fulfill economic plans. Exempt from many of the pressures that cause violations of law in the economic sector, both the intent and provisions of the law are carried through to a greater degree in social and cultural organizations than in factories.

In Rueschemeyer's research (1981a or 1981b: 23−7, 1982: 155−63) on professional collectives in the GDR, several examples of decision-making in the collectives, beyond those related to routine work tasks, were reported. Questions of promotion and salary premiums came before the work collectives. Members of one collective managed to rid themselves of a leader who was "ideologically and personally rigid" and replace him with another, more respected member of the group. To achieve this change, the union representative worked with the party secretary and the academic head of the section. In another instance the collective criticized a professor for not contributing his time to a new laboratory being constructed; he cooperated the next time the group met. In a collective with many members who were women with young children, hours were made flexible so that both men and women were able to work at home without difficulty. Problems of caring for sick children were also discussed at collective meetings and schedules were rearranged so that no pay would be lost. One collective refused to complete required readings for the next week's discussion over a weekend. They reduced the number of meetings and insisted on making gatherings more attractive.

Of course, not all professional collectives work well and achieve such everyday autonomy. The people in the collective may not like each other and therefore not work well together. Aside from personal tensions, problems remain. The rather steep hierarchic relations still characteristic of some professions such as medicine are not conductive to a well-functioning and at least somewhat self-regulating collective. Furthermore, even successful collectives fail to win every battle. The party may decide that a task must be discharged even if extra hours are added to an already heavy schedule. Many decisions are determined centrally, such as the number of teachers needed in a school, the research to be undertaken in an institute, or the necessity for students to take certain courses in philosophy, political economy, and scientific communism.

Professionals, however, can exercise some of the autonomy that the goals of the union formally allow, not only because their special expertise makes tight "outside" control difficult but also because they are able to invoke the broad goal of establishing a place for workers in the management of socialist society. Hence they cannot be as easily accused as others of having pursued self-centered short-term goals at the expense of long-term development.

The work collective in the German Democratic Republic varies in its potential for some degree of worker autonomy. While conditions differ and pervasive difficulties remain, it is clear that if the work collective successfully protects some autonomy, the solidarity of the group is reinforced and participation in the work organization as well as in union activities is encouraged. If the collective is unsuccessful, workers frequently react with passivity, cynicism, and absenteeism.

As in the other societies under examination in this volume, the unions in the GDR are partners at the highest level with the party, the state, and the top economic management. This relationship is reproduced at the enterprise level with such linkages limiting the unions' responsiveness to the needs and demands of their members. At the same time, managers and union leaders need the cooperation of the workers in order to pursue high production and other organizational goals. In extreme cases, dissatisfaction with work conditions and pay may result in apathy, neglect, and withdrawl as well as—given chronic labor shortage—high turnover. The constant need to improve productivity thus emerges as the ultimate source of whatever power the workers in the GDR may have.

Some of the factors which shape the underlying balance of power have changed considerably during the short history of the GDR. For example, both the labor force's level of qualification and the inherent complexity of work tasks have increased dramatically. As workers become more skilled, they become more aware of what is happening at work and in the union, more critical and more attuned to the possibilities for self-direction and autonomy. Other things being equal, they also become more difficult to supervise and control.

Nonetheless, large numbers of individuals cannot pursue their common interests effectively without collective organization, no matter how great their individual leverage. Two critical questions remain. To what extent are worker interests at odds with managerial interests? To what extent do such conflicts find organizational expression in the union? In spite of the ambiguities in union goals that result from the union's integration into the political system, there is no doubt that at the enterprise level the union does serve as an organizational conduit for some worker interests. Worker autonomy and direct worker influence seem greatest at the lowest organizational level in well-functioning work collectives. Even here, however, the conditions for success of work collectives vary by occupation, organizational structure, and other dimensions. At the same time, the official enterprise union organization cannot be dismissed as a mere instrument of managerial policy. It does share in control of workers and the mobilization of their energies, but it also provides channels for some worker participation.

Acknowledgments

We very much want to thank Dietrich Rueschemeyer for his comments during the preparation of this chapter.

The account of local union organization is based primarily on union statutes and on union literature concerned with the operation of production enterprises and their relationship to communities outside the larger metropolitan areas. Appropriate adjustments in structure and functional emphasis must be made when considering unions which depart from these prototypical conditions.

References

Barthel, Eckhardt, and Dickau, Joachim (1980), *Mitbestimmung in der Wirtschaft* (West Berlin: Colloquium Verlag).

Belwe, Katharina (1979), *Mitwirkung im Industriebetrieb der DDR* (Opladen: Westdeutscher Verlag).

Bohring, Gunther (1981), "Soziale Triebkräfte und Probleme der Bildung, der Qualifikation und des Berufes," in *Lebensweise und Sozialstruktur,* Materialien des 3. Kongresses der marxistisch-leninistischen Soziologie in der DDR (Berlin: Dietz Verlag).

Braunthal, Gerard (1978), *Socialist Labor and Politics in Weimar Germany* (Hamden, Conn.: Archon).

Bundesvorstand des FDGB (1969), *Hinweise für die Arbeit der Revisionkommissionen im FDGB und seiner Industriegewerkschaften und Gewerkschaften* (Berlin: Verlag Tribune).

Dahl, Robert A., and Lindbolm, Charles E. (1953), *Politics, Economics, and Welfare* (New York: Harper).

Diedrich, Karl and Kallabis, Heinz (1969), *Information and gewerkschaftliche Leitungstätigkeit* (Berlin: n.p.).

Erbe, Günther (1982), *Arbeiterklasse und Intelligenz in der DDR* (Opladen: Westduetscher Verlag).

Felgentreu, Herbert, and Menzzer, Heinz (1976), "Die Bewegung 'Sozialistisch arbeiten, lernen und leben' wirksam unterstützen," in *Die Arbeit*, n.v. 10, pp. 40−2.

Grebing, Helga (1969), *The History of the German Labour Movement* (London: Oswald Wolff).

Heck, Willi, *et al.* (1975), *Beiträge zur sozialistischen Arbeitskultur* (Berlin: Verlag Tribune).

Hiebsch, Hans, and Vorwerg, Manfred (1976), *Einführung in die marxistische Sozialpsychologie* (Berlin: VED Deutscher Verlag der Wissenschaften).

Hiebsch, Hans (1977), *Wissenschaftspsychologie* (Berlin: VEB Deutscher Verlag Der Wissenschaften).

Kahl, Alice (1981), "Zur Rolle des Arbeitskollektivs bei der Festigung der Betriebsverbundenheit," in *Lebensweise und Sozialstruktur*, Materialien des 3. Kongresses der marxistisch-leninistischen Soziologie in der DDR (Berlin: Dietz Verlag), pp. 77−81.

Krämer, R. (1976), "Zum Entwicklingsniveau der sozialen Beziehungen in Arbeitskollectiven, Diplomarbeit," Martin-Luther-Universität Halle-Wittenberg, Sektion Wirtschaftswissenschaften cited in Rudhard Stollberg, *Arbeitssoziologie* (Berlin: Verlag Die Wirtschaft).

Lenin, V. I. (1921/1960), "The Trade Unions, the Present Situation and Trotsky's Mistakes," in Institute for Marxism-Leninsim, *Lenin: Collected Works,* Vol. 32 (Moscow: Foreign Languages Publishing House, 1960).

Leptin, Gert, and Melzer, Manfred (1978), *East Germany: Economic Reforms in East German Industry* (Oxford: Oxford University Press).

Lieser-Triebnigg, Erika (1977), "Das neue Arbeitsgesetzbuch der DDR," *Deutschland Archiv,* vol. 10, no. 12, pp. 1286−9.

Manz, Günther, and Winkler, Gunnar (1979), *Theorie und Praxis der Sozialpolitik in der DDR* (Berlin: Akademie Verlag).

Menzzer, Heinz, Winkler, Gunnar, *et al.* (1968), *Ökonomisches System und Interessenvertretung* (Berlin: Verlag Tribune).

Protokoll des VII FDGB-Kongresses (1968), "Änderung der Satzung des FDGB" (Berlin: Verlag Tribüne; 2nd edn Cologne: Wissenschaft und Politik, 1979).

Richter, Helmut (1977), *Realization of Plans of Industry,* Texts for the Interregional Training Course on Industrial Planning (East Berlin: United Nations Industrial Development Organization).

Rueschemeyer, Marilyn (1981a), *Professional Work and Marriage: An East−West Comparison* (London: Macmillan and New York: St. Martin's Press).

Rueschemeyer, Marilyn (1981b), "Social and Work Relations of Professional Women: An Academic Collective in the GDR," *East Central Europe,* vol. 8, pts 1−2, pp. 23−37.

Rueschemeyer, Marilyn (1982), "The Work Collective: Response and Adaptation in the Structure of Work in the German Democratic Republic," *Dialectical Anthropology,* vol. 7, pp. 155−63.

Rueschemeyer, Marilyn (1982/3), "Integrating Work and Professional Life: An Analysis of Three Professional Work Collectives in the German Democratic Republic," *GDR Monitor,* no. 8, pp. 27−47.

Sabel, Charles F., and Stark, David (1982), "Planning, Politics, and Shop-Floor Power: Hidden Forms of Bargaining in Soviet-Imposed State-Socialist Societies," *Politics and Society,* vol. 11, no. 4, pp. 439−75.

Scharf, C. Bradley, (1976), "East Germany's Approach to Industrial Democracy," *East-Central Europe,* vol. 3, no. 1, pp. 44−57.

Schneider, Gottfried (1981), "Entwicklung und Nutzung der Bildung und Qualifikation der Arbeiter und der anderen Werktätigen," *Lebensweise und Sozialstruktur,* Materialien des 3. Kongresses der marxistisch-leninistischen Soziologie in der DDR (Berlin: Dietz Verlag).

Shelley, Louise (1981/2), "Law in the Soviet Workplace: The Lawyer's Perspective," *Law and Society Review*, vol. 16, no. 3, pp. 429−54.

Stollberg, Rudhard (1978), *Arbeitssoziologie* (Berlin: Verlag Die Wirtschaft).

Stollberg, Rudhard (1981), "Wissenschaftlich-technischer Fortschritt und sozialistisches Verhältnis zur Arbeit," in *Lebensweise und Sozialstruktur,* Materialien des 3. Kongresses der marxistisch-leninistischen Soziologie in der DDR (Berlin: Dietz Verlag).

Tisch, Harry (1982), "Bericht des Bundesvorstandes des FDGB an den 10. FDGB-Kongress," in *Protokoll des 10. FDGB-Kongresses* (Berlin: Verlag Tribüne).

van de Vall, Mark (1970), *Labor Organizations, a Macro- and Microsociological Analysis on a Comparative Basis* (Cambridge: Cambridge University Press).

Warnke, Herbert (1968), "Bericht des Bundesvorstands des FDGB an den 7. FDGB-Kongress," in *Protokoll des 7. FDGB Kongresses* (Berlin: Verlag Tribüne).

Weidig, T. (1978), Sozialistische Gemeinschaftsarbeit, cited in Stollberg, 1978, op. cit. (without complete bibliographic information).

Winzer, Rosemarie (1981), "Wissenschaftlich-technischer Fortschritt, Persönlichkeit und socialistische Lebensweise," in *Lebensweise und Sozialstruktur,* Materialien des 3. Kongresses der marxistisch-leninistischen Soziologie in der DDR (Berlin: Dietz Verlag).

Zimmerman, Hartmut (1970), "Wandlungen der Leitungsstruktur des VEB in soziologischer Sicht," *Deutschland Archiv*, vol. 3.

Zimmerman, Hartmut (1978), "The GDR in the 1970s," *Problems of Communism*, vol. 27, no. 2, pp. 1−40.

4

Czechoslovak Trade Unions under Soviet-Type Socialism

Joseph L. Porket

Introduction

When in February 1948 the Communist Party of Czechoslovakia (CPCS) took over power in Czechoslovakia, it promised to build up a new, higher type of society which in all respects would be superior to capitalism. It was to be a society in which there would exist a government of the people, by the people, and for the people; in which exploitation, unemployment, economic crises, poverty, and injustice would be absent; and in which culture would enjoy unheard-of opportunities for development.

By that time, the country had a relatively advanced economy, a literate population, experience of political democracy, a tradition of trade unionism and socialist movements, and a communist party which had served its apprenticeship years in a parliamentary state. Thus, in common with East Germany, Czechoslovakia was an exception among the countries which came under Soviet control following the end of World War II.

Not surprisingly, after the takeover of power neither the existing trade unions nor the existing participation in management escaped the consequences of the introduction of a Soviet-type political and economic system. And since over the years the nature of the system has not changed appreciably, despite the abortive attempt made in 1968–1969, the position and role of the official trade unions have not changed noticeably either.

Joseph Porkett, Risslip, Middlesex, United Kingdom.

The First Republic (1918–1938)

The beginnings of trade unionism on the territory of contemporary Czechoslovakia can be traced back to the second half of the nineteenth century, but its history under the Austro-Hungarian Empire lies in the scope of the present examination. Between 1918 and 1938, that is, during the existence of the First Republic, about half of white-collar and blue-collar workers were trade union members. As Table 4.1 shows, the density of trade union membership was highest in the industrially most advanced Czech Lands.

However, the trade union movement was badly split. Not a few of the many political parties then in being had their own trade unions and, in addition, there were a number of independent ones. By the end of 1937, when the trade union membership amounted to nearly 2.4 million, 709 unions were to be found, of which 485 were associated in eighteen union centers and 224 were unaffiliated (Zápotocký, 1948: 191). Communist trade unions were insignificant; in the late 1930s they comprised less then 6 percent of all organized white-collar and blue-collar workers.

As to participation in management, plant councils came into existence in coal pits and larger factories spontaneously, without legal sanction, as early as November, 1918. They lacked discipline and stability. Invariably, they were dominated by radical left-wing Social Democrats, future communists.

Participation in management was put on a legal basis by laws adopted in 1920 and 1921. The laws provided, *inter alia*, for plant councils in the mining industry and for plant committees outside it, and carefully laid down the mode of their election as well as their rights. Briefly, both plant councils and plant committees were to be elected by all persons employed in the plant, that is, not exclusively by trade union members. And both were conceived as more consultative and supervisory organs, which were not allowed to interfere in the management of the plant.

Table 4.1
Unionization of Czechoslovak White-Collar and Blue-Collar Workers, 1918–1938 (percentages)

	Czech Lands	Slovakia	Ruthenia	Czechoslovakia
1921				50.2
1930[a]				43.8
1935[a]	49.4	26.5	23.4	44.8
1938	53.1[b]	40.8	28.4	53.6[b]

[a] At the beginning of the year.
[b] The two figures appear inconsistent.
Source: Škurlo (1975: 65–6).

In practice, these councils and committees faced at least two problems in their relations with the trade unions. One arose from the latter's attempts to use the former for their own particular interests. Another arose from the latter's right to conclude collective agreements with the employees and the former's right to supervise the fulfillment of concluded collective agreements by the employers.

Despite their limited powers, these councils and committees were not without significance. If nothing else, they made possible a degree of coordination in a situation characterized by a plurality of trade unions at the plant level. Moreover, they were the only institution which was expected to represent the plant personnel as a whole, irrespective of whether organized or not.

Following the Nazi occupation of the Czech Lands in March, 1939, the Germans abolished the multitude of trade unions and substituted two trade union centers. Besides suppressing the independence of trade unions, they also suppressed that of plant councils and plant committees. On the other hand, they treated the Czech blue-collar workers gingerly, because they were interested in high productivity. They obtained it by using incentives rather than applying sanctions (Ústav, 1971: 531).

In Slovakia, after the declaration of a separate state, only one trade union centre was retained, to be dissolved by the end of 1941. Strikes were banned by the constitution, just as they were banned by the Germans in the Czech Lands.

The Pre-Takeover Stage (1945–1948)

After the end of the World War II, Czechoslovakia was reconstituted, albeit without Ruthenia. In the Czech Lands one single unified trade union organization was founded, called the Revolutionary Trade Union Movement (RTUM). This organization, the foundation of which had been prepared during the Nazi occupation, took over the property and funds of the two trade union centres established and controlled by the Germans. In April, 1946 the Slovak trade unions merged with it, so that the RTUM became a nationwide organization. Shortly afterwards, in May of the same year, it was granted a monopolist position.

Between the spring of 1945 and the spring of 1949 its membership grew steadily. Simultaneously, the density of trade union membership rose from 73.5 percent in April, 1946 to 88 percent in May, 1949 (Zápotocký, 1948: 226; *Protokol*, 1949: 143).

Theoretically, the RTUM declared itself to be independent of the political parties associated in the so-called National Front, but not politically neutral, having a class character and a socialist orientation. In reality, it was reliably under the control of the CPCS and most influential in aiding it (Kabinet dějin odborů při ÚRO, 1963: 386—90). Organizationally, it was built on the principle of democratic centralism and the principle "one plant—one trade union organization." It was tightly centralized, and the individual unions (originally twenty-one in number, later twenty-two) had no independence and were no more than integral parts of the RTUM.

If the CPCS controlled the RTUM, the RTUM in turn controlled the existing works councils and the worker's militia. Thus, at the pre-takeover stage the CPCS controlled the works councils and the workers' militia as well, albeit indirectly, through the RTUM, and was able to use them to further its interests in its struggle against the non-communist political parties and private owners. In the following, the workers' militia will be disregarded and only the works councils will receive attention.[1]

Hastily formed revolutionary works councils emerged in enterprises, plants, institutes, and offices immediately after the liberation of the country, and exerted considerable powers. They purged traitors, assumed responsibility for safeguarding property against sabotage and destruction, performed managerial functions, and influenced the appointment of managers.

Legally, the works councils were confirmed by a presidential decree of October 24, 1945, which put them under the exclusive guidance of the RTUM. They were to represent all persons employed in the plant, irrespective of whether these persons were trade union members or not, and had the right to receive information, to make suggestions, to be consulted on contemplated changes, and to supervise.

Although they were specifically prohibited from performing managerial functions, in practice they did interfere in the day-to-day running of plants. Moreover, they did not confine themselves to playing an economic role. They were politicized and played a political role as well, albeit not an independent one.

Originally, the works councils grew faster than the plant trade union organizations. There were 11,131 works councils and 8,030 plant trade union organizations by the end of 1945, and over 12,000 works councils and 10,340 plant trade union organizations in February of the next year (Kaplan, 1968: 245).

In the wake of the takeover of power by the CPCS in February, 1948 the party leadership abolished the works council as a separate institution, although retaining the name until 1955, and proclaimed the principle of one trade union organ in the plant (Kabinet dějin odborů při ÚRO, 1963: 10—27). At the same time, it transformed the entire industrial relations system. Not

---

[1]On workers' councils in this period, see Kaplan, 1966; Šumberová, 1968; Chabrová, 1980; and Porket, 1976.

surprisingly, the system was organized hierarchically, and the rules governing it were set unilaterally by the party leadership. At the societal level, its main actors became the party leadership, the government, the trade union leadership, and the working masses. At the enterprise level, its main actors became the enterprise director, the enterprise party committee, the enterprise trade union committee, and the personnel.

The RTUM was transformed into trade unions of the Soviet type (Porket, 1975, 1977, 1978), the position and role of which differ completely from the position and role of the trade unions existing in the developed industrial societies of the West.

The following discussion is based on the assumption that between the early 1950s and the early 1980s neither the nature of the industrial relations system nor the position and role of the official trade unions has changed fundamentally.

Main Features of the RTUM under Soviet-Type Socialism

The RTUM is a unified mass organization with a nominally voluntary membership, associating all employed persons, that is, blue-collar workers as well as white-collar workers, the nonmanagerial personnel as well as managers. It is authorized to represent both its members and nonmembers.

In theory, the RTUM is an independent organization, not a party or state organization, and no one is allowed to interfere in its activities or to impose decisions upon it. At the same time, however, it recognizes the leading role of the party and is required to be an assistant and collaborator of the party and of the state (Poláček, 1969; Giertl, 1977). Even in theory, then, its independence is confined to organizational independence and is not identical with political independence.

Actually, the RTUM is subordinate to the party and has to ensure the execution of assigned tasks. Consequently, its autonomy is low, it is an element of a system of levers and transmission belts (Kupka, 1974: 71−4), passing on party directives to the masses and providing the party with information about the masses and their moods.

Subordination of the RTUM to the party is achieved in two ways: first, through legal norms adopted on the basis of party directives and addressed to the RTUM; secondly, through party members who work in the RTUM and who are obliged to observe party directives. No wonder, then, that on the trade union organs party members tend to be represented disproportionately and that the higher a union organ, the greater the proportion of party members. In 1966, for instance, the proportion of party members on trade union organs was one third at the enterprise level, about one half at the district and regional levels, and 80 percent at the national level (*XIII sjezd,* 1967: 875).

Within the RTUM relationships and processes are dominated by the principle of democratic centralism which, although outwardly it combines democracy and centralism, implies a centralist and disciplinary bias. As a result, the RTUM has a hierarchical, centralized, and authoritarian structure. Its component units enjoy limited autonomy vis-à-vis superior trade union organs. Elections to trade union organs lack a genuinely democratic character and trade union functionaries are not truly responsible to the membership.

Because the RTUM is conceived as a unified mass organization constructed according to the production principle,[2] trade union members are not allowed to associate and dissociate at will, that is, to split off from the existing unions and to form new ones, either within or outside the RTUM. Consequently, it is not surprising that the number of unions is low.

However, during the Czechoslovak Spring (January to August 1968) dissatisfaction emerged with the existing number of unions. The original twelve unions were transformed into thirty Czech, twenty-six Slovak, and one statewide union. Moreover, and that still does not tell the whole story, the formation of over a hundred additional unions was demanded. But when effective normalization of the country began in April 1969, the number of unions was reduced to eighteen Czech and eighteen Slovak ones.

It is clear why the party leadership does not allow trade union members to associate and dissociate at will. The unity of the RTUM, and eventually even the principle "one plant—one trade union organization," would be endangered. The articulation of group interests would increase, as well as conflicts of interest and popular pressure on the enterprise management and the regime. In fact, the party leadership would lose control over the trade unions.

Trade union members[3] have impressive rights and extensive duties. The latter are of particular interest. They include, *inter alia*, to work consci-

---

[2]The production principle means that all persons working in one enterprise or establishment belong to the same trade union organization and to the same union, regardless of their position and role. This means that each union embraces all the white-collar and blue-collar workers in a particular branch of the economy.

[3]Bauerová and Jančovičová, 1983: 233 give the following data on the participation of women in the RTUM:

	1954	1977	1980
Percentage of women among members	34.8	42.6	42.1
Percentage of women among union officials	24.0	43.3	44.2

entiously; to observe work and state discipline; to defend and consolidate the socialist system; to strengthen the country's defense capabilities; to consolidate the alliance with the Soviet Union and other socialist countries; and to struggle for progress, friendship, peace, and internatinal cooperation in accordance with the principles of proletarian internationalism (RTUM Statutes, 1972: 115−6).

Following the Soviet invasion and the suppression of the indigenous reform movement, the density of trade union membership declined from nearly 92 percent in 1969 to slightly over 85 percent in 1971. However, afterwards it rose again, to reach an unprecedented 97 percent in 1977. Undoubtedly, pressure to join was one of the reasons for the increase.

At this juncture, a note on Slovakia is in place. Until August, 1960 there existed Slovak committees of the individual unions. These committees were abolished in the wake of the so-called Socialist Constitution adopted on July 11, 1960. In 1968−1969, though, steps were taken to put the RTUM on a federal basis. By the beginning of 1972, the RTUM had central (statewide) trade union organs, national (Czech and Slovak) trade union organs, Czech and Slovak organs of the individual unions, regional and district trade union organs, and basic (enterprise and local) trade union organizations.

Functions and Rights of the RTUM

Officially, the RTUM is assigned a number of functions. They include, *inter alia*, to promote production, to socialize politically, to defend worker's interests, to organize participation by the working people in management, to supervise the observance of labor legislation and of health and safety regulations, to raise the qualifications of workers, to carry out mass cultural activity, to provide opportunities for physical training, sport, and recreation, to administer social insurance, and to adjudicate labor disputes.

To perform its manifold functions, the RTUM is endowed with extensive rights (*Právnický slovník,* 1972: 718−21, 1040−41). Depending on the issue in question, trade union organs enjoy in relations with the state and the enterprise management the right to make suggestions; the right of prior consultation without their viewpoints being binding on the competent decision-maker; the right of codecision in the sense that a decision may come into force only with their consent; and the right of supervision. Yet, although these rights are impressive, their exercise is strictly regulated by legal norms and the directives laid down by superior organs, as well as circumscribed by the nature of directive economic management. And the same applies to yet another right of the RTUM, namely, the right to conclude collective agreements.

Being concluded under directive economic management, these agreements are not a result of collective bargaining in the proper sense. In any case, the RTUM has no real bargaining power. It lacks adequate means to defend and assert effectively the interests of white-collar and blue-collar workers, inasmuch as it is deprived of the right to strike.[4] The official dismissal of strikes is based on a reasoning dating from 1949: "Against whom would you strike? Should you strike against yourselves as the owners of the means of production?" (*KSČ*, 1962: 128).

Moreover, as follows from what has been said above, both the conclusion and content of collective agreements are regulated by legal norms and the directives laid down by superior organs. On top of that, their content must not contradict the economic plan.

Thus, collective agreements merely specify what is expected of employed persons and what the employed persons, in return, may expect to be allocated. And while responsibility for obligations contained in them may be of either a moral or political or a legal character, that of trade union organs is entirely moral and political (Kalenská, 1965).

Not surprisingly, in order to perform the manifold functions assigned to it, the RTUM needs not only paid officials but also elected trade union functionaries and trade union activists. As the available evidence suggests, the proportion of the latter is rather high. In 1966 they constituted nearly one quarter of all trade union members, by 1973 less than one fifth, and in 1977 about 23 percent. Yet whatever the exact proportion of elected trade union functionaries among trade union members, it in itself does not reveal how these functionaries fulfill their trade union duties. An attempt to give at least a partial answer will be made below.

The Production Role

The manifold functions assigned to the RTUM are sometimes grouped into two broader roles, which will be called here the production role and the interest role. To use official terms, the RTUM is supposed to take part in the development of the national economy, the fulfillment of the plan and the growth of production, and at the same time to care for the rights and interests of the workers, for the conditions of their work and life (Filka and Daněk, 1981: 62).

Officially, the production role is regarded as being more important than the interest role. As the Central Committee of the CPCS emphasized on January 30, 1970, the trade unions should participate not only in the distribu-

---

[4]Although strikes are banned in practice they are not prohibited by law. Indeed, strikes are ignored in legal norms.

tion of values, but in the first place in ensuring their creation (*Rudé právo*, February 2, 1970).

In playing the production role the trade unions are expected to mobilize the working people for the fulfillment of the state plan and the implementation of the party program, to strengthen work discipline, to raise labor productivity, to struggle against shortcomings in production, to uphold the authority of managers, and the like. Simultaneously, they are expected to foster in workers high political consciousness, a correct socialist attitude towards work, and dedication to the public interest, as well as to educate them in the spirit of tolerance to shortcomings, mismanagement, waste, a negligent attitude toward public property, antisocial tendencies, and survivals of the past in people's minds.

However, in practice the trade unions have never played the production role to the party leadership's full satisfaction. Between the early 1950s and the mid-1960s they were criticized, *inter alia*, for laxity, compliancy, formalism, and undue interference in management. In the 1970s they were criticized, *inter alia*, for formalism in the conclusion of collective agreements (Běžel, 1977) and excessive submissiveness to the enterprise management.

Naturally, any discussion of the production role of the trade unions would be incomplete without mentioning participation in management. On the one hand, trade union organs are entitled to participate in management. On the other, they are obliged to organize participation by the working people in management, the main forms of which are production conferences and socialist emulation.

As the available evidence shows, between 1970 and 1980 both the absolute number of production conferences and the absolute number of participants were increasing. In contrast, the average number of participants per production conference declined. Besides, by the end of the decade production conferences were attended on average by a mere 60–70 percent of those present at work (*Odborář*, no. 10, 1976: 10 and no. 1, 1982: 12–13; Doležal and Sedláček, 1981).

Over the same period, also, the absolute number of proposals submitted at production conferences was going up. Nevertheless, approximately one production conference out of three ended without any proposal, and about 20–30 percent of the proposals submitted were not made operative. In addition, although the activity of individual participants rose, it remained rather low. The number of proposals submitted per 1,000 participants evinces this: it amounts to 14.7 in 1970, to 27.7 in 1975, and to 31.6 in 1980.

What the available figures do not disclose is that in many cases the production conferences had an exlcusively informative character, were not properly prepared, suffered from formalism, discussed trade union matters, degenerated into social gatherings, took place during working hours despite directives to the contrary, and so on. On top of that, the available figures say nothing about the content and importance of submitted proposals, and other sources mention only some of the issues covered by them, such as problems of production, working conditions, safety at work, and socialist emulation.

Sociological surveys suggest that not a few white-collar and blue-collar workers are dissatisfied with the agenda and functioning of production conferences (Cysař and Dolejška, 1966: Petrovská, 1976: Pokorný and Duffek, 1978). Not infrequently they prefer to bypass production conferences and discuss problems with their immediate superior and with their colleagues.

If production conferences are one of the two main forms of participation by the working people in management, socialist emulation is the other. Simultaneously, both are regarded as outstanding manifestations of socialist democracy.

Socialist emulation dates from after the takeover of power. In the Czech Lands 232,000 white-collar and blue-collar workers took part in it in April, 1949, constituting 11 percent of all white-collar and blue-collar workers (*Protokol*, 1949: 124). Before the Czechoslovak Spring, socialist emulation reached its peak in 1964. Subsequently it began to decline, practically to disintegrate in 1968. During the 1970s it underwent a revival, though, and in 1980 it embraced nearly 85 percent of all white-collar and blue-collar workers or, if cooperative farmers were included, slightly over 78 percent of all economically active persons (Za štěstí a blaho lidu, 1978: 49–52; Statistická ročenka ČSSR, 1981: 123–206).

In 1966 Antonín Novotný criticized the trade unions for having allowed socialist emulation to be contained and discredited by empty formalism, barren registering, and the acceptance of questionable pledges. By that time, many a worker was dissatisfied with socialist emulation, and this was evinced by the results of a survey conducted in twenty-six engineering plants, the personnel of which amounted to over 52,000. The results are given in Table 4.2. In addition, when asked what they would suggest for a further development of socialist emulation, only 1,005 of the 5,300 respondents gave an answer. The two most numerous ones were to do away with formalism in socialist emulation (298 respondents) and to discontinue socialist emulation entirely (267 respondents).

Not surprisingly, post-1969 surveys ascertained somewhat less negative attitudes toward socialist emulation. Nevertheless, socialist emulation continued to suffer from formalism and other shortcomings, including insufficent support from union bodies (Krumpl, 1974; *Odborář*, no. 7, 1975: 4).

Currently the regime's interest in socialist emulation has not abated. Officially, care for the development of socialist emulation and further forms

Table 4.2
Attitudes toward Socialist Emulation (percent)

Socialist emulation helps fulfill the work tasks assigned		Socialist emulation improves the organization of work at the place of work		The pledges made cover tasks which	
Considerably	10.7	Strongly	7.7	Would not be fulfilled with a pledge	6.2
Partly	47.8	Slightly	39.6	Would be fulfilled without a pledge but with difficulties	24.5
Not at all	27.4	Not at all	37.8	Would be fulfilled even without a pledge	58.6
	85.9		85.1		89.3

Source: Svoboda, 1968; 60.

of workers' initiative belongs to the most important political and ideological tasks of every party organization, of every trade union organization, and of every manager (Kačírek, 1980).

All in all, in purely quantitative terms participation by the working people in management is quite impressive. Nominally, most white-collar and blue-collar workers are involved in it, and trade union organs are busy organizing it and, in general, playing the production role. In practice, though, trade union organs do not seem to perform the production role too effectively.

This is the verdict suggested by much of the empirical evidence. Surveys suggest that only about one-third of white-collar and blue-collar workers have positive attitudes toward participation in management, while another third have ambiguous ones and yet another third negative ones (Porkorný and Duffek, 1978: 93; Herman, 1980: 80). Secondly, working time is used insufficiently and improperly, that is work discipline is mostly quite slack. Late arrivals at work, prolonged breaks, and early quitting time abound. Workers spend much of their working time socializing, shopping, arranging their personal affairs, and moonlighting. In addition, the trade unions and other social organizations often hold meetings, seminars, and gatherings during working hours (Mikeš and Steinich, 1975: 24; Běžel, 1977: 6).

Of the managers interviewed in 1974, 13.2 percent estimated that in industry the losses of working time amounted to between 20 to 30 percent of the shift, 52.2 percent to between 10 and 20 percent, and 29.8 percent to under 10 percent (Mikeš and Steinich, 1975: 24). Later sources usually assert that in industry the losses of working time reach on average approximately 15 percent of the shift (Kováčová, 1979: 44; *Odborář*, no. 23, 1981: 20). The figures just quoted do not include absenteeism, that is, those cases when workers fail to report for work at the time they are scheduled to work.

Without doubt, losses of working time are not confined exclusively to industry. The factors which have an adverse impact on the use of working time include poor organization of work, the uneven supply of materials, limited material incentives for work, administrative interference from outside the enterprise, the informal culture of the enterprise, and a shortage of labor at the national level combined with overmanning at the enterprise level (Altmann, 1982).

Under these circumstances it is not surprising that the link between wages and performance is weak. Despite its efforts, the post-1968 regime has not succeeded in doing away with what is called unhealthy wage egalitarianism and achieving a greater wage differentiation. The reasons underlying wage levelling, as ascertained by a survey conducted in the mid-1970s, are given in Table 4.3. The first two deserve special attention because they make up between 60 and 74 percent of the answers, depending on the position and role of the respondents.

Coming back to the trade unions, the factors just discussed put limits on the effectiveness of the production role which the trade unions are expected to play. The unions therefore cannot be too effective in playing this role, they cannot achieve notable improvements in workers' performance, the quality of output, the utilization of the working time, and savings of materials and energy.

Table 4.3
Main Causes of Insufficient Wage Differentiation (percent)

	Trade union functionaries	Heads of work-and-wage departments	Shop-floor supervisors
1 Shortage of manpower	35.5	39.2	37.3
2 Managers' fear that persons employed in the plant would quit	27.1	35.1	23.2
3 Incorrect differentiation of bonuses and rewards	15.7	12.4	14.3
4 Varying quality of output norms	8.9	7.6	11.9
5 Unclear intentions concerning wage differentiation	7.3	4.4	6.9
6 No answer	5.5	1.2	6.3

Source: Bakajsa, 1977: 23.

If the trade unions are not (and cannot be) too effective in playing the production role, they also are not (and cannot be) too effective in the other role assigned to them, namely, the interest role. This role will now be examined in some detail.

The Interest Role

Officially, the RTUM is supposed to defend and represent the justified and rightful interests of the workers, that is, to protect the working people against excessive administrative zeal and bureaucratic distortions of individual functionaries of the state and economic apparatus, as well as against unconscientious workers and violators of work discipline (Mařík, 1980: 3−4, 6). In addition it is argued that the interests of the working people are protected not only by the RTUM but also by the state and the CPCS; that the RTUM must combine individual and group interests with societal interests; and that conflicts of interest between the RTUM on the one hand and the state and the CPCS on the other hand cannot arise because their interests are identical. Consequently, the interest role of the RTUM is both contradictory and limited−contradictory, since it must combine individual and group interests with societal interests; limited, since while it is allowed to protect the rightful interests of the workers against individual role-players, it is not allowed to define what the workers' interests are and to protect the workers against the state and the CPCS.

Thus there is a fallacy in the official formulation that increased production, productivity, and the like are a way to improved material and cultural well-being of the working people, and that the RTUM promotes the workers' interests by caring for economic growth. The fallacy lies in that the RTUM has no significant say in the distribution of national income and the determination of the working people's standard of living.

In practice, the trade unions have not always played the interest role to the party leadership's full satisfaction. Between 1954 and 1956 for instance, they were accused of remnants of reformism, of survivals of old thinking. Because many functionaries and members of the RTUM had worked for years in the reformist trade unions, one publication stated, they had become accustomed to regard the trade unions as an interest organization the concern of which was not the interests of the working class as a whole but merely partial demands (Kabinet dějin odborů při ÚRO, 1963: 423). The complaint was also made that many trade union functionaries, even communists, held and often expressed the incorrect view that under socialism the role of the trade unions was basically the same as under capitalism, that only forms and methods of the struggle had undergone changes, and that from such views followed the incorrect understanding of the question of the defense of the interests of the working people (*KSC*, 1962: 291).

Not surprisingly, the existence of survivals of old thinking had haunted the party leadership since it took over power. It was admitted that in Czechoslovakia the so-called cultural revolution (which aimed at creating a new socialist culture, a new morality, a new socialist way of life, at changing the thinking of people) had had specific features. These stemmed on the one hand from a high cultural level of the people, a strong progressive and popular tradition, and the size and maturity of the working class; on the other hand from a relatively strong influence on the bourgeois ideology and well-rooted petty-bourgeois illusions (Kabinet dějin odborů pri ÚRO, 1963: 411).

Later, in 1966, Antonín Novotný stressed that the trade unions must take a resolute stand against any manifestations of protectionism, against various conservative and backward moods, and against assertion of partial interests to the detriment of common interests of the working people (*XIII sjezd*, 1967: 54).

While in the party leadership's opinion of trade unions frequently neglected societal interests, not a few white-collar and blue-collar workers believed that the trade unions neglected individual and group interests. This was suggested by the results of a sociological survey conducted in one industrial enterprise in 1965. Of the 553 respondents, 18.8 percent were satisfied with the activities of the enterprise trade union organization, 17.7 percent were satisfied sometimes, 53.4 percent were dissatisfied, and 10.1 percent did not answer. At the same time nearly two thirds of the respondents thought that the basic task of an enterprise trade union organization was to defend the interests of its members (Cysař and Dolejška, 1966).

Indirectly, similar results were obtained by a public opinion poll of the first half of April, 1968. The question, put to a respresentative sample of 2,183 persons in the Czech Lands, asked whether the respondents thought that there existed an organization in the country that defended and advocated the interests and opinions of people. While 14 percent answered "certainly yes" and 15 percent "rather yes," 33 percent answered "rather no" and 28 percent "certainly no" (11 percent were uncertain or did not respond). As might be expected, party members gave more positive answers than non-party members (Piekalkiewicz, 1972: 133).

At the same time, and not surprisingly, the majority of the population perceived their influence on the management of society (on the activities of other people) to be either very low or nil. That was one of the findings of a statewide sociological survey conducted in November, 1967. On a twelve-point scale measuring perceived social influences, 85.1 percent of all respondents placed themselves on the lower half of the scale and 63.2 percent on the lowest third of the scale (Machonin *et al.*, 1969: 354−5: Porket, 1971, 1972).

Thus it is legitimate to assume that on the eve of the Czechoslovak Spring most white-collar and blue-collar workers were dissatisfied with the behavior of the trade unions as well as with relationships and processes within them. During 1968 then, their transformation was attempted. Basically, this transformation centered on four issues: (1) the role of the trade unions—the trade unions were to become an interest organization; (2) the independence and autonomy of the trade unions vis-à-vis the party; (3) the internal democracy of the trade unions; and (4) the right and opportunity of trade union members to associate and dissociate at will. In addition, the right to strike was demanded, and written into the statutes of the RTUM in March, 1969.

However, when effective normalization of the country began in April, 1969 the trade unions did not escape and their previous position and role were restored without delay. Besides, normalization of the country ended the extensive discussion of the concept of enterprise councils (workers' self-management) which had flourished during the Czechoslovak Spring, and abolished those enterprise councils which had been established, mostly in the wake of the Soviet invasion (Porket, 1976; Pravda, 1977).

At this juncture it should be asked how, in the post-1969 period, the trade unions have played the interest role assigned to them by the party leadership. For that purpose, some results of a survey conducted in 1974 in a number of organizations will be used. The respondents consisted of 1,456 managers, 1,409 functionaries of enterprise trade union committees, and 1,461 rank-and-file trade union members.

While 66.9 percent of the rank-and-file trade union members interviewed stated that enterprise trade union committees tried to defend workers' interests vis-à-vis the enterprise management and succeeded in doing so, 25.7 percent stated that enterprise trade union committees tried but failed, and 3.7 percent stated that enterprise trade union committees did not try at all. The remaining 3.7 percent gave other answers (*Odborář*, no. 21, 1975: 19). What is missing from the published results is the nature of the issues involved.

However, the structure of answers changed when it came to a somewhat more specific question, namely, how enterprise trade union committees defended workers' interests in disputes between an employee and the enterprise management. In this case 46 percent chose the first answer, 41 percent the second, and slightly over 4 percent the third, with about 9 percent unaccounted for (*Odborář*, no. 24, 1975: 19 and no. 1, 1976: 19). Yet once again the issues in dispute, as well as the ways they were resolved, were not examined.

Asked whether the current collective agreement expressed the interests and needs of the employees, 52.5 percent of the rank-and-file trade union members interviewed believed that it did so sufficiently and 34.2 percent

that it did so partially. Objective circumstances which the enterprise management was not able to change were identified as the main cause of the nonful-
fillment of some provisions of the collective agreement by 28.9 percent of the
interviewed functionaries of enterprise trade union committees, but 50.4
percent did not know the main cause or did not answer (*Odborář*, no. 5,
1976: 19−20). Two kinds of official complaint should be recalled in this
connection, namely, those of formalism in the conclusion of collective agreements, and those of the nonexistence of collective agreements in many plants
(Hoffman, 1980: 9).

Most functionaries of enterprise trade union committees as well as
most managers contended that the enterprise trade union committee enjoyed authority among the personnel. On the other hand, this authority
(which the researchers apparently conceived as informal authority, not as
formal rights) was seen by the respondents as stemming primarily from the
support given to the enterprise trade union committee by the enterprise
management, the enterprise party committee, and superior trade union
organs, as well as from the position of the RTUM in society, and only to a
lesser degree from the enterprise trade union committee's performance
(*Odborář*, no. 25, 1975: 20−1, and no. 1, 1976: 19).

While in the survey just quoted many managers regarded good cooperation between the enterprise trade union committee and the enterprise
management as one of the main factors determining the former's authority
among the personnel, in another large-scale survey conducted by the end of
the 1970s the managers interviewed expressed their opinion on whether the
legal rights of the enterprise trade union committee circumscribed their
scope for operational decision-making. While 41.3 percent stated that they
did not and 27.4 percent that they definitely did not, 27.5 percent admitted
that they might do so in some cases and 1.6 percent thought that these rights
did considerably circumscribe their scope for operational decision-making
(Navrátil, 1981: 101).

Several surveys confined to individual enterprises revealed that workers job related problems ranged over working conditions, wages, housing,
commuting, lack of career prospects, unused qualifications, and so on. Thus,
albeit indirectly, they also suggested what issues the workers would like the
trade unions to raise on their behalf.

One of these surveys deserves a separate note. The respondents
thought that the trade unions should pay more attention to workers' comments (66 percent), work-related problems (61 percent), social matters (59
percent), cultural and recreational activities (56 percent), interpersonal
relations in working groups (38 percent), education of trade union members
(37 percent), and socialist emulation (30 percent) (Herman, 1981: 80). The
low emphasis put on interpersonal relations may be explained by the respon-

dents' perception that they were relatively satisfactory, and that put on education and socialist emulation by the respondents' belief that they already had enough of them.

Despite their obvious limitations, the post-1969 sample surveys just quoted are not without significance, and together with the other evidence offered in the present examination make it possible to formulate some propositions about how the RTUM plays its interest role in practice. The propositions are based on the assumption that under Soviet-type socialism the official trade unions not only are not allowed to engage in open conflict with the party, the state, and the enterprise management, but try to avoid it because it does not pay.

At the societal level, due to their lack of real bargaining power, the trade unions are not able effectively to defend and assert the workers' interests, with two exceptions. One is through suggestions addressed to the party and the state in those cases when the party leadership defines a problem to be solved, and the problem is narrow and technical and requires expertise. The other is through toleration of deviant behavior on the part of lower trade union organs.

At the enterprise level, too, the trade unions lack real bargaining power and, consequently, here also we are unable effectively to defend and assert the workers' interests. Yet the situation at this level tends to be somewhat less dull than that at the societal level, albeit not widely advertised. To begin with, enterprise trade union committees may defend and assert the interests of the personnel by supporting the enterprise management in its attempts to get a soft plan, that is to maximize the enterprise's input in relation to the output demanded from it by superior organs and to minimize the enterprise's output in relation to the input allocated to it by these organs. Second, they may defend and assert the interests of the personnel by tolerating deviant behavior on the part of the workers (such as late arrivals at work, prolonged breaks, early quitting times, socialization, shopping, arranging of personal affairs, moonlighting during working hours, and so on) and by themselves initiating it (for example, by holding meetings, seminars, gatherings, and the like during working hours). Finally, they may defend and assert the interests of the personnel by tolerating a separation of rewards from performance, which means that wages are insufficiently linked to performance and contain a concealed social element, naturally not identical with any of the legally recognized social benefits.

It goes without saying that these ways of defending and asserting the interests of the personnel are a response to the nature of directive economic management and of the established industrial relations system, and are possible only to the extent to which enterprises have control over their internal processes, that is can make decisions autonomously, or are able to influence superior organs. It is obvious, too, that those ways of defending and asserting the interests of the personnel would be impossible without at least tacit approval on the part of the enterprise party committee. Expressed differently, in enterprises there seems to exist close cooperation or even collusion between the enterprise management, the enterprise party commitee and the enterprise trade union committee, directed not against the personnel but against superior organs.

When enterprise trade union committees defend and assert the interests of the personnel in the ways just described, their members tend to identify with the enterprise rather than with an external organization or the system as a whole, unless they are seeking a career outside the enterprise in the trade union, state, or party bureaucracy. After all, they (as elected trade union functionaries at the enterprise level) are employees of the enterprise and, therefore, have a stake in a successful and easy fulfillment of the state plan and in avoiding conflicts within the enterprise.

All this suggests, of course, that many white-collar and blue-collar workers are relatively satisfied with enterprise trade union committees precisely because the latter tend to be lax rather than strict, that is do not behave as officially expected, and that the latter tend to enjoy popularity rather than informal authority among the former. Moreover, all this suggests the existence and importance of the informal culture of the enterprise in a society that is highly formalized, imposes severe limitations on the population's freedom of action, and exposes individuals to constant strains and chronic shortages. The culture mitigates the strains and shortages, and thus makes life easier both at work and outside it.

Conclusion

The present examination has attempted to analyze the RTUM, established in Czechoslovakia as the official trade union, at four levels: the normative, which pertains to the sphere of official values, ideological commitments, and the patterns of behavior desired or expected by the regime; the institutional, which corresponds to the normatively prescribed sets of interrelated roles; the behavioral, which covers the observed behavior and interaction of individual role-players; and the attitudinal, which denotes beliefs and feelings about objects or situations in the social environment, expressed verbally by members of society.

It has been found that in Czechoslovakia (just as under Soviet-type socialism in general) the actual behavior of employed persons may be divided into typical and atypical (Porket, 1983). The former may in turn be subdivided into conformist (complying with the formal norms in force) and deviant (evading and violating the formal norms in force). The latter covers those less frequent (and irregular) cases when employed persons enter into open conflict with either a particular enterprise management or the regime. Officially, some forms of those conflicts (for example, employee–management disputes and union–management disputes) are recognized and strictly regulated, others (such as strikes, unlicensed demonstrations, riots, rebellions, and uprisings) are regarded as illegitimate. The events of 1953 and 1968 belong to the second category.

Typical deviant behavior is quite widespread and persistent. Moreover, it is displayed by white-collar workers as well as blue-collar workers, by managers as well as nonmanagerial personnel, by trade union members as well as those who are not unionized, and by party members as well as non-party members. It should be asked, then, why the regime tolerates it, although simultaneously it frowns upon its various above-mentioned manifestations, and describes at least some of them as phenomena alien to the nature of socialist society.

In the West one stream of writers on Czechoslovakia explains the current regime's tolerance of certain forms of typical deviant behavior in terms of a kind of tacit social contract, which has existed between the regime and the population since 1969. But this explanation is inaccurate (it disregards the pre-1968 regime's tolerance of typical deviant behavior) and incomplete (it neglects a number of important factors contributing to typical deviant behavior both before and after the Czechoslovak Spring).

To begin with, the political and economic system imposed on and maintained in the country is highly formalized, that is bureaucratized. As a result, informal behavior, informal communication, informal interaction, and informal structure inevitably arise, as they do in any formal (bureaucratic) system. Second, since the political and economic system established in the country is highly formalized, the volume of formal norms and administrative orders flowing from the top is vast. Besides, the norms and orders issued may alternatively overlap or fail to meet lay obligations without granting corresponding rights, etc. Consequently, in order to fulfill the tasks assigned to them from above and to protect their own economic interests, individual role-players must violate, evade, and ignore at least some of the formal norms and administrative orders addressed to them. Third, one feature of directive economic management is chronic shortages affecting consumers and enterprises alike. These give rise to the so-called second economy, the main function of which is to supply those consumer goods and services desired or needed by consumers and those materials, components, and equipment needed by enterprises which the official economy fails to supply. Finally, another feature of directive economic management is overmanning at the enterprise level, an important form of hidden unemployment. It too adversely affects the behavior of white-collar and blue-collar workers, and this is aggravated by a simultaneously existing shortage of labor at the national level, a more recent phenomenon.

In sum, the current regime does not tolerate typical deviant behavior only in order to appease the population. It *has* to tolerate it because it stems not only from attitudinal factors but also from systemic ones.

Naturally, there are limits to what the current regime is willing to tolerate, to its zone of indifference. They are given by the necessity to maintain the established political and economic system, which is regarded as irreversible.

Because of these limits, the official trade unions can hardly be expected to develop into an independent and democratic organization, capable of genuinely defending and asserting the interests of its members. That would be possible only if directive economic management gave way to a market economy; that in turn would require a different political system; and that again would require Soviet withdrawal from Czechoslovakia.

However, if a market economy did come into being, it would not only affect the position and role of the trade unions, it would also lead to the emergence of workers' self-management, for the simple reason that at present most of the means of production are in the hands of the state. At the initial stage at least, it would probably be both a form of enterprise management and a political device providing a safeguard against political power, with the former containing a contradiction between professional management and popular participation in management.

While at the time of writing these developments seem to be highly unlikely, the system is not entirely free of potential conflicts, of a possibility of popular unrest and sociopolitical instability. One of the underlying factors is economic; a certain tightening of the belt was experienced in the second half of the 1970s, and the prospects for the late 1980s appear dim. It should be remembered, too, that an officially unrecognized open conflict may be triggered off by an unforeseen event, having no direct connection with the causes of dissatisfaction.

On the other hand, despite the considerable gap between mass expectations and their satisfaction, there is a popular zone of indifference—the limits within which people are willing to comply with regime expectations despite worsening conditions, increasing hardships, and growing restrictions. Faced with the prospect of poor economic performance the party leadership may well try to improve union performance in order to siphon off dissatisfaction and widen the "zone of indifference."

References

Altmann, F. L. (1982), "Employment Policies in Czechoslovakia," in J. Adam (ed.), *Employment Policies in the Soviet Union and Eastern Europe* (London: Macmillan), pp. 72−95.

Bakajsa, V. (1977), "Odbory a aktuální otázky mzdové politiky," *Odborář*, no. 7, 23.

Bauerová, J., and Jančovičová, J. (1983), "Postaveni žen a rodin v ČSSR," *Sociologický časopis*, vol. 19, no. 2, pp. 225−237.

Běžel, V. (1977), "Úloha odboru v rozovoji národního hospodářství ve světle záveru IX vseodborového sjezdu," *Planované hospodářství*, no. 10, pp. 3−11.

Chabrová, V. (1980), "Závodní rady, dělnicka´ kontrola a znárodnění," *Obdory a společnost*, no. 1, pp. 45−54.

Cysař, J., and Dolejška, V. (1966), "Sociologická sonda v BSS," *Odbory a společnost*, no. 2, pp. 73−93.

Doležal, J., and Sedláček, Z. (1981), "Co ukázal průzkum vyrobních porad," *Odborář*, no. 2, pp. 10−11.

Filka, M., and Daněk, J. (1981), "Socialistické přeměny práce a úloha odborů," *Odbory a společnost*, no. 4, pp. 62−71.

Giertl, J. (1977), "ROH v súčasnej etape," *Nová mysl*, vol. 31, no. 9, pp. 42−48.

Herman, K. (1980), "Faktory rozvoje pracovních kollektivů," *Odbory a společnost*, no. 2, pp. 78−84.

Hoffman, K. I. (1980), "Veliká zkouška zralosti Revolučního odborového hnutí," *Odbory a společnost*, no. 1, pp. 1−11.

Kabinet dějin odborů při ÚRO (1963), *Nástin dějin československého odborového hnutí* (Prague: Práce).

Kačírek, B. (1980), "Leninské učení o odborech v podminkách budování rozvinuté socialistické společnosti," *Odbory a spolčenost*, no. 4, pp. 3−22.

Kalenská, M. (1965), "K pojetí a funkcí kolektivních smluv," *Právník*, vol. 104, no. 6, pp. 518−531.

Kaplan, K. (1966), "Hospodařská demokracie v letech 1945−1948," *Československý časopis historický*, vol. 14, no. 6, pp. 844−861.

Kaplan, K. (1968), *Znarodnění a socialismus* (Prague: Práce).

Kováčová, E. (1979), "Produktivita práce, effektívnost' práce, pracovné síly—ich vzájomná väzba i podmienenost'," *Plánované hospodařství*, no. 2, pp. 40−51.

Krumpl, J. (1974), "Stav a rozvoj iniciativy pracujícich," *Odbory a společnost*, no. 4, pp. 85−94.

KSČ (1962), *o úloze odborů při výstavbě socialismu: Sborník usnesení a dokumentu* (Prague: Práce).

Kupka, J. (1974), *Postaveni a úloha odborů za socialismu* (Prague: Práce).

Machonin, P., et al. (1966), *Sociální struktura socialistické společnosti* (Prague: Svoboda).

Machonin, P., et al. (1969), *Československá společnost: Sociologická analýze sociální stratifikace* (Bratislava: Epocha).

Mařík, V. (1980), "Usnesení IV všeodborového sjezdu o závodních výborech ROH—trvale aktuální dokument o postavení našich odboru," *Odbory a společnost*, no. 3, pp. 1−8.

Mikeš, E., and Steinich, J. (1975), "Problémy růstu produktivity práce v průmyslu," *Planované hospodařství*, no. 11, pp. 14−27.

Navrátil, O. (1981), "K některým výsledkům průzkumu uplatňování IV všeodborového sjezdu o postavení závodních výborů ROH," *Odbory a společnost*, no. 4, p. 92−105.

Petrovská, Z. (1976), "Z vypkumu aktivity robotníkov na výrobých poradách," *Odbory a společnost*, no. 3, pp. 80−84.

Piekalkiewicz, J. A. (1972), *Public Opinion Polling in Czechoslovakia, 1968–69: Results and Analysis of Surveys Conducted during the Dubcek Era* (New York: Praeger).

Pokorný, A., and Duffek, P. (1978), "Účast pracujících na řízeni a účinnost výrobních porad," *Odbory a společnost,* no. 3, pp. 93–97.

Poláček, K. (1969), *Rudé právo,* August 27.

Porket, J. L. (1971), "Czechoslovak Society in 1967," *British Journal of Sociology,* vol. 22, no. 4, pp. 448–454.

Porket, J. L. (1972), "The Communist Party of Czechoslovakia in 1967: Some Empirical Findings," *New Sociology,* vol. 1, no. 2, pp. 47–63.

Porket, J. L. (1975), "Participation in Management in Communist Systems in the 1970s," *British Journal of Industrial Relations,* vol. 13, no. 3, pp. 371–387.

Porket, J. L. (1976), *Industrial Relations and Workers' Participation in Eastern Europe from the late 1940s to the early 1970s.* St. Antony's papers in East European Economics, no. 49.

Porket, J. L. (1978), "Industrial Relations and Participation in Management in the Soviet-type Communist System," *British Journal of Industrial Relations,* vol. 16, no. 1, pp. 70–85.

Porket, J. L. (1977), "The Soviet Model of Industrial Democracy," *Annals of the American Academy of Political and Social Sciences,* vol. 431, pp. 123–132.

Porket, J. L. (1983), review of J. F. Triska and C. Gati (eds.), *Blue Collar Workers in Eastern Europe, Slavonic and East European Review,* vol. 61, no. 3, pp. 472–473.

Právnický slovník (1972) (Prague: Orbis).

Protokol (1949), *IX řádného sjezdu Komunistické strany Československa* (Prague).

Pravda, A. (1977), "Workers' Participation in Czechoslovakia", *Canadian Slavonic Papers,* vol. 19, no. 3, pp. 312–334.

RTUM Statutes (1972), in *Hlavní dokumenty VIII všeodborového sjezdu* (Prague: Práce).

Svoboda, L. (1968), "Nové cesty rozvoje iniciativy," *Odbory a společnost,* no. 2, pp. 56–68.

Škurlo, I. (1975), "Odbory na Slovensku," in *O revoluní odborovou politiku* (Prague: Práce).

Šumberová, L. (1968), "Demokratické orgány v závodech v předúnorovém období", *Odborář,* no. 11, pp. 7–9.

Ústav (1971) marxismu-leninismu ÚV KSČ, *Rudé právo 1939–45* (Prague: Svoboda).

ÚV KSČ (1978), *Za štěstí a blaho lidu* (Prague: Svoboda).

XIII sjezd (1967) *komunistické strany Československa* (Prague: Svoboda).

Zápotocký, A. (1948), *Nová odborová politika* (Prague: Práce).

5

The Politics of Romanian Trade Unions

Daniel N. Nelson

The Context of Romanian Trade Unions

There is considerable irony to the rule of a communist party in a peasant society. Lacking any of the socioeconomic characteristics Marx saw to be associated with revolutionary elan, the societies where most communists rule (the Northern Tier of Eastern Euope may be cited as an exception), offer few bases of party legitimacy. Where a politically conscious working class is nowhere to be found, a party which eschews peasants (as do orthodox Marxists) has, literally, no "place to go." Romania was, and is, such a case.

On the heels of the Red Army's offensive in the summer of 1944, a tiny communist party numbering perhaps 1,000 became the dominant—and quickly the only—political organization within Romania. Romania's communist party (the RCP) had poor or nonexistent connections with that country's workers and peasants, the latter constituting 80 percent of the workforce immediately after World War II and still 50 percent thirty-five years later. Although the peasant majority has declined greatly as the communist regime has promoted urban-based industry, it remains true that the vast majority of adult Romanians work in agriculture or are the first generation in their family to work away from the village. In that regard, Romania of the late twentieth century is still a peasant society, albeit one in transition.

Such a fundamental characteristic of Romanian society implies that a ruling communist party must not just mobilize industrial labor, but must create it. In such a process, there is no guarantee of working-class allegiance

Daniel N. Nelson, Department of Political Science, University of Kentucky, Lexington, Kentucky.

to the party, its leaders, or policies. Indeed, the entire process of "develop-ment" is one fraught with uncertainty for those in power, communist or not. But particularly in a communist system where the party came to power not by indigenous revolution (as in China, Cuba, Vietnam, or Yugoslavia), but via Soviet occupation, the effort to build an industrial society is one with enor-mous political risk. There is no existing "base" of support in such a circum-stance—there are no roots among the masses upon which to draw. Change inaugurated by the party's developmental policies could erode its own political control as an unsympathetic, unconvinced working class expands.

Cognizant of their distance from industrial labor, or at least, suspicious of workers' political consciousness, RCP leaders have followed a path taken many times by communist regimes—they have sought to keep industrial labor impotent via a total penetration of labor organizations, denying to workers any autonomous voice for collective action. A single trade union confederation under the aegis of the RCP, the General Trade Union Confera-tion of Romania (*Uniunea Generala a Sindicatelor dine Romania*, UGSR, or "Sindicat," the word for union in Romanian) is the hierarchy through which the party exerts its control of industrial labor. With 6 million members, the UGSR is a critical adjunct to RCP hegemony, penetrating through its local structures every branch trade union federation and each enterprise or institu-tion of that branch. Every wage-earner is expected to belong to the trade union and most do because benefits (pensions, day care, transportation, and so on) are contingent on membership (see Table 5.1).

Integration of trade union leadership with the party is complete. If one is a trade union leader at a local territorial level, one's membership in the RCP committee for that town, city, or county (Oras, Municipiu, or Judet) is expected. The party bureau at all territorial-administrative levels will include the Sindicat chief for that region or locale as well. At the national level, the

Table 5.1
Membership in Romanian Trade Unions, 1945–1983

Year	Total Membership	Total Number of Industry and Construction Wage-Earners in Population	Percent of Industrial Work Force Unionized
1945	519,000	1,700,000	30.5
1947	1,337,596	1,750,000	76.5
1954	2,5000,000	2,820,000	88.9
1972	(near)5,000,000	4,957,900 (1969)	Close to 100
1983	5,580,000	5,600,000	Close to 100

Source: Gilberg, 1975: 155; 1983 data are author's judgments based upon *Directives of the Twelfth Congress* of the Romanian Communist Party (Bucharest: Meridiane, 1980).

trade union leader (that is, president of the UGSR) will be a member of the RCP's highest formal organ, the Political Executive Committee, and may be as well a member of the Secretariat.

But the trade union edifice and the sheer weight of its bureaucracy confirm rather than deny the party's distance from Romania's working class. In its relationship with the worker, the RCP lacks historical links or the comradeship of revolutionary experience; it must thus "relate" to workers via Stalinist coercion or through some appeal which might transcend class interests, such as nationalism. But the threats and intimidation of Stalinism or the emotional appeals of nationalism have been insufficient to ensure proletarian solidarity for parties "of the proletariat," and the RCP has no reason to be sanguine about its legitimacy among workers either.

The roots of RCP distance from workers date from before the party's founding in May, 1921. A Romanian socialist movement, which was first organized as a party in 1893, identified closely with trade unionism, and had considerable success expanding unions (reaching 50 percent of industrial labor by 1920). But the industrial labor force was small, and most workers had strong ties with their native village. Communist-led trade unions could attract, then, only a fraction of all wage-earners to their cause—about 80,000, or less than 15 percent of industrial labor, by 1936−1937. Such a discrepancy was, in part, because the Social Democrats had made trade unionism *their* cause earlier, and the RCP could make little headway. Problems of an appeal from communists to an essentially peasant society, however, were also evident. It is not that Comintern and early RCP leaders did not talk of party activity within trade union; indeed, at Comintern direction, the RCP attempted to establish "unitary" trade unions in the mid-1920s apart from the Social Democratic unions. In April, 1929 a congress of these unitary trade unions being held in Timisoara ended in a clash between delgates, led by Vasile Luca, and police. Later, in 1933, Gheorghiu-Dej played an important role in organizing railyard workers at Grivita outside of Bucharest that resulted in a violent confrontation leaving scores of dead. As stated above, their membership peaked by early 1937 at around 15 percent of industrial labor.

But these events are transitory exceptions. Not only did the RCP fail in most of its organizational efforts, but it was also criticized heavily by other communist parties and by Comintern for its lack of contact with the masses and its inattentiveness to proletarian interests (King, 1981: 156).

Once the Red Army had secured Romania for the RCP in late 1944, the party worked assiduously to expand and to dominate trade unions—a task made easier as political opposition was eliminated by late 1947. The intimidation used against Social Democrats led, in large part, to RCP victory in elections for thousands of trade union officials in 1946 (58 percent of the vote going to communist candidates) (Russindilar, 1972: 108–16). Subsequently, the Sindicat has absorbed virtually the entirety of Romania's workforce with no alternative voice open to labor.

As one would expect, the RCP's account of its own contact with the working class over the past century is quite different. The exploitive nature of Romanian capitalism in combination with foreign "trusts" is alleged to have been evident earlier and to have encouraged, by the mid-1800s, workers' associations. The Marxist connection to such nascent unions is viewed as critical to their development (Ceausescu, 1971: 760–1). In the twentieth century Gheorghe Gheorghiu-Dej and other early party activists are credited with significant achievements in raising the political consciousness of workers during the late 1920s and 1930s when, in fact, they had great difficulty making any headway in organizing Romanian labor. The party's role in maintaining workers' opposition to Antonescu's fascist regime, in organizing workers during the August 23, 1944 insurrection, and other elements of wartime history has been expanded by present leaders.

Romanian trade unions thus exist within a context of retarded development in what continues to be a predominantly peasant society. The trade unions had minimal prewar connections with the Romanian Communist Party. Notwithstanding such weak historical linkages to the party, the RCP's rhetoric insists on a close identity with the working class—a relationship the party seeks to cement via the structures described in the following section.

Institutional Arrangements[1]

To students of communist systems, the hierarchy of Romanian trade unions will be very familiar (see Figure 5.1). As with most adjunct mass organizations which serve to extend party penetration of society, the trade unions exhibit an ostensibly democratic structure with over 13,000 enterprise or institutional unions as a mass "base." Every second year, at general assemblies of the enterprise (which are held twice a year), a president and an executive committee (Comitetul Sindicatului) are elected from unopposed slates. Those elected always include members of the RCP committee for the enterprise. Each time a Sindicat committee and president are elected, delegates to the town, city, or county (Oras, Municipiu, or Judet) conferences are also elected; most times, these delegates are the enterprise committee members. Each territorial-administrative unit will also have a trade union committee elected, once again from an unopposed slate, at the conference for that

---

[1]These institutional arrangements are discussed on the basis of "Statul-Cadrul al Sindicatului," published in *Minca*, March 8, 1971.

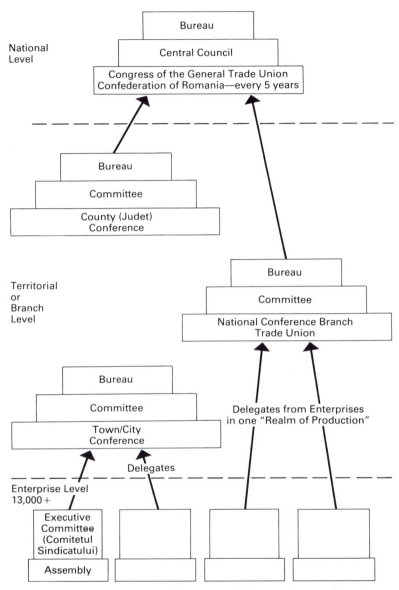

**National
Level**

Bureau

Central Council

Congress of the General Trade Union
Confederation of Romania—every 5 years

**Territorial
or
Branch
Level**

Bureau

Committee

County (Judet)
Conference

Bureau

Committee

National Conference Branch
Trade Union

Bureau

Committee

Town/City
Conference

Delegates from Enterprises
in one "Realm of Production"

Delegates

**Enterprise Level
13,000+**

Executive
Committee
(Comitetul
Sindicatului)

Assembly

Figure 5.1 Organizational diagram of Romanian trade unions.

locale held once every four years. The committee, in turn, elects an executive bureau of a president, one to three vice-presidents, and a secretary.

Delegates from factories or institutions in a particular realm of production—textiles, transport, machine-building, and so on—convene for national conferences as a branch trade union federation. These conferences, of course, also elect committees (*Comitetul Uniunii Sindicatelor pe Ramura de Productie*) and an executive bureau.

Once every five years, a congress of the General Trade Union Confederation of Romania is held, the last having been convened in early April 1981. These events, in which takes place the formal election of the Central Council of the Sindicat (*Consiliul Central al Uniunii Generale a Sindicatelor*), in fact serve as a forum for Nicolae Ceausescu's pronouncements to workers. While making promises to workers about greater consultation, Ceausescu used his 1981 opportunity principally to exhort industrial labor to raise productivity, conserve material, and so on. The final communiqué issued from the Congress assured General Secretary Ceausescu that the trade unions would devote "all their energies and forces toward implementing decisions of the Twelfth Congress and those adopted at union fora, to raise our country towards new progress and civilization" (Radio Free Europe, 1981). There was no debate evident to the public, and Cornel Onescu was approved as new UGSR chairman without any consultation of the mass membership (Dempsey, 1983: 20).

What took place at the last UGSR congress suggests, of course, that the institutional arrangements of Romanian trade unions exist for the RCP's benefit. No autonomous voice exists for workers with which to raise issues they regard as important and which they must seek to air through alternative means (e.g., the letters, protests, or strikes discussed below). Even decisions regarding leadership of trade unions are made at higher levels. But how can the party perpetuate this control of workers' institutions in Romania? In part, the answer lies in a smaller and younger Romanian industrial workforce, for which collective interests are unclear. But much more can be explained by examining the effect of the *nomenklatura* system and the principle of "democratic centralism."

The electoral mechanism of Romanian trade unions is predetermined because all candidates for leadership posts (that is, members of a committee) are selected by a higher level which has the power of appointment, dismissal, and promotion for a list of positions including those of the trade union committee. The *nomenklatura*, as described in other chapters as well, assures those in power (that is, the party intertwined with the Sindicat at every level) that they will be able to choose trade union officials before they are "elected" by enterprise workers. Through such a screening process, the potential for disaffected individuals to enter the trade union hierarchy is very low. Democratic centralism, moreover, insists that decisions made by superior officials or organs, ostensibly elected to that position of authority, are absolutely binding. The statutes for trade unions contain a direct statement to that effect, namely, that "it is obligatory to implement decisions" made at higher levels. Within the UGSR structures a committee of censure (*comisia de cenzori*) operates at all levels to enforce obedience using sanctions against workers which affect benefits and employability. Intimidation, then, silences complaints and minimizes slowdowns or strikes.

Such institutional arrangements thus speak clearly of their intended constraint on workers' interests and their articulation. Rather than being institutions to facilitate the expression of grievances and needs, Romanian trade unions exist to facilitate the party's control of labor.

Workers' Interests and Their Representation

The principle of "nonnegotiability" guides ruling communist parties' relations with workers. Such a principle is born out of the logic of self-justification by which erstwhile revolutionaries take the reins of government. Given that a state ruled by a communist party is a workers' state—that is, where the interests of working people are the *raison d' être* of the state as guided by a proletarian party—a normative dialogue between workers and party cannot exist. Ruling communist parties must seek to maintain the principle of nonnegotiability. Since the party sees itself as *the* spokesman for workers, it stands to "reason" that others would not negotiate with it on behalf of workers. Industrial labor is likely, then, to feel wholly unprotected, obliged to sell labor to a monopolistic employer, in this case a socialist state rather than monopoly capital (Casas, 1980: 249)

Maintaining the principle of nonnegotiability means depriving industrial labor (and all working people) of access to power. Put simply, political inequalities are used by ruling communist parties to constrain demands which arise from socioeconomic grievances. Because workers' demands—for more equitable distribution of resources, for a greater voice in enterprise decision-making and so on—threatened a communist regime which claims to already serve such interests, the proletarist is excluded from institutionalized access to power for policy influence and denied resources with which to construct autonomous participatory channels. That such inequality is perpetuated by the regime is all the more striking when one considers the domestic Romanian labor market, where (until economic slowdowns of 1979 through 1983) labor had been in short supply and increasing productivity was critical to meeting plans. Even when skilled labor was "scarce" in Romania because of rapid growth, the market did nothing to lessen political inequalities.

The USGR and its constituent branches thus speak to the workers *for* the party. To the extent that efforts are made on behalf of industrial labor, they are of a nature that can be termed "social welfare activities" such as organizing recreation or holiday activities, or expressing concern about health and safety matters at the workplace. Job security disputes, on rare occasions, are also a subject for trade union activity in Romania.

But principal among the Sindicat's concerns in Romania are workforce disicpline, productivity, and "socialist consciousness," themes repeated over and over again by General Secretary Nicolae Ceausescu whenever he discusses trade unions of labor (Ceausescu, 1981a). In such themes there is no room for any effort to carry the case for workers beyond the immediate workplace—and there is no record, public or otherwise, of Sindicat advocacy of positions at odds with party social or economic plans. Instead, fitting workers into allocative principles determined by national RCP elites is the major responsiblity of the UGSR.

This thesis of trade unions as mere transmission belts for a ruling party's policy is not new, and not unique to Romania, much less to communist sytems. The insistence with which Nicolae Ceausescu has identified such a responsibility for the UGSR, however, exceeds most other cases of communist regimes. At the height of Poland's Solidarity experience, in the spring of 1981, Ceausescu spoke at the opening session of a trade union congress where he demanded that the UGSR mobilize working people to implement RCP economic plans and to increase productivity (Ceausescu, 1981b). Such an outright denial of trade union autonomy followed by a decade of Ceausescu's promises to inaugurate new statutes for the trade unions and workers' self-management (Ceausescu 1981b). The new statutes have yet (as of late 1983) to appear; workers' self-management (discussed further in the next section) never went beyond establishing a formal structure of workers' councils (*consiliile oamenilor muncii*) until early 1978. In that year, a vehement propaganda campaign touting self-management (*autoconducerea*) was begun which likewise has connoted no substantive change (Nelson, 1981a).

Neither cultural nor political traditions of Romania would lead one to expect strong union advocacy. As reported above, trade unions were small and slow to develop as was all of Romanian nonagricultural employment. By turning unions into instruments of penetration and control after World War II, however, the RCP and its Soviet allies acted to assure themselves that such a tradition would not change. Where it once was desperate for any working-class sympathy, as in the 1930s, the RCP in power sought to deny any collective voice to labor in the political system.

Romanian workers understand quite well that their interests are not seen by the party as legitimate. They further understand that current channels for "representation" convey few of their needs, if any, to top RCP policy-makers. Romanian industrial laborers know that they are not consulted regarding decisions within the enterprise where they work, and appear to have been, in 1976, only a bit less sure of their impotence than were Polish workers (see Table 5.2).

It is not surprising, then, that union-organized "production meetings" (held in sections of institutions, production lines, or work teams in factories) are regarded as futile. Instead of encouraging workers to speak out about how to increase productivity, 63 percent of young workers, aged 30 and under (i.e., most workers) report that they never make proposals at such meetings. Almost half of the 37 percent who do participate at such sessions said that their proposals would have no effect (Badina, 1973: 74). The futility of appealing to "the system" for redress of grievances is also suggested by other data concerning the attitude of respondents in one Romanian survey, covering several thousand workers across industries, toward "excessive bureaucracy and arbitrary decisions." If confronted by such negative management behavior at the enterprise, only 6.6 percent said that they would "try to attract my superior's attention," while others said that they would not react because it would have no effect (30 percent of males, 13.3 percent of females) and very high proportions said that they would not respond at all (53.5 percent of women and 23.4 percent of men) (Dan-Spinoiu, 1974: 74).

While these data are too limited to provide more than a tentative portrait of workers' attitudes about their interests in the regime of Nicolae Ceausescu, I think it is warranted to conclude that industrial labor has made the same conclusion one might draw from the outside—namely, that the RCP continues to deny workers an access to power or an autonomous route for the articulation of their interests.

Workers' involvement in other sanctioned roles for political activity is limited as well. The proportion of RCP membership with industrial labor

Table 5.2
Consultation at the Enterprise in Romania vs. Poland

How Decisions Are Taken on the Job:	1976[a] Romania	1977[b] Poland
I'm always consulted	38%	4.5%
I'm frequently consulted		18.7%
I'm rarely consulted	62%	38.6%
I'm never consulted		31.8%

[a]Data are from two large industrial enterprises and are not a national sample; author's estimate based upon percentages reported by Cornescu, 1977: pp. 214–15.

[b]Question to Polish shipyard workers, 1979; "What influence does the rank and file worker have over what happens in the workplace?" Jacek Poprzeczk and Thomasz Sypniewski, "Stoczniowcy 81," *Zycie Warszawy*, as reported in McGregor, 1982: 11.

background, a very dubious statistic in any case, *has* risen since 1965 from perhaps 40 percent to a little above 50 percent (Ceausescu, 1981b). Yet the advance of skilled or unskilled labor within party ranks is constrained. As a consequence, a much smaller proportion of workers than of most professions is in the RCP. Most Ph.D.s, teachers, and almost all military officers, for example, are RCP members (Gilberg, 1975: 155; Mink, 1979: 109). By contrast, approximately 20–25 percent of all factory workers are party members, while another 15 percent are UTC members. By 1984, it appears that in some "model" factories more than half of the workforce will be affiliated with the RCP or UTC (Union of Communist Youth) (Nelson, 1982: 195). Yet local leaders are not workers, or have not been workers since their youth. Politically active Romanians, such as tens of thousands of people's council deputies, exhibit education and income well above the mean for all citizens, and offer a profile very different from the Romanian working class (Nelson, 1981b). Simply put, it is not just within unions that workers have no clout. Pervasive to Romania, and to other communist party states as well I think, is an effort to constrain political activity of workers. In Romania such an effort has been mounted in the face of an expanding industrial workforce, the productivity of which is desperately needed to maintain growth. The RCP, as it creates an industrial workforce, tries to keep it an impotent political force.

Role of the Trade Unions in Economic Management and Policy Processes

Official descriptions of the Sindicat's role in Romania suggest that trade unions "have their say" in general assemblies of enterprises and in workers' councils, the latter formally established in 1971. In such fora, the government argues, trade unions contribute "to the working out of the production plans in the organization of work and production, in the promotion of cadres, and stimulating the innovative spirit" of those institutions and enterprises (Blaga, 1977: 105). The "smooth unfolding of productive activity [and] of all economic plans . . . to strengthen order and discipline" and other matters related to this mobilization function have been emphasized increasingly at UGSR congresses (Timsmaneanu and Zaharia, 1977: 37). At the same time, trade unions ostensibly are "preoccupied with the continuous improvement of the working people's work and life conditions . . ." (Blaga, 1977: 105). Such dual functioning of trade unions in communist party states, discussed at length in this volume, alleges that the same organizations can at once strengthen discipline and socialist consciousness among workers while it simultaneously protects workers and serves as their advocate in social and economic decision-making.

Within state and party organs the "outstanding role" of trade unions is said to be institutionalized via the UGSR's presence in the Socialist Democracy and Unity Front (*Frontul Democratiei si Unitatii Socialiste*) and its representation in the Council of Ministers. In the formal organization, the Sindicat is the largest single component of the front organization which serves the party as a mechanism for nominating individuals for elections to state organs (e.g., people's councils and the Grand National Assembly). Such a tool of party control serves to perpetuate the party's contention that it can subsume interests of all people regardless of age, nationality, occupation, sex, and so on, but also unites the adjunct organizations aimed at such segments in one overarching hierarchy. The Front, however, provides no additional management or policymaking role to the trade unions, much less to the interests of working people. Since the only prominent function played by the Socialist Democracy and Unity Front in the Romanian political system is that of candidate nomination—from a list of individuals acceptable to the RCP committee of that territorial administrative unit—it provides no forum for the expression of working-class interests.

Following an announcement by General Secretary Ceausescu in 1967, the UGSR president has a place in the Council of Ministers, albeit no ministry post (Ceausescu, 1968: 601−2). But this formal role in government once again underscores the difficulty, if not impossibility, of functioning in a dual capacity—as mobilizer *and* representative of industrial labor. Indeed, between 1977 and 1981 the Minister of Labor was *also* UGSR president, and the image of autonomy was ignored entirely.

The Romanian Sindicat is, to put it succinctly, excluded from economic management and the making of national policy. As an organizational entity, it is impotent in both realms. This is not to say that the UGSR has no role important for those who *do* manage and who *do* decide about the allocation of resources (i.e., make policy). For the RCP elites, trade unions are meant to "carry through the program of Romanian multilateral development" (Blaga, 1977: 105). One must also recognize that important people within the party are given trade union responsibilities; some of the past and present UGSR leaders are involved in the management of Romania's economy and policymaking, quite apart from any effort to act as a spokesman for a union constituency.

Mobilization of human resources, particularly of the rural labor force for industry, is at the core of Romanian economic planning and management. Unable to depend on increasing capital resources to raise output, and confronting massive debt to foreign banks and governments, the Ceausescu regime has turned to the Sindicat, Union of Communist Youth (UTC), workers' councils (COM) and other adjunct organizations to increase productivity and further economize the use of material. All of these organizations, but particularly the Sindicat, are charged with the responsiblity of "educating" workers regarding the need for better performance and discipline. These activities are accomplished at the local level principally through general assemblies of the enterprise, production meetings (among work teams, groups of employees, and so on), and educational or cultural sessions arranged after hours. The agenda for general assemblies of the enterprise, as with all Sindicat-arranged events, is set not by the membership on the basis of their grievances but, rather, by central decision implemented through the RCP committee of the enterprise (all of whom are part of the trade union organization as well).[2] Mobilization efforts are enhanced by tying many important benefits to Sindicat membership and activity. Such basic services as transportation by bus or truck to a factory, day care for children, apartments at the Black Sea or in the mountains which can be rented for holidays, and others are provided to Sindicat members; individuals who become committee members for an enterprise or institution-level trade union will gain preferential service (for example, somewhat better apartments at the seacoast or first choice as to the time of reservation). For the peasant workers of Romania, who after living in a village through adolescence have been uprooted to depersonalized urban settlements, such Sindicat-provided services are critical.

But such enticements in no way bring manual labor closer to management or, for that matter, to policy making. Coopted workers, who fill places in establishment organizations such as the trade union, have no "input" role. Data cited earlier imply that workers have, themselves, made such a judgment. By every other indication, as well, the Ceausescu regime continues to decide about and implement policy regarding workers without regard to what may be presumed to be the preferences and needs of working people. That the RCP has been forced to *react* to labor grievances, violently expressed at incidents such as the Jiu Valley in 1977 and Motru mines in October, 1981 is unquestioned. But the regime continues its adament refusal to democratize management procedures or to consult with workers about national Sindicat leadership or economic policy. The UGSR chairman and Central Council still are appointed by President Ceausescu only later to be confirmed—unanimously—by the Congress of the UGSR as the last item of business (Radio Free Europe, 1981).

Decisions directly germane to workers, such as length of their work

[2]Data collected by Romanian sociologists imply an association between political affiliation and the centrality of one's role at general assemblies of the enterprise. Those employees who are RCP members help plan for such sessions much more frequently than do individuals whose "highest" political identity is UTC or Sindicat. I have reported on these and related data in Nelson, 1981d and 1981c.

week and workplace disciplinary statutes, have also been made as regime pronouncements—by Ceausescu at UGSR congresses, the party's Political Executive Committee, or the Council of State. The repeated promises and postponements regarding a shorter work week are a case in point. First promised by Ceausescu in June, 1972 as a goal for 1980, a 42-hour week was instead made a goal for 1990 in a plan announced in 1976, while a 44-hour week was to be inaugurated by 1980. One year later, in 1977, this was again revised, with the 42-hour goal being set aside entirely, and a 46- and 44-hour work week intended for 1980 and 1983 respectively. Interviews I conducted during 1979 indicated that the 46-hour goal had not been achieved until that point, particularly in critical export industries.[3]

Decree 400, promulgated by the Council of State (the highest executive organ of state) on December 29, 1981 further exemplifies the low priority given to workers' role in management and policy processes. In response to an explosion and fire at the Pitesti oil and chemical refineries earlier that month, which were widely thought to have been the result of purposeful negligence or outright sabotage,[4] the UGSR *endorsed* the regime's imposition of tough new penalties for any job-related "negligence" (*Munca,* December 29 and 30, 1981). A Western reporter, for instance, was told by a Sindicat Central Council member that "Decree 400 is necessary because the workers are not responsible at the moment" (Dempsey, 1983: 20).

Union Performance and Prognosis for Change

The illegitimacy of workers' interests and the exclusion of a collective voice for industrial labor from policy processes implies, as one might expect, a distance between trade union members and "their" union. Because they cannot rely on this adjunct organization to convey their needs to policymakers, or to make "a case" for workers' concerns outside an enterprise, it is not surprising that almost half of young workers interviewed in the early 1970s (a national sample) thought they had little or no influence on even local union leaders (Badina, 1973: 124). Data from the same national study, reported earlier, found that 63 percent of the 6,236 young workers in the sample regarded union performance as so unsatisfactory that participation was un-

---

[3]Conversations January—April, 1979 with people's council deputies in five locales (Timisoara, Cluj, Brasov, Iasi, and Consanta) included questions about workers' productivity and other labor-related difficulties.

[4]Conversations with several Romanian scholars, Fall, 1982 and April, 1983.

warranted, while another 15 percent took part in union-organized meetings but saw them as futile.

Such low regard for the Sindicat is, however, part of a wider indictment of "the system" in which diffuse support by industrial labor for the rule by a communist party—and especially the regime of Nicolae Ceausescu—has evaporated. Serious responses to their needs are not expected from state or party functionaries (Dan-Spinoliu, 1974: 74) and the potential for future confrontation with the Romanian Communist Party is understood to be quite real (Nelson, 1981c: 190–7).

A dramatic admission of Sindicat inadequacy was implicit in Nicolae Ceausescu's talk to a mass rally during the Jiu Valley uprising; only through the August 1977 strike of 35,000 miners could policy makers be reached, and only then by the extraordinary visit of the RCP leader to the scene of the strike activity (Ceausescu, 1978: 198–9). That Ceausescu's effort in 1981 to repeat the performance—appearing personally at the location of strikes by miners at Motru—resulted in an attack on his helicopter by an angry crowd further indicates the Sindicat's failure in the eyes of critical parts of Romania's workforce.

Other than strikes, workers' complaints are taking other routes including more emphasis on letters to party and state executive organs. To be sure, the party itself encourages this manner of expressing grievances for workers, perhaps to alleviate their discontent while providing "means of gathering information on society" (Radio Free Europe, 1982). That such complaint letters have "almost doubled" in number since the mid-1960s, and now involve about one in five employees, however, might exceed proportions deemed desirable by the Party (Radio Free Europe, 1982). Among trends apparent in such letter-writing is the tendency to submit complaints about broader issues, that is criticizing aspects of economic life beyond the immediate factory or community, and signing letters collectively rather than individually (Radio Free Europe, 1982).

Although vigorously suppressed, the rudiments of an independent trade union movement were begun in early 1979. The *Sindicatul Liberal Oamenilor Muncii din Romania* (or SLOMR) was announced in the West by Paul Goma, the dissident Romanian intellectual, in February 1979. At the same time, this effort was led in Romania principally by activists such as Vasile Paraschiv, Gheorghe Brasoveneau, and Ionel Cana. Paraschiv, known since the late 1960s for his criticism of the Ceausescu regime, spoke out vehemently against RCP trade union policy in a Western journal in 1978 (Paraschiv, 1982). One month after Goma's announcement, Paraschiv, Brasoveneau, and Cana were arrested and interned in psychiatric hospitals. Although the latter two were released in 1980, Parachiv's fate was unknown for several years, but he apparently remained incarcerated through 1982. SLOMR itself has not been able to develop further and the enterprises where any interest has been shown are rumored to be infiltrated by the Securitate (Romanian secret police).

Workers' attitudes about trade unions, infrequent but large-scale strikes particularly among miners, a rising tide of written complaints to officials and the first signs of an independent trade union organization—these are the most obvious indications that the Sindicat is evaluated poorly. To expect this discontent with the UGSR to widen and explode however, is unwarranted. For several reasons, the immediate prospect in Romania is unlikely to include either a national movement of Polish dimensions or strikes and protests across all segments of Romanian industrial labor.

Some of this assessment is based upon consideration of intangible elements of Romanian history and culture. It is not a novel observation that Romanians have, more than some other nations (the Poles are an obvious example), been quiescent under repressive governments. While I am reluctant to invoke a "national character" explanation for the lack of rebellion, perhaps other closely related concepts should be suggested. Prior socioeconomic conditions and cultural norms can, for example, account for part of the political behavior of contemporary Romanian workers. As discussed in the first section of this chapter, the late development of Romanian industry meant a small working class until the past two decades; the predominantly peasant origins of the present working class means that personal ties with the village remain strong, particularly since almost a quarter of industrial laborers commute to and from their native village (Cole, 1981: 178). Among those who do not commute, and who are thus deprived of village contacts (and who are frequently separated from their nuclear family), no organizational infrastructure exists on which to depend other than that provided by the party. Trade unions, while seen as ineffective and culpable for many of workers' grievances, are nevertheless the *only* option available for the young, peasant, politically inexperienced Romanian working class.

Far more than the older, established stratum of industrial labor in Poland, by comparison, Romanian workers are thus at the mercy of official trade unions. Although other communist party states are predominantly peasant in character, for example, China or Vietnam, the legitimacy of an indigenous revolution guided by the party strengthens the party's hold on an emerging working class. The Romanian Communist Party has none of that legitimacy, and has worn thin its claim as "national communists." An awkward "balance" is thus maintained in the Romanian labor force—between rejection of the party as irrelevant or antagonistic to the needs of working people *and* the inability of a relatively young and inexperienced industrial labor force to organize itself against the regime.

Further weakening the Romanian workers' ability to mount organized and autonomous political activity have been the party's efforts to undermine bases for worker's unity. Promises which placate all but the most disenchanted, wage increases coincident with price increases (the former not keeping pace, however), vociferous propaganda campaigns touting workers' self-management—these and other techniques have been used in the past decade and a half to dissipate the discontent of industrial labor. Ceausescu's record of promises, for example, encompasses his 1971 statement at a Sindicat congress that trade unions would no longer fulfill the role of "transmission belts," his commitments at the 1976 congress to consult workers for Sindicat leadership appointments, his repeated references (1971, 1976, 1981) to new UGSR statutes, and the extraordinary 1981 announcement that the party would no longer rule from the principle of a "proletarian dictatorship." Surely the latter grandiose promise has fallen on deaf ears, and Ceausescu's believability is minimal. But, in the shortterm, the party leader's promises have diverted attention from grievances.

It is unclear, however, how long such tactics and the customary quiescence of Romanian labor will suffice to constrain the alienation discussed in this chapter with the performance of the Sindicat and other sanctioned channels for workers' interests. No one who knows Romania well expects soon that the labor force will rise to challenge the party and Ceausescu in the organized fashion of Solidarity. But no one who has listened to disaffected workers in Romania during the last half-decade can expect them to accept without question the party's failure to heed their complaints or to fulfill its own promises to the social stratum for which it allegedly rules. As Romania becomes less and less a "peasant society," the party's unwillingness to regard as legitimate the interests of workers will exacerbate the RCP's own legitimacy problem. The party must, for ideological and developmental reasons, continue the creation and expansion of an industrial labor force. But to keep workers organizationally weak and subservient is thus likely to involve more conflict with each passing year.

References

Badina, O. (1973), "Participarea Tinerilor la Procesul de Realizare a Unor Inventil, Inovatii si Rationalizari," in O. Badina and C. Mamali (eds.), *Tineret Industrial* (Bucharest: Editura Academiei).

Blaga, I. (1972), *Romania's Population* (Bucharest: Meridiane).

Casals, F. G. (1980), "Theses on the Syncretic Society," *Theory and Society,* vol. 9.

Ceausescu, N. (1968), "Rapport la Conferinta Nationala a PCR—6 Decembrie, 1967," in *Romania pe drumul construirii societatii socialiste multilateral dezvoltate* (Bucharest: Editura politica), vol. 2.

Ceausescu, N. (1971), "Cuvintare la Congresul Uniunii Generale a Sindicatelor din Romania" (23 Martie 1971), in *Romania pe drumul* (Bucharest: Editura politica), vol. 5.

Ceausescu, N. (1978), "Cuvintare la marea populara din Petrosani cu prilejul vizitei de lucru in judetul Hunerdoara—9 Noiembrie 1977," in *Romania pe drumul. . .* (Bucharest: Editura politica), vol. 15.

Ceausescu, N. (1981a), "Rolul si Atributiile Sindicatelor din Romania" (Bucharest: Editura politica).

Ceausescu, N. (1981b), "Cuvintarela Congresul Uniunii Generale a Sidicatelor Din Romania" (Aprilie 1981) (Bucharest: Editura politica).

Cole, J. (1981), 'Family, Farm and Factory,' in D. Nelson (ed.), *Romania in the 1980s* (Boulder, Colo: Westview), pp. 71 – 116.

Cornescu, V. I. (1977), *Productivitatea Muncii si Factorul Uman* (Bucharest: Editura politica).

Dan-Spionoiu, G. (1974), *Factori Objectiv si Subjectiv in Integrarea Profesionala a Femeii* (Bucharest: Editura academiei).

Dempsey, J. 91983), "Romania Since Solidarity," *Workers Under Communism*, Spring, pp. 19 – 22.

Gilberg, T. (1975), "Romania in Quest of Development," in I. Volgyes (ed.), *Political Socialization in Eastern Europe* (New York: Praeger), pp. 147 – 190.

King, R. (1981), *History of the Romanian Communist Party* (Stanford, Calif.: Hoover Institution).

McGregor, J. (1982), "Polish Public Moods in a Time of Crisis," paper delivered at the annual meeting of the ISA, Cincinnati.

Mink, G. (1979), "Structures Sociales en Europe de l'est," in *Notes et études documentaires,2, Transformations de la classe ouvrière* (Paris: La Documentation Francaise).

Nelson, D. N. (1981a), "Romania: Participatory Dynamics in 'Developed Socialism'," in J. F. Triska and C. Gati (eds.), *Blue-Collar Workers in Eastern Europe* (London: Allen and Unwin).

Nelson, D. N. (1981b), "People's Council Deputies in Romania," in D. Nelson and S. White (eds.), *Communist Legislatures in Comparative Perspective* (London: Macmillan), pp. 85 – 110.

Nelson, D. N. (1981c), "Workers in a Workers' State," in D. N. Nelson (ed.), *Romania in the 1980s* (Boulder, Colo: Westview), pp. 174 – 97.

Nelson, D. N. (1981d), "Development and Participation in Communist Systems," in D. Schultz and J. S. Adams (eds.), *Political Participation in Communist Systems* (New York: Pergamon), pp. 234 – 53.

Nelson, D. N. (1982), "The Worker and Political Alienation in Communist Europe," *Polity* (Winter), pp. 182 – 201.

Paraschiv, V. (1982), "L'Itineraire d'un syndicaliste," *L'Alternative,* nos. 16 – 17, pp. 66 – 8.

Radio Free Europe (1981), Romanian Monitoring, April 8.

Radio Free Europe (1982), Situation Report, Romania, vol. 7, no. 23.

Russindilar, P. (1972), "Insemnatatea alegerilor sindicale din 1946 in cadrul luptei pentru consolidarea Frontului Unic Moncitoresc," *Anale de istorie,* vol. 18, no. 6, pp. 108 – 16.

Tismaneanu, L., and Zaharia, R. (1977), *Present and Prospect in Romania* (Bucharest: Meridiane).

6

Poland in the 1970s: Dual Functioning Trade Unionism under Pressure

Alex Pravda

Introduction

The 1970s began and ended with major crises involving the representation of labor interests. Trade unions were among the main institutional targets of criticism during the strikes of 1970–1971, and the establishment of independent unions figured prominently among strikers' demands. In 1980 the trade union issue was more central still. This time, though, reform of existing unions was side-stepped; wholly new defense-oriented unions were called for and successfully established. "Solidarity" marked the political bankruptcy of the union reform option. Radical change going beyond any modification of dual functioning unionism was seen as the only possible solution to the problems of the 1970s. With the suppression of Solidarity a modified dual functioning trade unionism has once again become the dominant model. The new official unions, now emerging slowly in Poland, mark very little advance on the reforms tried in the aftermath of previous crises. Thus the experience of the 1970s may have some bearing on the current situation.

Trade union development in the 1970s is also worth examining because of its significance in the context of unionism in communist states. One must be careful, of course, not to exaggerate the East European let alone the communist systemwide significance of Polish experience here. The extent to which the union developments with which this chapter deals are typical of dual functioning communist unionism as such hinges on the larger question of the national specificity of the 1970s in Poland. While this lies outside the

Alex Pravda. Department of Political Science, Stanford University, Stanford, California.

scope of the chapter, the issue of singularity permeates the kinds of question implicit in any examination of Polish unions in the 1970s. Were these unions weaker than their counterparts elsewhere in the communist world? Did they function in a distinct and peculiarly ineffective way or were Polish unions the victims of particularly extreme pressures and circumstances connected with the social, economic, and political enviornment in which they operated? The following survey of the role and performance of the Polish unions in the 1970s may throw light on these and other questions.

Historical Background and Development

Polish trade unions have a long and militant tradition going back well before World War I. In German and Austrian Poland unions operated from the 1880s; in the Russian part of the country they were banned and surfaced only sporadically in 1905−1907. By the 1930s over a million workers—about a fifth of the labor force—were unionized. Several hundred unions, predominantly industrial-based, belonged to various groupings and federations divided by religion and politics. While communists exercised considerable influence within some unions, the socialists were the dominant political force in the trade union movement as a whole (Gross, 1945: 145−50; Dobieszewski, 1977). Socialist influence among union rank-and-file persisted until the absorption of the party by the communists in 1948. Welded into one centralized association at the end of the war, the union movement underwent a thoroughgoing Stalinization beginning in 1949. As they were refashioned along Soviet lines, so the unions lost all vestiges of the influence they had exercised over factory management during the communist takeover period.

The subsequent development of Polish trade unions has been punctuated by three major crises: 1956, 1970−1971, and 1980−1981.

1956−1958

After the Poznań workers' protest in June 1956 the unions were thrown into ferment. The bureaucracy of the central union apparatus, the lack of power of local branches, and their dependence on management and communist party, all came under fire during heated discussions on union reform. Not surprisingly, far more was said than done. Limited steps were taken toward internal democratization but little happened to change the unions' role. The party leadership promised to allow unions more scope for interest activity but Gomulka outflanked the movement for more independent unionism by promoting workers' participation through newly established workers' councils. Once the general political crisis had subsided and the economic situation stabilized, these councils were emasculated and placed within party-controlled conferences of workers' self-management (Kolankiewicz, 1972; Gilejko, 1972: 91−112).

The 1960s saw a growing incorporation of the unions into the management-dominated establishment of the factory. Production tasks came to eclipse all others and the union movement came increasingly to be seen solely as the labor management arm of factory directors, goverment, and party. A gap opened up betwen rank-and-file members and shop-floor union activists on the one hand and the union apparatus on the other. While living standards rose, albeit slowly, this gap caused no more than grumbling; as real wages stagnated and began to fall in the later 1960s, such grumbling turned into vocal criticism of union failings (Ratyński, 1977: pt V; Barton, 1971).

1970−1973

As in 1956 worker protest, this time on the Baltic coast, brought the union issue to the fore. The strike committee of the Warski shipyard in Szczeciń called for the resignation of the entire Central Trade Union Council and the creation of independent trade unions that would defend and support the working class (*Przegląd Związkowy,* nos 11−12, 1972). Because protest was localized and soon brought under control, such radical demands made little headway nationally. At the twenty-first plenum of the Central Trade Union Council, union bureaucracy, inefficiency, and timidity in the face of management and government came under critical fire, but apart from a few changes in the union leadership little happened. The absence of a systemic crisis of 1956 proportions made it possible to contain reform within fairly close bounds. The line taken by the new party leader Gierek was that workers' interests could be fully protectd within the existing union structure; all that was needed was a tidying up of regulations and a change of style in the direction of "democratic consultation" between union officers and members (Gilejko, 1972: 123−41). Unions were asked to give priority to defending and representing their members' interests without being given any new rights to enable them to do so. No new union statute emerged and things moved slowly on the promulgation of a new Labor Code. As the party recovered from the debilitating effects of the 1970−1971 crisis, so it reasserted tight controls over the unions. By 1973 all talk of greater union autonomy had been replaced by the traditional emphasis on close union subordination to the party's "leading role."

1973−1980

Disappointment at the lack of union reform was softened by the rapid increase in real wages and living standards through the first half of the decade. As in the post-1956 period, material improvements cushioned the effects of immobilism on the union front. Only when faced with protests in 1976, linked with gathering economic decline, did political leaders make some efforts to improve union work. Yet these largely took the form of urging union officers to be less timid in using their rights to further members' interests. Rather than strengthen those rights, Gierek tried to shift attention to participation by upgrading the self-management conferences. Even under pressure from a growing strike wave and an influential albeit small movement for independent unions, the party came up with little other than well-worn calls for more vigorous union work. When the situation became critical in early 1980 the only change made was in the chairmanship of the unions, a move repeated on the eve of the Gdańsk agreement. Only then did the union leadership call for substantial reforms to upgrade the unions' policy role (Woodall, 1982: 172–82; Kolankiewicz, 1982: 130–3).

Shifting Interpretations of the Unions' Role

The 1970s saw considerable discussion of the basic role of trade unions in both academic and political circles. While there were no radical policy departures from the Leninist notion of dual functioning unionism, there were interesting shifts of emphasis in the course of the decade. Three phrases in policy may be distinguished here: a marked shift towards priority for defensive and representative functions (1971–1973); a return to tight party control and production priorities (1973–1976); and finally, after 1976, a growing emphasis on the importance of welfare improvement, participation, and shop-floor contact. The first phase produced by far the most interesting discussions and it is on those that I shall concentrate.

Exploration of the role of trade unions in the early 1970s developed lines of thought dating back to the late 1950s. For even after the waning of the union reform cause some academics made a strong case for raising the defense and representation of membership interests to first place among union functions. They argued that while dual functioning unions under socialism operated differently from their capitalist counterparts, the differences were far from absolute. Unions in Poland still had to perform "traditional" defensive functions alongside their "new" collaborative and participative ones. The existence even under socialism of a state apparatus with bureaucratic tendencies created the need for union protection of labor rights. The unions' "traditional" defense and representative role was further justified by the persistence of interest differentiation and conflict in socialist society. Of particular relevance here were differences of interest and perspective in the economic sphere. Ministries and central planning agencies focused on production growth while labor was interested in consumption.

To management wages were costs, to those who received them they were income. Self-evident though these points might seem, they represented a radical departure from established orthodoxy and had far-reaching implications for the role of trade unions. For if, as was generally accepted, unions existed to represent "employee" interests, their defensive function had to be placed on a par with those of production mobilization and labor "education" (Gilejko and Balcerek, 1965: chs V and VI).

The 1970–1971 crisis prompted union and party leaders to take note of such academic arguments. For the first time since 1956 defense and representation were given pride of place in official pronouncements on the unions' role. There was nothing unnatural about differences of interest in a socialist society, Gierek told the seventh trade union congress in 1972, nor about unions defending the interests of their members. He went on to say that this consituted "the essence" of the unions' task (Adamski, 1971: 16–17; Gierek, 1972: 15). This shift of emphasis in party policy was limited, however, by two sets of provisions which continued to circumscribe union defense activity.

The first set of provisions related to the ordering of interests. These remained ranked along hierarchical principles: short-term group or local interests were still to be subordinated to national, long-term ones. Most important, the definition of the latter continued to lie with the party. Thus the legitimacy and ranking of interests remained a matter of party decision; the legitimate defence of members' interests by unions or other bodies still depended on party approval.

The dependent status of unions as interest organizations was underscored by the second set of constraints, those limiting the means unions might legitimately employ in pursuing of their representative role. Since it was claimed that the degree to which interests varied and conflicted under socialism axiomatically differed in quality from the clash of interests under capitalism, Polish unions had no need of the weapons deployed by their Western counterparts. Strikes continued to be seen as an extreme last resort rather than as a legitimate and normal part of the union armoury (Gilejko and Balcerek, 1965: 77). So unions might act on occasion as defensive interest groups but never as pressure groups.

A Politburo resolution in April, 1973 marked the beginning of a shift in emphasis from representation by means of defense to representation of members' interests through the improvement of their material conditions (Szczepaniak, 1977: 112). Increasingly, union tasks were designated in orthodox terms of caring for workers' material welfare and paying attention to issues such as health, safety, and recreation. Alongside this came renewed stress on union responsibility for labor discipline and productivity. In the wake of the 1976 protests, the unions' role in the resolution of conflicts of interest came to the fore, as it had in 1956 and to a certain extent after December, 1970. This time, though, conflicts involving labor were depicted far more negatively, as pathological and as symptoms of union mistakes and failings rather than weakness (Kruczek, 1976: 6). The thrust of the message was that unions should preempt conflicts by concentrating on their role as spokespersons for employee interests and guardians of members' material welfare. Symptomatic of a further downgrading of the unions' defensive role was the promotion of their responsibility for organizing labor participation in production management. Only in later 1979 and early 1980 did defense make a last-gasp appearance in official statements about unions (Gierek, *Trybuna Ludu,* February 26, 1980). And even then defense was closely linked with the need for unions to maintain closer contact with the shop-floor and play a more prominent spokesperson role.

The Union in the Factory

Responsibilities and Rights

In Poland in the 1970s, as is the case in communist states generally, the factory was the main focus of union activity and the factory council the lynchpin of the union movement. In the mid-1970s the factory union network included approximately 30,000 factory councils, over 30,000 shop councils, and 175,000 trade union groups (Szczepaniak, 1977: 105). With the general shift through the decade toward a representation and participation oriented union role, the work of the factory-based organizations became increasingly vital.

Spelled out in the factory context, the dual function of the unions meant an extremely broad range of tasks and responsibilities. The union was supposed to perform its "production" role by participating in enterprise planning, educating members to work more productively, maintaining labor discipline, and supervising working conditions. Under the "interest defense and representation" heading the union was expected to administer welfare benefits, supervise management adherence to labor regulations, defend members' rights, resolve disputes, articulate demands, forward proposals, and, last but not least, generally represent members' interests and harmonize these with the interests of the factory and the economy as a whole ("Kompetence," 1976).

This would have been an impossible multiplicity of duties and responsibilities had union officers taken them all equally seriously. In fact they gave priority to certain duties and tended to neglect others. By far the most attention seems to have been paid by factory councils to welfare administration and general production responsibilities. Defense and representation of workers' interests came towards the bottom of their list of concerns. Among shop council officers priorities were only slightly different, with welfare and housing and articulation of members' interests figuring more prominently. Representation and care for members' interests did head the priorities of stewards who led the grass-roots union groups. They spend relatively little time on production and organizational tasks (Dziedzic, 1973: 67—74; Hirszowicz and Morawski, 1967: 294, 325).

The ordering of union priorities at the factory and shop council level reflected and was reinforced by the actual rights they possessed. Defense and representation of workers' interests was neglectd largely because union powers in this area were woefully inadequate. Union rights were essentially limited to consultation and verbal objection. Take, for instance, the factory council's powers in the key area of dismissals. Despite the fact that the Labor Code introduced in 1975 considerably broadened the scope for arbitrary dismissal, it placed the union in a very weak position. All the council could do was lodge objections against what it considered to be an unfair and illegal dismissal. It was up to the director whether he took account for the union's reservations. Even where the case was referred to a higher union authority, the director still retained discretion and could go ahead,union objects notwithstanding (Labor Code, 1979: 50; Mirończuk, 1977: 5).

The factory council's ability to further union members' interests by improving material conditions was also limited by a paucity of powers. These amounted to some decision-making rights only in areas such as recreation and health; in others, such as bonuses, the council could only offer its opinion.

Moreover, the scope for any negotiation on social benefits was reduced by the national standardization introduced by the Labor Code. This probably helped to reduce inequalities between factories but also further depleted union prerogatives. On vital issues such as hours and pay factory unions could anyhow do little since these were basically fixed centrally. The small scope for maneuver at local level—on matters such as payment for special conditions—was narrowed by the removal of large numbers of such decisions from the factory to the combines and associations (Woodall, 1982: 177 81). Thus the restructuring of Polish industry through the 1970s, revolving around the formation of the large economic organizations, siphoned off decisions from the factory and so further reduced the exercise of union rights on their members' behalf. Increasingly, all branch variations in pay, working conditions, and bonuses were included in the collective agreements concluded with the ministry by branch union headquarters. Unlike their counterparts in most of Eastern Europe, Polish factory councils could not negotiate a collective agreement directly with management, a disability that seriously damaged their standing with members and directors alike (Loch, 1980).

If the union thus had few resources with which to perform its defense and representative duties, the situation was little better where participation responsibilities were concerned.

In the course of the 1970s, the unions were involved increasingly in participation activities, with the apparent objective of improving their standing with rank-and-file members. As a result, however, unions were encumbered by additional responsibilities they found difficult to manage effectively and thus lost rather than benefited from their enlarged participation role. This role took three distinct forms. To start with, unions were charged with organizing production conferences which supposedly provided a general and accessible forum for discussing production issues. For the most part their proceedings were formal and added little to feelings of efficacy among rank-and-file unionists. A less well defined connection linked factory councils with the workers councils, a pale shadow of the original bodies set up in 1956. If during the 1960s workers' councils still provided something of a forum for airing labor grievances, in the 1970s few operated, as many council functions had been taken over by the union (Kolankiewicz, 1982: 131−3). Such colonization of participation brought the unions few advantages, though since their new rights were constrained by the umbrella framework of the conferences of workers' self-management. Not only did the conferences effectively neutralize any genuine workers' participation by their heavy bias to management (Hryniewicz, 1980: 95; Dziedzic, 1973: 87), they also reduced to a minimum the influence of the union on the broad range of issues that came under the general heading of participation in management. For while the union council was officially charged with organizing conference proceedings, these were dominated in practice by management and the party organization. The union emerged as very much the junior partner within the conference (Hryniewicz, 1980: 95; Dziedzic, 1973: 87).

The Union within the Power Structure of the Factory

Through the 1970s the union council remained a junior member of the factory establishment. At regular weekly meetings with the director, the party secretary and—until the mid-1970s—the chairman of the workers' council, the union council chairman took part in discussions dealing with the general running of the factory. Though formally described as the "management collective," colloquially known as the Big Four, the meeting was not distinguished by collegiality. True, the distribution of power varied from factory to factory and depended *inter alia* on the personalities involved. But generally power was not equally shared; it was concentrated in the hands of the director (only occasionally was the party secretary the dominant member) (Ozdowski, 1979: 75; Pokoj, 1979). To get some idea of the position of the union within the Big Four we need to consider its relations with the party and with the director.

Union and Party

No ambiguity existed, even in theory, about the subordination of the union to the factory party organization. As the local representative of the PUWP the factory organization exercised its "leading role" over all social organizations, including the unions (Dobieszewski, 1977: 544–5). In fact this was institutionalized during the late 1970s when the party secretary became the *ex officio* chairman of the conference of workers' self-management.

Party controls over the union were threefold (Ratyński, 1977: 393–407). In the first place the factory council was part of a democratic centralist movement which accepted the leading role of the party. This meant that the factory council was duty-bound to act within the framework of party policy as interpreted by the local committee. Since the party's responsibilities within the enterprise overlaped closely with those of the union, its directives often impinged on union work. Organizational supervision formed a second strand of control. And the upgrading of many party shop organizations increased the intensity of such monitoring of union activity. Lastly and most important, party influence was reinforced by the presence of large numbers of its members on union executives. Approximately one in three factory council members were card-carrying communists as were half the vice-chairmen and a majority of chairmen. Only among the union *aktiv* and stewards did party saturation fall to levels comparable with those in the industrial workforce as a whole (around a fifth) (Witłaec, 1978: 22). Bound by party discipline, these large strategic caucuses of communist-union officers coordinated policy in advance of union meetings and generally encountered little difficulty in getting this through. Few of the non-communist members would vote against a party group motion since they too were often vetted by the party organization. In the rare event of rank-and-file union electors rejecting a party nominated candidate for council office, an alternative party activist was usually successfully put up (*Robotnik,* no. 2, October 1977; "Spoleczno-politiczne," 1976: 45–6).

In addition to these direct channels of control, the party organization also exercised influence over union activity by virtue of its close relationship with management. Even if the party secretary rarely dominated the director, his influence, bolstered by the party committee, made them near-equal partners.

How one interprets the impact of such party influence over union work depends on the standpoints one takes. From the director's point of view, it simplified control over the running of labor affairs. Most decisions could be effectively taken within the forum of the party committee, or negotiated directly with the party secretary; the union would then follow suit. Middle management, however, seem often to have resented the party secretary's influence ("Partnerstwo," 1973; Ratyński, 1977: 393−5). From the vantage point of the central authorities, concerned with the smooth and efficient operation of the plant, the overlap of party and union work might have appeared as an advantage. Yet in reality the very duplication of functions made each of the organizations less effective. Union effectiveness was certainly reduced by the blurring of its identity. It was further diminished by the "negative selection" that typically resulted from the party's criteria for union office. Compliance and flexibility counted for far more than qualifications in selecting union activists. The domination of union councils by communist groups also deprived the unions of many of their most able non-communist activists. Overall, the stranglehold of the party over union activity seriously undermined all aspects of union work in the factory. According to Jurczyk, in 1980 head of the Szczecin interfactory strike committee, party secretaries' control over union council chairmen totally tied the hands of those council members who tried to carry out the union's representative and defensive functions vis-à-vis factory management (Passent and Wróblewski, 1980: 6).

Relations with Management

Union−management relations differed somewhat from those between union and party. To begin with, unions were supposedly partners rather than subordinates here. Party and union leaders alike urged factory officers to stand up to managers as equals (Gierek, 1972: 14−15). At the same time, the unions' assigned role and prerogatives made the notion of equal partnership an impracticable one. The continuing emphasis on co-responsibility for production and collaboration with management inevitably drove union councils towards dependence on the director. To be successful in improving working conditions, in getting more factory money for housing, and even in resolving disputes, union officers found that they needed to be on good terms with management. An identify with management was also fostered by the strong vested interest of most union officers in the prosperity of the factory. Their strong attachment to the factory brought them close to management. Career considerations led in the same direction. For while union officers could not be dismissed without the consent of their union superiors, they still remained employees of the factory and their longer-term advancement depended more on management (and party) decisions than on those of the union hierarchy (Śreniowski, 1978; Ozdowski, 1979: 69). Moreover, many of the most ambitious union officers aimed not at the limited number of full-time union jobs, but rather at securing a middle management post. The functions and rights of the union councils and the position of their officers placed them squarely within the director's sphere of authority.

To compound this power imbalance, managerial authority grew throughout the 1970s. Strong technocratic management was promoted by the party leadership as the path to rapid economic growth. Economic reform and reorganization boosted directors' power. Yet better training and higher educational qualifications notwithstanding, directors did not seem to wield their power any more sensitively than their elders (Greszczyk, 1978; Woodall, 1982: 134–42). The new directors were just as authoritarian. Unions and employees alike typically had to face an autocratic factory and combine management. What is more, union officers often had to cope with directors who doubled as union notables since something like one in three directors belonged to factory councils (Wasilewski, 1978: 187). Given their functional authority and information advantages director-members, as well as the other managers on union councils, tended to dominate discussion. One study in the early 1970s found this management group were thought to exercise most influence over council decisions (Hryniewicz, 1980: 109). Thus the circle of management dominance was completed; not only did managers dominate from their position within the executive hierarchy in the factory, they could also shape union policy from within (nor should one forget the influence they could exert through the party connection). And it seems that most directors used their power to manipulate the union. They tended to regard the union councils as "useful instruments to increase the effectiveness of their decision-making power" (Ozdowski, 1979: 62; Steszenko, 1973: 177–8). Accordingly, the great majority of workers saw unions as not just subordinate to but often as part of factory management, an agent acting on behalf of the director in the area of labor mobilization and social welfare ("Miejsce, rola i funkcja," 1980; Brodska, 1980).

Union Performance

By what criteria should one judge union performance in the 1970s? At first glance criteria appear to diverge according to which standpoint one takes. From the vantage point of central party and government authorities, industrial peace and high productivity mattered most. Thus union performance hinged above all on its traditional production role. For the factory manager, help in maintaining a compliant and productive labor force might have seemed the most important part of the union's work. By contrast, for the rank-and-file union member social welfare, working conditions, defense of legal rights, and representation of interests appeared to be the major yard-sticks for assessing union performance.

The 1970s in Poland saw some convergence between these different sets of criteria. Political leaders came increasingly to recognize that labor productivity was better served by improvements in conditions and climate than by traditional mobilization and discipline. To create the conditions favorable to labor contentment and hence higher productivity, more information and action was needed from the trade unions. To get information about workers' preferences and grievances, unions had to gain their members' confidence. Clearly, rank-and-file trust depended on the extent to which the unions fulfilled members' expectations. Increasingly through the 1970s, these expectations revolved around the defense and representation of membership welfare and interests (Hryniewicz, 1980: 92−3). It is therefore to these aspects of factory union performance that we now turn.

Welfare

For many workers the union's welfare role largely defined its day-to-day activity. It provided tangible justification for the union's existence and the payment of union dues. Without doubt the union's responsibilities for administering recreation, health, and housing earned it some popularity. At the same time, administering welfare benefits could prove a double-edged sword as dissatisfaction with the general level of provision could easily rebound against the front agent. For instance, the chronic housing shortage, which became more acute during the course of the decade, inevitably reflected at least to some extent on the unions which were involved in housing construction and distribution. Further, the way in which unions sometimes connived at housing preference being given to already privileged groups tended to generate resentment on this score ("Utrwalanie," 1976). Similarly, responsibility for distributing benefits from the factory funds sometimes proved to have mixed advantages. For this activity sometimes fomented divisions, even if these were typically between different shop union councils rather than between union and membership.

Large discrepancies existed too between the amounts of social benefit paid out to workers in different factories and sectors. Whether such disparities may be interpreted as reflecting differential union performance is highly doubtful since most of the differences can be explained by economic performance and workforce profiles (Krupa *et al.,* 1978). Judging by the substantial number of complaints to higher union authorities relating to social benefits, factory union performance was by no means invariably seen as satisfactory here. Nor was union performance in areas such as safety as effective as it might have been, given the increase in resources. Despite claims that union controls had improved, levels of safety remained low (*Robotnik,* no. 8, January 15, 1978). As for pay and premiums, the very limited amount the factory union could do here often irritated rather than satisfied members. Certainly complaints on this score rose through the early 1970s ("Utrwalenie," 1976; Pietraszewski,1976; Sanetra, 1980).

To sum up, it is difficult to assess precisely the performance of unions in the welfare sphere given the overwhelming importance of resources controlled by bodies and circumstances beyond union control. The picture is a mixed one. On the one hand, many workers seemed to think that the unions did a reasonable job in this area; on the other, their activities gave rise to growing numbers of complaints through the decade.

Defense and Representation

Assessing union performance becomes more straightforward when we consider the way in which unions acted as defenders and guardians of their members' rights. Union action here, and more generally in resolving conflicts in the workplace, may be examined in terms of two types of intervention: within the framework of quasi-judicial bodies, and in the course of day-to-day monitoring of management observance of labor law.

Trade unions played an important role in settling disputes within the factory through the arbitration committees whose composition was agreed jointly by union and management. Although unions were supposed to ensure these committees reflected the composition of the workforce, they often allowed the bodies to take on a heavy managerial bias. Unions did provide legal aid and defense for members who took their dismissals to the appeals committees for labor cases, though some doubt is cast on the effectivenes of such help by the large number of unfavorable verdicts passed. Thereafter workers' only alternative was to appeal to the district labor and social security court which heard a growing number of dismissal cases in the later 1970s. Here union legal aid seems to have been less useful—one report depicted the union representatives as definding members only when circumstances forced them to do so (Loch, 1975). In response to criticism of the unions' poor showing in arbitration and court proceedings, union officers contended that they settled the great majority of industrial disputes by way of informal consultation (Mirończuk, 1979). One has to set against such claims the repeated calls issued by higher trade union bodies for greater attention to be paid to the resolution of conflicts (Kruczek, 1977).

Factory councils apparently remained far too ready to accept the management view even where management had infringed employees' legal rights (Molenda, 1976; Mirończuk, 1979). Such timidity was particularly evident in dismissals which became a frequent cause of grievance after the introduction of the new Labor Code which made it relatively easy for directors to sack workers on the slightest pretext. As we have already noted, the factory council had the right to object in any case that seemed unjustified, thus delaying the decision and bringing it to the attention of a higher union body. In practice, unions proved extremely reluctant to use this right. Only a small fraction of dismissals were challenged even though a large number of them were found subsequently to have been illegal by the appeal committees and labor courts. Unions' failure to defend their members from unfair dismissal was particularly bad in small factories where union officers were of lower caliber and more afraid of challenging management (Molenda, 1976; Mirończuk, 1979). Union leaders were sufficiently concerned about the scale of the problems surrounding guardianship of members' rights to propose setting up small groups of opinion-leaders at shop level to help the councils combat management arbitrariness (Kruczek, 1977).

Highlighting the unions' timidity in defending their members in conflict with management may convey too black a picture of their performance as representatives. For survey evidence suggests that a sizeable proportion of workers considered unions to be a representative of sorts, albeit not a very effective one. A surprisingly large majority of industrial workers seemed to think that unions actually listened to their grievances and demands (Hryniewicz, 1980: 95, 102; cf. Steszenko, 1973: 177). What they typically meant by union was not the factory council but activists and officers at shop and grass-roots level. For here councils and stewards maintained far closer contact with rank-and-file members than did their factory superiors. All but a handful of stewards, in one study at least, claimed to be fully informed about their members' needs and demands (Kalinowski, 1979; Steszenko, 1973: 42; Strzoda, 1977: 148). Beyond a willingness to listen, union activists and shop stewards were also seen by most workers as trying to further membership interests. Even among those groups most critical of union performance, only a fifth thought that union officers made no effort to advance members' interests (Hryniewicz, 1980: 99; Steszenko, 1973: 177).

Where the unions appeared to fail in their representative role was in effectiveness rather than effort. Those low-level activists and stewards most willing to promote workers' interests simply did not have the power to do so in many cases. Quite often they encountered considerable difficulty in getting demands through to their own factory councils. Members of these councils, who had more opportunity to advance member's interests, were reluctant to run the risk of incurring management displeasure by pressing demands. Feebleness and timidity at factory level, then, rather than hostility or total indifference, flawed union performance as representatives from the shop-floor standpoint.

This widespread lack of confidence in unions as effective representatives prompted workers to take their problems more often to immediate supervisors, especially where conditions or pay were involved. Some industrial workers seem to have by-passed unions altogether, preferring to go to managers or to the party committee (Gilejko, 1979: 274–5; Hryniewicz, 1980: 110). Among the highly skilled and paid, collective action was also frequently cited as an effective way of getting things done in the factory—a damning reflection on the performance of the unions as representatives and defenders of labor interests. With the growth of direct industrial action through the later 1970s, the unions were pushed further into a position of inertia and avoidance of any conflict between labor and management. Where strikes broke out, union offices were often more retiring and critical of workers than their party or youth organization counterparts (*Robotnik*, no. 2, October 1977).

What of the overall evaluation of union performance by the mass membership; did this change in the course of the decade? If one compares workers' evaluations in the mid-1960s with ones by comparable groups ten years later, it seems as if general levels of confidence did fall. In the earlier period unions still commanded the trust of many older skilled industrial workers who used them to further their demands and interests within the factory (Ozdowski, 1979: 68; Dyoniziak: 1967, 162–4; Owieczko, 1966: 61). Their succesors, the skilled industrial workers of the mid-1970s, took a far more jaundiced view of the unions. Under no illusion that union councils were influenced by their worker members, this group of workers saw them as an administrative welfare agency and a tool of management (Wajda, 1976: 75). This increasingly unfavorable verdict on the unions stemmed perhaps not so much from an absolute decline in union performance over this period as from changing expectations (Hryniewicz, 1980: 110; cf. Steszenko, 1973: 148–9).

Workers seem to have a higher commitment to defensive, representative unionism. And it was among the highest skilled strategic groups that a preference for strong defensive unions was most deeply felt. The same group expressed greatest dissatisfaction with union overall performance for it was among them that the gap between expectations and union performance had become widest (Hryniewicz, 1980).

While much of the disenchantment with the unions can thus be attributed to the changing expectations of a better educated and more critical industrial workforce, the context in which unions had to operate also contributed to their declining popularity. Management were less indulgent in their treatment of labor than in the 1960s since the economic cost of such indulgence had risen and new managers were more technocratically minded.

Table 6.1
Education, Pay, and Polish Workers' Assessment of
Unions' Role

Education		Pay (zlotys per month)	
Main duty of the union is to represent workers' interests:			
Below elementary level:	85.5%	up to 1500:	77.8%
Elementary:	89.3%	3,001−3,500:	92.3%
Basic vocational:	89.7%	3,501−4,000:	95.9%
Secondary:	92.6%	5,000+:	93.9%

Source: Hryniewicz, 1980; 105, 107. The survey from which these data come was conducted
in eleven industrial enterprises in 1973−4; *N* = 3,000.

Moreover, the spread of bonuses and the increasing complexity of pay meant
that conflict issues multiplied. Labor relations, or more specifically their
perception, seem to have taken a turn for the worse between the mid-1960s
and the mid-1970s (Preiss, 1978: 64−5; cf. Matejko, 1969: 452). Tensions
seem to have been particularly high between middle and top management on
the one hand and skilled workers and technicians on the other. Factory
unions were thus squeezed between tougher, less indulgent management
and a more demanding and critical workforce.

Beyond the Factory

The trade union hierarchy above factory level did little to relieve the
pressure to those at the cutting edge of union activity. Indeed, weakness of
organization and policy influence at regional and national level arguably
contributed to the image of impotence that beleaguered their front line,
shop-floor counterparts.

Organization
Overcentralization, poor communication, and lack of responsiveness
within the union hierarchy were all issues singled out for critical comment by
union officers in the wake of the 1970−1971 protests. Their pressure for
democratization had some effect. The Central Trade Union Council apparatus
was slimmed down; factory councils' share of membership dues rose by
nearly half to between 50 and 70 percent of the total (Rudolf, 1973: 83−4).
Union leaders urged all intermediate union bodies to communicate regularly
with factory councils. Still, lack of responsiveness at branch headquarters and
regional offices continued to be a source of concern. Organizational reforms
designed to make the union structure more efficient and democratic some-

times had the opposite effect. The elimination of the district and regional offices of the branch unions (twenty-three of these comprised the Association of Trade Unions) removed the only directly elected body from the branch hierarchy. It also meant that factory councils were directly subordinated to head offices distant from them in physical location and often in outlook. The concomitant incorporation of regional branch offices into the regional interunion councils may well have facilitated the coordination of regional policy. At the same time, it meant a greater centralization of control within the union movement as a whole (Rudolf, 1973: 83−4). Most important perhaps, while factory councils were expected to supervise vast tracts of labor relations and production, their organizational structure lagged far behind the restructuring of industry. Very inadequate response was made by the unions—in the shape of combine councils and various union coordinating groups—to the emergence of the new industrial associations (Woodall, 1982: 177−8, 180). The unions found themselves ill-equipped to deal with the major corporate forces that increasingly came to dominate economic policymaking in the course of the decade.

Policy Influence

The scope for union influence on social and economic policy was considerable, in theory at least. The unions were supposedly partners of all administrative organs in running the state and managing the economy. Their co-management status was even ensconsed in the 1976 Constitution. Trade unions had the right to put forward legislative proposals on all matters affecting their members' welfare. More concretely, all government regulations relating to working and living conditions had to be agreed with the unions, and many regulations were issued jointly by the Presidia of the Council of Ministers and the Central Trade Union Council (Szubert, 1980: 67, 386). Furthermore, trade unions had the right to exercise supervisory control over a wide range of government agencies, particularly in the area of safety and prices. To enable the unions to fulfill this formidable policy and supervisory role, they were supposed to be afforded access to key decision-making bodies, including the planning commission. Impressive as these rights may have seemed, on closer inspection they all shared one major flaw—generality and vagueness. Unions had very few defined and hardly any binding powers over government and they remained of course subordinated to the leading role of the PUWP.

In the aftermath of 1970 some union officials called for improvements in their position which would change a situation in which policy gains were granted by government as favors rather than rights (Gilejko, 1971). But all that resulted from such discussion were injunctions from party leaders to government urging collaboration with the unions in all important policy areas. The unions had to continue to rely on conventional consultative arrangements and the goodwill of government decision-makers. At ministerial level, for instance, at least one union (the chemical workers) reported regular access to ministry executive meetings and detailed exchange of information. That such close collaboration enjoyed was far from universal is suggested by the fact that Gierek found it necessary to propose the institution of annual meetings between ministers and the chief officers of appropriate branch unions (Gierek, 1980: 3; "Owocne partnerstwo," 1976; Krall, 1972).

At the regional level, cooperation of a regularized kind was secured in some cases by agreements between regional interunion councils and local government counterparts ("Drogi umacniania," 1975; "Decyduje," 1979). These agreements at least provided for exchange of information and regular policy discussion. The actual effect of such contact was far less impressive than the arrangements themselves. To start with, exchanges of opinion seemed to be restricted to well-defined areas such as safety, health, and housing. Other major policy issues were not generally open for discussion. The main contribution made by unions to policy formation consisted in the provision of information plus occasional advice. In most cases this involved a change of emphasis in policy rather than a shift of any real substance. Such information input may have marked an advance on the 1960s, but it hardly added up to the co-policymaking role prescribed in theory. Union timidity prevailed here as in the factory; union officials often preferred to comment on draft proposals rather than put forward their own plans. Even had unions wished to oppose government schemes, however, they simply did not have sufficient leverage to make any impact on policy. They could only resort to indirect means such as persuading local party officials to their view and relying on them in turn to convince government decision-makers (Krall, 1972).

If some small gains were made in union access to policymaking at regional and ministry level, no corresponding advances were evident at the center. The top executives of unions and government reportedly held annual meetings to discuss key social issues only after 1976. Before then, such contact was sporadic; certainly the unions had a poor policy track record. The cases of policy influence cited by officials involved matters of detail in areas such as safety, pensions, and building regulations (Gierek, 1976: 3). Even where the unions supposedly participated in policy formulation, as on the Labor Code, they found that they could not exercise any effective positive influence. Union objections to the draft Code—an exceptional instance of union independent-mindedness—managed only to delay the legislative schedule. The final version did not incorporate any of the significant union amendments. Those relating to dismissal procedure would certainly have improved the unions' ability to defend their members' rights in this area ("Na polmetku," 1975). As it was, the failure to get a Code more favorable to labor and to the unions further undermined union performance and standing within the factory.

Ultimately more damaging to union status was their failure to make an impact on price policy. Entrusted with supervision over price levels and committed to price stability, the unions made no public effort to preempt the disastrous decisions of 1976 and 1980. Reportedly, even behind closed doors they failed to put up any real case against rises (*Morning Star,* December 13, 1976). The reasons for the unions' lack of policy impact are fairly clear. Quite apart from their lack of political clout and institutional power, union leaders simply were not the kind of men who opposed party leadership policy. After all, most of them had come to the unions directly from the party apparatus. Neither Kruczek or Szydlak had had any serious experience in union work before becoming chairman of the entire organization. Only very late in the day, in August 1980, did the party think it wise to select somebody with considerable trade union experience. And on his appointment Jankowski made a whole set of proposals aimed at strengthening the unions' policy role and making it a reality rather than perpetuating the fiction of the past thirty years (Potrzeba, 1980).

Concluding Remarks

The backward shadow cast by "Solidarity" inevitably colors any assessment of Polish trade unions in the 1970s. True, Solidarity was a social and
national movement in trade union form, produced by a national systemic
crisis and not merely by a crisis of trade unionism. Yet the srikes and protests
that produced Solidarity were a token of the failure of the unions to resolve
industrial conflicts, to channel workers' demands and translate them in part at
least into policy. In a sense Solidarity was a mirror image of the trade union
movement it effectively replaced; the major strengths of Solidarity reflected
the weaknesses of its predecessor. The contrast with Solidarity may help to
highlight the following problems and problem areas of Polish trade unionism
identified in the course of this survey.

*1   The difficulties of tinkering hesitantly with the dual functioning
role.* Policy discontinuity here helped foster uncertainty among union officials and members alike. It may even have contributed to the strengthening of
preferences among skilled worker groups for defense and representation
oriented unionism. In response, Solidarity, initially at least, insisted on an
unambiguous defense role.

2 The damaging effects of underpowered and overextended factory unions. The 1970s demonstrated the need to equip unions with effective rights to deal with increasingly powerful management. Solidarity declared itself fully independent of management and asserted its right to use whatever means were necessary to sustain effective collective bargaining.

3 Trade union performance did not deteriorate drastically in absolute terms. Rather, the unions proved unequal to the growing difficulties of the conditions under which they operated. These were shaped by tougher management and a more demanding and militant workforce. The squeeze on factory unions these developments produced tended to divide top council officers from their own *aktiv* as well as from rank-and-file members. The 1970s underscored the dangers of failing to adapt to changing expectations. Solidarity stressed the importance of maintaining a broad grass-roots influence within the movement.

4 Failure to adapt to changing conditions was also notable on the organizational front where union structures simply did not keep pace with industrial restructuring and the resultant shifts in loci of decision-making. Solidarity adopted a far more flexible structure and built up strong horizontal links and regional bases.

5 Policy impotence at regional and national levels contributed to the low status of unions in workers' eyes. It contributed indirectly to the mismanagement of economic policy that precipitated the collapse of the regime. The experience of the 1970s suggests that in conditions of economic discontinuity communist regimes cannot afford to combine union policy impotence with underpowered factory unions. Solidarity insisted on being a key actor in the national policy arena as well as a decisive force in the factory; indeed it was argued these roles were mutually dependent.

The development of Polish trade unions in the 1970s does not demonstrate conclusively that dual-functioning unionism in general is wholly bankrupt and entirely beyond reform. Rather, the Polish experience points up the fundamental weaknesses of the model and sheds light on the kinds of developments any communist leadership seeking to make dual functioning unionism more effective should seek to avoid. The official unions operating in post-martial-law Poland possess some rights, including a very circumscribed right to strike, not enjoyed by their pre-Solidarity equivalents. While the continuing climate of coercion in Poland makes the exercise of such rights extremely difficult, if not impossible, their very existence involves a modification of Classic Dualism which suggests that the lessons of union development in the 1970s have not been wholly lost on the Polish leadership.

References

Adamski, W. (1971), "Związki zawodowe—twórczym czynnikiem rozwoju budownictwa socjalisticzneygd," *Nowe Drogi,* no. 9, pp. 13–28.

Barton, P. (1971), *Misère et révolte de l'ouvrier Polanais* (Paris: Les editions ouvrières).

Brodzka, T. (1980). "Drukarze o związkach," *Zycio Warszawy,* August 27.

"Decyduje (1979) współdzalania," *Przegląd Związkowy,* Nos 7–8, pp. 31–4.

Dobieszewski, A. (1977) (ed.), *Organizacja politiczna społeczenstwa socjalisticznego w Polsce* (Warsay: Książka i Wiedza).

"Drogi umacniania (1975) wojewódzkich rad związkow zawodowych," *Przegląd Związkowy,* no. 9, pp. 10–20.

Dyoniziak, R. (1967), *Społecznc uwarunkowania wydajnośći pracy* (Warsaw: Książka i Wiedża).

Dziedzic, T. (1973), "Struktura formalna a faktyczny system podejmowania decyzji w socjalistiycznym przedsiębiorstwie przeymsłowym," Warsaw University, doctoral thesis).

Gierek, E. (1972), "Przeomówienie I Sekretarza Komitetu Centralnego PZPR," (to VII/XIII Congress of Trade Unions, November 13–15, *Przegląd Związkowy,* no. 12, pp. 8–16.

Gierek, E. (1976), "Polski ruch zawodowy reprezentuje interesy klasy robotniczej i dobrze służy ojczyznie," *Przeglad Związkowy,* no. 1, pp. 2–4.

Gierek, E. (1980), "O dalszy rozwoj socjalist y cznej Polska, o pomyślność narodu polskiego," *Nowe Drogi,* no. 3, pp. 55–97.

Gilejko, L. (1972), *Związky zawodowe w procesie przemian społeczne w PRL* (Warsaw: CRZZ), p. 215.

Gilejko, L. (1979), "Postawy społeczno-polityczne klasy robotniczcj i ich uwarunkowania," in Wajda, (1979), pp. 266–83.

Gilejko, L. and Balcerek, J. (1965), *Jwiązki zawodowe i samorząd robotniczy* (Warsaw: SGiP).

Gross, F. (1979), *The Polish Worker: A Study of a Social Stratum* (New York: Roy Publishers).

Grzeszczyk, T. (1978), *Dyscyplina pracy. Problemy społeczno-ekonomiczne i prawne* (Warsaw: PWE).

Hirszowicz, M. and Morawski, W. (1967), *Z badań nad społecznym uczestwictwem w organizacji przemysłowcj* (Warsaw: Książka i Wiedza.)

Hryniewicz, J. (1980), "Ocena związkow zawodowych i samorzadu robotniczego," in L. Gilejko (ed.), *Obraz swiadomości robotników wiclkoprzemysłowych w Polsce* (Warsaw: CRZZ). pp. 92–111.

Kalinowski, W. (1979), "Jak działa podstawowa komorka organizacyjna," *Przegląd Związkowy,* nos. 7–8, pp. 37–41.

Kolankiewicz, G. (1972), "The Working Class," in D. Lane and G. Kolankiewicz (eds.), *Social Groups in Polish Society* (London: Macmillan), pp. 88–151.

Kolankiewicz, G. (1982), "Employee Self-Management and Socialist Trade Unionism," in J. Woodall (ed.), *Policy and Politics in Contemporary Poland* (London: Pinter, 1982), pp. 129–47).

Kompetence (1976), i organizacja pracy rady zakładowe," *Przegląd Związkowy,* no. 5, pp. 47–50.

Krall, H. (1972), "Rozmowy na najwyższm szczeblu," *Polityka,* no. 45.

Kruczek, W. (1977), "Rzetelna praca i aktywność społeczna garancją naszej pomyślności," *Przegląd Związkowy,* no. 1, pp. 5–10.

Krupa, K., Mikluski, J., and Wiktorow, A. (1978), "Działalność socjalna warunkuje jakość pracy," *Przegląd Związkowy,* no. 2, pp. 17–25.

Kużba, A. (1975), 'Praworządność wymaga przede wzsytkim znajmósci praw i obowiazkọw', *Przegląd Związkowy,* no. 12, pp. 19−20.

Labor Code (1979) of the Polish People's Republic (Warsaw: Wydawnictwo Prawnicze).

Loch, J. (1975), "Świeczka i ogarek," *Polityka,* nos 51/2.

Loch, J. (1980), "Wzmocniony glos," *Polityka,* no. 8.

Lopatka, A., Bluszkowski, J., and Konstański, K. (1976) (eds.), *Organizacje partyne wielkich zakaładow pracy* (Warsaw: Książka i Wiedza).

Matejko, A. (1969), "Some Sociological Problems of Socialist Factories," *Social Research,* no. 3 (Autumn), pp. 448−80.

Miejsce, rola i funkcja (1980), związkow zawodowych w procesie tworczenia rozwiniętego społeczeństwa socjalistycznego," *Pregląd Związkowy,* no. 1, pp. 30−1.

Mirończuk, A. (1977), "Zapobieganie sporom pracowniczym zadaniem rad zakładowych," *Przegląd Związkowy,* no. 6, pp. 3−6.

Mirończuk, A. (1979), "Jak realizuje sie w praktyce kodeks pracy," *Przeglad Związkowy,* no. 9, pp. 6−8.

Molenda, I. (1976), "Musi uplynąć trochu czasu," *Przegląd Związkowy,* no. 3, pp. 18−19.

"Na połmetku (1975), kongresów związkowych," *Przegląd Związkowych,* no. 2, pp. 5−8, 18.

O Roli Związkow Zawodowych (1972): *wybór publiscystiki* (Warsaw: CRZZ).

Owieczko, A. (1966), "Działaność i struktura samorządu robotniczego w opinii załog fabrycznych," *Studia Socjologiczne,* no. 3, pp. 65−100.

"Owocne partnerstwo (1976) związku i ministerstwa," *Przegląd Związkowy,* no. 10, pp. 23−4.

Ozdowski, S.A. (1979), "Polish Industrial Enterprises—The Legal Model and Operational Reality," *Critique,* no. 12 (Autumn—Winter), pp. 55−80.

"Partnerstwo (1973) w zarządzaniu," *Przegląd Związkowy,* no. 6, pp. 31−6.

Passent, D., and Wróblewski, K. (1980), "Która droga jest w przód?," *Polityka,* no. 42.

Pietraszewski, J. (1976), "Roczne doświadczcnia sądów pracy i ubezpiczeń," *Przegląd Związkowy,* no. 9, pp. 25−7.

Pokoj, M. 1979), "Samorząd zacieśnia więzi pracowniczc," *Przegląd Związkowy,* nos. 5−6, pp. 11−13, 21.

Potrzeba (1980), głębokiej odnowy w ruchu związkowym," *Trybuna Ludu,* August 27.

Preiss, A. (1978), "Przemiany styla zarządzania w zautomatyzowanych przedsiębiorstwach pzremysłowych," in Instytut Organizacji i Zarządzania Politechniki Wrocławskiej, *Kierowanie zespołami pracowniczymi w organizacjach* (Wrocław: Wydawnictwo Politechniki Wrocławskiej).

Ratyński, W. (1977), Partia i związki zawodowe (Warsaw: Książka i Wiedza).

Rudolf, T. (1973), "Podniecienie rangi rad zakładowych," *Przegląd Związkowy,* no. 12, pp. 33−4.

Sanetra, W. (1980), "Zakladowa komisja rozemcza a współrządzanie pracownicze," *Praca i zabezpeczenie społeczne,* no. 11, pp. 19−28.

"Spolezcno-Polityczne (1976) podstawy działalnosci związkowcj," *Przegląd Związkowy,* no. 5, pp. 44−6.

Śreniowski, J. (1978), "Strajki w PRL," *Robotnik,* no. 17.

Steszenko, L. (1973), Rada zakładowa—z badań w przedisęborstwach przemysłu terenowego (Warsaw: CRZZ).

Strzoda, M. (1977), *Aktywność zawodowa i społeczna hutników* (Katowice: Śląski instytut naukowy).

Szczepaniak, M. (1977) (ed.), *Polityczna organizacja społeczeństwa w Polsce* (Poznań: Wydawnictwo Pozańskie).

Szubert, W. (1980), *Zarys Prawa Pracy* (Warsaw: PWN).

"Utrwalanie (1976) praworządności nadal ważnym zadaniem aktywu," *Przegląd Związkowy,* no. 8, pp. 17−20.

Wajda, A. (1976), "Jedność społecznych i ekonomicznych celów polityki partii w wielkich zakładach pracy," in Lopatka *et al.,* 1976, pp. 58−77.

Wajda, A. (1979), *Klasa Robotnicza w społeczenstwic socjalisticznym* (Warsaw: Książka i Wiedza).

Wasilewski, J. (1978), "Społeczne mechanizmy selekcji na wyzsze stanowiska kierownicze," *Studia Socjologiczne,* no. 2, pp. 181−206.

Witałec, A. (1978), "Organizacja partyjna pomocnikiem i inspiratorem związkowego działania," *Przegląd Związkowy,* no. 12, pp. 21−2.

Woodall, J. (1982), *The Socialist Corporation and Technocratic Power. The PUWP, Industrial Organisation and Workforce Control 1958−80* (Cambridge: Cambridge University Press).

"Wykorzystanie (1978), uprawnien warunkiem umocnienia autorytetu rad zakładowych," *Przegląd Związkowy,* no. 7−8, pp. 38−41.

7

Solidarity: The Anti-Trade Union

Tom Keenoy

The independent, self-governing trade union Solidarity, which was established following the Gdańsk strike of August 1980, was—and remains—a unique social phenomenon; not only to the command economies of Eastern Europe but also throughout the whole range of industrial societies. It was the social mechanism for a truly authentic expression, however confused and confusing, of the "will of Polish national consciousness," and the product of the social, political, and economic crises which had been developing since the "Polish October" of 1956.[1] Even a brief examination of the social movement which resulted from the 1980 crisis shows it to be an extraordinarily complex, ever-changing, and, at times, bewildering phenomenon. And, given the geopolitical significance of Poland to the defense of the Eastern bloc, it could hardly be otherwise; the world held its breath while Solidarity attempted the impossible.

In the account which follows there is no attempt to provide an analysis of the social experience that was *Solidarność*. The focus is on the idea of Solidarity as a trade union and, as such, it constitutes no more than an initial step in coming to an understanding of the historic social movement called *Solidarność*.

[1] For a detail historical background see Davies, 1981; for more specific accounts of the 1980 crisis see Ascherson, 1981; Singer, 1982; and McShane, 1981. Thus far, the most incisive analysis of *Solidarność* has been provided by Touraine *et al.,* 1983.

Tom Keenoy, Lecturer in Industrial Relations, University College, Cardiff, Wales, United Kingdom.

Solidarity: Organizational Structure

The movement for free trade unions was only one of a broad range of social protest movements which gained impetus throughout the 1970s, a decade in which the policies of the Gierek regime had dramatically accelerated the generalized decline in the social and political authority of those in power. The increasing disaffection was reflected in the emergence of a variety of "Self Defense" committees and organizations farmers, peasants, students, academics, political minorities, religious and civil rights groups as well as those seeking to create free trade unions were established (Raina, 1981). While each was focused on a particular aspect of the deepening social crisis—whether it was the clumsy attempt to expropriate private farmers through a new pension scheme or the efforts of KOR[2] to provide legal and financial support to those subject to arbitrary and "lawless" treatment by the police, the security police and others in authority—collectively, they represented a deep conviction of the need for social renewal. Reform would not be sufficient, for bureaucratic corruption had become too public and abuse of the law too flagrant; behind the floundering economy and public contempt for the political legitimacy of the PUWP (Polish United Workers' Party) lay a deeper and more fundamental malaise: a moral crisis.

It is only in this context that the organizational structure of Solidarity and the formal aims and objectives detailed in the statute of the independent self-governing trade union (Szajkowski, 1982: 275) can be analyzed.

In contrast to the preexisting union organization which, under the aegis of the Polish CCTU (Central Council of Trade Unions), was the typical East European democratic–centralist federation of industrial and occupational unions, of mobilization: the factory-level or district level, the regional level (the boundaries of this region were determined by the existing voivodship area of jurisdiction) and the national level (see Figure 7.1).

At the factory-local or district level the precise constituency of the Solidarity organization was governed by size: factories with 500 or more employees—irrespective of trade or occupation—could establish a Solidarity branch and elect the appropriate institutional structure; smaller enterprises were expected to form an interfactory Solidarity branch and formulate appropriate statutes to ensure the creation of the same institutional structure.

---

[2] The Committee for the Defense of Workers (KOR), originally established in 1976 by Jacek Kuroń and six other dissident intellectuals, had become a central focus for the expression of political opposition by 1980. It had extended the scope of its activities and added Committee of Social Self-Defense to its name—becoming KOR-KSS—but was invariably referred to by the original acronym, KOR.

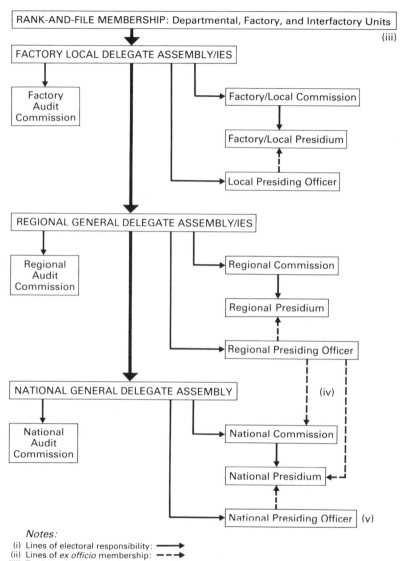

RANK-AND-FILE MEMBERSHIP: Departmental, Factory, and Interfactory Units

(iii)

FACTORY LOCAL DELEGATE ASSEMBLY/IES

Factory Audit Commission

Factory/Local Commission

Factory/Local Presidium

Local Presiding Officer

REGIONAL GENERAL DELEGATE ASSEMBLY/IES

Regional Audit Commission

Regional Commission

Regional Presidium

Regional Presiding Officer

NATIONAL GENERAL DELEGATE ASSEMBLY

(iv)

National Audit Commission

National Commission

National Presidium

National Presiding Officer (v)

Notes:

(i) Lines of electoral responsibility: ⟶

(ii) Lines of *ex officio* membership: ⤏

(iii) Trade/professional sections were established with parallel structures.

(iv) All regional presidents were members of the national commission; regional presidents of the six largest regions were also members of the national Presidium.

(v) In the original statutes the national President was to be elected by the national Presidium. This was revised at the national congress in September, 1981.

Figure 7.1. Solidarity: organizational structure.

(Thus, for example, a factory assembly would consist of delegates from all the member factories in proportion to the membership of those factory units.) The factory assemblies, meeting biannually, were to elect regional delegates who, in turn, would elect the regional officials (i.e., members of the regional commission, the regional audit commission—the primary function of which was to oversee the financial affairs of the union at regional level, and the regional presiding officer). The regional delegates were to elect delegates to the national congress which was intended to meet "once a year in ordinary session."

In keeping with the spirit of Gdańsk—and in total contrast to the democratic-centralist principles which had governed the "old" official union structure—the Solidarity organization was infused with "bottom-up" democratic procedures, incorporated checks and counter-checks on each level of officialdom, and took elaborate precautions to preempt any party or managerial infiltration. Every official was elected and could only remain in (the same) office for two years; the general assemblies of delegates at each level enjoyed supreme authority, being constitutionally responsible for setting and reviewing policy, scrutinizing the performance of officials, and for electing virtually all the officials of the union at each level. (The only exceptions were the membership of the Presidia which at the factory-local and regional levels were elected by the relevant commission while at the national level a more complex procedure—which included *ex officio* membership for the regional presidents of the six largest regions—operated.)

From the initial emergence of the founding interfactory strike committees during August and September of 1980 to the national congress in September 1981 there was a permanent and, at times, seemingly excessive concern with accountability. Singer ruefully relates one example which epitomizes the pervasive atmosphere of suspicion. On one occasion the Gdańsk delegates spent seven hours electing a commission and then, feeling it couldn't be trusted, immediately disbanded it. But, as he observes, "the discovery of democracy often took the form of an inordinate love of procedure. After years of broken promises the hated word was 'manipulation' and the rank and file mistrusted anybody, once elected" (Singer, 1982: 260). Such fears were also reflected in the statutory prohibition on all managers, supervisors, and their administrative subordinates from holding office in the union—there was a similar ban on all those "fulfilling managerial functions in political organizations."

The historical audacity of the new organization was matched only by its ambition with regard to whom it sought to organize within the trade union and what it sought to achieve. The statutes declared that: "The Union's area of operations is the territory of the Polish People's Republic"—though even this was to prove insufficient for the national congress in 1981 which, with typical

Polish flair for hyperbole, insisted on adding: "This shall include Polish workplaces outside the country" in order to ensure that those employed in Polish embassies could be asured of their right to join. Similarly, there was an equivalent all-pervasiveness in the scope of the statutory objectives. Apart from the fundamental generalized aim of providing an institutional means for the independent representation of workers' interest, the legitimate field of activity claimed by Solidarity went considerably beyond the conventional economistic objectives associated with trade unionism. The statute specified a political concern with the development of democratic modes of control and with the exercise of union influence on economic and social policy; an educational concern with the development and expansion of both vocational training and workers' education in general; a managerial concern with harmony at work; a specific social concern with the maintenance of the family; an ecological concern with the environment (this objective was not in the original statute but was added by the national congress); and a nationalistic concern with the "good of the Fatherland."

This national territorially based structure was to be buttressed by a parallel structure of affiliated "professional" and occupational trade unions created to represent the specific interests of particular categories of employee. But this parallel set of autonomous self-governing occupational trade unions—which were to emerge out of the ruins of the discredited CCTU "branch" unions—were clearly subordinated to the territorial structure both in the statute and, as was demonstrated, in practice. Only three brief paragraphs of the statute referred to the "professional and trade sections." These "are created by the Union's regional board [Commission], at the initiative of factory Union [i.e., Solidarity] locals." Once the regional authorities have come to some agreement, the national commission will create appropriate structures at the national level for the trade sections. Despite the insistence on autonomy, the statutes indicate that the constitutional powers of the trade sections were to be carefully regulated and limited; their functioning had to conform to the "internal statutes enacted by the National Commission" and while their officials could "prepare" and "state their opinions" of draft collective work contracts there was no right to bargain independently on behalf of their particular members, for the statute specified only that "the National Commission *may empower* the officials of the sections to make collective work contracts in its name" (emphasis added). Indeed, these are the only functions for which the "trade" sections were given specific responsibility in the statutes. Later, in the policy document approved by the national congress, their subordinate role was reinforced when the basic tasks of the sections were elaborated to include "representing the interests of a given group vis-à-vis the Union's authorities" and intervening, "on behalf of the Union's authorities" with the state administration. Other conventional trade union activities, such as regulating promotion, negotiating bonus payments, and *dissolving* work contracts were defined as being part of the factory-based Solidarity organizational functions. More significantly, in terms of the allocation of power within the overall dual structure, the decision to take strike action—which would normally be seen as an integral element of any collective bargaining process—was strictly the preserve of the members and officials of the territorially based Solidarity structures.

In part, this singular neglect of the trade sections reflected the widespread disenchantment and rejection of any form of structure which bore even a passing resemblance to the preexisting CCTU trade unions but, more fundamentally, this formal marginalization of specific occupational interests reflected the deeply felt conviction that no genuine independent trade union activity would be possible without first establishing a procedural basis for the legitimate pursuit of such activities. And, for this, what was required was an all-embracing national institution which could represent the *general* interest of workers in society, since the defense of their particularistic occupational or employment interests could not be pursued effectively without a legitimate and "independent" organizational base. This necessitated a radical change in the existing social institutions. Celinski, in presenting the NCC report to the national congress in September, 1981, pointed out that the initial period of Solidarity's existence had been dominated by the demands for long overdue material benefits and for the restitution of civil rights. The latter, in particular the guarantee of freedom of association, were essential to the legal establishment and continued existence of Solidarity as a social institution. Solidarity the social *movement* was the vehicle for the acquisition of such rights, while Solidarity the social *institution* was to be the protector and guarantor of these rights. It is only in this context that the structural ambiguities of the dual structure, with its inbuilt potential for conflict between the aspirations of the various occupational sections (Keenoy, 1982), can be comprehended.

Trade union organizational structure is often said to be a "function of purpose:" the initial—and critical—aim of Solidarity was to secure a legitimate role in Polish society. In the past, the material concessions granted following the worker protests of 1956, 1970, and 1976 were soon nullified and the less frequent political concessions—such as the workers' councils following the "Polish October" of 1956—had rapidly soured as the new institutions were incorporated into the cloying machinery of bureaucratic control. The monotonous experience of inevitable failure of all reform led to the conviction that only an institution which was truly independent of the party and the state could provide a genuine representation of worker interests. At one level, the organizational structure embraced a deceptively simple principle: in a workers' state, the workers should enjoy primary authority.

The question of issue, of course, was which form of organization, the party or the union, was best fitted to ensure a genuine representation and articulation of workers' interests. "Free" trade unionism—in any of the recognized meanings of that term—could not *begin* to exist until this question had been resolved in favor of Solidarity.

Solidarity in Action

In coming to an understanding of the complex array of forces which drove Solidarity into ever more irreconcilable conflicts with the government and the PUWP and which, in turn, impelled General Jarulzeski into declaring martial law in December 1981, it is impossible to ignore not only the obvious ideological incompatibility between the principles of democratic centralism and those of "free" or independent trade unionism but also the inherent *organizational* disjunction between these competing principles.

The contradictions and conflicts engendered by the social juxtaposition of these two sets of assumptions—which, practically, translate into quite incompatible organizational structures—was evident throughout the sixteen months of Solidarity's precarious and turbulent formal existence. It was reflected in the conflicts which, increasingly, occurred between the factions within the leadership of Solidarity; in the debates within the ranks of Solidarity—in particular, the arguments concerning the role the union could or should play in any structure of self-management; in the extreme reluctance of the government to establish any formally recognized and institutionalized means of discourse and negotiation with the new union; in the ideological and organizational crisis Solidarity precipitated within the PUWP; and, most obviously, in the continually overt and frequently bitter conflicts which characterized the relationship between the Solidarity officials—at all levels— and their counterparts in the state administrative apparatus from government ministers down through the provincial officials to local bureaucrats and enterprise management.[3] While the threat of external intervention and the

---

[3]This is by no means an exhaustive list of the institutions and organizations with which Solidarity came into conflict. In particular there were conflicts with the old "branch unions." In November, 1980, for example, they threatened to take legal action unless granted equal status with Solidarity in union–government negotiations. In the same month rail workers in Wrocław protested to preempt plans to base wage negotiations on proposals devised by the "branch unions." And, following the demise of the CCUT, the old unions—reorganized "independently" under a new coordinating committee—sought to embarrass and compromise Solidarity whenever possible. In May, 1981, for example, after Solidarity had declared a moratorium on pay increases, the NCC protested at the government holding pay talks with the "branch unions." Solidarity was also faced by "more comradely" competition from the new non-Solidarity inde-

fear of internal economic collapse were potent factors influencing the tone of the relationships between the government, the PUWP, and Solidarity, it was, equally, the irreconcilable clash of values with regard to how social, political, and economic institutions ought to be organized which ensured the perpetual atmosphere of deep suspicion and mistrust, prevented anything but token negotiations, and indicated that, short of social revolution, Solidarity could not be sustained. Empirically, this was reflected in three major issues which emerged following the legal recognition of Solidarity: the legitimacy of collective bargaining; the debate about self-management; and the demands for "horizontal" forms of organizational structure. Collectively, these issues represented a rejection of the principles of democratic centralism and, in particular, their expression in dual functioning trade unionism.

The Legitimacy of Collective Bargaining

It was clear from the statutes of Solidarity that collective negotiations were to be the primary method through which workers' interests were to be represented and pursued. A prerequisite for relatively peaceful and success-ful collective bargaining is the recognition—by both sides—of the right of the other not merely to exist but also to act as a legitimate representative. In order to conduct their business, the two sides usually establish procedural agreements which specify how to proceed in the event of a dispute. Such agreements specify the framework of rules by which both sides will be guided, if not regulated. While it would be historically naive to expect such mechanisms to be established without conflict, Solidarity, despite legal re-cognition and repeated government assurances, never enjoyed anything other that a *de facto* legitimacy from the government, and the creation of workable collective bargaining institutions never got beyond the talking stage. Celinski, at the national congress, admitted that the second major objective Solidarity had set itself, that of developing and establishing a negotiating strategy to deal with the government, had not been successful; the needs of the moment had always taken precedence over the discussion of general issues.

The organizational consequences of legitimizing collective bargaining include recognizing that authority to take decisions must be devolved throughout the various structures in order that specific problems can be

---

pendent trade unions organized within the Confederation of Autonomous Trade Unions—established in January, 1981— which eventually comprised some thirty trade unions represent-ing some 800,000 members. While these unions did not act as *agents provocateurs,* they competed for membership and representation rights.

negotiated at the appropriate level. Solidarity—in that authority "flowed upwards" from the base—was a structure specifically designed to engage in collective bargaining. In contrast, the existing governmental, party, and state administrative structures had been designed to preempt decision-making at all levels; executive authority was concentrated at the top.

Conflict between such diametrically opposed "organizational logics" was inevitable from the outset. For example, despite the apparent authority of the governmental negotiators at Gdańsk—led by Deputy Prime Minister Jagielski—even their decisions were, temporarily, modified by the Warsaw District Court when Solidarity went to register the statutes in September, 1980. Between then and the end of January some 650 "agreements" had ostensibly been reached between government officials and various Solidarity regional, branch, and factory organizations, yet it was not until February, 1981 that the government formally recognized the need to establish some institutional mechanism to regulate relations between itself and the new unions.

Trybuna Ludu, the PUWP daily newspaper, had called for the creation of some permanent negotiating machinery between the government and Solidarity unions on January 30. On the same day, the influential Polish journalists' union had appealed to the Sejm to set up a statutory public mediation body to resolve the problems of government–union relations. Jaruzelski, in his inaugural address as Prime Minister to the Sejm on February 12, announced the establishment of a special standing committee to coordinate government–trade union relations. This body, the Council of Ministers' Committee for Labor Union Affairs, first met on February 26, under the chairmanship of one of the new deputy premiers, Rakowski; but its functions were advisory, not executive, for it was only to *monitor* the implementation of agreements and create a *model* procedure agreement to regulate government–union relations. A week later the Sejm appointed its own special commission to monitor the implementation of the Gdańsk, Szczeciń and Jastrzebie agreements. It was hoped that this body, under Jan Szczepański, would also take on a mediating role. Neither of the two new commissions had the desired effect for, reporting to to the Sejm a month later, Szczepański pleaded with parliament, as a matter of urgency, to establish an arbitration commission to regulate the government–union relationship. In his view, such a body was imperative since the government could not act as an arbitrator in disputes to which it was itself a party. It is difficult to judge how seriously the government regarded its own formal attempts to create such machinery. Rakowski's special commission and its subcommittees met on several occasions, although there seems to be little evidence that the consultations ever got beyond formal declarations recognizing the enormity of the economic crisis, the need for both citizens and the government to observe the law, and for social cooperation between the government and the unions.[4]

Insofar as any effective mediators did emerge, the church seems to have played the most significant unofficial role (Szajkowski, 1983) while members of Solidarity's National Coordinating Commission (NCC) travelled the country "fire-fighting" in disputes between local Solidarity groups and Voivodship officials—most notably, perhaps, in the "Bydgoszcz affair" of March, 1981 when, among others, two senior Solidarity officals were beaten up by the security police. (The subsequent medical report insisted only that the injuries sustained "could not have been self-inflicted.") This was only one of countless occasions on which the existence of some form of independent arbitration machinery could have proved invaluable as a mechanism for defusing tension and ensuring some measure, however token, of perceivable "fairness" within the government–union relationship. It would also have permitted Solidarity officials to avoid being accused—as Wałęsa was during the Bydgoszcz dispute—of "selling out" to the government. The failure of Solidarity to force the government to establish institutional mechanisms for mediation and arbitration could be viewed as a critical weakness in their negotiating strategy to establish meaningful collective bargaining. However, since the achievement of such institutions would have been a negation of the organizational logic of democratic centralism, they would also have represented a critical defeat for the government, which, throughout the period, obstinately refused to devolve authority except as a matter of political expediency.

This last point is well illustrated by the pattern of dispute-resolution which came to characterize relations at all levels between Solidarity and the government. While Solidarity local and regional organizations were empowered to reach agreements, their attempts to do so were invariably frustrated by the fact that the local management, people's council, or Voivodship authorities did not possess equivalent authority. In consequence, virtually every dispute produced either a threatened strike, a "warning" strike—lasting several hours—a full strike by the group in dispute, or, less frequently, a general strike of workers throughout an area or region. In January, 1981, for example, the Jelenia Gora union threatened strike action unless the government sent someone authorized to negotiate on a variety of local demands—the most sensitive of which was the transfer of a new sanatorium built for the Ministry of the Interior to the public health service. The Ministry of Labor

---

[4] For details of the establishment and performance of these bodies, see RFE, Background Report/263 (Poland), *Poland: A Chronology of Events,* September, 1981, p. 88; and RFE, Background Report/Chronicle 3, *Poland: A Chronology of Events,* March, 1982, pp. 2–4, 11, 15, 35, 52, 58–9.

official who had been leading talks, it transpired, was not empowered to sign anything. Ten days later the action was suspended following the arrival of a deputy minister, Jablonski. After five days of negotiation it became clear that he too did not have authority to agree the transfer of the sanatorium; a general strike was called. Three days before it was due to take place, a new government delegation arrived to reopen negotiation and the general strike was suspended. Next—as was often the case in serious disputes—Wałęsa arrived with other Solidarity officials to try to calm the situation. All to no avail. The government negotiators could not agree to the demand; the general strike went ahead on February 9, and Wałęsa, together with local strike leaders and other Solidarity national officials, travelled to Warsaw to continue negotiations with yet another government team, this time headed by two deputy premiers. The next day the government conceded, transferred the sanatorium to the general health service, and the general strike was called off.[5]

This pattern of conflict-resolution, with each dispute becoming more bitter and protracted as it stumbled upward through the official hierarchy of authority, came to typify the relationship between Solidarity and the structures of officialdom. In effect, each and every dispute was rapidly transformed into a confrontation between government and citizens; a test of will so that almost every demand was magnified and came to be viewed as a direct challenge to the legitimacy of governmental authority. Politically, it may well have reflected the determination of the government and certain sections of the PUWP to "prove" that Solidarity was indeed the source of "anarchization" in Polish society. But it was not merely the result of political strategy. Analytically, this pattern of behavior represented more than the stubborn refusal to legitimize collective bargaining; it reflected an ideological incapcity to come to terms with the transformation of organizational authority which was essential *before* collective bargaining could become an appropriate and effective means of resolving disputes. In addition, there is evidence of a "trained incapacity" (Merton, 1952) within the bureaucratic machinery to adapt to the novel demands that were made on the existing structures; not surprisingly, after thirty-five years of democratic centralism, the autonomic response to all nonroutine matters of business had been to refer them upward for decision. Indeed, the demands made at all levels by Solidarity must have been experienced as a kind of bureaucratic nightmare; the apparatchiks were not merely incapable of "administering" collective bargaining: they were traumatized by the utterly alien adjustments it demanded to their way of life.

[5] For details, see RFE, Background Report/263 (Poland), *Poland: A Chronology of Events,* September, 1981, pp. 74, 91–2, 97, 99–102, 104.

The Self-Management Debate

The question of what form of self-management was to be created in order to democratize economic enterprises and administrative structures throughout Poland—the issue which dominated policy considerations throughout the summer of 1981 while the Sejm was preparing the new law on workers' self-management—underlined the incompatibility between the competing organizational logics and highlighted the inherent contradictions in the idea that Solidarity, as an independent trade union, could operationally coexist with a system of central planning, however flexible. And, in this context, the vexed question of what might be an appropriate role for the Solidarity unions in any structure of self-management was, essentially, a debate about the institutional identity of Solidarity.

Attempts to establish an acceptable and workable form of industrial democracy in Poland have a long and unsuccessful history. The factory councils of 1945 and the workers' councils of 1956 were incorporated not only, as Kolankiewicz (1982: 130) points out, because the "absence of external vertical or horizontal links between these councils inevitably iso-lated them, and their spontaneous nature left them within an institutional structure which gradually whittled away their internal sovereignty," but also because their relative autonomy could not be tolerated in an economic system dominated by the primacy of central directives. By 1980 Polish workers had clearly recognized the instrinsic limitations of the previous modes of self-management and experience had led to the conviction that independent representation was essential. Indeed, the free trade union groups which surfaced in the 1970s centered on the KOR-backed publication *Robot-nik* can be seen as pursuing a deliberate strategy designed to establish workers' organizations which could not be held responsible in any way for managerial decision-making and, thus, could not become shackled within the strictures of the dual functioning pattern (see Pravda and Ruble, Chapter 1, above) characteristic of East European societies.

Criticism of the CCTU branch unions centered on their failure to defend workers' interests both generally and in disputes with management (see Pravda, Chapter 6, above). In the first edition of *Robotnik*, for example, only three objectives were set: "Solidarity in defence of *worker interests;* increased participation of employees in *determining the level of wages;* support of independent workers representation which should replace the moribund institution of the Trade Unions" (Raina, 1981: 371; emphasis added). Such a focus articulated the belief not only that worker interests were clearly demarcated from those of management but also that their effective defense and pursuit required independent representation. The extent to which conventional trade union economistic demands had been neglected within the existing industrial relations structures was also reflected in the

1977 Charter of Workers' Rights, signed by free trade union groups from all over Poland. This document listed six major demands: the reform of the wages system to ensure greater equity; the introduction of the 40-hour working week together with the abandonment of the practice of enforced overtime; improvements in safety regulations and the system of accident investigation—notably that "the post-accident commissions and the plant doctors should be completely independent of factory management;" the elimination of special privileges enjoyed by party members and the militia—in particular preferential treatment at work and in the allocation of housing, holiday accommodation; consumer goods, medical treatment and social welfare benefits; an end to the practice of "forcing people to act against their conscience," such as informing on colleagues or being forced to produce defective goods; and, finally, it demanded a new Labor Code since the 1975 code "introduced regulations that are disadvantageous to the workers. The articles contained therein are interpreted to conform with the interests of the employer" (Raina, 1981: 375 ff.). The creation of Solidarity seemed to provide an institutional mechanism through which such grievances could be remedied but, if previous experience was any guide, success would be dependent on the extent to which the new union could maintain its institutional autonomy, and thus disclaim any responsibility for interests other than those of its members, the Polish workforce.

The question which arises is why, given the mantra of "self-managing independence," the Solidarity activists allowed themselves to be drawn, through their active participation in the enterprise self-management debate, into co-responsibility for the management of the economy.

A surface inspection of the historical dynamics of the fifteen months from August, 1980 suggests that Solidarity was simply trapped by a series of economic and political forces over which it had no control and little influence. Fundamental to both the emergence of Solidarity and the course of events which overtook it was the economic crisis; between 1979 and 1981 it is estimated that national income dropped by 25 percent in real terms; in the first ten months of 1981 money wages rose by 26.4 percent while the supply of goods and services decreased by 11 percent (Singer, 1982: 248); one Solidarity economist estimated that 33 percent of the population's purchasing power remained unused (McShane, 1981: 87). Bujak, the chairman of the Warsaw region Solidarity, is reported to have described the new union as "a union of seamen on a sinking ship," while Nove, hardly renowned for histrionics, has concluded: "Poland's leadership adopted an economic policy of possibly unique unsoundness, and the resultant destabilization was all the more risky because the political foundations of the regime were so weak" (Nove, 1983: 147). Alongside the progressive economic devastation—and, in part, clearly responsible for it—was the seemingly terminal decline in the political legitimacy and authority of the party and the government; a process which had accelerated dramatically throughout the 1970s with the more unashamedly public incidence of conspicious consumption among the ranks of the political, administrative, and military elites. It seemed clear to all where the foreign dollars—borrowed for economic growth—were being spent. The former KOR activist, Romaszewski (1983: 99) seems to capture the flavor of feeling:

> Officials signing contracts at home and abroad swallowed the bacillus of consumerism and infected the whole apparatus of power which, not being subject to any public control, became a mafia and cynically exploited society for their own ends. When challenged, it became paralyzed with fear which rendered it unable to cope throughout the fifteen months of the crisis.

Empirically, this inability to cope was reflected in the succession of mass defections and expulsions from the party—for example, fifty-one former directors, including a former minister of foreign trade and maritime economy, were expelled in December, 1980; an inability to introduce anything other than token reform into the system of economic management—not least because the relationship between the central planning mechanisms and the reality of productive activity of enterprise level had deteriorated, in many instances, to little more than a paper formality; as Blazyca concludes: "Polish central planning had disintegrated" (Blazyca, 1983: 24).[6] Thirdly, as noted above, it was reflected in the clumsy ineptitude which typified daily relations with Solidarity at all levels, the primary consequence of which was to reinforce the downward spiral of confidence in the government and the PUWP.

The cumulative effect of the twin political and economic crises was the *de facto* assumption of social power and authority by Solidarity, a reality which was evident from the success of the Gdańsk negotiations but not easily accommodated by those in power. In January 1981 Kania was still insisting to a meeting of party secretaries that "there is no room in our state for a duality of power." The hollowness of this claim is highlighted by Szczepanski's report to the Sjem in April, 1981 in which he suggested that an analysis of the major agreements indicated that Solidarity had, for some months, been the joint ruling institution in society. By this time Solidarity officials at both the national and regional levels had become deeply involved in a very wide range of social, economic, and political issues and every grievance against "the authorities," no matter how trivial, was processed through Solidarity. The agenda of the NCC meeting at Gdańsk on January 7, for example, included items on the establishment of the 5-day week, the censorship law, the

---

[6] For detailed analyses of the nature and significance of the economic crisis see also Blazyca, 1982; Drewnowski, 1982; Nuti, 1981; and Shapiro, 1981.

position of political prisoners, the registration of Rural Solidarity, and the government's refusal to release the film *Workers 80*. Indeed, there seemed to be few areas of social relations—excepting perhaps the military and internal security forces—which were not penetrated by the authority of Solidarity. In August 1981, for example, the Radom regional Solidarity representatives met with the Voivodship officials to discuss access to the mass media, market supplies, and the election of the authorities for the Radom Higher School of Engineering. To stand aside from the debate over what form enterprise self-management should take, given that Solidarity had become the effective voice to every strand of "self-management" elsewhere in society, would have been a completely incongruous policy position, however ambivalent the members of Solidarity might feel about such involvement. It was in this context that the Solidarity "Network" group, established in April 1981 and composed of representatives from about seventeen of the major enterprises throughout Poland, set out to formulate the series of proposals which were to become the Solidarity policy document on enterprise self-management.[7]

But it would be mistaken to conclude that Solidarity drifted into a concern with self-management just to fill the usual vacuum created by the authorities' incompetence or neglect. While, in general, Singer's (1982: 252) assessment that "the government, unwilling to share power and unable to exercise it on its own, was leading the country to ruin" seems accurate, enterprise self-management was among the few issues upon which the government had been actively drawing up new legal proposals. It was the anticipated character of these proposals and their consequential impact on the organizational logic of Solidarity which seems to have provided a major stimulus to involvement.

Prior to their active participation in seeking to influence government policy on the issue, Solidarity had inevitably been drawn into day-to-day managerial functioning through the actions of the membership in their pursuit of "trade union" issues at plant level. With the declared objective of improving managerial effectiveness, many managers, deemed to be incompetent or unacceptable, had been removed from their posts and, more positively, there had been an increasing number of instances where workers, through the new Solidarity organization, had established *de facto* self-management structures tailored to their own particular circumstances (Kolankiewicz, 1982). The initial impetus for these *ad hoc* arrangements was often pragmatic; the new union had to have much better information on how the enterprise operated in order to conduct its "union business" in an

---

[7] For details of the Solidarity proposals see Network, 1981; for text of the government legal proposals on state enterprises and workers' self-management see *Poland: A Chronology of Events,* August–December, 1981; RFE, July, 1982, pp. 165–93.

effective manner. But this, in turn, raised the more difficult and critical issue of enterprise autonomy, for if the union was to represent worker interests in the manner intended, management too had to be autonomous or, at the least, to enjoy a much greater degree of independence than could be tolerated within the preexisting centrally directed structures. Much of the overt conflict centered on the authority and accountability of the enterprise director—notably in the LOT airline employees' strike of July 1981 over the right to appoint the new director, and the attempt in September 1981 to oust the director of the Huta Katowice Steelworks following his closure of an allegedly anti-communist union journal. Nevertheless, while these episodes represented a coherent attempt to undermine the party "personnel selection" system of *nomenklatura,* of greater organizational significance was the realization that any genuine attempt to satisfy the aspirations of Solidarity also demanded a fundamental change in the degree of autonomy granted to the enterprise as an economic unit. Without such a change, Solidarity's role as a trade union would have remained marginal if not impossible—even in the unlikely event of their being able to appoint their own enterprise directors. For without localized control over output, production targets, wages, prices, and the employment relationship, "free" trade unionism is not viable.

Thus, the debate over self-management focused on two critical issues: who would appoint the director, and the relationship between the enterprise and the state planning institutions. Once again, at the core of these arguments lay the competing organizational logics of free trade unionism and central planning. The logic of the Network proposals, in which the director would be appointed and dismissed by the employees' council—which was to be the key institution of the new self-management structure—and the enterprise would exercise control over the resources allocated to it, was to establish an organizational compatibility between the enterprise and the trade union: the "new" enterprise was to be responsive to trade union demands. In effect, the Network position was that central planning was to disappear, for overall responsibility for economic plans was to be vested in the Sejm, the existing economic brance ministries were to be merged into one ministry of trade, and while "the Government should also possess its own planning staff," these, "of course, shouldn't impose any decisions on enterprises" (Network, 1981: 2). In addition, there were to be territorially based representative self-management institutions—obviously designed as structures to run parallel with regional Solidarity structures—which, along with individual enterprises, would prepare their own plans which would only be "related to the central plans by means of economic instruments established by acts and also by means of information exchange" (ibid.: 4), although even this gesture of acknowledgment to the overall National Socioeconomic Plan was conditional, for "enterprise and territorial authorities make their own decisions concerning plans, their range and time span" (loc. cit.).

Like the concomitant attempts to establish a procedural framework for collective bargaining, such demands struck at the core of the existing organizational and ideological touchstones while also highlighting the degree of dissensus within Solidarity itself. While there was probably a national consensus on the need for economic reform, the question of how radical this reform ought to be and which direction it ought to take was a major source of internal conflict. At the Solidarity congress three major positions came to be identified: the minority view, of what might be called the "nationalist anti-communists," which insisted upon an extensive self-managing marketization of the economy—a strategy which would have openly abandoned any commitment to planning from the center; a larger and more influential view, of the "radical socialists," who argued for even greater devolution of power in order to establish genuinely democratic socialist planning; and the majority position, that of the "trade unionists," which endorsed the Network policy document. This majority view, while undoubtedly reflecting the most politically expedient position, evaded the central issue: that of the relationship between *any* form of democratic socioeconomic planning and the logic of trade unionism (Crouch, 1982). There were only the vaguest of indications as to what might occur in the event of a conflict between the newly democratized self-managing enterprises and either the self-managing trade union or the "general" interest of a region or society as represented by the regional self-management bodies or the Sejm. The debate about self-management highlighted the progressive "identity crisis" which plagued Solidarity throughout its brief formal existence: in becoming involved Solidarity could not avoid a significant measure of responsibility for the management of the economy yet, in doing so, it was forced to relinquish its claim to be no more than the representative of particularistic group interests. At the same time a policy of noninvolvement was impossible, not least because to leave the governmental proposals uncontested would have permitted the construction of a degree of democratic centralism which would have proved inimical to the functioning of independent trade unionism. Self-management proved to be the political, economic, and organizational "Catch 22" of the Solidarity movement.

"Horizontal" Organization

The third symptom in the social process of delegitimizing democratic centralism was the movement to establish "horizontal" associations. Although this notion did not appear to take on a concrete organizational form until the emergence of the Toruń Party Forum in April, 1981, the principles upon which it rested were embedded at the center of the 1980 crisis. In short, "horizontalism" was a euphemism for self-managing, independent, democratic social institutions and, as such, was the complete antithesis of democratic centralism.

Its emergence as the means through which the membership of the PUWP intended to restore the political legitimacy and vitality of the PUWP was significant insofar as it represented the final dénouement of the preexisting social and political institutions. Its origins lie in the multitude of self-defense organizations which sprang up in the 1970s and the workers' self-defense committee, KOR, which established positive links between workers and the intelligentsia, can be regarded as the first significant "horizontal" association. Indeed, insofar as it is possible to identify critical incidents in the emergence of Solidarity, it seems likely that the creation of KOR in 1976 should be treated as one of them. The extent to which KOR represented a novel organizational form and a novel political strategy is indicated by the degree of antipathy which had previously characterized the relationship between the workers and the intelligentsia. In 1968 the workers had stood by while the student protests were suppressed, the universities were purged, and some 30,000 people went into exile; two years later, in 1970, the students refused to support the strikes and riots which broke out along the Baltic seaboard cities in response to Gomulka's food price increases. The success of KOR in building a relationship of trust between themselves and other sections of society contributed to the conviction that, with the appropriate form of organization, radical reforms could be achieved. Solidarity, in that it was an organization of workers as workers, was, of course, the "horizontal" organization which destroyed the vertical demarcations which had characterized the associations of workers within the branch unions under the CCTU. And, while the organizational form which it adopted was to mirror the structural configuration of the party and state administrative apparatus, authority and the impetus for action came from below and not from the top; responsiveness and accountability were ensured through the insistence on genuinely competitive electoral mechanisms.

Within the PUWP the already fragile legitimacy of its electoral procedures had been finally shattered by the Gdańsk events, and those who did not leave the party set about the delicate process of reforming it.

Public confessions, purges of the leadership, and expulsions were not, of course, a novel phenomenon; they had accompanied the crises of 1956, 1970, and 1976 but they had never taken place on the scale seen after the signing of the Gdańsk agreement. Week after week there were demands for the sacking or replacement of officials—often at the instigation of Solidarity branches but sometimes such demands came from rank-and-file party groups.

The party hierarchy—anxious to retain some degree of political legitimacy in a rapidly deteriorating milieu—could do little but comply.

This process of purification was accompanied by a parallel process of democratization—the so-called "horizontal" movement. The new organizational principles established by Solidarity were rapidly diffused throughout the lower levels of the party and, in the attempt to redefine the role of the party and reestablish its political legitimacy, became the central plank of the demands for renewal; a self-managing "trade union" had to be balanced by a self-managing party. In January, 1981, for example, party activists in Poznań met, without party approval, to discuss how the party might be made more responsive to the membership and how it might best serve the workers. Similar groups sprang up elsewhere and culminated with the Toruń Forum in April which was attended by over 700 delegates from fourteen Voivodships. The most significant demands were those for the democratization of the party which, once effected, would have entailed a very considerable weakening, if not the abandonment, of the organizational principles of democratic centralism. Had their democratic reform become an institutional reality, then the basis for a genuinely collaborative relationship with Solidarity would have been created. But, in the process, the party would have been transformed. Martial law, it would seem, may have been as much a response to the possibility of a self-managing PUWP as it was to the socioeconomic crisis for which Solidarity was held responsible.

Solidarity: The Anti-Trade Union

Lech Wałęsa, speaking to the press at the ILO in June, 1981, indicated his preference for the shape of the new order when he said: "The government should govern, the party should look after party matters, and the unions should protect the interests of their workers." Such a conception represented an idealized expectation of some future configuration in which the functional role and functional interdependence of the three institutions would be clearly demarcated and recognized. What it would have required was not merely the granting of a genuine measure of legitimacy and autonomy to Solidarity, but also a clear separation of the state and party structures together with—as suggested above—a fundamental reorientation in their organizational structures and methods of operation. The implication of Wałęsa's statement is that social and political harmony depended upon no more than a redefinition of the existing pattern of administrative responsibilities and a clearer separation of functions. Solidarity, it would seem, had done no more than replace the preexisting but ineffectual CCTU trade union structures with a new and more efficient union organization. This was an image which was encouraged by Solidarity's leadership and seized on by the Western media. Editorials extolled the virtues of free trade unionism and Western political leaders insisted on the right of free association as the touchstone of the democratic society.

At this simple, and often simplistically construed, level of analysis, Solidarity could be described as a trade union. The progressive inability of successive governments since the mid-1950s to reform the management of the economy to meet either the increasingly complex needs of an advanced industrial society or the rising expectations of a better educated and more urbanized workforce had been marked by social protest of increasing generality and, ominously, with shorter periods of relative social peace. Given what can now only be described as the catastrophic decline in Poland's economic fortunes, a surface reading of this historical context suggests that the events of 1980 were merely the culmination of a series of previous attempts by workers to institute a more equitable distribution of economic rewards and establish some acceptable and effective measure of industrial democracy. As in any form of society, the failure to meet economic expectations and demands creates instability, social discontent, and, invariably it seems, a politically conservative response. So too in Poland; and the strikes, sit-ins, demonstrations, and riots of 1956, 1970, and 1976 were coercively suppressed—as was the student–intellectual protest of 1968. The proven inadequacy of previous reforms and the increasingly self-evident inability of the state economic managers to effect any positive reforms in the structure of central planning led to the conviction that the only solution lay in the independent articulation of worker interests. If the PUWP could not or would not represent worker interests, then Solidarity would.

Hence, according to this perspective, Solidarity was exactly what it said it was: an independent self-governing trade union. McShane, for example, while recognizing the problematic distinction which is often drawn between "trade union demands and political demands," could nevertheless insist that "the work of Solidarity is mainly devoted to defending and extending the well-being of its members, their families and the community in which they live" (McShane, 1981: 9–10). It is true that the initial response to the 1980 crisis seemed to be economistic in origin; the July strikes against the price increases produced compensatory pay awards. But within weeks the content of the demands began to expand in scope. At Lublin, for example, apart from the predictable pay demand, the strikers also demanded family allowance increases to bring them up to parity with the police and the militia, the end of press censorship and even a demand for trade unions "that would not take orders from above" (Ascherson, 1982: 131). These latter demands were traded in for the pay increase but clearly presaged the agenda which was to become the basis of the final agreement at Gdańsk. It is also true that the

Gdańsk dispute was triggered by a specific worker grievance—the victimization of Ann Walentynowicz—and only developed, seemingly opportunistically, into a *generalized* dispute about the whole range of grievances long felt by the Polish industrial proletariat. Indeed, nearly all the accounts of the "revolt of the incapacitated" at Gdańsk suggest that spontaneity as much as prescience determined the character of successive demands and the eventual outcome of negotiations. (See, for example, Staniszkis, 1981.) The extent to which the dramatic victory at Gdańsk surprised even the workers themselves is reflected in Jacek Kuroń's response when he heard about the government's agreement to an independent trade union: "It was impossible, in fact, I know it is impossible."

Even after the eventual registration of the new union, the leadership, and especially Wałęsa, continued to insist, albeit somewhat ingenuously, that the union did not seek to play a political role; it sought merely to represent worker interests to management, local authorities, and government. While no one—least of all the Poles themselves—could have been in any doubt as to the political significance of the Gdańsk strike, its objectives were consistently portrayed as being of the "trade union variety." And, at least in the first few months, there seemed to be some among the leadership who did think that some form of collaborative coexistence could be realized. However, as argued above, even a brief examination of the character of the power–dependence relationships (Keenoy, 1981) between Solidarity, the government, and the party illustrates the operational incompatibility between the logic of "free" trade union activity and the principles of monocratic bureaucracy which inform democratic centralist institutions.

A brief examination of the conventional role of trade unions in command economies demonstrates why it is analytically mistaken to see Solidarity as a form of trade unionism. There is a widespread measure of agreement in the literature on what Porket calls "the Soviet-type Communist political system" concerning the role and functions of trade unions in centrally planned economies. Despite the "exceptionalism" of Hungary and possibly Yugoslavia, Porket insists that virtually all these societies should be regarded as "variants of a single type" (Porket, 1978: 70). Since the fundamental structural cause of industrial conflicts, private property, had been eliminated, trade unions no longer have to fear or fight employer exploitation. Hence the relationship between workers and management was transformed from one which was fundamentally conflictural to one which is fundamentally cooperative. Such asumptions are the basis upon which the social legitimacy of "dual functionary" trade unionism had been constructed (see Chapter 1 above). The only legitimate managerial ideology is one which stresses what Fox (1966) has called the "unitary frame of reference" with regard to the employment relationship; trade unions become a critical support in the managerial process and to management authority, they subordinate themselves to the guiding role of the party, and have a role to play in ensuring that workers' rights under the complex legislation regulating the employment relationship are respected. Analytically, for Porket, this translates into three major trade union functions: the promotion of production and productivity; the political education of workers; and the (legal) defense of workers' interests. Subsequently, Ruble (1979), in a more sympathetic and analytically more incisive account, established the concept of dual functioning trade unionism to describe the essential features of this historical form of trade unionism. In particular, he, like Porket, clearly recognizes the apparently contradictory role placed upon trade unions—in that they are expected to reconcile the specific interests of the worker with the more general interests of society— and both point to the seemingly deleterious consequences this is likely to have for the energetic pursuit of specific worker interests. (See also Pravda and Ruble, Chapter 1, above.) Nonetheless, in the context of central planning, such trade unions are *necessarily* supportive of managerial objectives and the scope for autonomous collective bargaining is, given that priorities are determined centrally, also necessarily of a very limited nature.

In contrast, sociopolitical factors lie behind the movement for independent allocation of function and authority within the employment relationship. As such, its success could only be measured by the extent to which the other parallel institutions were also radically transformed. Given the "normal" dual functioning character of trade unions in centrally planned economies and the distinctly compliant relationship of management and the party, it would be analytically naive to conclude that Solidarity merely represented an attempt to create a more effective form of worker representation. To have accorded Solidarity any genuine social legitimacy within the existing societal power structure would have required the government to relinquish the principle of democratic centralism and, in all probability, also abandon any prospect of ever maintaining a genuine commitment to central planning. Thus, insofar as the conventional models of trade unions in the Soviet bloc are of any use, they would suggest that solidarity be regarded as an "anti-trade union" in that it sought to reverse the "normal" pattern of authority. The trade union was to police management, not the workers; and the powers of the central planners were to be severely constrained through "self-management" by an institutionalist structure of workers' control.

This is one of the primary reasons why Solidarity cannot be regarded as a trade union—at best, it could be analyzed as a unique form of revolutionary trade unionism (Hyman, 1971; Ridley, 1970). In this context Solidarity was the leading edge of a political revolution and the institutional expression of a mass social movement which, perhaps out of ideological necessity, called itself a trade union and, insofar as its organizational characteristics took a

Acknowledgments

I would like to thank Bogden Szajkowski not only for providing many of the documentary sources used in this discussion but also for translating many of them.

References

Ascherson, Neal (1981), *The Polish August* (Harmonsworth: Penguin).

Blazyca, George (1982) "The Degeneration of Central Planning in Poland," in Woodall (1982), pp. 99–127.

Blazyca, George (1983), *Planning is Good for You* (London: Pluto Press)

Crouch, C. (1982), *Trade Unions: The Logic of Collective Action* (London: Fontana).

Davies, Norman (1981), *God's Playground: A History of Poland* Vol. II (Oxford: Oxford University Press).

Drewnowski, Jan (1982) (ed.), *The Crisis in East European Economies: The Spread of the Polish Disease* (London: Croom Helm).

Fox, Alan (1966), *Industrial Sociology and Industrial Relations*, Research Paper No. 3, Royal Commission on Trade Unions and Employers' Associations (London: HMSO).

Hyman, Richard (1971), *Marxism and the Sociology of Trade Unionism* (London: Pluto Press).

Keenoy, Tom (1981), "The Employment Relationship as a form of Socio-Economic Exchange," in G. Dluglos and K. Weiemair (eds.), *Management Under Different Value Systems* Berlin: Walter de Gruyter).

Keenoy, Tom (1982), "The Organisational Structure of 'Solidarity': Some Observations," in B. Szajkowski (ed.), *Documents in Communist Affairs 1981* (London: Butterworth).

Kolankiewicz, G. (1982), "Employee Self-Management and Socialist Trade Unionism," in Woodall (1982), pp. 129–147.

McShane, Denis (1981), *Solidarity: Poland's Independent Trade Union* (Nottingham: Spokesman).

Merton, R. K. (1952), "Bureaucratic Structure and Personality," in Merton *et al* (1952), pp. 361–371.

Merton, R.K., Gray, A., Hockey, B., and Selvin, H. C. (1952), *Reader in Bureaucracy* (Glencoe, Ill.: The Free Press).

Network (1981), *Position on Social and Economic Reform of the Country* (Gdansk: Solidarity).

Nove, Alec (1983), *The Economics of Feasible Socialism* (London: Allen & Unwin).

Nuti, D. M. (1981), "The Polish Crisis: Economic Factors and Constraints," *Socialist Register* (London: New Left Books).

Porket, J. L. (1978), "Industrial Relations and Participation in Management in the Soviet-Type Communist System," *British Journal of Industrial Relations*, vol. 16, no. 1 (March), pp. 70–85.

Raina, Peter (1981), *Independent Social Movements in Poland* (London: LSE/Orbis Books).

Ridley, F. F. (1970), *Revolutionary Syndicalism in France* (Cambridge: Cambridge University Press).

Romaszewski, Z. (1983), "August 1980–December 1981: What Next?" *Communist Affairs*, vol.2, no.1, p. 91–104.

Ruble, B. A. (1979), "Dual Functionng Trade Unions in the USSR," *British Journal of Industrial Relations*, vol. 17, no. 2 (July), pp. 235–241.

Shapiro, Ian (1981), "Fiscal Crisis of the Polish State: Genesis of the 1980 Strikes," *Theory and Society,* vol. 10, no. 4 (July) pp. 469–502.

Singer, Daniel (1982), *The Road to Gdansk* (New York: Monthly Review Press).

Staniszkis, J. (1981), "The Evolution of Forms of Working-Class Protest in Poland: Socioloical Reflections on the Gdansk-Szczecin Case, August 1980," *Soviet Studies,* vol. 33, no. 2 (April), pp. 213–14.

Szajkowski, B. (1982) (ed.), *Documents in Communist Affairs—1981* (London: Butterworth).

Szajkowski, B. (1983), *Next to God ... Poland* (London: Frances Pinter).

Touraine, Alain, Dubet, F., Wieviorka, M. and Strzelecki, J. (1983), *Solidarity* (Cambridge: Cambridge University Press).

Woodall, Jan (1982) (ed.), *Policy and Politics in Contemporary Poland: Reform, Failure, Crisis 1970–1981* (London: Frances Pinter).

8

Trade Unions and Workers' Interests in Hungary

István Kemény

Historical Background

The Hungarian industrial working class evolved in the course of the development of capitalism in the second half of the nineteenth century and the early years of the twentieth. In 1880 there were 110,000 workers in factories and 400,000 employed in small-scale industry; by 1910 these groups had grown to 510,000 and 490,000 respectively. The country's level of industrial development was considerably lower than in Western Europe, but substantially higher than in Russia. The same was true of trade union development. In 1907 the 130,000 unionized workers came mostly from the skilled groups which made up 70 percent of the industrial labor force in 1910. The number of those who took part in strikes fluctuated between 20,000 and 40,000 per annum just before World War I (the annual number of strikes fluctuated between 130 and 260 from 1910 to 1913). Most of the unionized work force were members of the Social Democratic Party which advocated the nationalization of the means of production.

World War I saw a strengthening of the workers' movement. By the end of 1917 there were more than 200,000 organized workers, by the end of 1918 their ranks had tripled to over 700,000. The losses of territory brought by the Treaty of Trianon meant a halving of the population (from 18.3 million to 7.8 million) and a more drastic fall still in the number of industrial workers which dropped from 1 million to 400,000. In the 1930s one in four of these workers belonged to trade unions and strikes were frequent. The Great

István Kemény, Centre de Sociologie Historique, École des Hautes Etudes en Sciences Sociales, Paris, France.

Depression brought a setback in the union movement which lasted through the 1930s. Nevertheless, immediately prior to the German invasion of Hungary in March 1944 the unions grouped 100,000 workers.

In 1945, in the wake of the victory of the Soviet army, a united trade union movement was formed with Communist and Social Democrat participation. All union offices, from the lowest to the highest, were divided up between the two workers' parties on a parity basis. Up to 1948 there was bitter infighting between the two parties, despite slogans proclaiming unity. The majority of those who had longstanding ties with the organized workers' movement supported the Social Democrats, while newcomers and younger workers tended toward the Communists. In 1945, in the first and last free postwar elections, the Communist Party won 17 percent of the vote, with the Social Democrats taking 15 percent.

It was in 1946 that the Communist Party first came out with a slogan calling for the fusion of the two parties and in the summer of 1947 it launched a merger campaign. Up to February 1948 this met with strong and unanimous rejection from the Social Democrat side, but the Communists managed to overcome such resistance by using methods amounting to a *coup d'état*. To start with they expelled from the party every single Social Democratic leader of international standing; they then had them arrested and sentenced. The same treatment was meted out to middle-rank officials; altogether 1,000 Social Democrats were imprisoned. After the formal merger, 300,000 Social Democrats were expelled from the new united party. Within the trade unions Communists started off with a 2:1 advantage over Social Democrats in official posts. Gradually they eased out all former Social Democrats from union office in the course of a humiliating campaign of harassment throughout industry.

After the war, Hungary suffered from unprecedented inflation. This was halted by the stabilization of 1946, when salaries were at 50 percent of their 1938 level. During the period up till 1948–1949 prices rose by 67 percent, and nominal salaries kept pace. In 1953, owing to the rapid rise of the consumer price index, real wages were no more than 79 percent of their 1949 value. During the same period industry throughout the country adopted the system of production norms, which increased faster than the salaries. Consequently, real wages showed a downward trend. Furthermore, a deterioration in the quality of consumer goods coincided with the shortage in food products and a halt in housing construction. The standard of living of the older workers (and of former craftsmen who had become skilled factory workers) declined considerably.

As the number of workers was actually growing rapidly, this drop in the level of real wages and in the standard of living would have been impossible had workers not been prohibited from changing jobs or avoiding a work contract, even if they considered the wages they were being offered by no means satisfactory.

A jobless worker was in fact liable to charges of vagrancy. At all events, it was impossible to change one's place of work; the new employer was under an obligation to refuse to employ anyone who had not received permission to change jobs from his previous employer—this authorization being registered in his work record book. With the disappearance of the labor market, salary negotiations became impossible. And finally, any organized struggle for the safeguarding of class interests was quashed. Although trade union representatives were in theory elected, in practice they were appointed. The trade unions, no longer able to protect the interests of their members apart from ensuring that they paid their union dues, had no other task than to mobilize the workers in support of Communist Party policy and increased production rates. Even the workers' cultural and sports organizations were disbanded or reorganized and placed under party control. In order to stifle the deep discontent that prevailed, the authorities sentenced to concentration camps or to hard labor not only those who dared to protest openly but also those who let slip the slightest disparaging remark, even in intimate circles. There was hardly a workers' family in Hungary which did not have at least one member who had been subjected to police harassment.

1956 and After

During the 1956 revolution, workers' councils took over the running of the factories. Efforts were made to establish independent trade unions. On November 4 Soviet troups intervened, and after bloody fighting, shattered the armed resistance. But the workers' councils continued to function, and the deputies from the workers' councils of the Budapest factories formed the workers' council of Budapest, which soon became the representative organ of all workers' councils in the country. As soon as government power had been reconsolidated with the aid of the army, the workers' councils were dissolved. The trade unions were reassigned their former insignificant role, and a ban was placed on all labor organizations that did not come under direct party rule and political police control.

Between November 1956 and the end of 1958, according to some estimates, between 20,000 and 25,000 people received prison sentences. (This number does not include those arrested for a couple of days or weeks.) A further 2,000 people were sentenced to death and executed. The overwhelming majority of those given the death penalty and executed were workers. Tens of thousands of workers left Hungary between November 1956 and January 1957. The organized labor movement was simply decapitated; any assertive workers were intimidated or beaten up by the "workers' militia" or the police.

All the same, some concessions were also made in order to "normalize" the situation. Although they had no institutional underpinning, the concessions marked a compromise between the new regime and manual labor. On the one hand, the new regime was to have a monopoly of all decision-making. It would not allow any organized struggle for the protection of economic interests, nor any organization or league formed by the workers themselves. On the other hand, the authorities undertook to ensure the provision of wages higher than those gained before the disturbances. They promised to provide a far larger supply of consumer goods than was available in the other communist states. Finally, they agreed not to penalize those involved in unofficial demonstrations of solidarity; this meant it would be possible for pressure groups to emerge, albeit within a restricted framework.

In the factories—at shop-floor level—those now in charge would take account of individual qualifications and productivity. As a result of this clause, and through the influence of unofficial solidarity, the highest skilled workers in all factories began to gain influence. At the same time the "petty aristocracy" of the workers—the local party functionaries and officials from the youth and trade union organizations—began to lose ground, even though they continued to play a part in the period that followed.

In the 1960s combining extensive industrialization with technological progress proved untenable. For by the mid-1960s the rural areas had ceased to be overpopulated, and the sources of available unskilled manual labor were drying up locally. So, while between 1949 and 1960 the number of workers in industry grew by 100 percent, between 1960 and 1970 it rose only by a third. And this increase was confined entirely to the first half of the 1960s; by the mid-1960s the industrial labor force had stopped expanding. Hungary had become an industrial society and was now on the path leading to a post-industrial society. The proportion of rural workers in industry had dwindled to a quarter of the total workforce, while the ranks of salaried employees had grown to almost the same level.

In order to maintain the growth in industrial production it became necessary to stake everything on the development of technology and to switch from extensive to intensive industrialization; no longer was it possible to rely on an increase in the number of manual laborers. Economic reform was given an impulse by a widespread shortage of goods, by mounting stock-piles of very low quality and unsaleable merchandise, by the inability to export, and by a disequilibrium in the balance of payments. However, the decisive reason for this reorientation of economic strategy was that industry was unable to function in conditions of labor shortage.

The preparation for the reform began in 1964 and continued for three years. Discussions and suggestions were not published, but some experts participated in them who did not belong to the establishment or belonged only to its outer reaches. It was suggested, for example, that trade unions become organizations for protecting workers' interests and that the right to strike be guaranteed by law. These proposals also received support from some members of the establishment. The reform introduced on January 1, 1968 was a compromise; the possiblity of carrying it further was left open. Had the international and domestic balance of forces remained unchanged, it probably would have been taken further. But the Warsaw Pact intervention and the subsequent "normalization" of Czechoslovakia put an end to such expectations. As for safeguarding workers' interests, only one concession was made: the right of veto, which is discussed later.

The most important reform measure, as far as the workers were concerned, was the lifting in 1968 of various sanctions against workers who changed their jobs. This measure transformed the position on the labor market of workers in general and of the skilled in particular. Although still unable to make demands, workers were now able to quit their jobs, and some did not pass up the opportunity to do so. Management thus came to realize that these workers were indispensable to factory production; wage increases were therefore granted. As a result, the reform led to a rapid and considerable increase in the real wages of skilled workers, and likewise to an improvement in the wages and the standard of living of the other strata of workers.

Subsistence, Pay, and Income

Hungarian workers can be divided into four main categories on the basis of their wages and income. The first category includes those who are satisfied with their basic wage, which they can earn at the factory without overtime. This basic wage amounts to a monthly average of between 2,000 and 4,000 forints. Most of the unmarried young are to be found in this category. As a rule, young workers marry before the age of 24, shortly after completing their national service; after marriage, they try to earn more and work more, especially after the birth of their first child. This category also includes most unmarried women, as well as the majority of married women living with their husband and children in Budapest or any of the major provincial cities. In fact, married women with children cannot, for family reasons, take on overtime work. (Women make up 60 percent of semiskilled and 16.5 percent of skilled workers.)

Workers in the second category will not accept any overtime, but they do supplement their basic income with seasonal work in farm cooperatives or by working on private projects. One worker in five has a member of his family working in a cooperative; two thirds of worker families have plots of their own; among workers living in the country, this ratio is a high as four fifths. Work on the smallholdings (on average 20−25 hours per week per family) is done either after the day's work at the factory, at the weekend, or during paid or sick leave. Many industrial and construction workers, however, alternate their industrial work with seasonal farmwork by getting themselves hired for a few weeks or even months by agricultural cooperatives, often with the permission of factory mangers. While such seasonal farmwork brings in more money over a shorter period of time, factory work sees them through the winter months. Were it not for this form of alternating work, Hungarian agriculture would come to a standstill. It is these same workers who undertake the toughest jobs in industry.

Workers in the third category do not take on overtime; instead, they supplement their wages by doing general handyman jobs, helping craftsmen on piecework, or working on the black market. Their total wages from the factory and from their side-jobs range between 5,000 and 8,000 forints, even more in exceptional cases, but to earn this they have to work 10 to 12 hours a day and often weekends as well.

The fourth category includes workers who regularly take on overtime and who work 12 hours a day. Overtime thus represents a common interest for factory management and worker. The only way the factory can hold on to its best qualified workers is by providing them with correspondingly good wages; but not even with a top-scale wage are they able to earn over 4,000 forints for an 8-hour day. With normal overtime, and double time on Sundays, such workers can earn up to 8,000 forints, occasionally more.

To summarize: a sizeable majority of young workers, a large proportion of female workers, and about one-tenth of married workers earn an average of 3,000-4,000 forints for a 44-hour week; a considerable number of women and the great majority of married men work a 72-hour week and earn well above the average income.

Trade Unions and Organizations for Defending Workers' Interests in Hungarian Factories

The statutes of the Hungarian trade unions, as revised at their twenty-fourth congress in December 1980, sum up the aims and functions of Hungarian trade unions in a page and a half. The following are key passages in the order in which they appear:

> The Hungarian trade unions are mass organizations of the working class in power . . . They function . . . under the ideological and political guidance of the

Hungarian Socialist Workers' Party . . . they convey the policy of the party . . . they help the building of socialist society. They strengthen the power, unity, and leading role of the working class. They organize and mobilize the workers to increase the political and economic power of the working class . . . Through their educational, instructive, and organizational activity they contribute to . . . the shaping of socialist man. They educate the workers in the spirit of socialist patriotism and proletarian internationalism. As organizations for defending workers' interests, they represent and safeguard the interests of their members, the workers, in accordance with regard to the interests of society.

I have quoted eight objectives, and only one of them—the last—concerns the defense of workers' interests. It would be to no avail, however, to draw any firm conclusions from these sentences or from the order in which they appear. Actual practice may meet the objectives laid down in the statutes, or may differ from them.

All Hungarian firms have a three-layer structure. At all levels there are three organizations operating parallel to one another: the firm management, the party, and the trade union. The Hungarian literature often uses the phrase "firm triangle" to refer to this situation; at the firm level, this means the director of the firm, the secretary of the firm party committee, and the secretary of the trade union committee of the firm. The management hierarchy is as follows: fifteen to thirty workers are supervised by a foreman, three to five foremen by a works manager, two or three works managers by a managing director, and the managing directors by the company manager. Alongside the foremen there are trade union and party stewards; works managers and the managing directors have works and company trade union committee counterparts.

The 1968 Labor Code includes an article giving unions a right of veto:

As a more efficient means of defending the workers' interest the Labor Code has introduced a new right, investing the firm trade union organ with the power to raise objections when in its opinion a measure taken by the economic management violates the regulations on labor relations or does not conform to the agreement concluded with the trade union. Firm trade union organs may also raise objections to any decisions taken by the management in the field of labor relations that are incompatible with socialist morality.

From the organizational structure I have outlined and from the above-mentioned right of veto of the trade unions, the reader might conclude that if the trade union committee raises objections, the measure in dispute cannot be implemented until higher managerial and trade union authorities reach agreement on the question and give their joint verdict. If we examine how things work in practice, however, we find that this is a premature conclusion. By looking at the results of concrete investigations, I shall endeavor to indicate the real place trade unions occupy in defending workers' interests on the one hand, and how workers fight to safeguard their interests on the other.

Informal Groups and Industrial Relations in the Enterprise: Case Studies

One of these investigations was described by Lajos Héthy and Csaba Makó (1972). They conducted their investigation in one of the biggest factories in Hungary, the Raba Works. Among other things, they studied the fitters working on the construction of railway freight cars. At the time the investigation was made, two kinds of freight cars were manufactured in the factory unit; on one the workers earned good money, while on the other they earned little. In February and March, 1968 the firm management decided that 80 percent of production would consist of the manufacturing of the nonprofitable cars, as a result of which the earnings of the fitters fell catastrophically. At the same time, overtime was halved. In April, they started manufacturing the freight cars that paid well, but no extra overtime or special bonus was allowed. The workers decided that they would deliberately reduce their output from the usual 105−6 percent to 77 percent. As a result of this action they suffered considerable financial loss, as they received very little in wages, but at the same time they "torpedoed" production—to use an expression in common use in Hungary. As a result of the "sinking" not only the railway car manufacturing unit but the whole firm found itself in very serious trouble. In May, the firm management gave in: the overtime allocation was raised and considerable special bonuses were set. The workers' output increased from 77 percent to 132 percent of set norms. In the following months production continued to increase, reaching 154 percent in September. At the same time, the workers also put in a monthly 80 to 100 hours overtime, and their monthly earnings thus increased to approximately triple the average manual wage packet. In October and November, however, they reduced their output to 107 percent, because they had learned through their contacts that all those whose output surpassed 108 percent in these two months would have their norm raised in January 1969. They used the same ruse to avoid being affected by another norm hike in April 1969.

Taking all this into consideration Héthy and Makó conclude (1972: 116, 123)

> The production and wage tactics of the fitters were perfect of their kind; both the offensive and defensive forces were highly developed and conformed with one another. The degree of organization and coordination which was necessary for this was ensured by a highly developed, uniform informal organization . . . The division of functions is also manifest within this organization; there are

leaders who coordinate and direct the activities of the members of the organization and there are persons who are led. There are relations of subordination and superordination, and the acts and behavior of the men are specified by rules. Information flows through specific channels, and the mechanism of decisions is also strictly defined. The informal organization even has its own controlling mechanism; it can reward or penalize the actions of the members. In a word, it is an organization within the organization and even within the organizations.

By various methods the authors also discovered who had directed the fight for the defense of interests and how they had done so (pp. 124–5).

A restricted collective body came into being: "the Six." All were hardworking men, who excelled in their work. The most important among them was a quiet and reserved worker, who never intervened in discussions with the managers but always remained composed and tried to arrange things in such a way that it would be relatively beneficial for all workers . . . but also for the factory management. He had a real gift for "compromises" . . . Two other members of "the Six" were similarly inclined to compromise. The fourth and the fifth members were considered the best even among the excellent workers, they were thought "even to think too much of what they know" but otherwise "good lads." They were the ones who would "bang their fists on the table." They had heated debates with the management, and "when they cut up rough, they would not give and inch." The sixth member was also an interesting person, the workers called him "the great philosopher." When there were problems, the managing directors always thought to have reached an agreement with him, and only when he had left the office did the foremen realize that he had not yielded an inch and things were exactly as they had been.

Héthy and Makó also examined the rules prevailing in the informal organization. They conclude that the workers worded these rules like slogans, in simple sentences. As far as solidarity was concerned: "one for all, all for one," "principles and wages can only be defended collectively, individually they can only be defeated." With regard to production: "We work a lot, and hard, but only if there's a reason," "Man is not like a machine," "There's no sense in going at full speed; it's pointless for me to do 40 percent over the norm today if they take it all off my wages tomorrow." "You shouldn't act hastily. You should think twice before raising a hammer." "If somebody overdoes it pointlessly, it's because he wants to impress the boss, and we don't like that." "Those who want to break the work norms in every way they can are the migrant type; they skim off what cream there is and then move on, leaving the others in the thick of it." It was also a rule that only "reliable" persons were let into the secrets and tricks of the fitter's trade. The informal organization of the fitters ostracized and pushed out of the team any workers who violated its rules.

Héthy and Makó also call attention to the prudent flexibility of the rules. For instance (pp. 126–7), a worker had been "picked out" by the managing directors who showered him with financial and other bonuses. Yet the informal organization did not cast him out, but put him in a harmless position, since they were fully aware of the value of the information with which the worker in question was able to provide them from management and party sources. There came a moment when the managing directors realized that the workers could handle their man better than they could themselves.

From this case, Héthy and Makó draw the conclusion that "the power of the workers was able to rival the company management ... It was said about the six-men collective leadership of the fitters in the factory: 'If those six set out, everybody goes after them. But if those six stop, everybody stops.' "

What was the role of the trade union in this fight for the workers' interests? Héthy and Makó say (pp. 180−2):

> It was precisely in the question which affected the workers the most closely, that is, the question of output and wages, that the trade union was unable to obtain any say. Formally it had the right, but not the power, to obtain a say, since the balance of power between the management and the trade union had become upset in favor of the former .... The firm trade union committee accepted the arguments of the firm management in favour of raising the norm.

Héthy and Makó explain this attitude of the trade union committee— which disregarded the workers' interests—by the fact that the secretarial post of the firm trade union committee was occupied by a foreman, and the presidential post by a works manager, and three of the members were administrative employees. "The trouble is that the trade union leaders are also paid by the factory," the workers said. Every year, the trade union leaders submitted the list of their officials to the firm management, so that the latter might, within the legal limits, recompense their voluntary activities financially, which the firm in fact did. Certain foremen used their trade union job as a stepping stone to higher management posts. The higher functionaries of the trade union were full-time officials in theory, but according to the collective agreement they received a share from the profits in a similar way to the management of the firm. Thus it is no wonder that the workers gave Héthy and Makó a very bad opinion of the activities of the trade union. For example: "Here the trade union is only a name, it is equal to zero," or "The firm and the trade union work hand-in-glove" (pp. 174, 176−7, 178−80).

Somewhat later Héthy and Makó conducted a similar study at a Budapest building firm, focusing on groups of workers including maintenance electricians. These electricians worked individually or in groups of two or three at more than twenty building sites. In spite of being scattered over so many sites they stayed in close contact with one another. Because of their key positions they earned very high wages, and with overtime made two or even three times as much as the average worker. In 1970 a new company manager was appointed, who abolished overtime, thus reducing the electricians' high wages to the average manual level. The secretary of the firm trade union committee tried to persuade the workers to accept the firm manager's policy. The electricians tried to win over their foremen and the building engineers, but without success. They therefore resorted to force. One of their actions fused an entire electric circuit which they had put down in overtime. In 1971 new machines were connected to the network. The electricians refused to make the necessary alterations, as they were only willing to do this in overtime. When the whole circuit fused, the firm immediately began to pay them overtime.

The electricians usually resorted to the same action; they worked to rule and observed all regulations to the letter.

> When for instance an electrician had his overtime suspended, he immediately went out and looked round. He reported that one of the cranes was working with a cable of over regulation length. He warned the building engineer, telling him that if they did not bury the cable it would be his duty to switch off the crane. The building engineer shrugged his shoulders, telling him not to be silly, because the crane had been working like that for two years. Two days later the electrician switched it off. There was a scandal, then bargaining began. When the man got the money he thought was acceptable, "normal service" was restored.

The differences over the overtime led to a conference in which all the interested parties took part, including the electricians' delegates. There the electricians succeeded in carrying their point as a result of the kind of actions which have been described (Héthy and Makó,1972: 12−13; Héthy, 1978).

In the late 1970s in the above-mentioned Györ Raba Works Károly Fazekas (1981, 1982) conducted an extensive investigation. Fazekas states that in the course of twelve years the Raba Works had grown six- or sevenfold by gradually absorbing several provincial factories and premises. One of the main reasons for the expansion was labor shortage. The firm lost most of its original workforce, and since Györ had run out of labor reserves, the Raba management tried to solve its problems by expanding. They also attempted to tackle the labor shortage by extending the system of individual piece-wages, or as the workers say, the "output press." Thus, for instance, the individual piece-wage system was introduced in the tool workshop. Immediately, the workers' output started to rise, as did their wages, until the workers had gained an increase of 2 forints per hour. Then output growth suddenly stopped; from then on the workers put in for their individual hourly wages plus the 2 forints. The reason for this was that the workers had learned that the manager of the Raba Works had envisaged a 2-forint wage rise to meet his plan; they had also understood that if they went on increasing their output, the norms would be raised. Therefore they stopped. All this was possible because all the workers in the tool-making unit were skilled metal-workers, all were expert at their job, and all knew the rules of the wage struggle in the factory and therefore regulated their output collectively and very strictly. Output rose again, but still only temporarily. Once again the workers knew how far they could go. The piece-wages have been stable ever since, yet it is difficult to imagine how somebody does precisely the same amount of work every month. What happens when, for one reason or another, he produces much more? In that case the workers do not put in the extra wage tickets, but, when they have a chance to do so, they carry them over to the next month or give them to those who have not managed the necessary output levels. And if they really cannot do anything with some of the tickets, they prefer to tear them up than use them.

What determines the weight of an individual worker in this collective system of hierarchy and solidarity? His competence, experience, ability, diligence, and two more very important factors: his own tools and his relations with others in the workshop. Thus, as we have seen, in the tool workshop the introduction of piece-wages did not bring the results the manager of the Raba Works had expected, but at least it did not cause any serious trouble.

However, Fazekas found things were different in the motor factory. In this unit the majority of the workers were not skilled but semiskilled workers, or workers who were not qualified as metalworkers. The products were manufactured on machines working in a closed cycle, and thus individual skills did not play a significant part. In such workshops there was no sense in introducing the piece-wage system. Yet the general manager insisted on doing so, hoping that by increasing output it would be possible to reduce the labor shortage. The method consisted of each worker having to work at several posts, for instance, operating several machines simultaneously.

In fact some of the workers raised their output. Others, the old skilled workers, gradually left, and the Raba Works lost them forever. Lastly, an increasing number of workers simply idled or worked badly. Instead of diminishing, the labor shortage increased, the number of manual workers of the factory gradually dwindled, and the quality of the products deteriorated considerably.

Owing to similar measures and to other causes, labor discipline declined not only in the motor factory but in the entire Raba Works. This fact led in late 1978 to a measure which is still being talked about in Hungary. The general manager dismissed 900 workers and refused to employ any worker who had not applied through the compulsory labor exchange channels. The trade union committee naturally supported his decision, just as it had supported the extension of the piece-wage system. The labor situation of the factory did not improve, however, and the general manger was compelled to life the ban on employment. Neither the expansion, nor the piece-wage system, nor the dismissals had solved the problems of the company.

Janos Kollő, examined the situation of wages and interests in a textile factory in a large provincial town (Kollő, 1981, 1982). His studies give a survey of the history of the Hungarian cotton industry, in which he distinguishes three periods: a period of excess labor, one of transition, and one of labor shortage. To some extent even in the period of transition, but more notably in that of labor shortage, the managers of the cotton mills have tried to solve emerging problems by increasing the labor intensity.

The trade unions, which, according to their statutes should defend the workers' interests "in accordance with the interests of society," naturally supported the managers' endeavors. In the cotton mill where Kollő conducted his investigation, however, most workers also accepted the rules of the "output press." All those women workers who were bringing up their child on their own, who had parents to support, whose husbands had small salaries, or who were young and saving for a flat or a house, were obliged to do so. The only workers who did not play the game where those who could afford not to do so; older women who had already brought up their children, women whose husbands had a good salary or who could benefit from the parallel economy.

No solidarity developed in this cotton mill and wage-bargaining was not carried out collectively. No collective strategy could develop because the weavers lacked the means of power necessary for it: skill, experience, and their own tools.

(The above studies partly confirm and partly modify the conclusions which I drew from my own research between 1969 and 1972, reported in my book *Magyar Munkások* (Hungarian Workers), written in 1972−1973 and distributed in Hungary in manuscript.)[1]

---

[1]In 1974 I studied the situation at the assembly-line of the motor cycle unit of the Csepel Works. The hourly wages of the workers of the assembly line moved between 9.60 and 14.10 forints in that year. With these wages the factory would not have been able to keep its old, highly skilled workers. Thus, the so-called "overtime team" became the pivot of the work process: with 120 to 180 hours of overtime a month, its members were able to earn 4,000 to 6,000 forints a month. This team consisted of workers of very great experience, who were experts in all phases of the assembling process and were able to deputize for anybody at any time. These "short-notice replacements" were always "undertakings" on the part of these workers, the price of which they settled by bargaining. The members of the overtime team were the ones who could mend the motor, so that despite the strict hierarchy, not only were workers not at the mercy of manage-

In every factory there is an elite. It is composed of the most intelligent workers, those with the highest qualifications, who through their personal relations and their long experience are also familiar with the entire life of the factory. Their knowledge of how the factory operates is not merely technical, it is also human; they are well acquainted with interpersonal relations in the factory, at both worker and management level.

The trade union does not embody the workers' cause; but the workers, guided by their own elite, do succeed in following through constant collective action for the protection of their interests, an action that may take two distinct forms.

In one type of factory, the technical preconditions are such that the workers have to divide into groups of five to seven members, as production is the result of their collective work. In such communities relations of subordination do exist, and certain members are even exploited by others. At the head of the group one person is always to be found; if not officially appointed to the position of leadership, he will find himself spontaneously placed there. He dictates the pace of work, designates jobs, and at the same time assumes the role of spokesman for the group. Any action for the defense of interests is collective; the whole group stops work, if necessary, and if there is a complaint to be lodged, the entire group follows the spokesman.

In the other kind of factory, each worker is required to perform individual work; there are no opportunities for organizing collective action of the type mentioned above, and this is a source of constant complaint from many of the skilled workers. In such circumstances, the spontaneous organization of workers will nevertheless occur, but in a different form, no longer limited to groups, but incorporating all workers in a section who have the same qualifications and the same kind of job. They all act according to the advice of their elite, or, more exactly, in pursuit of the traditions established by this elite. It is therefore no longer a community but an association of individuals engaged on equal terms.

In addition to the spontaneously chosen elite in the factories, there exists another elite comprising workers protected by the management. Such workers can afford more frequent breaches of discipline, and they also have

---

ment, but the relationship of dependency was rather the reverse. One condition of the balance of power which thus developed was the solidarity between the members of the overtime brigade. But they could only defend the interests of their own, smaller, community, and not those of all the assembly-line workers. In 1974 the workers on the line were promised a 2-forints rise in their hourly wages for the last two weeks of the first half-year if they met the half-year plan. The plan was met, but they did not get the 2 forints rise. A wildcat strike broke out. The works manager, who was at the same time the trade union steward, thwarted the strike by warning the workers of the grave consequences to be expected. See my essay "La chaine dans une usine hongroise," *Acte de la récherche en sciences sociales,* no. 24 (November, 1978), pp. 62–77.

access to the best-paid jobs. Generally, they earn more than the members of the other elite; nevertheless, they are not directly cold-shouldered by the collective. Likewise, where political issues are involved, it is the opinions of the spontaneously chosen elite that carry authority.

The factory, then, is in fact governed by two powers—the management and the spontaneously formed elite—both of which seem to carry equal weight.

The collective actions undertaken by these spontaneous organizations serve to bring the workers together, and this unity always lies behind their more or less powerful sense of solidarity. This feeling of togetherness, however, does not preclude personal differences or the often underhand settling of old scores, nor does it prevent a certain brutality in human relations.

This is why workers, when questioned, say they would like to have a more powerful organization, one which would transcend the stage of spontaneous association. In any case they consider solidarity as a value to be as or even more important than work and productivity.

Whether the workers are in a power position or are defenseless, it is they alone who can defend their interests, independently of the trade unions. If the trade unions play any part at all in safeguarding workers' interests, this consists of supporting the factory management, or of taking the side of one or the other party in the faction fights between leaders which are so frequent in Hungarian factories.

All this does not mean that the trade union stewards never take any part in the fight for workers' interests. I could quote many cases when the trade union steward was a member of the workers' highly developed informal solidarity organization—not in his capacity as trade union steward, however, but as one of the workers. I also know of cases when the workers, as part of their collective strategy, were able to have the person of their choice appointed trade union steward. When this happened, it usually did so in a roundabout way. In Hungarian factories the trade union stewards are elected from a list of candidates drawn up by the party committee and the administrative management of the factory, as a result of which those appointed are elected in a seemingly democratic way by the workers. Often the workers familiar with the clash of interests in the factory fights manage, in very complicated ways, to get candidates of their choice included in the lists. Following the temporary victory of Solidarity at the end of August 1980, in a few Hungarian institutions in the course of elections the workers openly rejected the person appointed by management and elected trade union stewards in a truly democratic fashion, and even got the approval of higher trade union organs for this.

Indirect proof of the above may be found in the programme for union reform proposed in issue nos 5-6 of the samizdat opposition review *Beszélő* :

The system of the defense of interests needs thoroughgoing reform. It is the reform of the lower—basic—levels of the trade union hierarchy which seems to be the most urgent.

It would be the task of the National Council of Trade Unions to draw up new organizational statutes which would ensure that trade union officials at workplace level really be responsible to those who have elected them. A few basic principles might be the following:

—All officials are to be elected by secret ballot, there should be no preliminary lists. Only the electors would be able to recall those who have been elected, higher trade union organs could only propose their removal.

—When their mandate has expired, the full-time officials should return to their original job. Only with the approval—by secret vote—of the electors can they be appointed to the apparatus of a social organ or to a more advantageous job at their place of work.

—The higher trade union organs can give advice, make proposals, and inform the officials at the workplaces but not instruct them.

What is the most superfluous thing in the world? The trade union—according to a well-known Hungarian joke. How idle the whole enormous apparatus seems from the workers' point of view is well illustrated by the collective agreements. These are concluded in Hungary too, just as in countries where there are real trade unions. In 1969 I made a representative study among the workers of Pest County, and among the questions there were some concerning the collective agreements. In the largest and most developed county in Hungary, 31 percent of the skilled workers, 46 percent of the semiskilled workers, and 48 percent of the unskilled workers had no knowledge of the fact that a collective agreement had been concluded in their factory. It is even more typical, however, that immediately before my investigation the collective agreements had been expanded to include a few apparently important provisions, for example, the right of veto of the trade unions. Seventy-five percent of the skilled workers and 88 percent of the semi- and unskilled workers knew nothing about these new provisions.

Trade Unions and Workers' Interests at a National Level

There is something else that supports the hypothesis of a corporatist model; the fact that it comes about not at a firm but at a national level. A few words of the speech made by Sándor Gáspár, the Secretary General of the Hungarian trade unions at the twenty-fourth national union congress on December 12−14, 1980, seemingly confirm the existence of such a possibility (XXIV Congress, 1981: 15, 18−20):

Nowadays, in no essential question concerning the life and work conditions of the working people of the development of society in general can decisions be made without the trade unions. . . . In our country, the trade union movement does its work autonomously but not independently. Should some decisions of a state or economic organ curtail the workers' interests . . . firm measures shall be taken. . . . We must do our best in order that the individual and strata interests should find their expression at the democratic forums and get solved in harmony with the interests of the society. As a consequence, within the activity of the trade unions for the defense of interests, the competent evaluation of interests and their satisfaction through reasonable compromise will now come to the fore.

These words lose much of their value if we think of the fact that they were uttered in December, 1980, after the victory of Solidarity in Poland. Let us, however, suppose that the Secretary General of the Hungarian Trade Unions Council represents the workers' interests in the Political Committee of the party—of which he is a member—and that in that committee the interests of the party, the state, and the workers are coordinated. We may examine such a possibility in connection with the decisive change which the 1968 reform brought in the Hungarian workers' life. Emboldened by the invasion of Czechoslovakia, the Hungarian party apparatus started its counterattack in 1969, but was unable to develop it fully. Between 1969 and 1971 it sounded out the Soviet leaders.

From 1969 on the apparatus primarily demanded the prohibition of the free movement of labor. As a result, in 1970 the mass media started a campaign against the "migrants"; in 1972 the first restrictive measures were taken; in 1974 further restrictions were introduced, and in 1976 legal obstacles were again put in the way of changing workplaces. Simultaneously, the wages of the workers of cooperatives were regulated so that they would earn less than the workers of state companies. In early 1976 a large-scale norm-raising took place throughout the industry.

One of the leading personalities in this battle fought by the party apparatus was Sándor Gáspár; for years the Secretary General of the National Council of Trade Unions fought to divest the workers from the only real achievement of 1968, the free choice of their workplace. Gáspár's campaign included organizing a false, fake workers' initiative after the reform was introduced. In order to win over the managers, the "father" of the reform, Rezso Nyers, promised them new bonuses if they produced profits. It was easy for Gáspár, or rather for the Central Committee's section dealing with mass organizations, to mobilize those functionaries in the factories under their authority, especially at Györ, to oppose these bonuses, and then to depict this action, organized from above, as a genuine workers' initiative. For the sake of completeness I must add that finally the workers did manage to preserve their rights. Thus, after the raising of the norms in 1976, the majority of the workers—who were in a power position—refused to take on any overtime, as a result of which in the first three months of the year the factories were already unable to meet their production plan. As a solution, in most of the country's factories the managers then concluded informal agreements with the workers. In late summer 1983, Gáspár launched another campaign against the reform. "Well-informed" circles had no doubt about his victory. This time, however, 1972 was not repeated. Gáspár was relieved of his office which was given to the faceless Mehes, up to then Minister of Industry.

The statutes of the Hungarian trade unions emphasize that the trade unions are not independent of the party. They are independent not of the party but of the workers, who have no influence on the functioning of the apparatus. That apparatus defends its own power and material interests.

One cannot use terms such as "recession," "particularly deep crisis," to describe the present state of the Hungarian economy. One has to say that it has reached a state of impossibility. There is only one way out: structural economic reform. This problem falls outside the scope of this chapter but one of its most important preconditions must be mentioned nevertheless.

At present two powers exist side by side in Hungarian factories: that of the management and that of the workers. The workers are able to control production and productivity by their own informal means. This workers' power now stands opposed to factory management, factory party organization, and the leadership of the whole country. This power cannot be eliminated. However, there is a way in which this power could be harnessed to increase production and productivity: by recognizing the workers' power by involving workers in labor organization and in directing factory and investment.

One essential purpose of the reform now under preparation is to increase the export-capacity of Hungarian industry. New techniques, however, cannot be introduced without the active cooperation of workers and engineers. The informal organizations of workers exist not only in order to bargain for better wages and to defend themselves against the exploitation of their labor. They are also a means to safeguard their human dignity. Recognition of this human dignity is a precondition of any real economic reform in Hungary. Indeed, reform is possible only if it is entirely based on this dignity.

References

Fazekas, K. (1980), "Intenziv termékváltás es terjeszkedés," in M. Tardos (ed.), *Vállalati magatartás—vállalati környezet* (Budapest: Közgazdasági es Jogi Könyvkiadó).

[2]Gáspár retained effective control of the trade unions in his new post as chairman; he also remained on the Politburo.

Fazekas, K. (1982), "Bér- teljesítmény alku a belső munkaerőpiacon," in P. Galasi (ed.), *A munkaerőpiac szerkezete és mű ködése Magyarorszagon* (Budapest: Kőzgazdasági es Jogi Könyvkiadó).

Héthy, L. (1978), "Bérvita az épitkezésen," *Valóság*, January.

Héthy, L., and Makó, C. (1972), *Munkásmagatartások és a gazdasági helyzet* (Budapest: Akadémiai Kiadó).

Kollő, J. (1981), "Taktikázás és alkudozás as ipari űzemben," *Kozgazdasági Szemle*, July-August.

Kollő, J. (1982), "A külső és belső munkaerő piac kapcsolata egy pamutszövödében," in P. Galasi (ed.), *A munkaerő piac szerkezete és mű ködése Magyarországon* (Budapest: Kozgazdasági es Jogi Könyvkiadó).

XXIV Congress (1981) of the Hungarian Trade Unions, Abridged Minutes (Budapest).

9
Yugoslavia: Unions in a Self-Managed Society

Bernard Carter

Shortly after the partisans came to power in Yugloslavia in 1945 a new trade union national center was established, which later took the name of the Confederation of Trade Unions of Yugoslavia (CTUY). The CTUY traces its own beginnings back to 1919 when the first trade union center was founded in what was then the new nation-state of Yugoslavia ("Always on a Progressive Course," 1979). Trade unions and other worker organizations had been active, however, in certain parts of Yugoslavia well before World War I, particularly in the Habsburg lands of Croatia and Slovenia where manufacturing industry was more developed. Tito himself joined a metalworkers' trade union in Zagreb in 1910 (Auty, 1970).

The interwar period was a difficult time for the Yugoslav unions, whose organization fragmented because of internal political and national divisions and the unrelenting harassment of trade unionists by successive governments. After the war the new regime under Tito created a more cohesive state out of the chaos of the interwar years. The CTUY has benefited from this relative order and its membership has constantly increased in line with the expansion and industrialization of the economy. The CTUY has, however, faced some major challenges over the last thirty-five years. It has been necessary for the CTUY to reassess periodically its organization and role to ensure their compatibility with developments in the complex system of self-management. There have been at least four major constitutional revisions since 1950 when the self-management system was inaugurated and the first workers' councils established. These changes, together with the passing of innumerable laws defining and codifying self-managed relations in Yugosla-

Bernard Carter. Crazies Hill, Wargrave, Berkshire, United Kingdom.

via, have fundamentally reshaped Yugoslav society ensuring, at least in a formal sense, that self-management is practiced in virtually all aspects of life in the country. At each stage in this process the Yugoslav unions have had to adjust.

Trade unions, perhaps more than other Yugoslav institutions, have needed to question what function they could usefully perform in this new system. Under self-management the very existence of trade unions had to be justified. For against whom or what were workers to be protected by unions when the workers themselves were meant to manage their enterprises' activities and through their delegates directly to influence policymaking in society at large? It would be an anathema to the system if unions were to usurp the authority of workers' councils or other organs of direct workers' control within enterprises.

The relatively free play of market forces has been associated with the development of self-management, particularly since the Economic Reform of 1965. This aspect of Yugoslavia's system, which is not shared by any other communist country to such a degree, has brought with it many difficulties as well as its positive contribution. Inequities and market disruptions have accompanied Yugoslavia's rapid economic and industrial development over the last twenty years. The Yugoslav unions have had to cope with disturbances to the labor market, which are not so apparent in other communist countries. In particular, the problem of large-scale unemployment has afflicted the economy for many years. Unemployment according to official figures stood at 950,000 in 1983 and looked certain to pass the 1 million mark. Unemployment has its regional dimension in Yugoslavia reflecting the marked inequalities between the north and the south of the country. Whereas Slovenia has enjoyed almost full employment, the poorer republic of Macedonia had over 22 percent of its workforce unemployed in 1981 (Savezni Zavod za Statistiku, 1982). Also, large numbers of Yugoslavs, approximately 600,000 in 1983, have been allowed to seek temporary employment abroad. It has been one of the tasks of trade unions to look after the interests of these workers while abroad and on their return to Yugoslavia.

Cyclical fluctuations in the rate of economic activity are more evident in Yugoslavia than in most countries discussed in this volume. Sharp variations in the real earnings of workers have resulted, a factor which is also explained by the existence of a persistent inflationary problem and by periodic attempts to control inflation through the suppression of personal incomes.

The Yugoslav labor market is also characterized by a large private sector, which in 1981 employed 120,000 workers in nonagricultural activities. It is common for Yugoslavs to hold more than one job and receive several sources of income. According to one estimate, at least 40 percent of Yugoslav families derive some form of income from the "black" economy in such sectors as catering, construction, or farming (Slijepćević, 1983). If these figures are accurate, it suggests that a large section of the employed in Yugoslavia may be poorly organized in the official private sector or are not organized at all in the black or informal economy.

Yugoslav unions in the modern period have therefore been faced with a two main challenges. First, without any precedents to follow, they have had to define a useful role for themselves to play within the self-management system. Second, they have needed to cope with labor market conditions which were less regulated than in other communist countries. This chapter discusses how unions function in contemporary Yugoslavia and assesses how successful they have been in meeting the demands placed upon them.

Source materials on Yugoslav trade unions are very limited. Without the materials produced by the Yugoslav trade unions themselves in their weekly paper *Rad* and in their monthly journal *Sindikati* (Yugoslav Trade Unions), information would be very sparse indeed. Little attention has been devoted to Yugoslav unions by Western commentators and most studies of self-management make only passing reference to the subject. For their part Yugoslav authors have tended to concentrate on the theoretical role of unions in a self-managed society, rather than their actual performance (Kardelj, 1978; Kavčić, 1981; Pavlović, 1975; Radević, 1981; Vidaković, 1970). In their own contributions two former presidents of the CTUY have also focused on the normative aspects of trade union activities (Petrović, 1977; Vukmanović-Tempo, 1962–1967). Though the Yugoslav unions are remarkably candid and self-critical of their performance, their published materials do not contain close analyses and statistical evaluations of their activities. This absence of material on unions is regrettable in itself and in consequence the role of trade unions in Yugoslavia has tended to be overlooked. This chapter seeks to cast some light on this neglected subject and demonstrates that unions peform a low-key but potentially vital role in the organization of Yugoslav society and its unique self-management system.

The Organizational Framework

Over the last thirty years the trade union movement in Yugoslavia has adapted its organizational structure on several occasions to fit in with the institutional reforms which have frequently accompanied the development of workers' self-management. The current shape of trade union organization in Yugoslavia reflects the major steps taken to redesign the self-management system embodied in the 1974 Constitution and batch of important laws, principally the 1976 Law on Associated Labor, which were introduced thereafter. This legislation stressed that the fondation of workers' control over economic, social, and political affairs should rest firmly on the self-management bodies established within enterprises in the so-called basic organizations of associated labor (BOALs). BOALs represent discrete organizational units inside enterprises with each possessing its own workers' council and executive board. Through these bodies BOALs manage their own business affairs, coordinating their activities with those taken by other BOALs in their enterprises.

As a general rule a basic trade union organization will be established in each BOAL within an enterprise to which all workers in the BOAL belong. It is these basic organizations of trade unions (BOTUs) which are the cornerstones of trade union organization in Yugoslavia. Each BOTU is an autonomous trade union cell. Though each will collaborate closely with other BOTUs within their respective enterprises, they are in most regards independent and possess their own executive organs. This arrangement mirrors the independent status of BOALs within enterprises in the self-managing and accounting senses. A typical BOTU will have no more than 1,000 members and may well be much smaller. This feature of trade union organization in Yugoslavia reflects a strong desire to decentralize authority in the trade union movement. Indeed, there is a body of opinion in Yugoslavia which considers that the BOTU is too large a unit to organize workers and distances the trade union from its membership ("Continually in Action," 1980; "Better Decisions," 1981). There are many examples where trade union groups or branches have been created within BOTUs to represent sections of workers in individual departments within BOALs. In BOALs operating multishift systems it is common for a trade union group/branch to be established to organize each shift. These trade union groups/branches can be very small units representing fewer than a hundred workers. The exact relationship between the groups and the BOTUs will be defined in the individual statutes of each BOTU.

Figure 9.1 illustrates schematically the full structure of the trade union movement in Yugoslavia. It is worthwhile emphasizing that the arrangements established in Yugoslavia are designed to build a trade union organization from the bottom up rather than the reverse. Hence the figure identifies the BOTU as the centrepiece of the structure on which all other trade union organization is built. The figure shows that each BOTU will typically develop three links or affiliations to higher levels of trade union organization in the system.

First, each BOTU will need to establish close working relationships with other BOTUs within its enterprise. Naturally, the configuration of the trade union structure within enterprises depends on the size and complexity of the enterprises concerned. Most Yugoslav enterprises are associations of

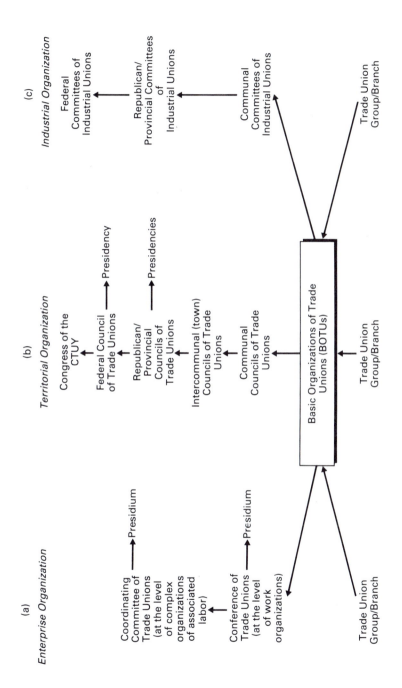

Figure 9.1 Structure of the trade union movement in Yugoslavia.

BOALs termed work organizations (WOs). On occasion, however, larger enterprises have been created by joining a number of WOs, sometimes from different sectors, into integrated combines called complex or composite organizations of associated labor (COALs). All WOs, irrespective of whether they are associated with a COAL or not, will possess their own workers' councils and other self-managing organs, which are additional to the corresponding machinery within their constituent BOALs. Likewise, when WOs are grouped into COALs, there will be established a third layer of self-management organization at the COAL level. (For abbreviations see Glossary of terms on pages 215−16.)

What this means in trade union terms is that trade union machinery must be established at each level in an enterprise where self-managing machinery exists. Within a WO, a body called a trade union conference is usually found which has a presidium as its executive arm. Each BOTU in a WO will send its representatives to the conference. The exact proportion of BOTU representatives in the conference and the presidium will vary from case to case depending on the statutes of the conferences. In some cases, representation will correspond to the size of the membership in each constituent BOTU; in other cases each BOTU will be equally represented. In those cases where WOs are associated into COALs, another tier of trade union organization, called trade union coordinating committees, will be established at the COAL level.

Second, Yugoslav trade unions are tightly organized on a territorial basis within the overall framework of the CTUY. Each BOTU sends delegates to the local council of trade unions in the commune in which it is based. Communal trade union councils act as links between BOTUs and the hierarchy of the trade union movement in Yugoslavia at republican and federal levels. The political activity of the movement is channeled through the communal councils to trade union organizations within enterprises and, in theory, from BOTUs upward to the republican and federal bodies. Some, but not all, communal councils employ full-time officials who should advise and assist BOTUs in their work. In some localities, primarily in the big cities like Belgrade, Zagreb, and Sarajevo, this communal organization will be supplemented by intercommunal councils.

Each of the six republics possesses a republican trade union council. In the cases of Vojvodina and Kosovo—the two autonomous provinces within the republic of Serbia—the corresponding organizations are provincial trade union councils. In Yugoslavia's decentralized system where considerable powers are conferred on the republican governments and the republican arms of the League of Communists, it is not surprising that the republican councils exercise an important role in the overall trade union structure. It is their task to exert political influence within their republics and establish attitudes for their delegates to take at meetings of the federal bodies of the CTUY. On occasion republican councils can follow apparently independent courses of action, as occurred recently when the Croation Trade Union Council took the federal government to Yugoslavia's Constitutional Court over a dispute about the guidelines on incomes for 1983 contained in the economic plan for 1983 ("Resistance to the Negation ...," 1983).

The republican councils operate through congresses held every four years or so at which the councils themselves are elected, together with their smaller presidencies which perform the executive duties. These arrangements are mirrored at the federal level where the federal Trade Union Council and Presidency are elected at federal congresses. The statute of the CTUY guarantees equal representation on the Council and Presidency for each republic. From among its membership the federal Presidency elects a President each May. No President is allowed to stay in office for more than a year and each republic and province is meant to take the Presidency in turn. In 1983–1984, for example, the President was a Macedonian, Stojan Stojčevski, who took over this role in May, 1983 from Bogoljub Nedeljković, a representative from Kosovo. This system of rotating leadership is applied across all sociopolitical organizations and institutions of government in Yugoslavia, though the term of office may be longer than the one-year period of tenure laid down in the CTUY's statute. This national policy was prompted by a speech given to the eighth congress of the CTUY in 1978 by President Tito, in which he expressed his concern that individuals and groups might abuse their position of extended authority and undermine the internal democracies of these organizations. He was also motivated by the desire to prevent any one national or ethnic group within the federation from appearing to gain ascendancy in these institutions. This policy is now under some attack in Yugoslavia on the grounds that the rotation of leadership is creating discontinuity and organizational inefficiency (Čuruvija, 1983).

Third, unions are organized on an industry-by-industry basis. There are currently fifteen industrial (or professional) unions in Yugoslavia covering the major sectors of manufacturing industry and the public services. In principle, each BOTU is affiliated to one or other of these fifteen unions. However, in practical terms such industrial affiliation may mean very little to BOTUs. Whereas the trade union structure in territorial terms is elaborate and well defined, the reverse is true for the industrial organization of trade unions. The links between the organs of the industrial unions and BOTUs may be very tenuous. The industrial unions mostly operate at the federal and republican/provincial levels where committees for each of the unions exist. These committees may not possess permanent secretariats independent of the republican and federal councils to which they are attached and on whose premises they usually meet. Few, if any, of the industrial unions produce regular journals or newspapers to publicize their activities to affiliated BOTUs. Beneath the republican levels, the organization of industrial unions is thin and uneven. Some communal councils may establish ad hoc committees of industrial unions in sectors which are important to the local economy but they are not obliged to do so.

Despite their low profile, the industrial unions can still perform important functions. In terms of setting industrial policies for individual sectors, especially as they affect health and safety and other working conditions, the top-level committees of the industrial unions can make a major input into decision-making and can be a party to important decisions. For example, the Yugoslav union for fuel, power, and petrochemical workers helped to negotiate a major agreement in 1982 laying down the minimum standards of working conditions for miners ("Obligatory Minimum. . .," 1982). However, in organizational terms it is evident that the industrial unions are not major forces. BOTUs will identify more closely with the union structures within their communes and enterprises than with their appropriate industrial union.

This arrangement is a far cry from the position which existed prior to a major reform of the trade union movement effected in 1978 at the eighth congress of the CTUY when a new statute for the CTUY was promulgated ("General Principles. . . ," 1978). Up to this time, industrial unionism was a more distinct feature of the Yugoslav movement. BOTUs used to contribute a proportion of their revenues to the industrial unions, a practice which ended after the reform. Before 1978 BOTUs did not affiliate directly to the communal councils but could do so via their industrial unions. The industrial unions also nominated representatives to the federal and republican councils of the CTUY. The reform measures of 1978 reversed this approach. Industrial unionism was thought to be outmoded for the stage of development reached by a self-managing society. The industrial structure of union organization was considered to accord more closely to the conditions prevailing under capitalism or the state control of industrial and economic planning which typified Yugoslav development in the early postwar years. Some even argued in 1978 that the industrial unions should be abolished altogether ("Action Not Only . . . ," 1978). In the end a compromise was reached which fell short of this extreme solution. Nonetheless, the 1978 trade union reform in Yugoslavia had as its main intention the objective of elevating the status of communal councils and BOTUs. This was achieved at the expense of the industrial unions.

The numbers organized in trade unions have greatly increased throughout the postwar period as Table 9.1 shows. This growth reflects the sharp rises in the total numbers employed in the socialized sector. Though no worker is compelled by law to join a trade union, in practice virtually everybody does as a matter of course, particularly in the socialized sector. The

Table 9.1
Trade Union Membership, 1945—1981

	Members (in thousands)	Percent of Workforce Unionized
1945	662	—
1949	1,560	—
1953	1,456	88.9
1968	3,255	90.7
1972	3,721	88.4
1976	4,599	93.4
1980	5,389	92.9
1981	5,484	91.9

Sources: Statistički Godišnjak SFRJ, 1954, 1974, and 1982.

degree of union organization varies somewhat from republic to republic. Both the most advanced republic, Slovenia, and the poorest regions, Montenegro and Kosovo, are heavily unionized. The agricultural areas of Macedonia and Vojvodina are the least organized with unionization standing at 84 percent and 88 percent respectively in 1980 (Savezni Zavod za Statistiku, 1981). The relatively high levels of nonunionized seasonal work associated with farming may offer a partical explanation.

Yugoslav unions employ only a small number of full-time union officials. In 1982 there were 1,074 full-time union officials in Yugoslavia assisted by over 800 professional advisers and experts with about 1,500 administrative staff. The ratio of full-time officers to members is 1:5,360. ("De-Proféssionalization . . . ," 1982). This is a low ratio by international standards, where it is usual for a full-time official to cover 1,500—2,000 members. Most officials are based in republics and communes though as many as 50 percent of communes were without full-time officials in 1978 ("Action Not Only . . . ," 1978). This arrangement suggests that many BOTUs will experience few direct contacts with full-time officials and must rely on their own resources to sort out their problems. This position is the result of a deliberate policy on the part of the CTUY to "de-professionalize" unions. It was considered inappropriate in a self-managed society for full-time officials and political workers to carry out the tasks assigned to union organizations and their lay representatives within companies.

In keeping with Yugoslavia's nonaligned stance in international affairs, the CTUY is not affiliated to the International Confederation of Free Trade Unions, the World Federation of Trade Unions, or the World Confederation of Labor. The CTUY has contacts with these international organizations, particularly the WFTU, but it cannot at present become a member of any of them as this would indicate a particular alignment on the part of the CTUY in East—West affairs. It is of interest that the CTUY is eager to develop its ties with the European Confederation of Trades Unions, an organization represenating trade unions in the EEC and EFTA countries. This may suggest a desire on the part of the CTUY to balance its involvement with WFTU and to tighten its links with the EEC (Franić, 1982). By union standards the CTUY engages itself in a very active program of international visits and exchanges. It is particularly common for delegations from trade union centers in developing countries to be invited to Yugoslavia. This fact displays a close involvement by the CTUY in North—South issues.

Unions as Guardians of Self-Managers' Rights

It was with the intention of making union services more relevant to the needs of workers in their role as self-managers that the institutional and organizational reforms discussed above were implemented. The reforms introduced in the 1970s were overdue. Unions had not adapted sufficiently in the 1950s and the 1960s to developments in the system of self-management. Confirmation of this came in 1958 when the first recorded work stoppage or strike under self-management took place at Trbovlje. Following the strike a more authoritative President, Svetozar Vukmanović-Tempo, was installed at the head of the CTUY. This change of leadership was successful in reestablishing the position and power of unions at a national level but it did little to realign the role of unions within communes and enterprises to provide the services their members needed as self-managers. The stormy sixth congress at the CTUY in 1968, at the end of Vukmanović-Tempo's period as President, again exposed worries about the effectiveness and representativeness of trade unions to their members (Carter, 1982).

The legislative changes effected in the mid-1970s through the 1974 Constitution and the 1976 Law on Associated Labor signalled a recovery in the position of Yugoslav unions. Under this legislation unions were given a heavier workload and the place in the overall system of self-management was more sharply defined. Many tasks, numbering over sixty in the case of the Associated Labor Law, were allocated specifically to unions. The reforms of the 1970s created a more purposeful role for trade unions within the system but this was achieved without giving them any major executive functions to perform. Their enlarged role had to be performed mainly through the persuasion of those who possessed executive authority in the system. Unions by themselves cannot directly veto or overrule the decisions of self-managers taken in workers' councils and elsewhere.

The following sections examine the main areas where the unions' function has now been defined in the system.

Establishing and Maintaining Self-Managing Relations

Under the Law on Associated Labor unions are charged with several important duties to ensure that the correct form of internal democracy within enterprises is instituted and that the appropriate procedures are observed. In the first place, unions at enterprise level must ensure that the appropriate number of BOALs within WOs and COALS are established. There have been many cases where managers or other groups within enterprises have resisted full "BOAL-ization" out of the wish to maintain centralized executive control within enterprises. Second, unions oversee the electoral and candidature procedures within enterprises as workers choose their representatives on workers' controls, executive boards, and disciplinary commissions. They should also have a voice on the selection boards appointing enterprise directors and other senior managers. Thirdly, impeachment procedures against members of workers' councils or other elected enterprise representatives can be initiated, but not carried through, by unions. Fourth, unions must ensure that no organ of self-management within an enterprise oversteps its authority by usurping the decision-making function of any other organ within an enterprise. Legal requirements and the internal statutes of enterprises define which issues can be resolved by executive boards and workers' councils and which, say, should be left to votes by the entire workforce at ballots or mass meetings.

As unions are responsible for ensuring that the machinery of self-management is correctly installed within enterprises, so are they obliged to ensure that it then functions appropriately and that the correct decisions are taken. BOTUs and other union bodies at enterprise level should keep abreast of events under discussion within BOALs and enterprises, and should issue advice on how self-managers should tackle individual questions. On issues of particular importance to workers such as job description, work practices, and incomes, no decision can be reached by a workers' council or any other self-managing body without consulting the union involved and seeking its opinion. This legal arrangement allows unions a direct say, but not a controlling influence, in the decision-making process within enterprises in these key areas. The self-managing organs are obliged to discuss what recommendations and conclusions the unions have to offer before making a final decision. If the union advice is rejected, reasons must formally be submitted to the relevant union organization.

These arrangements have been instituted because it is tacitly acknowledged that various shortcomings can enter into the functioning of self-management within enterprises. These aberrations principally involve abuses committed by the professional managers of enterprises and state officials. According to Kardelj, such deviations can arise because " . . . the technocratic itch to wield control over labor and the means of production, the centrapetal forces of administrative centralism in the government and the system of associated labor, the bureaucratic callousness toward working people, the low level of political consciousness among some sections of the working class, the abuses of self-management rights which foster idleness, irresponsibility, breakdown of work discipline . . . provide fertile soil for violations and the suppression of the rights and interests of working people" (Kardelj, 1978).

To protect their members from these dangers, unions must closely monitor and check the functioning of each enterprise's internal democracy. Various institutional arrangements and legislative requirements help unions perform this task.

First, they can insist on the publication in full of all relevant information relating to business performance. In theory, there is very little information which cannot be disclosed to unions and workers. What happens in many circumstances, however, is that such information is not regularly disclosed, or if it is disclosed, it is not made available in a form which is of use or readily understood.

Second, unions are obliged actively to participate in the negotiation of self-management agreements, termed *samoupravni sporazumi,* which regulate internal relations within BOALs and enterprises. Such agreements cover such matters as transfer pricing among BOALs and WOs, joint marketing, and R&D programs. Unions must also sign those agreements which dircetly regulate work relations or income distribution. In these cases, there is a clear-cut way for unions to formulate the necessary compromises to establish harmonious relationships within enterprises. This unifying influence could be important in those enterprises in which various group interests and difficulties have surfaced. Problems will inevitably arise when BOALs take contradictory positions within WOs and COALs. There is also a tendency for the professional managers at WO and COAL levels to dictate the terms of inter-BOAL relations. Through their involvement in negotiating self-management agreements, unions are in a position to help BOAL representatives resist such pressures from centralized management. They must also ensure that those BOALs in a stronger market position do not exploit the weaker BOALs in their intra-enterprise dealings.

In negotiating these self-management agreements unions, and the other parties involved, must also take heed of the parameters for enterprise negotiations laid down in social compacts *(društveni dogovori)* agreed at the communal, republican, and federal levels between the sociopolitical communities (central and local governments) and the sociopolitical organizations. Each republic will, for example, have a social compact laying down criteria for the distribution of income and others indicating investment priorities. The appropriate arm of the CTUY will probably be a signatory of these social compacts.

It is not clear, however, whether the union structure in Yugoslavia, with its heavy emphasis on BOTUs, will be able to carry out an effective coordinating role. For if BOALs have problems in reconciling their positions on overall enterprise policy, so too may BOTUs. They also may reflect the group interests of the part of the enterprise they represent. What will be controversial questions for the self-managing machinery of a WO or COAL to resolve may also be a source of disagreement and even interunion disputes among BOTUs. A high level of public purpose will be required on the part of the lay officials in BOTUs if the problems of finding satisfactory relationships among BOALs are not to carry over into their own work in the WO union conferences and the coordinating committees of COALs. It will be the task of the communal councils to identify and remove such potential conflicts among BOTUs.

Third, unions should make major contributions to the work of the workers' supervisory committees—*samoupravna radnička kontrola*—within enterprises. These bodies are independent of workers' councils and all other self-management machinery. No member of a workers' supervisory committee can be a member of any other self-managing body. It is the task of these committees *inter alia* to supervise the legality of decisions reached by workers' councils, to ensure respect for relevant self-management agreements and social compacts, and to monitor the implementation by professional managers of decisions reached by workers' councils. Its potential powers are considerable and can lead to the investigation of an enterprise's activities by the relevant authority based in the local commune.

In defending the position of self-managers much depends on the effectiveness of union organization within enterprises, particularly at the BOTU level. From the slim evidence available, it appears that all is not well in this area. An unpublished study recently prepared by the Belgrade Center for Workers' Self-Management is one of the first to analyze trade union organization within enterprises. According to some accounts (Jovanović, 1983; Erak, 1983), the study indicates that unions are not as actively engaged in enterprise activities as they should be. In many of the thirty-eight Serbian WOs studied, BOTUs did not issue advice to worker representatives on current enterprise affairs. Nor did they lead prior discussion on issues to be decided at mass meetings of workers as they are obliged to do. It is suggested that many BOTUs are only formally involved in the self-management process and prefer to deal with peripheral social issues at enterprise level like organizing sports and leisure activities. This study has provoked the CTUY to examine its BOTU organization. A provisional finding of this internal examination reported in *Rad* confirms this poor evaluation of BOTUs and suggests that many BOTUs "live in the shadow of professional managers" (ZRV, 1983).

It is also an indictment of BOTU performance that workers' supervisory committees are generally held in low esteem. Many have been slow to develop their role. Complaints have often been made that they pay insufficient attention to self-managing rights and the weaknesses of professional managers by concentrating on disciplinary questions and resolving the grievances of individual workers ("Supervision over Supervision," 1983; Strahinjić, 1983). Of the thousands of cases taken to the courts of associated labor concerning the violation of self-managing rights, only a handful have been initiated by supervisory committees or unions directly ("Workers' Supervision . . . ," 1982). In view of the widespread criticism of workers' supervisory committees, some major reform of their activities appears inevitable.

Even in their formal duties at enterprise level, some BOTUs are apparently underperforming. The Croatian Trade Union Council has criticized BOTUs in its republic for their failure to be sufficiently active in enterprise elections. It is a frequent occurrence for BOTUs to accept without question the candidacy lists prepared by the local branch of the League of Communists rather than draw up their own lists of potential representatives through discussions with their members. Unions, it is suggested, have "no influence at all" in the selection of senior managers as the procedure is dominated by the municipal authorities of local communes ("Unfulfilled Expectations," 1983).

If BOTUs and other trade union organizations at enterprise level are to function effectively, then adequate trade union education must be provided. With wide-ranging and complex tasks to be performed by BOTUs, and with a relatively small number of full-time officials to help them, their representatives are in need of special training and support. This training should emphasize the legal and constitutional position of workers and their self-managing rights. It should also draw attention to the wide variety of self-managing practices around the country which can be drawn upon to solve problems within enterprises. Most communes in Yugoslavia possess facilities to train trade union representatives in institutions variously entitled workers' universities, people's universities, or self-managers' clubs. These premises are usually used as centers for adult education but they also have a range of leisure and cultural facilities. In some senses Yugoslavia is well placed to provide trade union education on a large scale. About 60 percent of all workers in Yugoslavia have received some form of education connected with their function as self-managers (Pašić *et al.,* 1982). Much of this training takes the form of basic courses in Marxism or self-management theory. More detailed education geared to the needs to trade unionists, which may analyze in detail the approaches used to resolve the problems and contradictions of self-management, is less common, however. As a rule, it is only the President and the executive of the WO union conferences who attend courses of this kind ("Trade Union Schools . . .," 1980). In addition, trade unionists encounter resistances from local management in permitting time off with pay to attend trade union courses ("In the Function of Associated Labor," 1980).

Income Distribution

The system explicitly acknowledges that unions must take a close interest in decisions relating to the distribution of enterprise income. Personal income is seen as the most important issue of concern to workers. In exercising their influence in this area, unions will be confronted with four major tasks or objectives. First, BOTUs and other bodies within enterprises will constantly seek to maximize the income achieved by enterprises. This may sound axiomatic but this aim places the unions in difficult positions where they are seen as relentlessly pressing workers to increase productivity or where they are asking workers to increase investment and thereby forgo earnings in one year for the sake of higher incomes in the years ahead.

Second, unions will endeavor to ensure that the total income of an enterprise is allocated to BOALs in the agreed fashion laid down in a self-management agreement, which reflects equitably the contribution of each BOAL to achieving this income. This is a delicate matter and may frequently result in disagreements among BOALs. For instance, it may be claimed that the underperformance or overachievement of a particular BOAL was due to exceptional market factors beyond its control for which some adjustment should be made—increasing or reducing its income.

Third, unions must work within enterprises to achieve an equitable distribution of income to meet the competing needs. They will have to help formulate a view within self-managing bodies on what proportion of income should go to investment, reserves, joint consumption, expenditure in social fields, and personal incomes. It is beholden on unions to ensure that personal incomes do not take a disproportionate share. As it is commonly supposed that workers under self-management are constantly awarding themselves excessively large personal incomes, it follows that unions must with equal determination try to resist this tendency. Both suppositions may, however, be wrong in the majority of instances. For, if anything, workers under self-managing conditions have tended to be too ambitious in their investment decisions rather than their allocation to personal incomes. It is interesting to note that as part of the current stabilization drive in Yugoslavia to control inflationary tendencies in the economy, unions are more concerned to limit excessive investment and expenditure on social and communal facilities than to restrain personal incomes.

Fourth, unions will be pressing for an equitable distribution of personal incomes among the various workers in enterprises. It will generally be their aim to put into effect a system of remuneration which rewards personal effort and initiative. Under self-management, the authorities wish workers to receive incomes relating to the results of their work. If this concept is to be faithfully applied, it suggests that each worker's contribution will have to be measured. However, this is not the case; Yugoslavia is not an economy where everyone operates a "payment by results" system. Instead, what occurs is an attempt to evaluate each category of job within a BOAL, laying down broad production and performance standards where possible. Unions are closely involved in this task of setting norms and internal differentials. Naturally, the work on fixing these job schedules attracts much attention from workers, who must agree to the adoption of any new schedule by referendum.

On the question of personal incomes, unions should also be conscious of the need to protect the living standards of the lowest paid. This can be done by raising the income levels of the lowest paid or by pressing enterprises to improve common facilities such as subsidized meals and transport. Whichever way is chosen, the effect will be to squeeze differentials, an outcome which is frowned upon in Yugoslavia. These twin objectives—setting income payments by results and the protection of the living standards of the lowest paid—can be difficult to reconcile. An undesirable leveling of incomes can result, thereby reducing incentive in the system (Slijepćević, 1983).

Grievance Procedures and Work Stoppages

Every enterprise and BOAL will have its own grievance and disciplinary procedures written into its statute.

If the professional management or executive board authorizes disciplinary action against any worker or workers, then the union must be informed immediately. The union is required by law to represent the workers involved at any disciplinary hearing, if the workers so desire. Unions are also directly represented on the disciplinary commissions themselves. The protective role of unions is therefore secured in theory, though it is not easy to judge from the evidence available how well they perform this function.

Workers can also accuse their professional managers and workers' councils of ill-treatment and can raise grievances. In most cases these grievances will involve questions about the distribution of personal incomes, the denial of self-managing rights, or the misuse of the disciplinary procedure. A major grievance area also concerns housing. In Yugoslavia, enterprises have an important role to play in housing policy by financing the building of apartments in the socialized sector for their workers or by giving credits to workers to build or acquire their own properties. Enterprises should distribute apartments as they become available according to an agreed formula which attaches priority to workers with long service, a good disciplinary record, and family need. However, such are the housing difficulties in most Yugoslav cities where demand, despite a heavy building program, greatly outstrips supply that the agreed procedure may be misapplied as workers attempt to jump the queue.

When a grievance is lodged by a worker there will be attempts to resolve any difficulty through the agreed procedure defined in the statute. Again, the union is obliged to represent a worker, if so desired. On the many occasions where this internal procedure does not succeed in resolving grievances, a dissatisfied worker can try alternative approaches. In particular, there is the opportunity for a worker to take his or her case to the local court of associated labor. These courts are peripatetic, with floating memberships. If a case surfaces in a particular enterprise, then the court will probably decide to hold its hearing in that enterprise. Most courts have three independent magistrates who take evidence and pass verdicts. Most magistrates are not legal experts: for example, only one in ten of them in Montenegro are full-time judges ("Decisions in Favor . . . .," 1982). The method of work of the courts is an informal one designed to make them easily accessible and relatively attractive to workers. It appears that the courts have been successful in this respect and most republics have kept their courts busy with an average of 3,000−5,000 cases processed annually. This high work-rate must also be attributed to the fact that in 60−70 percent of cases, the courts have ruled in favor of the workers concerned and against enterprises and their self-managing organs ("Workers Take Their Disputes . . . ," 1979). Such chances of success must encourage workers to press their grievances through the courts.

In principle, unions are obliged to represent workers at these courts at the request of the workers concerned. If unions are closely in touch with their members, it should be anticipated that unions will themselves lodge many of the workers' complaints before the courts. In fact, few operate in this fashion. In Bosnia, for example, unions brought a worker's case before the court in less than 5 percent of cases between 1976 and 1978 ("Workers Take Their Disputes . . . ," 1979). This is a cause of concern for Yugoslav unions, apparently reflecting their isolation or inactivity at enterprise level. Furthermore, there have been cases where unions have actually testified against workers before the courts, which then have ruled in favor of the workers.

Collective grievances held by large groups of workers in enterprises can arise. The serious disturbances in this area mostly concern the level of personal incomes, the operation of bonus systems, work evaluation, and the inability of enterprises to pay incomes on time ("When the Self-Management Mechanism Falters," 1981; Crnjaković, 1983). On occasion, such grievances result in work stoppages or strikes, though, more frequently, "go-slows" or "white strikes" result (Džadžić, 1983). There average about two hundred or so strikes per year, most of which take place in manufacturing plants in Croatia and Slovenia. They are usually spontaneous events lasting for a few hours only.

Officially, the CTUY takes an ambivalent line on such occurrences and rarely dissociates itself entirely from the striking workers. Strikes are not illegal in Yugoslavia but nor are they explicitly authorized in the constitution. The CTUY suggests that strikes are not demonstrations against the self-management sysem as such but against the unfaithful implementation of the system within enterprises. This suggests that it is mostly in those enterprises where union organization and self-management practices are least developed that problems arise ("A Signal About the Malfunction . . . ," 1983).

In the only detailed study of work stoppages yet published, Jovanov asked representatives of communal trade union councils in areas where strikes had occurrred about the official union attitude to strikes. He found that in 11 percent of cases unions supported the strike activity in their areas and in a further 45 percent unions supported the position of the workers but not the use of the strike weapon (N. Jovanov, 1978 and 1979). Nearly two thirds of the union officials questioned saw the union's role as preventing strikes by removing their causes or, when they break out, by resolving them as quickly as possible. This finding accords with Županov's view that unions rarely adopt an adversorial stance against management when conflicts arise (Županov, 1978). Unfortunately, Jovanov's work was based on information collected in the late 1960s. It is likely that different attitudes would be adopted today when union organization in enterprises is more developed. It would be interesting to test what proportion of strikes in recent years have been supported by BOTUs. However, no information has as yet been published on BOTU support or opposition to work stoppages.

The Unions' Place in Political Life

It is a major feature of self-management that workers' control is not limited solely to matters within the factory gates. An elaborate and extensive system of direct democracy has been established in Yugoslavia which, in principle, allows workers to exercise considerable influence in policymaking at local and national levels. This aspect of workers' control in Yugoslavia takes two main forms. First, the enterprise is the root of the political system. Worker delegates from enterprises are sent to attend local assemblies at municipal and communal levels, and from there, possibly, to the republican and federal parliaments. Second, delegates from enterprises directly administer the functioning of the main social services in their communities like education, health, and social security. In this area, special institutions called *samoupravne interesne zajednice* (SIZ-ovi) have been established at which workers from the services themselves and from local enterprises meet to lay down agreed policy.

To regulate democratic procedures in these two areas, the delegate system was introduced into Yugoslavia in the 1970s. Under this system each enterprise will elect from its workforce a delegation. This delegation will serve as an interface between the enterprise and the sociopolitical communities and SIZ-ovi. Members of the delegation will be sent as delegates to the various bodies in these two categories upon which the enterprise is represented.

It is the union's role to ensure that the delegate system operates effectively. With over a million workers elected to delegations, this is clearly a formidable task. As with elections to other self-managing organs, trade unions have to organize the candidature and electoral process for delegations. They will monitor the activities of delegations and make known their views on individual issues. Trade unions must also promote the practice of regular reporting-back by delegates. In this area, the delegate system is not functioning as well as it should. Delegates, through the pressure of events and the need to expedite decisions, are often unable to report back to their delegations to seek advice. Delegates can be manipulated by the cadres who organize the activities of the SIZ-ovi and the sociopolitical communities by withholding information or massaging it to favor their positions. In such conditions, even if a delegate faithfully reported back, the delegation would not be properly equipped to decide its position ("In the Function....," 1980). The delegate system is central to the activities of the communal trade union councils. It will be within their remit to define, where possible, common trade union positions on issues discussed within the communal assemblies and SIZ-ovi. In advancing their policy positions the communal councils are helped by being directly represented within local assemblies in the so-called chambers of sociopolitical organizations.

The federal and republican councils of the CTUY coordinate the trade union input into the delegate system. They run awareness campaigns on issues of the day and establish common positions for trade union activists at the communal level to follow. The highest organs of the CTUY can also make a direct imput into the formulation of government policy at republican and federal levels. In its direct lobbying activities there are three main groups which the CTUY will be trying to influence and will in turn be influenced by.

First, there is the executive arm of the Yugoslav government, the Federal Executive Council (FEC). The FEC will be lobbied on policy matters by various interest groups such as the League of Communists and the governments of the republics and autonomous provinces. Trade unions are not a lobbying force on the scale of the republican governments or the League of Communists, but they too can wield some influence, particularly on issues relating to incomes and working conditions. The constitution allows the CTUY to submit policy proposals direct to the FEC, which must be given due consideration and responded to. This arrangement permits trade unions to make known to the FEC any initiative they may have on almost any policy issue.

Second, unions will try to influence the Federal Assembly and the equivalent assemblies in the republics. At the federal level unions find it more difficult to exert influence over the Federal Assembly than they do within the communal and republican assemblies. For, unlike the other assemblies, the federal parliament has no chamber for the sociopolitical organizations. If they are to get across their views, then unions must lobby the delegates to the Chamber of the Republics and Provinces who come direct from the republics or the delegates in the Federal Chamber who are representatives from communes (Galeb, 1982).

Third, the CTUY will try to coordinate its policy positions with other sociopolitical organizations. This can be achieved through the Socialist Alliance of Working People of Yugoslavia, which is an umbrella organization including the CTUY, the League of Communists of Yugoslavia (LCY), the Socialist Youth, and other sociopolitical bodies in its membership. The CTUY seeks particularly close liaison with the LCY, the most powerful sociopolitical body. It should be stressed that the CTUY is in a formal sense independent of the LCY. The LCY can no longer issue directives to the CTUY (Ribičič, 1982). Nor does it now become officially involved in the procedure to elect top union officials (Radević, 1981). Many LCY members are, however, union activists and through them the LCY will have ample opportunity to influence unions from within. The LCY is a mass party with over 2 million members and 26 percent of workers in the socialized sectors are members (Stanič, 1982). Each level of union organization is mirrored by similar LCY organization. In many BOALs there are basic organizations of the LCY and party cells will also operate at WO and COAL levels. These bodies perform similar functions to union organizations in enterprises in advising worker delegates on stances they should adopt.

Once the federal parliament and the FEC have developed their policy stances, they will often need to implement these policies through the medium of social compacts. These compacts represent a way to elaborate and implement policies on issues of broad community interest involving in the drafting process those organizations most directly affected. Trade unions, other sociopolitical organizations, departments of the federal and republican governments, the chambers of commerce, SIZ-ovi, and enterprises are among those bodies which are regular signatories of these compacts. In drafting and negotiating the social compacts, unions have a further opportunity to exert influence on such important policy issues as prices, employment, foreign trade, planning, income distribution, and the environment.

It is very rare for unions to step far out of line from the views of the FEC and other influential bodies on major policy issues. For example, there is no indication, as far as can be detected, that the CTUY seriously challenges the thinking behind the current stabilization program, the centerpiece of the country's economic strategy of retrenchment. Nonetheless, in their pro- nouncements on national policy issues the Yugoslav trade unions make their own distinctive input designed to protect the position of the 5 million employed workers they represent. The current long-term stabilization pro- gram throws up some good examples of this point. For unions have been very vociferous and entered into controversy on individual policy questions within the overall program.

In the first place, the CTUY has sought to ensure that the austerity packages should not just hit workers' incomes. It has constantly urged the case for inflation-control in Yugoslavia to be achieved by reducing excessive investment and public expenditure and not by restraining incomes and consumer spending ("Associated Labour Adheres . . . ," 1981). In this area the CTUY has not been as successful as it would have wished. Workers appear to have borne the brunt of the stabilization measures and average incomes in real terms have fallen by an astonishing 33 percent over the last four years (Lončar, 1983). It is not surprising in these circumstances that unions are resolutely opposed to suggestions that personal incomes should now be frozen. It is the CTUY's view that greater flexibility is needed in pay determi- nation to reduce anomalies and create incentive (Neđeljković, 1983).

Second, the CTUY has attempted to highlight the severe problems of the lowest paid workers whose living standards have fallen sharply in recent years. To this end the CTUY has pressed strongly for a more active social policy to be introduced in Yugoslavia to support those most in need. Unions have advanced the idea that to identify where greatest need exists enterprises should draw up "social cards" in which details of each worker's family posi- tion and income are listed (Slijepćević, 1983). This idea has met with considerable opposition on the grounds that the food and rent subsidies needed to support the families of the lowest paid would place an excessively high burden on enterprises and the economy ("Domet Socijale," 1983). It is argued that workers should not rely on subsidies to protect their standard of living but should work more effectively.

A third area of controversy where unions are concentrating their efforts is prices policy. Of the main sociopolitical organizations, unions are the most favorably disposed toward the introduction or maintenance of rent and price controls, particularly on basic foodstuffs. The CTUY is losing the argument in this area as recent measures have been introduced to deregulate prices. The CTUY has protested at the consequences of this decision which led in the summer of 1983 to a plethora of price increases on basic commodities such as bread and milk. Unions have asked for these increases to be reversed as they took place without the proper procedures, including consultation with republican trade union councils, being observed (Miljević, 1983; Z. Jovanov, 1983).

What is perhaps most surprising about the current activity of the CTUY is that there is no apparent strategy emerging to resolve the problem of unemployment. Yugoslavia has a good record on employment creation, and unions can take some credit for this, but such is the severity of the imbalance in the labor market that a major rethink of current approaches is required if it is to be resolved (Singleton and Carter, 1982). Whereas unions in Western Europe have campaigned strongly for a reduction of working time as a means to reduce unemployment, the CTUY has been relatively silent on this subject. It is only recently that the issue of working time (each full-time worker in Yugoslavia works a 42-hour week) has been taken up seriously as a policy option. However, the public discussion of this matter has not featured a trade union input (Milošević and Peterman, 1983). The CTUY's reluctance to contribute to this debate may be the result on the emphasis it places on improving productivity and raising industrial output. In common with unions in other communist countries, the CTUY concentrates on campaigning to improve economic and industrial performance. It is very active in encouraging innovation and reducing waste. Indeed, unions are currently running a drive against idleness and indiscipline in workplaces. The Slovenian trade union council has even gone as far as supporting legislation in Slovenia to penalize "idlers" by removing some of their employment rights ("Losses and Poor Work . . . ," 1982).

Conclusions

Many characteristics of dual functioning unions are as apparent in Yugoslavia as in other East European countries. Union officials, especially at the WO and COAL levels, work very closely with the professional managers of enterprises to raise productivity and promote the efficient use of socially owned capital. However, since the 1978 reform and the ensuing de-professionalization of their activities, unions have been conscious that such collaboration with management should not go too far and impair their ability to represent the separate interests of workers and perform their protective function. In addition, the constitution requires unions to be deeply involved in ensuring the faithful implementation of the self-management system on the gound. Union activities should be directed toward assisting and guiding workers to exercise their self-managing rights within enterprises and beyond. So central should be this aspect of their work that it may be appropriate to view unions in Yugsolavia as having a triple function to perform with the care and maintenance of the self-management system appearing as their third major role. At the current stage in self-management's tortuous and complex evolution, unions should play an active role in ensuring that the system overcomes those forces, particularly technocratic and bureaucratic, which threaten the rights of workers as self-managers. As long as these imperfections in the system remain, unions should not be redundant institutions in Yugoslavia.

From the slim evidence available it is difficult to assess how effectively Yugoslav unions perform their triple function. There are grounds to believe, however, the Yugoslav unions are failing to realize the potential offered to them under the constitution and its associated laws. For the enterprise organization of unions is insufficiently strong to carry out the major tasks allotted to them. In a system which places a pronounced emphasis on building from the base upwards, the recent revelations about ineffective BOTU organization are indeed very worrying to the CTUY (Djodjić, 1983). In some quarters it has been suggested that unions are organizationally incapable of carrying out their wide remit and should concentrate on those matters of direct concern of workers ("Kako prepoznati klasu," 1983). As this debate is occurring at a time when the real earnings and living standards of Yugoslav workers are falling sharply, it appears that Yugoslav unions are facing a major challenge to their credibility as the representative voice of Yugoslavia's working class (Lovrić, 1983). If unions cannot find the necessary answers to their current problems, then not only they but also the system itself and the position of self-managers may be weakened.

Glossary of Terms

Basic Organizations of Associated Labor (BOALs)
Subdivisions within enterprises in which workers can exercise their self-management rights on a decentralized geographical or departmental basis.
Basic Organizations of Trade Unions (BOTU)
The basic trade union structure within enterprises corresponding to the BOAL structure.
Complex Organizations of Associated Labor (COALs)
Business combines in which groups of enterprises join together to achieve vertical or horizontal integration.

Confederation of Trade Unions of Yugoslavia (CTUY)
 The trade union national center of Yugoslavia.
Drustveni dogovori (social compacts)
 Agreements entered into by the main social-political organizations to effect govern-
 ment decisions on social, industrial, and economic policies.
Federal Executive Council (FED)
 The federal government.
Samoupravna Interesna Zajednica (SIZ-ovi)
 An institution created to manage a social service or a public utility on which the
 users and producers of these services jointly decide policy.
Samoupravna radnička kontrola (workers' supervisory committees)
 Bodies within BOALs and enterprises on which elected worker representatives
 monitor the performance of local management in respecting the self-manage-
 ment rights and decisions of workers.
Samoupravni sporazumi (self-management agreements)
 Agreements entered into by workers, management, and, sometimes, communal
 authorities with the principal aim of regulating the internal relations of BOALs,
 WOs, and COALs.
Work Organizations (WOs)
 Groupings of BOALs, which are frequently constituted as independent enterprises.

References

"Action Not Only (1978) in Associated Labor but in the Political System as Well," *Yugoslav Trade Unions,* 113 (May−June), pp. 2−6.
"Always on a Progressive Course" (1979), *Yugoslav Trade Unions,* 119 (March−April), pp. 1−3.
"A Signal about the Malfunction (1983) of the Self-Management Mechanism," *Yugoslav Trade Unions,* 114 (May−June), pp. 5−6.
"Associated Labor Adheres (1981) to Agreed Upon Policy," *Yugoslav Trade Unions,* no. 134 (September−October), pp. 3−4.
Auty, P. (1970), *Tito: A Biography* (London: Longman).
"Better Decisions" (1981), *Yugoslav Trade Unions,* no. 136 (January−February), pp. 12−13.
Carter, A. (1982), *Democratic Reform in Yugoslavia: The Changing Role for the Party* (London: Frances Pinter).
"Continually in Action" (1980), *Yugoslav Trade Unions,* no. 124 (January−February), pp. 12−13.
Crnjaković, M. (1983), "Stajkovi Mjenjaju Smjer," *Danas,* no. 84 (September 27), 1983, pp. 14−16.
Čuruvija, S. (1983), "Dugi Razgovori O Kratkim Mandatima," *NIN,* no. 1687 (May 1), 1983, pp. 10−12.
"Decisions in Favor (1982) of the Workers," *Yugoslav Trade Unions,* no. 136 (January−February), pp. 9−10.
"De-Professionalization (1982) and Priority to Excellence," *Yugoslav Trade Unions,* no. 140 (September−October), pp. 11−12.
Djodjić, L. (1983), "Bez Ijednog Izuzetka," *Rad,* September 30, 1983, p. 3.
"Domet Socijale" (1983), *Ekonomska Politika,* no. 1639 (August 29), p. 13.

Džadžić, T. (1983), "Strajkovi Protiv Belog Strajka," *NIN,* no. 1705 (September 4), 1983, pp. 19−21.

Erak, Z. (1983), "Pozajmljivanje Tuđe Volje," *NIN,* no. 1701 (August 7), 1983, pp. 14−15.

Franić, J. (1982), text of speech to the Committee for International Trade Union Cooperation at the ninth congress of CTUY, *Yugoslav Trade Unions,* no. 141 (November−December), 1982, p. 18.

Galeb, R. (1982), "Independence—the Vital Link in the Work of Trade Unions," *Yugoslav Trade Unions,* no. 136 (January−February), 1982, pp. 1−3.

"General Principles (1978), the Role and Tasks of the CTUY," *Yugoslav Trade Unions,* no. 116 (November−December), pp. 25−7.

"In the Function of Associated Labor" (1980), *Yugoslav Trade Unions,* no. 125 (March−April), pp. 8−9.

Javanov, N. (1978), "Strikes and Self-Management," in J. Obradović and W. Dunn (eds.), *Workers' Self-Management and Organizational Power in Yugoslavia* (Pittsburgh, PA: University Center for International Studies), pp. 339−73.

Jovanov, N. (1979), *Radnički Strajkovi u SFRJ* (Belgrade: Zapis). (1983)

Jovanov, Z. (1983), "Ludovanja novog cjenika," *Rad,* August 12, p. 3.

Jovanović, R. (1983), "Tko Pita Sindikat," *Rad,* August 19, p. 2.

"Kako Prepoznati Klasu" (1983), *Ekonomska Politika,* no. 1640 (September 15), p. 10−11.

Kardelj, E. (1978), *Democracy and Socialism* (London: Summerfield Press).

Kavčić, B. (1981), "Trade Unions in the System of Workers' Self-Management in Yugoslavia," in K. Sethi *et al.* (eds.), *Self-Management and Workers' Participation: Indo-Yugoslav Experiences* (New Delhi: Scope Publications), pp. 209−40.

Lončar, D. (1983), "Kako Nas Štiti Sindikat," *Danas,* no. 78 (August 16), pp. 9−10.

"Losses and Poor Work (1982) under Attack," *Yugoslav Trade Unions,* no. 139 (July−August), pp. 1−2.

Lovrić, J. (1983), "Je li Divljanje Cijena Zužnost," *Danas,* no. 81 (September 6), pp. 12−13.

Miljević, V. (1983) "Dogadja se nešto neodgovorno," *Rad,* August 19, p. 3.

Milošević, M., and Peterman, B. (1983), "Milion glava dva milliona ruki," *NIN,* no. 1690 (May 22), pp. 7−10.

Nedeljković, B. (1983), "Nesposobni moraju otići," *Rad,* July 29, p. 4.

"Obligatory Minimum (1982) for Miners," *Yugoslav Trade Unions,* no. 139 (July−August), pp. 14−15.

Pašić, N., Grozdanović, S., and Radević, M. (1982), *Workers' Management in Yugoslavia: Recent Developments and Trends* (Geneva: ILO).

Pavlović, V. (1975), "Saviz Sindikata Jugoslavije," *Jugoslovenski Pregled,* January, pp. 13−20.

Petrović, D. (1977), *Self-Management in Yugoslavia* (London: The Summerfield Press).

Radević, M. (1981), "The Trade Union in the Self-Management Society," *Socialist Thought and Practice,* no. 4, pp. 19−35.

"Resistance to the Negation (1983) of the Income Principle," *Yugoslav Trade Unions,* no. 143 (March−April), pp. 4−5.

Ribičič, M. (1982), "Honor and Power to Labor," *Yugoslav Trade Unions,* no. 141 (November−December), p. 12−14.

Savezni Zavod za Statistiku (1981), *Statistički Godišnjak SFRJ 1981* (Belgrade: SZZS).

Savezni Zavod za Statistiku (1982), *Statistički Godišnjak SFRJ 1982* (Belgrade, SZZS).

Singleton, F., and Carter, B. (1982), *The Economy of Yugoslavia* (London: Croom Helm).

Slijepćević, S. (1983), "Tanka Linija Solidarnosti," *NIN,* no. 1705 September 14, pp. 7−8.

Stanič, G. (1982), "Članstvo Saveza Komunista Jugoslavije," *Jugoslovenski Pregled,* March pp. 145−150.

Strahinjić, C. (1983), "Samoupravna Radnička Kontrola," *Jugoslovenski Pregled,* January, (1983), pp. 11−16.

Supervision over Supervision" (1983), *Yugoslav Trade Unions,* no. 144 (May–June), p. 12.

Trade Union Schools (1980)—Centers for Knowledge and Experience," *Yugoslav Trade Unions,* no. 129 (November–December), pp. 9–10.

'Unfulfilled Expectations (1983)", *Yugoslav Trade Unions,* no. 144 (May–June), pp. 6–7.

Vídaković, Z. (1970), "The Function of Trade Unions in the Process of Establishing the Structure of the Yugoslav Society on a Basis of Workers' Self-Management," in M. Broekmeyer (ed.) *Yugoslav Workers' Self-Management* (Dordrecht: Reidel), pp. 42–60.

Vukmanović-Tempo, S. (1962–7), *Sindikati U Novim Uslovima* (Belgrade: Biblioteka Drustvano—Politicke Studije).

"When the Self-Management Mechanism Falters" (1981), *Yugoslav Trade Unions,* no. 133 (July–August), pp. 3–4.

"Workers' Supervision (1982) Is Still Not Sufficiently Felt," *Yugoslav Trade Unions,* no. 138 (May–June), pp. 7–8.

"Workers Take Their Disputes (1979) before the Court," *Yugoslav Trade Unions,* no. 122 (September–October), pp. 8–9.

ZRV 1983), "U Sjeni Poslovodnih Struktura," *Rad,* September 16, p. 4.

Županov, J. (1978), "Two Patterns of Conflict Management in Industry," in J. Obradović and W. Dunn (eds.), *Workers' Self-Management and Organizational Power in Yugoslavia* (Pittsburgh, PA: University Center for International Studies), pp. 390–400.

10
The People's Republic of China

Jeanne L. Wilson

Compared with their East European and Soviet counterparts, Chinese trade unions operate in an environment of considerably reduced influence and increased uncertainties. A distinguishing feature of Chinese trade unions is their institutional weakness even in comparison with unions in other communist states. The explanation for such weakness lies in a series of interrelated historical, social, political, and economic factors. Contrary to the classic dictates of Marxism, the Chinese Communist Party (CCP) came to power through the employment of a peasant-based strategy of revolution in a peasant society. The virtual exclusion of the proletariat from participation in the revolutionary struggle after 1927 placed the trade unions out of the mainstream of the Chinese communist movement. The Chinese trade union movement lacked an extensive revolutionary tradition even in relation to the Soviet case. Chinese trade unions represented a weak, numerically small working class in a peasant society that, Marxist-Leninist ideology aside, was rooted in a Maoist appreciation of peasant rather than proletarian virtues.

The Chinese trade union movement thus started out in the post-1949 period from a particularly disadvantaged position that left it ill-prepared to set about carving out a place in the industrial hierarchy. Lacking any tradition of autonomous action, Chinese trade unions were quickly subordinated to the CCP as an auxiliary structure. In accordance with the Chinese decision to follow the Soviet model, the emerging Chinese trade union apparatus adopted the Soviet-style trade union format complete with the dual functioning ideological rationale. In theory, the Chinese interpretation of the dual functioning principle was completely orthodox. In practice, few other commu-

Jeanne L. Wilson, Department of Government, Wheaton College, Norton, Massachusetts.

nist societies have provided such a stark highlighting of the inherent tensions of the concept. The strains of striking some sort of balance between workers and the party, and between welfare and production, have been intensified in the Chinese case by the extreme politicization of the Chinese enterprise. For much of the post-1949 era, party policy onesidedly identified production as virtually the exclusive focus of trade union activity, condemning evidence of trade union concern with workers' welfare as "economist," reflective of an unhealthy preoccupation with material benefit.

Nonetheless, the general reorientation of Chinese economic, political, and social policy by the post-Mao leadership has included a reassessment of the role of the trade union. In contrast to past priorities, present policy specifies the representation of the workers' interests as the main focus of trade union work. The current Chinese perspective in no way exceeds the boundaries of the dual functioning role—flexibility being a hallmark of the dual functioning precept—but it does indicate a significant shift in Chinese policy. The current trade union line constitutes the most unequivocal expression of party support for the trade union's welfare role made in the post-1949 era. Moreover, although the trade union remains subordinate to the party, current policy recognizes the legitimacy of a limited trade union operational autonomy. The revised trade union constitution unveiled at the Tenth Congress of the All-China Federation of Trade Unions (ACFTU) in October, 1983 noted for the first time the importance of independence in trade union work (*Zhongguo Gonghui Dishici*, 1983:51). But if what was previously considered as "economist" and "syndicalist" now constitutes the basis of trade union policy, the fundamental issue facing the trade union movement is its ability to translate policy into empirical reality.

History of the Chinese Trade Union Movement

Although guilds were a feature of work organization among handicraft workers in traditional Chinese society, the establishment of trade unions in China was essentially a twentieth-century phenomenon. The Chinese trade union movement evolved more in response to political than to economic factors, with its fate closely linked to the dynamics of the political struggle between the Kuomintang (KMT) and the CCP. Under the direction of the Comintern, both the CCP and the KMT pursued an urban-based strategy in the 1920s aimed at the organization and recruitment of workers. The establishment of the First All-China Labor Congress in May 1922 marked the national organization of a trade union apparatus in China. The Chinese labor movement reached a highpoint in 1927 with an estimated 3 million workers organized into trade unions (Epstein, 1949:57). Chiang Kai-shek's attack on the CCP in 1927, however, struck a near-fatal blow not only to the CCP but also to the fledgling Chinese trade union movement. The subsequent flight of the CCP from the cities and its reorganization, first in Jiangxi and later in Yenan, in the countryside signalled the development of a peasant-based strategy of revolution. After 1927, CCP links with urban workers were tenuous at best. With Chiang Kai-shek firmly in control, KMT activities in the trade union sphere were also repressed. The KMT Labor Law of 1928 effectively stripped trade unions of any effective powers reducing them to a state of virtual inactivity. Although the formation of the second KMT-CCP alliance in 1936 initially sparked some hopes of a revival, the Chinese trade union movement essentially remained dormant throughout the war years. Despite some efforts to organize trade unions in the communist-held base areas, the CCP did not become involved in the large-scale organization of industrial workers until early 1948 when its armies overtook Manchuria. The convocation, under Communist Party auspices, of the Sixth All-China Trade Union Congress in Harbin, Manchuria in 1948 marked the first national trade union meeting to be held since 1929.

The Chinese leadership's decision to "lean to one side" (that is, to follow the Soviet model) with the founding of the People's Republic of China on October 1, 1949 meant the Chinese adoption of the Soviet model of trade union organization. Lacking extensive organizational experience on their own, the Chinese borrowed heavily from the example of the Soviet "elder brothers." The leadership's attempt to organize unions according to the dual functioning precept, however, almost immediately ran into difficulties. Within the span of a decade, the Chinese trade union movement was twice subject to political purges that reflected the trade union's inability to reconcile its two-pronged role. The so-called "first trade union crisis" of 1950–1951 involved a struggle between the party and the union leadership over the right of the trade union to exercise a limited operational authority in defense of the workers' interests. While the party identified production as the foremost task of trade union work, the union leadership argued for a functional division of labor in the enterprise which would allow the unions to concentrate upon workers' livelihood as a primary endeavor. The trade union's efforts to establish a specialized niche in the enterprise hierarchy was seen as an unacceptable challenge to political authority. In the ensuing conflict, ACFTU Chairman Li Lisan and a host of his identified supporters were purged as advocates of "economism" and "syndicalism."[1]

---

[1] As a former chairman of the CCP (1928–1930) and a longterm resident of the Soviet Union (1930–1946), Li Lisan must have been anathema to Mao Zedong in any case. He suffered only as a concession of the Soviets. For a further analysis of the "first trade union crisis," see Harper, 1969: 171–205. As an illustration of trade union attitudes at the local level toward party

Nonetheless, the recourse to the imposition of political controls provided at best only a short-term solution to an unresolved problem, and conflict over the trade union's role resurfaced during the political liberalization of the Hundred Flowers period of 1957. The issues defining the "second trade union crisis" paralleled those of the first; trade union cadres—including the party's carefully selected replacement appointments to the union leadership—protested that the union's subordination to the enterprise leadership precluded the possibility of acting to represent the working class. In his highly publicized (later to be infamous) ten-city tour of China in the spring of 1957, ACFTU Deputy Director Li Xiuren complained that he had not been able to find even one case in which the trade unions had stood up to the enterprise leadership in defense of the workers (Li, 1957: 10-13). Frustration with ineffectual trade union performance was such as to lead some trade union cadres to protest that the unions in their present format were "useless" as structures of worker representation and might as well be abolished.[2] As during the first trade union crisis, the trade union leadership maintained the necessity of trade union operational autonomy—the trade union's right to "independent activities" in the words of ACFTU Chairman Lai Ruoyu—within the enterprise (Harper, 1969: 232). The abrupt termination of the Hundred Flowers experiment, manifest with the initiation of the Anti-Rightist Campaign in June 1957, resulted in an attack on the union leadership for its economist and syndicalist deviations. Although ACFTU Chairman Lai Ruoyu was not a direct target of criticism (presumedly due to his terminal bout with cancer), he was attacked posthumously and the leadership structure of the ACFTU was subjected to a wide ranging purge at both the national and the regional levels.[3]

---

policy stressing the primacy of production and the necessity of accommodation with capitalist factory owners as a prerequisite to economic recovery, see *Zhejiang Ribao*, 1950; *Zhejiang Ribao*, 1951a; *Zhejiang Ribao*, 1951b.

[2]The question of the utility of the unions constituted a central issue during the second trade union crisis in 1957. ACFTU Chairman Lai Ruoyu, in his otherwise hardline post-rectification analysis, nonetheless acknowledged that the unions were perceived as "useless" by some elements due to their inability to represent the working class (Lai, 1957: 2). Even after the launching of the rectification campaign, trade union cadres continued to protest that the union's role should properly be directed toward workers and not production. At the Zhejiang Provincial Trade Union Congress, held in October, 1957, for example, a portion of the representatives, led by one Su Chenhai, argued that the trade union served no useful purpose in the enterprise unless it be granted sufficient autonomy to promote workers' welfare as a primary endeavor (Chen, 1957: 2; *Zhejiang Riabo*, 1957).

[3]The subject of the second trade union crisis is treated at length in Harper, 1969: 219–54.

The Anti-Rightist Campaign marked a watershed in the PRC in its signalling of the ascendancy of Maoist values. As the Anti-Rightist Campaign merged into the Great Leap Forward of 1958–1960, Maoist ideology superseded Soviet managerial ideology as the preeminent managerial ethos in the enterprise, with highly detrimental consequences for the already weakened Chinese trade union movement. The development strategy of the Great Leap, with its stress on voluntarism, mobilization, and the heritage of the party's experience in Yenan in the Anti-Japanese War era, relegated the trade unions to the periphery of the enterprise, patently Soviet-style structures in an increasingly anti-Soviet environment. The Maoist precept of "politics in command" guaranteed the absolute subordination of the unions to the party while the ambitious output goals of the Great Leap Forward reaffirmed the trade union's obligation to pursue production as a primary endeavor. The politicization of the enterprise during the Great Leap led the party to usurp many of the trade union's designated functions in the administrative realm. Since trade union cadres were among the first to be sent down to the factory floor to labor in production during drives to simplify and reorganize production, personnel were often unavailable to perform trade union tasks. At the height of the Great Leap Forward, the trade unions ceased performing even routine administrative functions and the union structures atrophied as a consequence of neglect.

Although the trade union made a comeback of sorts in the wake of the Great Leap Forward with the return of trade union cadres and the partial recovery of its designated administrative duties, the unions remained passive organizations subordinated to the party's will. The trade union's very acquiescence to the party, however, only rendered it more vulnerable to the political conflagrations of China's next campaign, the Great Proletarian Cultural Revolution of 1966–1976. The trade unions were an early target of radical attack at the onset of the Cultural Revolution in 1966; in January 1967 the ACFTU was dissolved at both the national and the local levels. The trade unions were denounced as thoroughly revisionist structures that had betrayed the ideals of the Chinese revolution, the same change that was leveled against all of the Chinese mass organizations—the Young Communist League, the All-China Women's Federation, and so on—that shared the ACFTU's fate of dissolution. But as with the rest of the mass organizations, the underlying reasons for the union's demise lay in its fatally close identification with the party bureaucracy.

It is not possible to disassociate the experience of the trade unions during the Cultural Revolution from the broader dynamics of the political conflict that engulfed the CCP and extended throughout Chinese society. In the intensely politicized environment of the Cultural Revolution, no issue was without its political implications to be used as ammunition in the internecine struggle. Although segments of the political left had argued for the permanent abolition of the trade unions, the party eventually opted for the reconstitution of the trade union structure, formally announced in January 1973. Efforts to reconstitute the unions, however, soon became enmeshed in an intra-party conflict about which faction would exercise control over the emergent trade union apparatus. In the first rounds, the leftists gained control over the reestablishment of the trade union councils, with Wang Hongwen elected head of the Provisional Trade Union Congress in Shanghai, and Zhang Chunqiao and Yao Wenyuan prominent participants at the Provisional Trade Union Congress in Beijing.[4] Although the leftists maintained their dominance over the reemerging trade union network at the local levels, the rightists had enough influence to postpone the Ninth National Congress of the ACFTU originally announced in 1975. The national reconstitution of the trade union structure, however, had to await the death of Mao, the arrest of the gang of four, and the consolidation of power in the hands of Deng Xiaoping. Finally, in October, 1978, the Ninth National Congress of the ACFTU was held in Beijing with Deng Xiaoping the keynote speaker. After an eleven-year hiatus, the formal institutional operation of the trade unions was resumed.

The Influence of the Labor Market on Unions

Aside from political forces, the Chinese trade union movement has been substantially shaped by the structure of the Chinese labor market. In the Chinese case, this is almost wholly a unilateral relationship. Current Chinese labor policy is determined at least as much by demographic factors as by ideological convictions. Chinese trade unions have no significant role to play in decisions taken over the allocation of labor, acting as passive recipients rather than active formulators of policy. The specific features of the Chinese socioeconomic environment, however, set China apart from its more advanced communist kin. With an estimated 1982 per capita income of 232 dollars, the PRC belongs squarely in the ranks of Third World nations. Eighty percent or approximately 800 million of China's 1 billion people live in the countryside. China's urban population of 200 million includes an urban workforce of 118 million people (State Council, 1985: 255). While this makes the Chinese urban workforce second in size in the communist world to that of the USSR, it also minimizes the social, economic, and political significance of that workforce within China itself. The structure of the Chinese labor force reflects the interplay between demography and state policy.

---

[4]Wang, Zhang, and Yao, of course, made up three of the members of the so-called "gang of four," the remaining member being Jiang Qing, Mao Zedong's wife.

Rural—urban migration, despite some leakage in the system, is proscribed as a means of limiting urban growth.[5] Although peasant incomes have risen markedly in recent years with the institution of a system of household contracting of production and encouragement of individual forms of initiative, the still sharp differential in the standard of living between the cities and the countryside makes anything but a forced repatriation of urban dwellers to rural areas unrealistic, a point implicitly conceded by the state in the discontinuation of its widely unpopular program to send urban youths to the countryside on a permanent basis.[6] Deborah Davis-Friedmann estimates, in fact, that despite significant gains in peasant income since 1979, the urban—rural wage differential has remained fixed at the pre-1979 ratio of 3:1 (Davis-Friedmann, 1985: 178).

Although Chinese urban dwellers are an elite compared with their less fortunate compatriots in the countryside, they are nonetheless a highly differentiated elite in which conditions of work and remuneration are dependent upon job classification and place of employment. The major distinction in employment among Chinese workers in the post-1949 era has been between employment in the state-run enterprises, characterized as examples of "ownership of the whole people," and employment in the theoretically less advanced collective enterprises. As of the end of 1983, there were 87 million employees in collective enterprises in the PRC (State Council, 1984).[7] Not only are wages in the state sector typically higher—estimates range from 20 to 40 percent—than in the collective sector, but employees in the state sector of industry tend to receive a wide range of welfare benefits such as medical care, retirement pay, factory housing, and so on, that are available on a reduced scale or not at all to workers in the collective sector (Davis-Friedmann, 1985; Whyte and Parish, 1984; Walder, 1984).[8] A further employment distinction is between employment as a permanent or nonperma-

---

[5]John Emerson has estimated that 13 million contract workers, largely peasants recruited from rural communes, succeeded in remaining in the cities between 1966 and 1976 (Emerson, 1982, 1983).

[6]A country survey of 31,435 rural households reported an average per capita income in 1984 of 355.3 yuan; a countrywide survey of 12,050 urban households reported a per capita income of 608 yuan (State Council, 1985: 255). Actual per capita income of peasant families was reported to have increased an estimated 98.4 percent compared with 1978 while the average per capita living expenses of urban dwellers was reported to have increased by 42.7 percent (Zuo, 1985).

[7]By the end of 1984, the number of workers in the collective sector was reported to be 32 million (G. He, 1985).

[8]Workers in small-scale collective enterprises located at the *xian* (country) level and below generally do not receive welfare benefits at all (Xue, 1983: III; 99—101; Whyte and Parish, 1984: 71—6).

nent worker. As in other communist states, permanent workers in the PRC have traditionally enjoyed a virtually unshakable job security with little fear of being fired except on political grounds or for outrageous acts of dereliction in job performance. Nonpermanent workers, estimated in the late 1970s to constitute somewhere between 4 and 7 percent of the Chinese labor force, generally, but not always, receive lower wages than permanent workers and additionally are usually ineligible for most welfare benefits (Emerson, 1983; Walder, 1981, 1984). Current Chinese labor policy strives to make a clear-cut distinction between contract and temporary workers. Contract workers, hired on the basis of specified labor contracts, are supposed to receive the same welfare treatment as permanent workers. Temporary workers, however, are excluded from participation in welfare plans (J. Wang and Li, 1985). Since 1979, moreover, the Chinese urban labor force has been further differentiated by the growth of a private sector of individual entrepreneurs. Current policy actively encourages the development of tertiary industry and forms of individual economy. By the end of 1984, over 3 million urban dwellers were reported as self-employed, a twentyfold increase over 1978 (G. He, 1985). Wages in the self-employed sector of the economy are subject to considerable variation but self-employed workers do not qualify for state welfare benefits.

In comparison to those of its communist counterparts, the Chinese labor market has been distinguished for its institutional rigidity and lack of job mobility, currently considered a serious structural defect by the state. By the late 1970s the Chinese labor market had become highly stratified, with little movement of labor between the state and collective sectors of industry. Employees were assigned their jobs by the state and turnover was close to marginal—rarely approaching rates of 5 percent per annum—in the state sector of industry (Walder, 1981:48). The limited opportunities for access to state sector employment were reinforced by the development in the early 1970s of the so-called "substitution" system in which retiring parents handed down their job in a state-run enterprise as a generational inheritance (Shirk, 1981; Emerson, 1982; Walder, 1984; Davis-Friedmann, 1985).[9] The demographic pressures of population growth, seen in the doubling of the Chinese population since 1949, have exacerbated the problems of labor allocation. Although reported figures vary widely, there is no doubt that unemployment constitutes a serious problem in the PRC.[10] Most of China's unemployed are

[9]Majorie Wolf notes, however, that women are far more likely than men to take early retirement to allow employment for a child. She reports, on the basis of her field research, that cases of male early retirement were symbolic rather than actual with men being retained by the workplace and shifted to work in another capacity (Wolf, 1985: 75).

[10]Whyte and Parish report that Chinese sources at the start of 1979 estimated unemployment at between 5 and 12 million or 5–11 percent of the nonagricultural labor force (Whyte

secondary school graduates seeking to enter the labor force for the first time drawn from the estimated 6 million youth who enter the labor force each year (G. He, 1985). The severity of China's unemployment problem, moreover, has been intensified by the return of millions of urban youth from the countryside since 1978.

Thus a major thrust of Chinese economic reform efforts has been directed toward restructuring the role of the state in the allocation of labor and increasing competition and labor mobility with a "socialist job market" (see Wei, 1985). In 1981, authorities announced that the state could no longer be responsible for procuring employment for all urban jobseekers, nullifying the state's longstanding guarantee of employment. By 1983, moreover, the state was actively promoting various forms of contract hiring envisioned as an eventual replacement for the system of permanent employment. Competition among workers based on meritocratic criteria is seen to replace the much-maligned "iron rice bowl" system of permanent job security. While the 1984 Reform Decision clearly identified state-run enterprises as the "leading force in China's socialist economy," collective and individual undertakings were presented as necessary complementary and adjunct forms of production (Reform Decision, 1984: XIII). As a practical matter, an estimated 70 percent of jobseekers entering the Chinese workforce from 1978 to 1984 found employment in the collective or individual sectors of the economy (G. He, 1985). Although the future course of the Chinese economic reforms, still in an incipient stage of implementation, remains uncertain, the constraints imposed by Chinese demography make it seem unlikely that the current stress on development of the tertiary sector of the economy will be abandoned.[11]

Trade Union Organization

With the historical, political, and socioeconomic context of current trade union activity having been established, it is now time to direct attention

---

and Parish, 1984: 42). Emerson notes that Chinese estimates of urban unemployment ranged from 10 to 25 million in 1979 (Emerson, 1983: 1−2). More recent Chinese accounts, however, have tended to present a more optimistic view of the unemployment problem. The 1983 *Almanac of China's Economy* reported that the government had found jobs for 4,750,000 young people in 1982 with the employment problem solved in twenty-three provinces, cities, and autonomous areas (Xue, 1983: III 96−7). The 1984 State Bulletin report on the Chinese economy listed 3,530,000 people as "waiting for work" at the end of 1984 (State Council, 1985: 255).

[11]The tendency for original reform goals to undergo permutation is evident, for example, in Chen Liang's article on contract workers in which he suggests the possibility that after the expiration of the first contract period "five to ten year and even longer long-term contracts" be given to workers (Chen, 1985).

to the unions themselves. In this connection, it is important first to examine the organizational structure of Chinese trade unions as an institutional arrangement which has its roots in the Soviet-style model. The Chinese construction of the trade union apparatus after 1949 was characterized by an unabashed borrowing from Soviet experience. Many Chinese documents on trade union work and trade union organization were simply verbatim translations of the Russian originals.[12] Consequently, Chinese trade unions look very similar to Soviet trade unions on formal institutional structure. As in the Soviet case, Chinese trade unions are organized according to a production principle held together by democratic centralism. Enterprise trade unions have a dual accountability both to an industrial trade union structure and to an immediate superior in the regional hierarchy (see Appendix, p.245). A machine-building factory in Tianjin, for example, would be accountable to both the branch office of the national level Machine Building Workers' Trade Union and to the citywide Tianjin Trade Union Council existing under the national authority of the ACFTU.

As with the Communist party whose organizational format it imitates, Chinese trade union organization is pyramidal in structure. Trade union members at the enterprise level elect trade union committees and standing committees which are charged with overseeing trade union work within their domain. These committees form the bottom rung of a complex organizational hierarchy which extends upward through the municipal (or city or township) and provincial levels, culminating in the national structure of the ACFTU at its apex. The ACFTU constitutes the "supreme" repository of trade union authority in the PRC which is empowered with the general administration of trade union policy. Elected for a five-year term by representative trade union congresses at the various levels, as of October 1983, the ACFTU had a 241-member Executive Committee headed by ACFTU Chairman Ni Zhifu. A 34-member Presidium and an 11-member Secretariat, selected by the Executive Committee, carry on the daily organizational and supervisory work of the ACFTU.

Although Chinese trade unions display a striking structural congruence with the Soviet model, the resemblances that exist on paper tend to break down in practice. Compared with their Soviet counterparts, Chinese trade unions exhibit a lower level of institutional development. While trade union membership is close to universal in the Soviet Union, a substantial proportion of Chinese wage-earners are not unionized. In units in which the trade union was organized, 73,310,000 staff and workers out of a workforce of

---

[12]The Soviet legacy in trade union work is still marked with the Workers' Publishing House in Bejing continuing to publish Soviet tracts on the trade union movement in translation. See, for example, Junwannuofu, 1985.

85,866,000 were reported to be trade union members at the end of 1982, a membership rate of 85.3 percent (Xue, 1983: 1–39). But not all units have a trade union organization. With a Chinese urban workforce of 112 million at the end of 1982, around 27 million Chinese worked in units without a trade union organization, or approximately 23 percent of the total Chinese wage-earning population. Although trade union membership is on the increase, as of the end of 1982 only about 67 percent of the total Chinese wage-earning population belonged to trade unions.[13]

The likelihood that an enterprise will have a functioning trade union varies considerably according to such variables as type and size of the enterprise and geographic location. State-run enterprises, especially large-scale state-run enterprises, are more likely to have established trade union organizations than collective enterprises. Trade union organization tends to be more developed in the cities than at the quasi-rural level of the county or the township. Enterprises located in the coastal areas of China typically display a higher level of trade union institutionalization than enterprises in the remote hinterlands or in the national minority regions. Trade union membership in the PRC thus tends to follow the dualistic divisions of the Chinese labor market. A present aim of Chinese trade union policy, however, is to increase trade union membership through the establishment of trade union structures in rural areas and through the recruitment of workers in collective industry and contract workers who were often deliberately excluded from joining the trade union in the past. In April 1983 the Organizational Department of the ACFTU circulated a "Notice on Contract Workers' Trade Union Membership," requesting local level trade union committees to recruit contract workers into the trade union (*Gongren Ribao*, 1983d; *FBIS*, 1983a). The resolution of the Second Session of the Tenth Trade Union Congress in December 1984, moreover, specifically noted the need to build up trade unions in rural enterprises which employed 30 million peasants turned workers ("Resolution," 1985).[14]

The institutional weakness of Chinese unions is in part a consequence of the political turbulence of the post-1949 period. In particular, the Chinese

[13]In 1949, 38.9 percent of workers and staff belonged to trade unions in units in which the trade union was organized; in 1964 the trade union membership rate was 77.4 percent; and in 1979 the trade union membership rate was 74.6 percent (Xue, 1983: 1–39). It should be noted, however, that these statistics do not deal directly with the question of what percentage of Chinese *industrial* workers belong to unions since trade union membership is open to all Chinese wage-earners (with the exception of those excluded for political reasons) regardless of occupational position.

[14]The resolution also noted the need to establish trade unions in the Special Economic Zones ("Resolution," 1985: 124–5). For a discussion of trade union operation in the Special Economic Zones see *Ta Kung Pao*, 1984.

trade union movement has been faced with the challenge of overcoming the legacy of its twelve-year demise during the Cultural Revolution. Although organizational work to restore enterprise trade unions was initiated in the early 1970s, the national convocation of the Ninth ACFTU Congress in October 1978 preceded the actual reconstitution of trade unions at the enterprise level in some instances. Reports of trade union reconstruction in the Chinese press extended into 1980 (see *JPRS*, 1980a; 1980b). Current trade union policy continues to identify the need to strengthen the organization of trade unions at the basic level. In accordance with the decentralizing impetus of the Chinese reform movement, the December 1984 Resolution of the ACFTU specified that trade unions at basic levels be delegated increased authority to ensure their successful operation ("Resolution," 1985).

Enterprise Authority Relationships: The Party in the Factory

The politicization of Chinese society has meant a direct party leadership over the enterprise. Unlike some other communist states, China only rarely placed an emphasis on managerial expertise and technical efficiency during most of the post-1949 period. In the "red versus expert" debate of the Maoist era (a debate played out during the early stages of socialist state construction in each of the societies under examination in this volume), the political "red" invariably won out over the technocratic expert as the arbiter of policy. The CCP maintains its control over the enterprise through a series of formal and informal mechanisms, none of which is actually unique to China as a communist society but some of which exhibit a higher degree of organizational development than in other communist systems. As with other communist states, the PRC relies on democratic centralism as a means of exercising organizational control. The ACFTU exists as an auxiliary structure of the party under the direct leadership of the party committee in the enterprise. Within the enterprise, the operation of democratic centralism serves to concentrate power in the hands of the enterprise party committee. Second, the existence of an "interlocking directorate" positions party members in leadership roles throughout the enterprise. Typically most of the members of the enterprise trade union committee are simultaneously members of the party and the enterprise trade union chairman usually serves on the enterprise party committee.[15] Similarly, the overlapping of party and

---

[15]With the initiation of elections to select the trade union leadership, the theoretical prospect of a non-party member being elected the enterprise trade union chair has received some attention in the press. In a question and answer session on the role of the trade union

managerial positions has often made the attempt to distinguish between party and management in the enterprise rather futile. Although China lacks the formal institution of *nomenklatura* as it exists in the Soviet Union and elsewhere in Eastern Europe, the party nevertheless retains a key control over the designation of enterprise leadership posts.

While the party's occupation of key enterprise positions ensures its predominance within the enterprise hierarchy, its basis of power is simultaneously reinforced through informal channels of interaction. In fact, enterprise employees are likely to view these informal networks, which tend to parallel existing leaderships, as the key determinant of the enterprise distribution of power (Walder, 1981: 132). As in other communist systems, patron – client relationships are important in the PRC and oftentimes critical in delineating the structure of enterprise relationships. The party's ability to define values and make decisions over the allocation of resources within the enterprise places other enterprise actors in a subordinate position conducive to complaint behavior. Leaders of career advance and the distribution of enterprise rewards are both controlled by the party.

By and large, the post-1949 operations of the Chinese enterprise have been geared less to meritocratic standards of performance than to political criteria and expressions of political loyalty as the basis for the distribution of rewards. Communist Party control within the enterprise gave rise to a system of incentives that placed a high priority on politically acquiescent behavior. Trade union cadres learned very early on, through the union purges of the 1950s, the costs of defying the priorities of the political leadership. If trade union policy in theory enjoined trade union cadres simultaneously to strike a balance between production and workers' livelihood, the party's earmarking of production as the union's primary task made cadres, knowing their prospects for promotion and movement up the enterprise hierarchy were on the line, hard-pressed to defend the workers' interests. Rather, the politicization of values within the Chinese enterprise served to encourage trade union cadres to espouse the most militant expressions of obedience to the party line, leaving those who might be inclined to articulate a dediant point of view highly susceptible to the dreaded charges of economism and syndicalism. As Kang Wenhua, the chairman of the Mukdan Trade Union Committee noted (Kang, 1983): "In the past we felt that to grasp production was safe; to grasp livelihood was dangerous. To follow the tide was safe; to independently take responsibility for developing movements was dangerous. To be responsible to the leadership was safe; to be responsible to the masses was dangerous."

---

appearing in *Workers' Daily* in March, 1984, for example, it was asserted that the trade union chair should be elected by the workers, not selected by the enterprise party secretary even if it resulted in the election of a non-party member *(Gongren Ribao,* 1984a). (In fact, given party control over the selection of potential candidates, the possibility would appear to be remote.)

The party's ability to ensure compliance extends beyond institutional actors down to the workers' themselves. The party's control over the enterprise reward structure, which is accentuated by the reliance of workers in the state sector on the enterprise for the provision of such scarce resources as housing and delivery of social services, has led to a situation identified by Andrew Walder as "organized dependency" (Walder, 1981, 1983).[16] Walder's research has emphasized the extent to which the organizational structure of controls exercised by the party within the enterprise has been instrumental in the development of a dependency relationship linking workers to the party in a highly personalized network of interactions. Compared to the East European or the Soviet case, the Chinese enterprise has been distinguished by the pervasiveness of political controls. Although workers in the collective sector of Chinese industry have been subject to less stringent organizational controls than workers in state-owned industry, political organization in the Chinese enterprise has typically extended down to the workshop floor. The party monitors workers through such measures as the maintenance of dossiers, files kept on each enterprise employee which includes a political evaluation, and reliance on a network of activists whose responsibilities include reporting on worker behavior to party authorities.

Enterprise employees, moreover, are organized into small groups, conducting political study and periodic criticism and self-criticism sessions, which serve as an additional agent of political control. Within the Chinese enterprise, the shop-floor foreman, who possesses considerable discretionary powers over the work team, invariably acts as an agent of the party, keeping tabs on the political as well as the productive performance of rank-and-file workers. In sum, the domination exercised by the party in the enterprise is reflected organizationally by the development of vertical rather than horizontal patterns of interaction. The separate vertical ties binding both the unions and the workers to the party act to discourage the formation of linkages between the unions and the working class. The Leninist conception of the unions as a transmission belt situated midway between the party and the workers remains unrealized since neither union cadres nor workers are motivated to identify the union–worker relationship as more important than the cultivation of direct ties to the party.

The party's monopoly of control over enterprise operations, however, has been the target of repeated attacks by the Deng Xiaoping leadership which formally announced its intention to replace the Maoist system of party leadership over the enterprise with the system of factory manager responsi-

---

[16]This discussion of party–worker relationships is based upon the research and analysis of Andrew Walder who discusses the mechanisms of party control in the enterprise in Walder, 1981 and 1983.

bility in the 1984 Reform Decision (Reform Decision, 1984). What was a virtue in the Maoist era is now seen as a distinct liability in weakening the growth of spheres of autonomy, the division of labor, and the development of specialization and technical expertise within the enterprise. Although not expressed in so many words, the reform in reality strives to reinstitute the Soviet-style system of "one-man management" that was briefly—and imperfectly—adopted in Chinese factories in the early 1950s.[17] Whether the Deng Xiaoping leadership will be able to push through enterprise depoliticization, or even how the leadership conceives of enterprise depoliticization, remains an open question. The projected transfer of operational control from the party to the factory director inevitably arouses the opposition of enterprise party committees. But if successfully instituted, the factory manager responsibility system does hold out the promise of a shift in enterprise authority relationships, allowing for a greater differentiation of interests within the enterprise. The implementation of the factory manager responsibility system would bring China closer to the mainstream of Soviet-style practice in enterprise management and, in so doing, increase the prospects for the unions to perform their envisioned dual functioning role as the simultaneous representative of both the party *and* the working class.

Enterprise Reforms and Enterprise Democracy

Since the watershed Third Party Plenum of the Eleventh Party Congress in December, 1978, renewed attention has been paid to the concept of socialist democracy. "Without democracy," according to Deng Xiaoping, "there can be no socialism" (Q. Wang *et al.*, 1984). Among the measures taken to strengthen Chinese democracy since the death of Mao, the implementation of enterprise democracy has figured prominently. Speaking at the Ninth ACFTU Congress in September, 1978, Deng Xiaoping noted (*Zhongguo Gonghui Dijiuici*, 1978: 4):

> In order to achieve the Four Modernizations all our enterprises without exception should have democratic management and this should be combined with centralized leadership. Workshop directors, section chiefs, and group heads in every enterprise must in the future be elected by the workers in the unit. Major issues in an enterprise should be discussed by workers' congresses or general membership meetings at which leadership cadres of the enterprise must listen to the views of the workers and accept criticism and supervision by them.

[17]In the early 1980s, however, articles appearing in the Chinese press openly extolled the virtues of "one-man management." See, for example, Wang, 1981; 37−44; Ma, 1980: 5.

Deng's speech has subsequently served as a sort of blueprint for the institution of democratic management in Chinese enterprises. Workers' congresses have been established as representative meetings of enterprise staff and workers; enterprise elections have been promoted as a key component of worker participation in enterprise management; and the role of the trade union has been redefined to allow the trade union greater independence to act as the representative and defender of the workers' interest.

In comparison with its Maoist predecessor, the current regime has exhibited little concern with democratic management as a means of transforming relations of production, directing instead a predominant attention to its strategic utility in achieving pragmatic regime goals. Democratic management has been seen as a means of underpinning regime legitimacy, illustrating the decisive role taken by the working class in the operation of the economy and the links binding the proletariat to its vanguard. Democratic management is assumed to perform an integrative function in enhancing workers' sense of efficacy and strengthening their sense of identification with the system. As with other communist systems, notably in Eastern Europe, enterprise democracy has been conceived of as a factor of productive efficiency, and a means of motivating employees in production (Reform Decision, 1984: VI; Su, 1981). The major thrust of Chinese analyses of enterprise democracy in the post-1978 era, however, has been to link enterprise democracy to the restructuring of enterprise authority relationships. A key issue, as discussed in the previous section, has been the need to dislodge the party's monopoly of control through an increasing differentiation of spheres of authority in enterprise operations.

By mid-1980, proposals to reform the enterprise leadership structure had evolved to a format that envisioned a tripartite sectioning of responsibility within the enterprise. The division of authority envisioned in the Chinese reform proposals, antithetical to the "politics in command" ethos of the Maoist era, seems to have drawn its inspiration not from any Madisonian notions of checks and balances but from the differentiation of "lines of authority" in the Yugoslav model.[18] Three forms of authority in enterprise management were distinguished in the Chinese analysis: policy authority, command authority, and supervisory authority. Rather than the party exercising control over all three aspects of enterprise authority, the reform advo-

---

[18]For a description of the division of spheres of authority in the Yugoslav enterprise, see Zukin, 1981. The initial phases of the experiment to grant Chinese enterprises increased self-management authority was accompanied by increased speculation about the possibilities of instituting forms of workers' participation along the lines of Yugoslav workers' councils. For a discussion of the influence of the Yugoslavian model on Chinese reformers see Kosta, 1984; Halperin, 1985. As illustrations of Chinese interest in the Yugoslav system see Siaqieweiji, 1977; Meng, 1978; *Nansilafude*, 1979; Pang, 1980.

cated a threefold division of responsibility with the workers' congresses assuming policy authority, the management assuming command authority, and the party exercising supervisory authority in enterprise relations. Each actor was to play a functionally separate role, enjoying operational autonomy, and a more or less equal status in enterprise operations. The party, while still in charge of carrying out the broadly defined policy line within the enterprise, was seen as disengaged from the minute details of daily operations. In its most daring form, the reform went so far as to advocate the replacement of the "factory manager responsibility system under the leadership of the party committee," with the "factory manager responsibility system under the leadership of the workers' congress" (H. Ma, 1980; Zhang, 1980; Tian *et al.*, 1981; Shanghai Dishier Mianfang Zhichang, 1981). Nor did the reform proposals remain a matter of rhetoric alone as the "factory manager responsibility system under the leadership of the workers' congresses" was adopted at selected keypoint enterprises on an experimental basis during 1980 (H. Ma, 1980; Shanghai Dishier Mianfang Zhichang, 1981; Tian *et al.*, 1981).

Nonetheless, the suggestion that the workers' congresses assume a policy authority within the enterprise did not survive the swing to the political right in China in late 1980 when antireform forces in the party managed to halt the momentum of the reform movement. The "Provisional Regulations Concerning Congresses of Workers and Staff Members in State-Owned Enterprises," issued in June, 1981, governing the establishment of workers' congresses were a conservative reconfirmation of the political status quo in the PRC. The regulations in essence reconstituted the workers' congresses in their pre-Cultural Revolution format, shorn of substantive powers and definitively subject to the authority of the enterprise party committee (Scherer, 1983: 28−31). But in the subsequent power struggle waged within the top echelons of the Chinese leadership over the direction of post-Mao policy, the fundamental goal of enterprise depoliticization has endured. The 1984 Reform Decision lays to rest, at least in theory, the "factory manager responsibility system under the leadership of the party committee," replacing it with the "factory manager responsibility system" (Reform Decision, 1984: VI). In the revised format, the conception of a differentiation of spheres of authority is still seen to constitute a critical aspect of enterprise operations. However, the autonomous authority delegated to the factory management does not extend to the workers' congresses which remain under the leadership of the enterprise party committee.

The leadership's reassertion of the primacy of political controls over mechanisms of worker participation stands in complete correspondence with longstanding Marxist-Leninist convictions about the relationship of the party to the proletariat. Nonetheless, the decision to discard the proposal that the workers' congresses assume a policy authority over enterprise operations was possibly also reinforced by the outbreak of the Polish crisis in the summer of 1980. Despite the geographical and cultural distance separating China from most of its communist brethren, the Chinese leadership has long been sensitive to the political implications of internal domestic events within the communist bloc.[19] After meeting with State President Li Xiannian in July, 1980, then president of the European Parliament Simone Veil reported that she had been told that China would face a crisis similar to that in Poland unless current economic reform efforts were successful (Sh. He, 1981: 72). Despite the weakness of Chinese unions, the memory of the union purges in the 1950s and the spectacle of the establishment of an independent trade union movement in Poland apparently created a certain anxiety within the Chinese leadership about the potential dangers of trade union autonomy.

The enterprise reform debate, as it unfolded in 1980, was notable in its failure to consider the role of the unions in the enterprise. Although the reconstitution of the ACFTU in 1978 was accompanied by a conventional Leninist emphasis on the unions as an institutional link between the workers and the party in the enterprise, the trade unions received almost no attention in discussions of reforming enterprise authority relations in 1980 and the few references made to the trade unions were uncharacteristically cryptic and tentative.[20] Despite the reformers' preoccupation with differentiating spheres of authority in the enterprise, no mention was made of the possibility of the institution of an operational autonomy for the trade union. It was not until after the enterprise leadership debate took a more conservative turn, asserting the primacy of political controls, that the trade union role reemerged as a topic of discussion. In correspondence with pre-Cultural Revolution practice, the 1981 Provisional Regulations on Workers' Congresses designated the unions as the working organs of the workers' congresses, in charge of carrying out tasks of the congress between sessions and handling the preparatory details connected with the convocation of the congresses (Scherer, 1983: 31).

It seems likely that the emergence of Solidarity strengthened the hand of those segments of the political leadership who were uncomfortable with the notion of establishing autonomous spheres of influence in the enterprise at the expense of the enterprise party committee. Silence over the role of the

---

[19]For a discussion of how political unrest in Poland and Hungary in 1956 influenced the Chinese leadership's decision to embark upon the "Hundred Flowers" period in 1957, see Solomon, 1971: 268–329.

[20]Wang Mengkui, for example, devoted three sentences to what he ambiguously referred to as the "organizational problems of the trade unions" in his article on problems of the enterprise leadership system in the January 1981 issue of *Economic Research* (Wang, 1981). See also Shanghai Chaiyou Jichang, 1980; Shanghai Dishier Mianfang Zhichang, 1981.

trade union may have been one indication of uneasiness; the decision to abandon the notion of the workers' congresses as autonomous enterprise structures possessing policy authority may have been another. Although the workers' congresses lacked the potential, theoretically possessed by the unions, to unite workers at the national level, the Chinese leadership still apparently found the concept of workers' congresses operating independently of direct party controls to be a threat. Present trade union policy goes further in identifying an independent role for trade unions than at any time in the post-1949 period. But the Chinese leadership apparently still continues to view the trade unions with some trepidation. State President Li Xiannian was reported to have acknowledged the existence of sympathizers to Lech Wałésa in the PRC in the midst of an attack upon Solidarity as an example of "sham trade unionism" (*jia gonghui zhuyi*) delivered at the Tenth Congress of the ACFTU in October, 1983 (*Zhongbao*, 1984). Scattered reports, moreover, have indicated attempts to establish Solidarity-style trade unions in China with no notable signs of success (Bernstein and Parks, 1980; Parks, 1981; Sh. He, 1981; Oka, 1983). A continued fear of the trade union's potential capacity for nationwide mobilization was evident in the guidelines issued by the Second Session of the Tenth Congress of the ACFTU in December 1984 specifying that "national, transregional, and transindustrial mass activities should by all means be discouraged" ("Resolution," 1985: 126). in short, current policy decrees that unions should be independent but not too independent. For all the talk of autonomy, the trade union policy line upholds the leadership role of the party over the unions.

The Chinese experience with enterprise democracy since 1978 has reflected the inherent contradictions between expanding the basis of worker representation in the enterprise and the simultaneous perceived need to maintain political controls. Following Deng Xiaoping's guidelines laid down at the Ninth ACFTU Congress, Chinese enterprises have reconstituted workers' congresses, instituted workplace elections, extending in some cases up to the level of the enterprise director, and sought to increase the authority of the trade union to act in defense of the workers' interest. The profusion of forms of democracy has apparently been accompanied by some confusion over differentiation of roles. Guo Feng, the First Secretary of the Liaoning Provincial Party Committee, noted in an article appearing in *Worker's Daily* in June 1985 the lack of a "clear and rational relationship between the workers' congresses and the trade unions" (Guo, 1985: 3).

A more serious impediment to the institution of democratic management, however, has been the continued domination of the party over the implementation of democratic management. By interjecting its personnel in key roles and relying upon the direct and indirect methods of control at its command, the party has been able to exercise a guiding hand over the institution of workplace democracy. Article 11 of the 1981 Provincial Regulations on the establishment of workers' congresses directly specified the positioning of party members on the workers' congress presidium (Scherer, 1983: 31). The operation of the interlocking directorate, moreover, has acted to ensure that the chairman of the workers' congresses be a concurrent member of the enterprise party committee. Under these circumstances, it is unsurprising that workers have been reported to complain that workers' representatives to the workers' congresses are "not selected by workers but designated by leaders" and that the presidium of the workers' congress is virtually synonymous with "a joint meeting of party branch secretaries" (*FBIS*, 1983b: K18). In a similar fashion, the structure of political controls within the enterprise acts to preordain electoral outcomes. The institution of limited choice elections of the enterprise leadership is a Dengist innovation which lacks a direct parallel to the pre-1978 period. Nonetheless, the preparation of the slate of electors for leadership posts takes place under the supervisory guidance of the enterprise party committee, making it extremely unlikely that a non-party approved candidate would appear on the ballot. Moreover, despite the movement toward decentralization sanctioned by the 1984 reform decision, the PRC still constitutes an example of a centrally planned economy which has retained the family resemblance to the Soviet-style model. Thus, the range of decisions open to deliberation by the workers' congresses remains limited and the institution of limited choice elections within the enterprise indicates a choice between individuals rather than between competing policy programs.

The strains of the current leadership's efforts to balance democracy and centralism, to realize a pluralist accommodation of interests within the workplace without simultaneously acknowledging the legitimacy of societal conflict is exemplified by the leadership's ambiguous and contradictory analysis of the role of the trade unions in supporting strikes. The right to strike, which was first installed, at the Mao Zedong's behest, in the Chinese Constitution of 1975, and retained in the Constitution of 1978, was eliminated in the 1982 Constitution.[21] Although the right to strike was castigated as an example of extensive democracy verging on anarchism, the idea of the right to strike has nonetheless lingered on as an item of discussion by the trade union leadership. Speaking at a press conference on the eve of the Tenth ACFTU Congress in October, 1983, ACFTU Executive Committee member Wang Jiachong noted that Chinese unions could support strikes in exceptional cases such as those involving industrial safety (Chang, 1983). In early 1984 ACFTU Chairman Ni Zhifu also suggested in an interview that workers

---

[21]The constitutional right to strike notwithstanding, Mao Zedong did not hesitate to dispatch the People's Liberation Army to quell strikes which erupted in China in 1976.

might legitimately be driven to strike in situations in which working conditions were intolerably dangerous and management deaf to workers' exhortations. The strike, according to Ni, could be viewed as an extraordinary measure used in a case of last resort to combat bureaucratism. The responsibility for organizing the strike and serving as an intermissary between workers and management would be that of the trade unions (*Zhongbao*, 1984). The quasi-legitimacy accorded to worker collective action directed against a recalcitrant management was reiterated in the resolution of the Second Executive Session of the Tenth Congress of the ACFTU which stated that "trade unions should support workers in exercising their rights to boycott those who direct production in violation of regulations" ("Resolution," 1985: 123). As a practical matter, given the subordination of union cadres to their political and managerial superiors in the enterprise hierarchy, the prospect of the unions organizing the workers to strike against management appears remote. Both Wang and Ni declined to provide any concrete examples of legitimate forms of collective action in Chinese factories although Wang stated that such kinds of industrial action had "already taken place" and Ni noted two examples—one the infamous Bohai Oil Rig Disaster in which twelve workers died—of managerial negligence. One might speculate that here, too, the specter of the Polish situation underlies Chinese attempts to strengthen union ties to the workers and to channel worker protests into a regulated format. Nonetheless, the idea of the right to strike is noteworthy for its implicit acknowledgment of the existence of conflicting interests in Chinese society. It is an idea, moreover, that goes beyond the conventional boundaries of ideological discourse in the communist bloc.

Chinese Reform Efforts

The Chinese reform movement initiated by Deng Xiaoping at the Third Plenum of the Eleventh Party Congress has occasioned dramatic changes in the economic and political structure of Chinese society. Instituted in many instances as an explicit rejection of policies pursued during the Maoist era, the post-1978 reforms have given a high priority to goals of political institutionalization economic modernization. From the viewpoint of the members of the current Chinese leadership, most of whom suffered as victims during the continual political campaigns of the Maoist era, political stability is not only a paramount regime goal but a necessary precondition for modernization. Under Deng Xiaoping's guiding influence, the Chinese Communist Party has embarked on a course of internal self-criticism and rectification designed to purge the party of Maoist sympathizers, dislodge the geriatric old guard, and elevate a younger, better educated, and more technically disposed generation of cadres to political leadership. Chinese experimentation with economic reforms has been carried furthest in the agricultural sector where the institution of the agricultural responsibility system in the Chinese countryside has been accompanied by the dismantling of collective production at the level of the production team in favor of a system of household contracting of production. Nonetheless, a series of industrial reforms that began initiation on an experimental basis in 1978 received an official sanction for nationwide implementation at the Third Plenum of the Twelfth Party Congress in October 1984. Although it is as of yet uncertain how the reforms will evolve in the course of concrete implementation, the 1984 Reform Decision embodied a vision of industrial organization somewhat akin to the Hungarian model. The Chinese reforms include a decentralization of decision-making authority from the center to the lower levels, a reform of the price system to reflect the interplay of supply and demand, the use of profit as an indicator of performance, and an increased reliance on economic rather than administrative levers to operate the economy. Despite the steps taken toward a reliance on market mechanisms, the extent to which the Chinese reforms represent an abandonment of the Soviet-style system should not be exaggerated. Rather, in certain vital respects, the outline of the economy contained in the 1984 Reform Decision constitutes an effort to rid the Chinese industrial system of its Maoist eccentricies and return to the Soviet-style model that was only imperfectly instituted in the PRC in the 1950s. The Chinese efforts to depoliticize the enterprise, to increase spheres of autonomy in enterprise operations, to promote technical expertise, professionalism, and specialization in the division of labor trace their origins to the Soviet-style system.

The current attempt to increase the independent role of the trade union can be seen as an interrelated facet of the broader reform efforts to restructure enterprise authority relationships so as to allow for the development of spheres of autonomy in enterprise operations. If successful, the implementation of the 1984 Reform Decision holds out the prospect for an enhanced scope of action to the unions allowing for a concentration upon the representation of the workers' interests rather than production as a primary endeavor. Nonetheless, the impact of the industrial reforms upon the trade unions appears to be mixed, at least in the short run. Preliminary evidence suggests that the initial institution of certain reform decisions has either failed to tackle longstanding problems of the trade union's role or has had unintended detrimental consequences for the trade union movement.

Since the 1950s when trade union cadres complained that they were "fourth rate" cadres, the trade union has occupied a vulnerable position in the enterprise hierarchy. Neither the party nor the management has displayed a consistent commitment to the institutional development of the trade union. The high levels of enterprise noncompliance at paying the trade union fee as required by trade union law prompted a formal rebuke of the enterprise management by the State Council in December 1980 (State Council, 1981). By and large, trade union work tends to rank as a low priority item on enterprise party committee agendas. In discussing how to implement a Central Committee directive on strengthening the quality of party leadership over the unions, Ma Wenrui, a Central Committee member and the First Party Secretary of Shanxi Province, recommended that enterprise party committees set time aside to discuss trade union work once every six months (*Gongren Ribao* 1983i). The party has also often proved unwilling to relinquish certain functions officially within the trade unions' domain such as the organization of campaigns and socialist emulation work that were incorporated into the party's sphere of operations during the Cultural Revolution. The continued existence of this problem was noted by the Second Session of the ACFTU in December 1984 which stressed the importance of creating distinct spheres of responsibility between the party and the unions and the management and the unions to ensure the independence of trade union work ("Resolution," 1985: 125).

The subordinate position occupied by the trade union in the enterprise hierarchy is also revealed in the current leadership's efforts at "administrative readjustment," aimed at replacing longtime political appointees with a younger, technically competent, pro-reform breed of cadres. Evidence indicates that enterprise leaderships, faced with the task of administrative streamlining, have not only moved capable cadres out of the trade union to other departments but have also used the trade union as a repository for surplus cadres eliminated as a consequence of the readjustment.[22] Speaking about this problem, Liu Zhengwei, First Party Secretary of Henan Province, noted that the overall quality of union cadres was actually being lowered as a result of the administrative readjustment as older cadres with a low cultural level were being transferred into the organization (Liu, 1984). The use of the trade union as a sort of final resting place for surplus cadres who are unwanted elsewhere in the system obviously has detrimental implications for the future of trade union institutionalization. Even more so than is the case elsewhere in the communist world, politically ambitious cadres have tended to view trade union work not as a career commitment but as a stepping stone to other, more prestigious jobs within the enterprise.

In addition, evidence also suggests that the trade union's susceptibility

---

[22]The Chinese press has often been very candid about the propensity of the enterprise leadership to use the trade unions as a sort of dumping ground for surplus—often the old and the infirm—cadres. See, for example,*Gongren Ribao*, 1983h, and 1983l. A related problem has been the tendency of enterprise leaderships to rely upon trade union cadres as a source of temporary labor, to be used to fill vacancies and perform investigation work throughout the system. See, for example, *Gongren Ribao*, 1983c.

to the enterprise leadership has been accentuated by the movement to decentralize decision-making authority in the PRC. Although tensions between centralization and decentralization have long been endemic in the PRC, the mandate given in the 1984 Reform Decision to run the enterprise as a "relatively independent entity" indicates a shift of some significance in the overall distribution of power between the center and the localities. The lessening of controls between the national and the enterprise levels, however, does not appear to be advantageous to the trade union's position in the enterprise relative to the enterprise leadership. As an extreme example, an article appearing in *Workers' Daily* in early 1983 reported that some enterprise leaderships had used their newly granted powers to abolish the trade union as an enterprise structure, merging its duties with other administrative departments and transferring trade union cadres to other positions throughout the enterprise (*Gongren Ribao*, 1983g).

The trade union's newly designated responsibility to defend the workers' interests as a primary endeavor, moreover, tends to place the unions in an adversarial position to the enterprise leadership on the issue of wage reform. Even in the trial stages of economic reform, some enterprises, operating in an environment of increased autonomy, interpreted the party's injunction to break the "iron rice bowl" and link distribution to work as a mandate to cease or reduce payments for workers' insurance benefits and subsidies.[23] Enterprises, especially small-scale enterprises in the collective sector, have been reported to have engaged in such practices as slashing medical and retirement benefits, closing down enterprise clinics, dining halls, and nurseries, and abolishing or reducing sick leave.[24] Women workers in particular seem to have been a target of discriminatory treatment with enterprises reported to have closed down factory nurseries, abolished nursing time and pregnancy leave, and pressured women to quit the workforce through placing them on extended leave.[25] Although the Chinese leadership initially reacted to condemn cutbacks in welfare expenditures as violations of Chinese labor law, its current response is more ambiguous. A report appearing in *Workers' Daily* in late 1984 acknowledged without criticism that the majority of the 316 units

---

[23]The practice of providing extensive subsidies to residents of Chinese cities, which was estimated to make up 40–50 percent of the costs of the state budget in 1984, is slated to be eliminated under the 1984 Reform Decision.

[24]See for example, Xue 1983: Part III, p. 101; *Gongren Ribao*, 1983b.

[25]In Liaoning Province over 18,000 pregnant or nursing women were reported to have been given leaves of absence, some of whom were subsequently denied the right to return to the factory (*Gongren Ribao*, 1983k). According to additional incomplete statistics from Liaoning province, over ninety-eight nurseries and nursing rooms had been shut down in the economic reform movement as of the fall of 1983 (*Gongren Ribao*, 1983n).

in Wuhan's Number Two light industrial, textile, machinery, and metallurgical systems that had reformed the original labor insurance regulations had reduced sick leave and medical treatment; only one unit of the 316 had improved the standard of retirement benefits for staff and workers as a consequence of the reform (*Gongren Ribao*, 1984b). The resolution issued by the Second Session of the Tenth ACFTU Congress in December 1984 noted the necessity of reforming social welfare policy and labor insurance regulations, while seemingly leaving open the possibility that a restructuring of the system to link worker performance more closely to wages would indicate a decrease in benefits for at least a portion of the workforce ("Resolution," 1985: 118). Current policy thus places the enterprise trade union committee in an unenviable position. Trade union cadres who protest at the dismantling of workers' insurance benefits leave themselves open to the charge by the enterprise management of sabotaging the enterprise reform efforts.[26] Nor does the trade union policy line provide a reliable guide to action. The December 1984 ACFTU resolution exhorted trade union cadres to "dare to protect the legitimate rights and interests of the workers and staff members" without, however, distinguishing which rights and demands were legitimate and which were not ("Resolution," 1985: 120).

Conclusion: The Future of Trade Union Performance

Chinese trade unions fare poorly in a comparison with most of their communist counterparts. Such factors as the Chinese peasant-based revolutionary heritage, the PRC's continuing status as an underdeveloped agricultural society, the primacy given to political values within the Chinese enterprise, and the political instability of the post-1949 period have all contributed to the weakness of the Chinese trade union movement. Although the Chinese state has been in existence for over three decades, the oscillations of the Chinese political struggle, culminating in the Cultural Revolution, have served to impede the basic task of trade union institutionalization. By and large, Chinese trade unions do not play a role in the definition of policy either as national actors or within the enterprise. The Chinese industrial system lacks the structures—nominal or otherwise—that provide for trade union participation in other regimes. The Chinese trade union movement tends to play a passive role acting in response to, rather than as an initiator of, policy.

---

[26]A letter to the editor in the June 15, 1983 issue of *Workers' Daily*, for example, recounted the situation of a trade union cadre whose protest against a decrease in sick pay for workers resulted in the charge that he was out to "destroy" the reform efforts. Further efforts by the trade union cadre to protest resulted in the Party Secretary instructing the enterprise finance department to cut off his wages (*Gongren Ribao*, 1983j).

Yet despite all of the problems connected with the trade unions, the Chinese leadership has remained committed to the Leninist concept of the trade union as a necessary structure within the socialist enterprise. In the final analysis, the perception of the trade union as a link between the party and the workers is seen as indispensable in a state that bases its legitimacy on its claim to be the vanguard of the proletariat.

The future performance of Chinese trade unions is dependent upon a series of extraneous factors outside of its control. The long-term prospects for the Chinese trade union movement are inextricably connected to the ability of the PRC to deal with demographic and structural variables, curbing population growth, providing employment for Chinese urban dwellers, and attaining the goal of modernization. But in the short run, political variables assume an immediate primacy. The success of the current attempt to give the trade union greater operational autonomy within the enterprise as a spokesman for the workers' interest will be decided as a political issue. At the time of writing, the projected depoliticization of the enterprise remains a nebulous concept in the Chinese political vocabulary. It is not clear what the current Chinese leadership envisions as enterprise depoliticization, to what extent it will be successful in its efforts, or whether the as yet unknown future leadership will remain equally committed to this goal. What is clear, however, is that this is a measure which pits the Dengist leadership against the enterprise party committees which can be depended upon to fight a rearguard action against the reform.

Attempts, however, to increase the autonomy of the trade unions will be doomed to failure unless they are accompanied by a restructuring of enterprise authority relationships such that the act of defending the workers' interests is seen as a legitimate activity that will not sound the death knoll for a union cadre's career. The enterprise leadership also needs to exhibit a hitherto absent interest in the task of trade union institutionalization. Partly as a consequence of its Soviet-style heritage, it would seem that the trade union's prospects for exercising authority are greatest in a centralized system with a high degree of vertical integration. Short of a union sytem based on totally new principles beyond the dual functioning model, the closer the Chinese approximation to the Soviet-style system, the better the chances of the trade union to maximize its position. The reform program of the Deng Xiaoping leadership places China on the liberal end of the continuum of communist state behavior. But in a comparative sense, China appears to be moving closer to the communist mainstream in contrast to its previous location during the Maoist era on the outer fringes of the communist bloc. Current Chinese trade union policy places the PRC squarely into line with its communist counterparts. Whatever the inherent tensions of the concept, the dual functioning role, should it actually be instituted in practice as well as articulated in theory, offers the Chinese trade union movement greater autonomy than it experienced in the Maoist era.

Appendix

I   Organization of the ACFTU

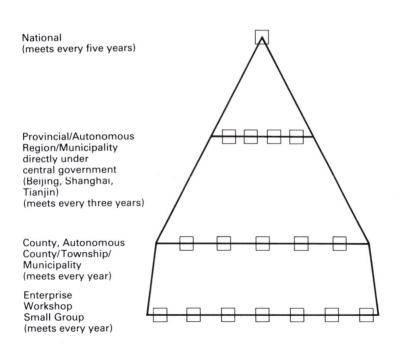

National
(meets every five years)

Provincial/Autonomous
Region/Municipality
directly under
central government
(Beijing, Shanghai,
Tianjin)
(meets every three years)

County, Autonomous
County/Township/
Municipality
(meets every year)

Enterprise
Workshop
Small Group
(meets every year)

II Statistical Information for the PRC Population, Employment, and Wage Data

	Population	Employment	Wages
Total	**1,036,040,000** (1984)[a]	**460,040,000** (1983)[b]	
Urban	241,280,000 (23.5%) (1983)[c]	118,240,000 (1984)[a]	608 yuan per capita (1984)[a]
Rural	782,670,000 (76.5%) (1983)[c]	342,580,000 (1983)[b]	355 yuan per capita (1984)[a]
Type of Organization			
State Enterprise		87,710,000[e] (1983)	836 yuan[f] (1982)
Collective Enterprise		32,000,000[d] (1984)	671 yuan[f] (1982)
Self-Employed		3,000,000[d] (1984)	

Female Employment among Staff and Workers[b] (1983)
Total: **41,988,000 (36.9%)**
In Collective
Enterprises 13,841,000 (50.7%)
In State
Enterprises 28,147,000 (31.8%)

Birth Rate (1984) 1.75%[a]

Sources: [a]State Council, 1985; [b]PRC Yearbook, 1984; [c]Bannister, 1984; [d]He, 1985; [e]State Council, 1984; [f]Congren Ribao, April 40, 1983.

III Trade Union Membership and Organizational Data

*Type of Member**
Trade Union Members[b] (1983)	73,310,000
Trade Union Activists[b] (1983)	9,300,000
Trade Union Cadres[c] (1983)	256,000
Company Cadres (1980)	11,700
Industrial Cadres (1980)	15,100
Country Level and above cadres (1980)	26,100
Enterprise Cadres[a] (1980)	190,000

Type of Organization†
Primary Trade Unions[b] (1983)	432,000
Workshop Trade Unions (1980)	449,000
Trade Union Small Groups[a] (1983)	5,479,000
Chinese Communist Party Members (1983)[‡]	40,000,000

Notes:
Trade Union Activists are full-time workers who are not divorced from production.
Trade Union Cadres are paid trade union functionaries
[†]*Sources:* Xue, 1982: 716; [a]Ni, 1983: 2; [c]Congren Ribao, 1983m: 1.
[*]*Sources:* Xue, 1982; 716; [a]Gongren Ribao, 1983a; [b]Ni, 1983: 2; [c]Congren Ribao, 1983m:
[‡]*Source:* Ta Kung Pao, 1983; 1.

Acknowledgment

I would like to thank Andrew Walder for his very helpful comments on an earlier draft of this chapter.

References

Bannister, Judith (1984), "Population Policy and Trends in China, 1978−1983," *China Quarterly* , no. 100 (December), pp. 717−41.

Bernstein, Harry, and Parks, Michael, (1980), "Labor Unions Emerging as a Major Force in China," *Los Angeles Times*, (December 29), p.1.

Chang, Elizabeth (1983), Paris AFP in English 17 October 1983; in *FBIS*, (October 20), K9.

Chen, Ce (1957), "Bixu jianchi shehui zhuyi de gonghui yundong" (It is necessary to maintain a socialist trade union movement), *Zhejiang Ribao*, (October 17), p. 2.

Chen, Liang (1985), "Contract System Workers Are Not Temporary Workers," *Yunnan Ribao*, (October 19, 1984), p. 3; in *JPRS-CEA-85-033,* (April 4), pp. 232−3.

Chen, Xueyan (1983), "The Rise and Fall of the Solidrity Trade Union in Poland," *Liaowang*, no. 2 (February 1983), pp. 30−1; in *JPRS*, no. 83433 (May 9), pp. 24−9.

Davis-Friedmann, Deborah (1985), "Intergenerational Inequalities and the Chinese Revolution," *Modern China*, vol. 11, no. 2 (April), pp. 177−202.

Emerson, John Phillip (1982), "The Labor Force of China, 1957−1980," in John Hardt (ed.), *China Under the Four Modernizations: Part 1*, (Washington, D.C.: United States Congress Joint Economic Committee), pp. 224−67.

Emerson, John Phillip (1983), "Urban School Leavers and Unemployment in China," *China Quarterly*, no. 93 (March), pp. 1−16.

Epstein, Israel (1949), with a supplement by Juilian R. Friedman, *Notes on Labor Problems in Nationalist China*, (New York: Institute of Pacific Relations).

FBIS (1983a), Xinua Domestic Service in Chinese 1232 GMT April 25 1983; (April 27), K14.

FBIS (1983b), "Workers' Congresses Only Nominal Power Organs," *China Daily*, (September 4, 1983), p. 4; (September 7), K18.

Gongren Gongzuo Wenda (1981) (Questions on Trade Union Work) (Beijing: Gongren Chubanshe).

Gongren Ribao (1983a), "Cong tigao zeren gan zuoqi" (Raise responsibility and dare to act), (April 2), p. 3.

Gongren Ribao (1983b), "Baohu zhigong hefa quanli zujin gaige xunli jinxing" (Uphold the legal rights of the workers, advance the proper route in the reform), (April 21), p. 1.

Gongren Ribao (1983c), "Buyao suibian choudiao gonghui ganbu zuo qitade shi" (Don't casually transfer trade union cadres to do other work), (April 23), p. 3.

Gongren Ribao (1983d), "Hetongzhi gongren keyi canjia gonghui (Contract workers can join the trade union), (April 25), p. 1.

Gongren Ribao (1983e), "Guanyu 1982 nian guomin jingji he shehui fazhan jihua chixing jieguo de gongbao" (Bulletin on the results of the implementation of the 1982 state economic and social development plan), (April 30), pp. 2−3.

Gongren Ribao (1983f), "Yiyi yiqian duo wanren" (Over a billion people), (May 1), p. 1.

Gongren Ribao (1983g), "Shaoshu qiye chexiao gonghui zuzhi shi cuowude" (The small number of enterprises that have abolished the trade union organization are mistaken), (May 13), p. 1.

Gongren Ribao (1983h), "Zong mou fuchangzhang dao gonghui renzhi shuoqi" (Speaking of the Assistant Factory Manager holding a post in the trade union), (June 2), p. 1.

Gongren Ribao (1983i), "Renzhen guanche Dang Zhongyan dui gonghui gonzuode zhishi" (Diligently carry out the Central Committee's directive on trade union work), (June 6), p. 2.

Gongren Ribao (1983j), "Gonghui ganbu xuan shang dangde zhengce you shacuo?" (Is it really the case that trade union cadres that publicly criticize the party's policy have nothing to fear?), (June 15), p. 1.

Gongren Ribao (1983k), "Jingji gaige buneng qinfan ba nugong chuanli" (The economic reform cannot violate the rights of women workers), (July 8), p. 1.

Gongren Ribao (1983l), "Buyao ba nianlao tiruode ganbu anpai dao gonghui" (Don't arrange to move old and infirm cadres into the trade union), (July 22), p. 2.

Gongren Ribao (1983m), "Wo guo gongui jianshe wunian lai qude henda chengji" (Our country has attained very great results in the past five years of construction), (October 12), p. 1.

Gongren Ribao (1983n), "Buying dang suiyi chexiao tuoyou yuansuo (Don't casually abolish nurseries), (November 12), p. 1.

Gongren Ribao (1984a), "Zhuanbian zuofeng, shenru shiji kaichuang gonghui gongzuo xin jumian" (Transform work styles, enter deeply into reality, open up trade union work to a new phase), (March 14), p. 3.

Gongren Ribao (1984b), "Laodong baoxian shi dui laodongjie jiben shenghuode baozhang" (Labor insurance is the safeguard of the workers' basic livelihood), (November 14), p. 3.

Guo, Feng (1985), "It is the Common Duty of the Party, Administration, and Trade Unions To Do Well in the Democratic Management of Enterprises," *Gongren Ribao*, (June 12, 1985), p. 3; in *FBIS*, (June 27), K14−16.

Halperin, Nina P. (1985), "Learning From Abroad: Chinese Views of the East European Economic Experience, January 1977−June 1981, *Modern China*, vol. 11, no. 1 (January), pp. 77−109.

Harper, Paul (1969), "Political Roles of Trade Unions in Communist China", unpublished PhD dissertation, Cornell University.

He, Guang (1985), "Talk on the Question of Labor Employment," Bejing Domestic Service, (April 28, 1985); in *FBIS*, (May 2), K14−16.

He, Shen (1981), "The Solidarity Union of Poland and China," *Zheng Ming*, 10 (October 1); in *JPRS, no. 79689, pp. 72−80.*

JPRS (1980a), Guizhou Education Trade Union Forum January 25, 1980 (March 5), no. 75255, p. 73.

JPRS (1980b), Guangzhou Trade Unions March 14, 1980, (April 21), no. 75533, p. 51.

Junwannuofu (1985) (ed.), *Kexue Jixu Geming Yu Gonghui* (The Technical Revolution and the Trade Unions) (Beijing: Gongren Chubanshe).

Kang, Wenhua (1983), "Dan zhongyan ban gonghui zhichule zhengquede fangziang" (The Central Committee points out the correct direction for trade union administration), *Gongren Ribao*, (May 2), p. 1.

Kosta, H. G. (1984), "China on the Road to a Market Economy," RAD Background Report/226 (China), *Radio Free Europe Research*, (December 30), pp. 1−8.

Lai, Ruoyu (1957), "Guanyu gonghuide zuoyung yu diwei" (On the trade union's function and position), *Zhejiang Ribao*, (November 20), p. 2.

Li, Feng (1957), "On an 8,000 Li Tour of Hurried Observation," *Renmin Ribao*, (May 9, 1957); in *Survey of China Mainland Press*, 1551, pp. 10−13.

Liang, Yung-chang (1954), *The Kuomintang and the Chinese Worker* (Taipei: China Cultural Service).

Liu, Zhengwei (1984), "Bixu gaibian gonghui ganbu nianchi yuepei yueda de qingkuang" (It is necessary to correct the situation of trade union cadres' becoming increasingly aged), *Gongren Ribao*, (March 24), p. 2.

Ma, Chao-chun (1955), *History of the Labor Movement in China*, (Taipei: China Cultural Service).

Ma, Hong (1980), "Guanyu gaige gonye giye lingdao zhidude tantao" (Discussion on the reform of the enterprise leadership system), *Renmin Ribao*, (November 20), p. 5.

Meng, Yunjeng (1980), "Nansilafude shehuizhuyi zhidu" (Yugoslavia's socialist system), *Jingji Yanjiu*, 12, pp. 53−9.

Nansilafude (1979) *Shehuizhuyi Zizhi Zhidu He Jingji Fazhen* (Yugoslavian Socialist Self-Management and Economic Development) (Shanghai: Renmin Chuban She).

Ni, Zhifu (1983), "Zai shehui zhuyi wuzhi wenming he jingshen wenming jianshe zhong fayang gongren jieji de zhureng weng jingshen" (In the midst of building a material civilization and a cultural civilization, promote the spirit of the proletariat being the masters of society), *Renmin Ribao*, (October 27), p. 2.

Oka, Takashi (1983), "China Gives Workers a Voice to Prevent Solidarity-Like Movement," *Christian Science Monitor*, (October 21), p. 10.

Pang, Chuan (1980), "Nansilafude zizhi zhidu" (Yugoslavian self-management), *Jingji Guanli*, 7, pp. 13−18.

Parks, Michael (1981), "Chinese Leaders Fear Loss of Control," *Los Angeles Times*, (November 19), p. 1.

People's Republic of China Yearbook 1984 (1984) (Beijing: Xinhua Publishing House).

"Reform Decision of the Central Committee (1984) of the Communist Party of China on the Reform of the Economic Structure," *Beijing Review*, vol. 27, no. 44, pp. I−XVI.

"Resolution (1985) of All-China Trade Union Federation," Bejing Xinhua Domestic Service in Chinese, (December 27, 1984); in *JPRS-CEA-85-008*, pp. 118−126.

Saiqiewieji, Miaudelige (1977) (Miodrag Zecevic) *Nansilafu Daibiao Zhidu* (The Yugoslav delegate system) (Bejing: Chuban She).

Scherer, John L. (1983) (ed.), "Provisional Regulations Concerning Congresses of Workers and Staff Members in State-Owned Industrial Enterprises," *China Facts and Figures Annual 1982*, (Academic International Press), pp. 28−31.

Shanghai Chaiyou Jichang (1980), "Women shi dzemyang kaihou zhigong daibiao tahuide?" (How can we do a good job of organizing the workers' representative congresses?), *Jingji Guanli*, 5; pp. 33−5.

Shanghai Dishier Mianfang Zhichang (1981), "Shixing zhigong daibiao dahui lingdao xiade changzhang fucizhi," (Institute the factory manager responsibility system under the leadership of the workers' congress), *Jingji Guanli*, 4; pp. 42−4.

Shirk, Susan (1981), "Recent Chinese Labor Policies and the Transformation of Industrialization in China," *China Quarterly*, no. 88 (December); pp. 575−93.

Solomon, Richard H. (1971), *Mao's Revolution and the Chinese Political Culture* (Berkeley and Los Angeles, Calif.: University of California Press).

State Council (1981), "Zhonghua Chuanguo Zonggonghui, Zhongguo Renmin Yinhang, Caizhengbu guanyu yange an 'Gonghui Fa' guiding fajiao gonghui jingfeide tongzhi" (Notice of the ACFTU, the People's Bank of China, and the Ministry of Finance on paying strict regard to the regulations of the "Trade Union Law" in the transmission of the trade union fee), *Zhonghua Renmin Gongheguo Guowuyuan Gongbao 348*, (March 1), pp. 31−2.

State Council (1984), "Zhonghua Renmin Gongheguo Guojia Tongjiju guanyu 1983 nian guomin jingji he shehui fazhan jihua zhixing jieguode gongbao" (Bulletin of the Statistical Bureau of the People's Republic of China on the results of the implementation of the 1983 plan for the national economy and societal development), *Zhonghua Renmin Gongheguo Guowuyuan Gongbao 430*, (May 20), pp. 287−301.

State Council (1985), "Zhonghua Renmin Gongheguo Guojia Tongjiju guanyu yijiu basi nian guomin jingji he shehui fazhande tongji" (Economic and societal development statistics of the Bulletin of the Statistical Bureau of the People's Republic of China), *Zhonghua Renmin Gongheguo Guowuyuan Gongbao 461*, (April 10), pp. 243−56.

Su, Shaozhi (1981), "Economic Development and Democratization," *Selected Writings on Studies of Marxism*, no. 8.

Ta Kung Pao (1983), "CPC Adopts Decision on Party Constitution," (October 13), p. 1.

Ta Kung Pao (1984), "SEZ Trade Unions Reconcile Labor Disputes", December 27, p. 4.

Tian, Fang, Qi, Dong, Liu, Xun, Yun, Zhen, and Zheng, Ji, (1981), "Zhongqing shi kuangda qiye zizhu chuan shidiande chubu diaocha" (An initial investigation on experiments in enlarging the right of self-management in Chongqing's enterprises) *Jingji Yanjiu*, 3, pp. 28−35.

Trade Union Law of the People's Republic of China (1956) (Beijing: Foreign Languages Press).

Walder, Andrew G. (1981), "Work and Authority in Chinese Industry: State Socialism and the Institutional Culture of Dependency," unpublished PhD dissertation, University of Michigan.

Walder, Andrew G. (1983), "Organized Dependency and Cultures of Authority in Chinese Industry," *Journal of Asian Studies*, vol. 43, no. 1 (November), pp. 51−76.

Walder, Andrew G. (1984), "The Remaking of the Chinese Working Class, 1949−1981," *Modern China*, vol. 10, no. 1 (January), pp. 3−48.

Wang, Jingu, and Li, Haihu (1985), "Progress Made on Nationwide Practicing on Contract Labor System," *Gongren Ribao*, November 28, 1984, p. 1; in *JPRS-CEA-85-033*, (April 4), pp. 221−2.

Wang, Mengkui (1981), "Qiye lingdo zhidu zhongde yige wenti" (A central problem of the enterprise leadership system), *Jingji Yanjiu*, 1, pp. 37−44.

Wang, Qianghua, Jingrui, Liu, Yide, Zhang, and Tao, Kai (1984), "Why Must We Thoroughly Negate 'Extensive Democracy'?." *Guangming Ribao* (September 13, 1984), p. 2; in *FBIS*, (September 20), K7.

Wei, Jie (1985), "A Socialist Job Market Should Be Set Up," *Guangming Ribao*, (August 10, 1985), p. 3; in *FBIS*, (August 21), K4−5.

Whyte, Martin King, and Parish, William L. (1984), *Urban Life in Contemporary China* (Chicago: University of Chicago Press).

Wolf, Majorie (1985), *Revolution Postponed: Women in Contemporary China* (Stanford, Calif.: Stanford University Press).

Xue, Muqiao (1982) (ed.), *Almanac of China's Economy 1982*, (Hong Kong: Chinese Economic Yearbook Limited).

Xue, Muqiao (1983) (ed.), *Almanac of China's Economy, 1983* (Hong Kong: Chinese Economic Yearbook Limited).

Zhang, Yiwei (1980), "Lun shehuizhuyi qiye guanlide jiben tezheng" (A discussion on the fundamental characteristics of the socialist enterprise), *Jingji Guanli*, 11, pp. 14−22.

Zhejiang Ribao (1950), "Hang siying tagon buchang gonghui shi zenyang lingdao gongren mianxiang shengchande" (How the trade union of Hangzhou Impartial Privately-Owned Cotton Factory leads the workers to face the needs of production), (August 15), p. 3.

Zhejiang Ribao (1951a), "Chuansheng gonghui gongzuo huiyi bimu kuangfa jiaoliu gonghui gongzuo jingyan" (Provincial trade union work meeting concludes; broadcasts the experience of the trade union's exchange experience work), (March 20), p. 1.

Zhejiang Ribao (1951b), "Hangzhoushi cong gonghui sisan yue gongzuo cong jiexing jinhou renwu" (Hanzhou city trade union meeting summary of the past thirteen month's work and present and future tasks), (April 7), p. 1.

Zhejiang Ribao (1957), "Gongren yundong bixu shi shehui zhuyide" (The workers' movement must be socialist), (October 20), p. 1.

Zhongbao (1984), "Mudi zai yu guanliao zhuyi duihang gongren keyi anqian liyou bagong"

(Workers can strike on grounds of safety in order to oppose bureaucratism), (February 20), p. 1.

Zhongguo Gonghui Dijiuci (1978) *Chuanguo Daibiao Dahui* (The Ninth Representative Congress of the All-China Federation of Trade Unions) (1978) (Beijing: Gongren Chubanshe).

Zhongguo Gonghui Dishici (1983) *Quanguo Daibiao Dahui Zhuyau Wenjian* (Principal Documents of the Tenth Congress of the All-China Federation of Trade Unions) (Beijing: Gongren Chubanshe).

Zukin, Sharon (1981), "The Representation of Working-Class Interests in Socialist Society: Yugoslav Trade Unions," *Politics and Society*, vol. 10, no. 3, pp. 261–316.

Zuo, Wosheng (1985), "Price Reform and Improvement of the People's Livelihood," *Jingji Ribao*, (April 29, 1985), p. 3; in *FBIS*, (May 8), K9–11.

11
Communist and Capitalist Trade Unionism: Comparisons and Contrasts

Craig R. Littler and Gill Palmer

Chapter 1 set out a model of Classic Dualism and then considered the specific national variations of this model. Thus the succeeding nine chapters have surveyed the varieties of communist trade unionism in relation to the Leninist-derived notion of dual functioning unions. Such a survey invites comparison with capitalist trade unionism; indeed, Western discussions of communist unionism often assumes an implicit model of *capitalist* unions, based, typically, on the Anglo-American experience and involving formation by grass-roots activists, union independence, and adversarial collective bargaining. Such simplifying assumptions ignore the evidence that many capitalist unions have been set up or shaped by external interests and that confrontational collective bargaining is only one of the methods used by trade unions within capitalism. Consequently, this chapter aims to set out the varieties of capitalist unionism and to analyze their functions, so as to examine noncapitalist unions in a clearer light.

In one sense the above objective is an impossible task; the varieties of unionism and industrial relations within capitalist societies, both developed and developing, are so huge that any generalizations tend to crumble before persuasive counterexamples. Second, the very act of comparison can be misleading. Trade unions are located in economic and social structures which involve different principles, such that the roles and functions of unions are very different in competitive capitalism, corporate capitalism, or under state planning. Nevertheless, these problems of comparison and compression are true of all cross-cultural study and it is important to begin the

Craig R. Littler, School of Social and Industrial Association, Griffith University, Queensland, Australia.

Gill Palmer, Queensland Institute of Technology, Brisbane, Australia.

theoretical effort so that theories of trade union formation and trade union functions are not confined to one political economy.

The Dynamics of Union Formation

Organizations called "trade unions" represent different phases of organizational emergence. Stinchcombe has suggested that the history of most types of organization shows that there are great spurts of foundation of organizations of a particular type, followed by periods of relatively slower growth; perhaps to be followed by new spurts, generally of a fundamentally different kind of organization in the same field (Stinchcombe, 1965). This clustering of organizational emergence associated with a relative stability of organizational form is a useful way of looking at the development of trade unions. In general there have been three phases of development, each a response to markedly different conditions.

Occupational institutions designed to protect member interests in product and labor markets predate the processes of industrialization. The feudal guilds were powerful economic, social, and political institutions in the cities of Europe from the twelfth to the fourteenth century. The guilds were not worker organizations in a strict sense, but their organizations were based around the possession of an occupational skill and their economic objective was to preserve and increase the value of that skill on the market. Using Weberian terminology, we can say that they adopted policies of economic closure (Weber, 1947: 139−43). In other words, they sought to close access to their advantageous market position by restricting recruitment and preventing outsiders from breaking their monopoly over the supply of skills. They unilaterally regulated market and management issues by laying down a network of rules, determined in guild parliaments, which covered the apprentice system, methods of work, manning levels, the pay of apprentices and journeymen, and the prices at which supplies should be bought and goods sold.

Guild controls decayed with the growth of industrialism, indeed many industrial entrepreneurs sought to evade such controls by relocation in different cities and regions. Nevertheless, closure policies continued to act as a model, a desirable goal, for groups of skilled men who sought to maintain occupational controls within the new capitalist markets and firms. Early craft unions and the traditional professional associations attempted to restrict recruitment and maintain the internal discipline needed to impose their own regulations on the buyers of their labor. When circumstances were favorable, they could impose unilateral controls over such areas as wages, hours, and conditions (Palmer, 1983: 96−103).

Occupational controls are most successful where rivals are weak, that is, in conditions where employers are small and competitive and where the state is relatively passive. The *sine qua non* of occupational closure is the ability to maintain a monopoly over valued and nonsubstitutable skills, and, since the height of craft and professional association control in the mid-nineteenth century, this ability has been successfully challenged by the developing powers of employers and the state. The ability of employers to challenge occupational controls has been strengthened in two ways, both by the reduction in nation-based employer competition associated with business concentration and also by the development of bureaucratic techniques of managerial control designed to reduce employer dependence on marketable skills (Edwards, 1979; Littler, 1982). This shift from the conditions of competitive capitalism to those of corporate capitalism has given rise to the emergence of different forms of unionism which we will discuss below. But it is also important to underline that occupational controls have not disappeared. Such employee institutions are still important in preserving the status of older professional groups, especially in the United Kingdom and United States. They operate partly through the traditional closure policies, but also are heavily involved in informal political bargaining through pressure-group lobbies of government. Where they face a major employer (as the British Medical Association does in relation to the National Health Service) there has been a movement toward a form of collective bargaining with its production of bilateral regulations. Some skilled manual workers in Britain have retained the outer forms of craft unionism, but they have largely lost their ability to impose unilateral controls. Manual workers have never had the lobbying power of middle-class occupational groups, and where their organizations survive they have largely been forced to adopt the less certain tactics of collective bargaining.

In capitalist societies which industrialized in the late nineteenth century or the twentieth century the period of competitive capitalism, characterized by small employers and low capital-intensity, was often brief. Japan is a good example of this; the period of competitive capitalism was so short that no extensive tradition of industrial craftsmanship was ever established. Equally, in capitalist economies which have been extensively restructured since World War II (such as West Germany) the old craft forms of unionism have not survived.

Most workers in the developing capitalist economies of the nineteenth century had no clearly defined skill which could be used to support policies of closure and monopoly control. In the United Kingdom and United States many attempts were made to mobilize unskilled workers to try to improve their conditions, but these efforts faced constant difficulties because unskilled, low-paid, and ill-educated workers had few resources with which to build effective organizations. Protesting workers could all too easily be replaced by new recruits from the reserve army of labor. As a result it was not until the late nineteenth century that there was the spread of a "new unionism" across Europe and the United States creating general or industrial unions. The second spurt of unionization created very different unions from the earlier, craft unionism. In place of craft elitism and exclusivity was an ideological underpinning of a united working class. In place of organization around strictly sectional, economic objectives (increasing the value of particular skills and thereby the social and economic status of the holders) was the mobilization of a general discontent in which objectives ranged from reducing work hours to revolutionary social and political change.

The resources and therefore the methods of the craft and new unions were different. Craft unions were well resourced; they could enhance membership solidarity and discipline by the provision of extensive welfare benefits and they sought to achieve their economic goals by monopolistic closure and the imposition of unilateral controls. In contrast the low pay of the new unionists entailed low subscriptions, low funds, few benefits, and minimal organizational resources. The weak economic base of the new unions pulled them toward two types of action: support for new left-wing parties at the political level and collective bargaining at the industrial level. The form that collective bargaining took was shaped in Britain by employers' associations. They imposed industrywide procedure agreements on the trade unions, which restricted formal employer−union bargaining to the industry level, and to the labor market issues of pay, hours, and conditions of work. Managerial issues of the detailed control of the labor process were largely untouched by the formal collective bargaining system that developed.

In Britain the general and industrial unions which emerged at the turn of the century have tended to become conglomerates, organizing skilled and unskilled workers in a number of sectors and often including organizational subsectors for white-collar workers. In societies where governments or employers have sought to rationalize union organization, a more industrial structure has been reinforced as in the United States, the Netherlands, West Germany, and Sweden.

The different organizational forms of craft and new unions introduced cleavages into union movements which long persisted in many capitalist societies. In Britain a pragmatic coexistence has survived within the TUC. In the United States the craft American Federation of Labor and the unskilled Congress of Industrial Organizations constituted rival federations until 1955. On the continent of Europe the importance of ideology as an underpinning for the new unions has left a heritage of union rivalry based on political or religious affiliation.

The new unions developed in reaction to the labor markets of early, competitive capitalism which were characterized by unbridled employer power to hire and fire for the purposes of labor cheapening plus consistent employer efforts to intensify labor by extending the working day. This market context resulted in the major objects of union regulation being the standardization of wages plus the length of the working day. The classic example is the British case, where a large part of trade union administration was created in order to deal with piece-work and standard price lists for work tasks. Equally, the demand for the 9-hour day was often a rallying point around which many unions were first established or enlarged beyond local groups.

In contrast to the conditions of early capitalism, under corporate capitalism with bureaucratic work organization and internal career structures the nature of the labor market is markedly different. It is characterized by a multisegmented labor market with many firm-specific internal labor markets. Large size and the possibility of an organizational career structure introduce the potential for unions to be based entirely on one employer. Enterprise or company-based unions are now a common feature of capitalist labor organization. This, then, is the third phase of the development of unionization.

The society which exemplifies most clearly the pattern of company-based unionism is Japan. Large conglomerate corporations (the zaibatsu) formed early in Japanese industrial history, and faced with tendencies to unionization sought to contain the pressures by the formation of company unions. Today, nearly all Japanese unions are "enterprise unions," that is, autonomous units organized by company or enterprise rather than industry- or craft-based. Almost all bargaining is conducted between the enterprise unions and their managements with the bargaining representatives limited entirely to members of the enterprise union (Cook, 1966: 28–56).

Enterprise unions are not simply a transient employer device to head off wider patterns of unionization; a fragile facade which will eventually be burst open by working-class pressures. It is true that some Western industrial history suggests this interpretation. For example company unions have long been a feature of labor relations in the United States; in 1926 company unions had about half as many members as the main union federation and were a significant factor in the failure of independent unionism to spread before the 1930s. During the mid-1930s there was a period of factory occupations in the United States and the spread of militant unionism in such industries as automobiles, steel, and rubber. Similarly, company unions in Britain have, until recently, taken the form of staff associations which are often no more than formalized systems of joint consultation, without bargaining or strike powers, and intended to legitimate top management decisions. Such associations have been common in the financial sector and white-collar work generally, and many staff associations have tended to give way in the face of the rapid spread of white-collar unions in the postwar period. However, this path of union history is only part of the story.

As we have said, under corporate capitalism the nature of the labor market changes; wages are no longer the price of labor as a factor of production in a neo-classical sense, but become relatively inflexible; work hours are regulated both by law and bureaucratic rules, and job security in some degree underpins the career structure. Under these circumstances any labor unions which are formed will tend to center their regulations on job security and dismissal procedures, promotions, and job transfers. Dismissals and redundancies become an extremely important object of regulation because internal labor markets mean that it is difficult to move to another firm and the cost of doing so in terms of lower wages, poorer working conditions, lost promotion, and pension rights is very high. Thus company unions may serve the interests of workers as well as employers, particularly if a worker has acquired non-transferable skills based on work experience rather than generally recognized certified training. Internal labor markets, company unions, and enterprise bargaining can protect the interest of a new "labor aristocracy" based on organization position rather than protected craft status. Thus in the United States, company bargaining has been used by the unions to negotiate rigid seniority criteria for promotions and to institutionalize the practice of "bumping," whereby people in redundant posts can displace and take the place of newer recruits.

Trends in Britain and elsewhere suggest that company unionism is linked to the development of corporate capitalism. Despite the strong traditions of craft and industry unions in Britain, several recent analyses have noted that there is a widespread shift to company-level industrial relations because the structure of interests which union representatives have to deal with have frequently been factory-specific interests (TUC, 1984). Bargaining is increasingly showing some of the characteristics institutionalized in Japan, with a union organization whose commitments and loyalties extend no further than the enterprise itself. This pattern is particularly visible in "greenfield" factories, where several unions have concluded agreements including sole recognition, equal conditions for manual workers and office staff, advisory boards of elected staff representatives, and negotiating procedures ending in compulsory arbitration (*Financial Times*, January 9, 1984). This pattern is sufficiently distinctive to have been called the "new industrial relations."

Equally, Japanese industrial relations have become a model for many other societies, especially developing economies. Some governments, such as Singapore, have encouraged, or even legislated for, the replacement of industrial unions with enterprise-based unions. As it happens, in both Africa and Asia much of the unionism that developed in the late colonial and early independence periods tended to center on particular enterprises. Some analysts, such as Dore (1979), suggest that this pattern is typical of late-developing economies, with a dualistic structure of economic development, juxtaposing a traditional economic sector with national, large, modern plants or multinational operations.

Thus, the third phase of unionism—enterprise unionism—tends to be associated with late corporate capitalism in the developed societies (though with a mixed pattern of different forms of union) or with economic dualism in the developing societies.

There is a fourth type of unionization - namely, state-regulated or state-controlled unionization—which also tends to be associated with late industrialization. Thus, this form of unionism can be conceptualized as an alternative path for capitalist developed and developing societies to choose compared with enterprise unionism. It is from this perspective that one can view the emergence or establishment of unions in the communist societies. The nature of state-controlled unionism is considered in the next section.

State-Controlled Unionism

It is a cornerstone of liberal democratic philosophy that the government should distance itself from the regulation of economic affairs and in particular from the detailed regulation of employment. This philosophy, often turned into rhetoric, obscures the realities of relations between trade unions and the state in capitalist societies. Many modern, capitalist trade unions have been structured by the state or operate within a legal framework which closely regulates their activities and permitted functions. Even in the British case, the originator of liberal democracy, the famous voluntarism of British industrial relations may have been contingent on specific historical events. Wedderburn (1982) points out that during the near-revolutionary labor struggles in the three years leading up to World War I, intervention by legislation to fix wages was felt by many to offer one avenue of escape from disastrous strikes. So great was the interest of the British government in the Canadian system of industrial relations at that time and in particular in the Lemieux Act, under which any dispute in certain industries had to be submitted to a board of conciliation, that Lord Askwith was sent across the Atlantic to report on the system for the government. Wedderburn concludes that "we cannot tell whether the nonintervention of law in collective labour relations would ever have evolved out of this stormy period had not the World War submerged it" beneath strong feelings of patriotism that cut across both classes (ibid: 1−2.)

The British tradition of voluntarism, now under sustained and probably fatal attack from recent governments, was always unique. In all societies industrializing after Britain, the role of the state has been more active and evident. Legislation which regulates union activities is found across Western Europe, in Japan, and in Australia and New Zealand. In the latter two societies, legislation which provides for compulsory arbitration if bargainers fail to agree has radically altered the nature of employer−union relations. Instead of the nominally bilateral control of collective bargaining, all the details of employment issues have become subject to a complex tripartite regulation of unions, employers, and courts. On the continent of Europe and in many ex-colonial societies, legislation not only sets a legal framework around collective bargaining but also establishes statutory work councils at workplace level, or central institutions for the control of incomes, or for economic planning at the national level. The role given to unions within these structures varies, but their presence inevitably helps shape the scope of union action.

The tension between the liberal democratic ideal of a neutral state and the reality of state intervention in structuring union−employer relations forms the focus of the "corporatism" debate within political sociology and industrial relations (see Schmitter and Lehmbruch, 1979; Crouch, 1977; Panitch 1980; and the summary in Palmer, 1983). As Kastendiek (1983) notes, governments in Western Europe have, in recent years, swung between more or less liberal or corporatist policies. Liberal policies seek to achieve the institutional segregation of economic and political spheres and liberal governments usually rely on some form of collective bargaining as the best way of depoliticizing the institutionalization of industrial conflict. In contrast, more corporatist policies move away from this separation of collective bargaining from management or state structures of control, and seek to incorporate employee representatives more closely into the administrative government or management apparatus. Collective bargaining is restrained by incomes policies which may or may not be negotiated with unions. Conflictual negotiations on basic conditions of employment are supplemented or, hopefully, displaced by more cooperative bargaining or "concertation" (Crouch, 1977) conducted in statutory works councils or in tripartite central bodies like the West German concerted action institutions or the British National Economic Development Council.

In the developed world the relative merits of these different public policies have become the subject of a continuous debate which has intensified with the economic crisis of the 1980s. The role of the state in structuring the trade unions' role has become a major issue, and despite the revival of liberal, anti-corporatist policies with the administrations of Thatcher and Reagan, the corporatist integration of union and employee representation is practiced, to some degree, in most developed societies and remains on the political agenda in the remainder.

In developing societies an uneasy relationship between the state and trade unions seems to be a worldwide phenomenon. An aggressive labor movement is seen as a threat to development, because such a movement constitutes an organized pressure for consumption rather than a high investment strategy. In addition the state−union relation has a sharply edged political dimension; in many African and Asian societies trade unions can mobilize urban discontent and are in a unique position to weaken or even overthrow governments. As a result, most Third World governments have developed union containment strategies involving some mixture of wage and price controls, specific legislation aimed at moulding union structures and functions to the requirements of economic development as perceived by the power-holders in society, plus spasms of moral and ideological pressures centered on nationalism. But most of the typical measures used in developing societies—limiting the right to strike; building compulsory arbitration into the system; removing certain areas from collective bargaining (as under the 1968 Singapore Industrial Relations Act); restrictions on the political activities of trade unions; and promoting decentralized and fragmented structures—do not necessarily add up to a model of state-controlled unionism. Instead, they provide a picture of state-regulated union activity, often indeed with tight constraints, but usually with a residue of liberal collective bargaining.

Corporatist policies can clearly vary from the highly pluralist central bargaining of West European concerted action policies to the coercive state manipulation of puppet unions in, for example, the National Socialist (Nazi) or Mussolini regimes. Corporatism needs clear definition and subclassification and for the purpose of this chapter it is useful to distinguish between *voluntarist* or bargained, and *statist* or coercive, corporatism. "Under statist corporatism, the State is both active and coercive, while under . . . voluntarist corporatism the State is active, but by and large non-coercive, depending on bargaining and accommodation with other organized interests" (Crouch, 1977: 35). An ideal type model of state-controlled trade unions under statist corporatism involves the following elements:

(1) Co-option of unions on to the ruling state machinery.
(2) Participation of unions in economic administration, if only at the lowest levels.
(3) Participation in regulated political activities.
(4) Appointment of union officials by the government or party or veto power over such appointments.
(5) Absence of collective bargaining. Instead of the resolution of economic or social conflicts at the level of civil society, there is a

tendency for all significant interaction between individuals and groups to be mediated by the state and its organizations.

(6) The main function of trade unions becomes mobilizing the working class behind the objectives of the regime.

Perhaps the best example of state-controlled unionism within a state capitalist framework is that of Mexico. Most Mexican unions are members of the major trade union federation (the Confederacion de Trabajadores Mexicanos, or CTM). The CTM is an integral part of the ruling party and endeavors to maintain support for the existing regime. As Dore points out, Mexican politicians depend on the CTM for support and in return union officials obtain government posts (Dore, 1979: 352). At the level of the factory this pattern of corporatism is duplicated; union organizers collude with the employers to keep "trouble-makers" away from the factory, and receive sizable sums of money accounted for as "contributions to union sports activities" in the company budget (ibid.). Such is the incorporation of Mexican unions within the structures of the existing regime, that the 1970s witnessed a surge of attempts to create autonomous unions in Mexico, a response with striking similarity to the events in Poland (Nelson, 1983: 25).

Nevertheless, Mexico does not amount to a pure type of state-controlled unionism. Within the tight political constraints imposed by the government, collective bargaining exists in the modern sectors of the Mexican economy, especially in mining, transport, and communications. This bargaining is often not coordinated across plants or sectors, but this indicates another qualification; the imprint of the government on Mexican industrial relations is partly maintained by the fragmentation of the labor movement, resulting in some indications of enterprise unionism. For example, General Motors (the US multinational) has two plants within 75 miles of each other near Mexico City. Despite this proximity and common ownership, each plant has a separate union, affiliated to rival confederations, and they have never attempted to coordinate bargaining (Thompson, 1983: 74).

Thus the Mexican case suggests that governments, even with a pattern of state-controlled unionism, find it difficult to squeeze out all collective bargaining from the system. Trade unions tend to become mediating institutions, on pain of being replaced by more independent labor organizations. Second, state-controlled unionism may coexist with elements of enterprise unionism. Finally, it should be noted that Mexico is typical of many industrializing economies, with widespread unemployment and underemployment, estimated to be between 25 and 50 percent (Thompson, 1983: 65). This, as we point out later, provides an important contrast with communist societies.

Distinctions between statist and voluntarist or more pluralist corporatism rest primarily on the degree of state control over trade unions and the extent that trade unions genuinely act to promote the interests of their members, rather than acting as instruments of worker mobilization and control. However, even in societies heavily influenced by liberal democratic ideology, trade unions are not entirely autonomous, nor are they immune from the tensions, evident under corporatism, between exerting power *for* their members and exerting power *over* their members; between the representation of employee interests and the mobilization of employee cooperation in the maintenance of central policies. This functional dilemma is considered in the next section.

Trade Unions as Intermediary Organizations

Hyman provides the best starting point for the analysis of trade unions in capitalist societies. He argues that trade unions are not simple, representative institutions, but are "the institutional meeting point of the contradictory demands and interests of different sectional groups of workers, of employers and state functionaries." In other words, they represent a focal point in a complex network of power relations (Hyman, 1976: 101). Following similar lines of analysis, Muller-Jentsch has developed a theoretical framework within which trade unions are conceived as mediating agencies, or as he terms them, "intermediary organizations." The complete integration of trade unions into modern capitalist society cannot be expected because of inherent conflicts of interest. Nevertheless, Muller-Jentsch argues that there are certain structural trends in society which tend to push modern unions almost inevitably into the role of a mediating agency between capital and labor (Muller-Jentsch, 1982: 1 − 2). Revolutionary unions have either accepted the compromise of bargaining with existing employers or political structures, or retreated to localized syndicalist groups (as in Spain), or ceased to exist (like the International Workers of the World). Equally, craft unions have accepted collective bargaining, and the maintenance of unilateral controls has retreated to the province of solidary work groups in particularly favorable conditions.

In understanding the role of trade unions in capitalist societies, it is important to underline two points about the relation between union leaders and the rank-and-file members. First, union leaders, like many organizational elites, enjoy a considerable area of autonomy in their day-to-day work. But there is a curious quality to the work autonomy of trade union officials which arises from the accountability procedures constraining union representatives in many societies. Essentially, the area of autonomy is constituted by four factors: first, the amount of tolerated secrecy (and some union leaders have been notoriously secretive); second, the time period before union representatives are held accountable; third, the election and reelection procedures (many union officials hold office for life); and fourth, the typical mandate or constitution (many are studiously vague). It is this area of institutional autonomy (constantly under attack either by the state or by sectional groups of workers) which allows union representatives to mediate the conflicting pressures bearing in on them from different social sources (Hyman, 1976; Michels, 1959).

The second aspect of the relation between union officials and their membership is the reverse side of the coin. Contrary to some popular views about "over-mighty barons," trade unionists experience a running sense of vulnerability. As Eccles puts it (1979: 158):

> Apart from the rivalry between unions, a vast army of employed are not in unions, there is a persistent rank and file resistance to union polices, a variable willingness by workers to act on union decisions and a marked reluctance on the part of some unionists to pay their union dues at all. It is not unexpected that trade unions are wary of any proposal which could reduce what they see as their precarious hold on events.

This felt vulnerability pushes union representatives toward caution and compromise, toward negotiation with the powers-that-be. Moreover, trade union officials are often pulled in the same direction—by government pressure, by employer threats of factory closures, by ideological appeals, by the morning newspaper, and the night-time brick through the window.

Once unions accept the compromise of negotiation, they then accept the inevitability of a bargained exchange. What unions exchange for their collectively bargained joint determination of pay and conditions of work, or their corporatist voice on managerial and state policy, is peace. Their bargaining weapon is the delivery of worker cooperation.

There is, therefore, a configuration of typical pressures which frequently turn capitalist trade unions into the "manager of discontent." Even in the collective bargaining systems which are premised on an incompatible conflict of interest, issues and grievances are narrowly defined, so as to ease the path toward compromise and settlement. The force of these pressures can be seen reflected in the recent TUC document on union strategy. It stresses the need for the right to strike, but insists that, contrary to media images, such a right is rarely used and that "All parties have to be diligent in avoiding unnecessary strikes." It sees proper collective bargaining as the way to avoid disputes, maximize efficiency and secure an acceptance of change, including technological change: "Unions are the vehicle for winning the consent of individuals as workers for policies that employers and governments wish to pursue and that need the cooperation of workers if they are to succeed" (TUC, 1984).

If the concept of capitalist unions as intermediary organizations is correct, and if the thesis that there is a structural bias toward a cooperative style of union representation in capitalist societies is accurate, then the notion of dualism in relation to communist labor unions cannot be seen as totally distinctive. Instead, the position of communist unions in terms of function can be regarded as the extreme case of a general tension which characterizes the position of all trade unions—capitalist or communist. All labor organizations are faced with a contradiction between representation of the interests and grievances of their rank-and-file members versus mobilizing workers for production goals. Even in capitalist firms with a long history of militant unionism there is a duality—side-by-side with the workers' resistance to subordination lies the fact that workers have an interest in the maintenance of the capital–labor relation and the continued viability of the units of capital which employ them.

Comparisons and Contrasts

So far in this chapter we have analyzed capitalist unions, but what does this broad survey of the development and nature of capitalist unions imply in terms of comparison with communist unions? The first step is to go back to the model of Classic Dualism set out in Chapter 1 so that we can contrast it with the "classic adversarial" model of capitalist unions, before developing the extent and level of comparison (see Table 11.1).

Through the course of Chapters 2 to 10, we have seen the qualifications which need to be made to the Classic Dualist model of communist unions, especially in relation to the situation in Hungary, Yugoslavia, and Poland. From the start of this chapter we have sought to criticize the classic adver-

Table 11.1
Capitalist Unions and Communist Unions Contrasted

Communist Unions *(Classic Dualism)*	*Capitalist Unions* *(Classic adversarial model)*
1. Unitary view of economic interests. It is axiomatic that no "industrial conflicts" exist.	1. Pluralist view of economic interests.
2. The production function is paramount.	2. Representative function is paramount.
3. Protection of members' rights is secondary.	3. Production function is either (i) not acknowledged, or (ii) secondary.
4. Subordination to the party.	4. Autonomous organizations.
5. No collective bargaining. Union practices exclude the use of adversarial means.	5. Adversarial collective bargaining is the typical process of industrial relations.

sarial model of *capitalist* unions as excessively simplistic or, at best, as only referring to a particular slice of the capitalist world. At the opposite extreme to the classic adversarial model, a significant subgroup of capitalist unions, it has been argued, are state-controlled unions. In terms of Table 11.1 a model of state-controlled unionism implies a unitary view of economic interests; the production function is given primacy; the subordination to the state though with some, residual, collective bargaining. Do these obvious parallels with the classic communist union pattern imply that we should not see communist unions as *sui generis*, but as a particular version of state-controlled unionism? Such an argument is tempting, but it represents a crude method of comparison. What is left out of account by such an argument is the context of the political economy. The characteristics of the labor market and the economic framework of the enterprise are such as to radically alter the nature of comparison. Consequently, it is useful to analyze and compare the political economies in terms of the differing economic situation of the worker and the economic situation of the factory manager or bureaucrat. We have attempted to do this briefly in Table 11.2.

Table 11.2 underlines that there are critical differences between capitalist and Soviet-type economies in relation to the processes of capital accumulation. In Soviet-style economies the unit carrying out the accumulation process is not the firm but the national planning agency, such that the choice of techniques is made by planners not by managers. Second, whereas profit is the primary objective in capitalist corporations this is not so for communist enterprises; shareholders' interests are not at stake so that enterprise managers do not experience the same pressures felt by capitalist managers to reduce the size of their labor force in response to economic downturns or in order to "rationalize" production. Third, capitalist economies are characterized by rapid reallocation of capital funds seeking the most profitable avenues of investment and by intercapitalist competition leading to a continual reorganization of the production process and the concentration of control and ownership. In contrast. the processes of accumulation in Soviet-type societies are not stimulated or reinforced by market competition; they are governed by a plan rationality and not a market rationality. Clearly, market-based economic reforms in communist societies modify these stark contrasts, but only Yugoslavia and Hungary, so far, constitute significant deviations. Even in China, despite the victories of Deng Xiaoping, market reforms have not altered the fundamental economic structures of society up to the present.

If we turn to the economic position of the worker, then, clearly, the neo-classical view of the capitalist labor market, entailing a single market in which all employers and all workers operate such that workers flow into and out of jobs freely according to marginal differences in wages, is not an accurate model of capitalist reality. We have already noted that monopoly

Table 11.2

Soviet-Type Economies	Capitalist Economies
1. State establishes all the conditions of the contract of labor, including the principles of remuneration for all categories of labor.	1. The employer establishes some of the conditions of the contract of labor. The rest is established by collective bargaining and the state.
2. No employment benefits. Employment becomes not only a legal obligation, but a direct material necessity. (However, the second economy qualifies the nature of the wage relation and the employment dependency.)	2. Unemployment benefits in developed societies. None in developing societies. Benefits reduce the personal costs of being out of work and thus lessen dependence on an employer. (Paralleling the second economy effect is the situation of the 'peasant-worker' in many developing societies.)
3. Qualified freedom to change workplace in search of higher wages or better working conditions. (Not true of China; see Chapter 10.)	3. Freedom to change workplace.

Economic Situation of Management

1. Monopolists of some particular good.	1. Market situation varies. Many large corporations are oligopolistic within a structure of international competition.
2. Little knowledge of markets. Economic demand enters into the process only at the beginning in the form of bureaucratic estimates or negotiated targets.	2. Well-developed market knowledge.
3. Cannot simply shut down units of production operating at a "loss" or terminate non-remunerative manufacture of articles without providing substitutes.	3. Can close factories and terminate nonprofitable lines. Frequently occurs, especially during periods of "economic crisis."
4. Unemployment cannot be institutionalized.	4. Unemployment is common. History punctuated by periods of mass unemployment.

capitalism tends to be associated with segmented labor markets including some internal labor markets characterized by job security. Nevertheless, there is a vast difference between the capitalist labor market, with its fluctuating levels of employment, and a Soviet-type labor market. The latter is typically a labor shortage situation, with enterprise managers seeking to hoard labor, which, obviously, puts workers and job-seekers in a relative position of power (see Hare *et al.*, 1981: 43–4). In tight labor market conditions, such as those of the GDR (see Chapter 3), unskilled and semi-skilled workers can be dismissed for indiscipline and immediately get another job. Only China and Yugoslavia can really be described as "labor surplus" economies and even in these contexts there is still the labor market freedom to take leisure at work. For example, here is the account of one worker describing the daily routine in an oil products factory in Changsha, China:

> Before long I knew the routine. Every day we had to report exactly on time, but after that we were on our own. The first item on the agenda was what the workers liked to call "Socialist news"—tales of the neighborhoods where those who didn't live in the factory dormitories had homes. These stories of pickpockets and local scandals usually lasted an hour. After that, we "changed into work clothes," which took another half hour. Then, suddenly, the shop was empty. Some had gone to the clinic for minor medical complaints, some to the outhouse, some to the financial office to get expenses reimbursed. Others worked repairing their bicycles or making things for friends and relatives like locks, coal burners, and iron chairs. A third group gambled for cigarettes behind the big emergency water tanks.
>
> Organization was near perfect. If any factory leaders came to check the shop or look for someone, there was always a sentry to say, "Oh, they were just here. Maybe they went to the stockroom to get some materials." If anyone wanted to know about a repair job that had been approved and stamped by the repair workshop, it was, "Sorry, we're understaffed today," or "Sorry, no materials." Sometimes the same jobs fluttered on the bulletin board for weeks.
>
> By 11 a.m., everyone magically reappeared, and we sat and chatted until 11:30, when the group leader checked us out for lunch and a two-hour nap. In the afternoon the morning's performance was repeated. It added up to a full eight-hour day. (Liang and Shapiro, 1983: 220)

This example should be seen in context. It describes the situation in the mid-1970s, when there was considerable demoralization and cynicism on the shop-floor. In addition, it reflects not just work group control but the inefficiencies of the management and production systems which resulted in vast stretches of time during which there was nothing to do even if the workers wanted to. Nevertheless, when all qualifications are made, the fact is that even in labor surplus communist societies industrial workers have a degree of shop-floor power irrespective of any formal union organization. This is even more true in state socialist societies with permanent labor market shortages.

At a different level, the leaderships of all state socialist societies, except Yugoslavia, have not been able to reintroduce large-scale unemployment, however much this might seem desirable (to the party leaders) as a means to solving the problems of labor discipline, productivity, and turnover. Discussion about weakening the walls of job security has been going on among Soviet economists since at least the 1960s, but very little has actually happened. Similarly, there have been attempts to promote experiments in labor contracts in China but there has been resistance at all levels of Chinese society to "breaking the iron rice bowl" (i.e., the situation of job security) and replacing it with a "mud rice bowl" (Lockett and Littler, 1985). Partly resistance stems from the fact, as Holubenko argues, that social relations in Soviet-type societies are more transparent, such that the reintroduction of job insecurities would be seen as a conscious decision by the ruling group rather than the hidden hand of Adam Smith (Holubenko, 1975: 6−7).

The different labor market and management structures in state socialist societies result in different patterns of social control compared to capitalist societies. In the latter societies, structures of control are largely a consequence of managerial strategies and ideologies but, in contrast, in state socialist societies the structure of control is not a function of managerial strategy, but a consequence of state strategies. For example, decisions to introduce production brigades, workers' congresses, or to start a new discipline campaign are made at the state level. Equally, without the threat of unemployment and the pressures of a reserve army of labor on workers, the relations between the party as the ruling group and the unions become critical. The labor unions become part of the bureaucratic apparatus of control as in Mexico or similar state capitalist societies, but without the underlying pressures of unemployment and underemployment which rack such capitalist economies. This results in an uneasy relation between the notion of trade unions and the state in state socialist economies. These relations typically revolve around a structural contradiction of the necessary mobilization of the mass of workers behind economic policies versus continued party control. A perennial tension is created between the legitimacy of party-linked unions on the one hand and a tendency toward party−union conflicts on the other hand, if union leaders endeavor to expand the scope of their union role in response to rank-and-file demands for effective representation of their interests. Some state socialist societies have "solved" this problem by ensuring that trade unions are ineffective representational organizations—this is particularly true of Czechoslovakia since 1968/9 (see Chapter 4) and Romania (see Chapter 5). Nevertheless, worker demands for some representation cannot be totally ignored, because worker dissatisfaction with conditions and pay may result in apathy, work slowdowns, a retreat to the second economy, or (in the case of Eastern Europe and the Soviet Union), a high labor turnover. China still has a system of job allocation, which is one factor limiting the shop-floor power of Chinese workers and which has served to mark off the Chinese system from other state socialist economies. However, Chinese workers, as we have seen, still retain a *de facto*, shop-floor bargaining power based on an ability to determine labor productivities. Despite the political adventures of the Cultural Revolution and the abolition of the Chinese unions from 1967−1973, even the Chinese leadership has not been willing to abolish the trade unions on a permanent basis (see Chapter 10).

The shadows of the Polish crisis, plus the present economic problems of Soviet-type economies, have created an intensified interest in the contradiction described above, and several East European societies, as well as China, are struggling to work out an acceptable solution. In seeking to solve the contradiction of a union role, there appears to be a recurring policy alternative between allowing more independence to official, national unions as opposed to promoting workers' councils or workers' congresses as a channel for the expression and debate of grievances. The latter policy entails some degree of increased enterprise autonomy within a pattern of economic reforms in order to function meaningfully. The use of enterprise participation in order to defuse grievances is limited by the nature of the centrally planned economy. If all major economic decisions are taken outside of the plant, then there is nothing to participate in. Thus, the political problem of the containment and channeling of worker grievances is tied in with the question of economic reforms in the state socialist societies, not just in a material sense, but in a structural sense.

In conclusion, though there are clear parallels between unionism in state capitalist societies and unions in state socialist societies, and there is a necessity to avoid simplistic analyses, nevertheless the differing political and economic contexts mean that these parallels cannot be theoretically reduced to a single model. The nature and dynamics of social control in state socialist societies are distinctive. Finally, the underlying question of this book—can trade unions defend workers' interests within the context of a Soviet-type system, especially given the de-legitimation of Western trade union methods? —must on present experience receive a negative answer.

References

Cook, A. H. (1966), *An Introduction to Japanese Trade Unionism* (New York: Cornell University Press).
Crouch, C. (1977), *Class Conflict and the Industrial Relations Crisis* (London: Heinemann).
Dore, R. P. (1979), "Industrial Relations in Japan and Elsewhere," in A. M. Craig, (ed.), *Japan: A Comparative View* (Princeton, NJ: Princeton University Press), pp. 324–70.
Edwards, R. (1979), *Contested Terrain* (London: Heinemann).
Hare, P., Radice, H., and Swain, N. (1981), *Hungary: A Decade of Economic Reform* (London: Allen & Unwin).
Holubenko, M. (1975), "The Soviet Working Class: Discontent and Opposition," in *Critique*, no. 4, pp. 5–25.
Hyman, R. (1976), "Trade Unions, Control and Resistance," in *Open University, DE 351*, Unit 14 (Milton Keynes: Open University Press).
Kastendiek, H. (1983), "A General Restructuring of Society? Problems Affecting an Attractive Hypothesis," mimeo, presented to the Cambridge Colloquium on Economic Crisis and the Politics of Industrial Relations.
Liang, H., and Shapiro, J. (1983), *Son of the Revolution* (London: Chatto & Windus).

Littler, C. R. (1982), *The Development of the Labour Process in Capitalist Societies* (London: Heinemann).

Lockett, M., and Littler, C. R. (1985), *Management and Industry in China* (London: Heinemann).

Michels, R. (1959), *Political Parties* (New York: Dover Publications).

Muller-Jentsch, W. (1982), "Trade Unions as Intermediary Organizations," Institut fur Sozialforschung, Frankfurt, mimeo.

Nelson, D. N. (1983), "State Capitalism, State Socialism and the Politicization of Workers," University of Kentucky, mimeo.

Palmer, G. (1983), *British Industrial Relations* (London: Allen & Unwin).

Panitch, C. (1980), "Recent theorizations on corporatism: reflections of a growth industry", *British Journal of Sociology*, vol. 31, no. 2, pp. 159–87.

Schmitter, P., and Lehmbruch, G. (1979), (eds.) *Trends Towards Corporatist Intermediation* , (London: Sage).

Stinchcombe, A. L. (1965), "Social Structure and the Invention of Organizational Forms," in J. G. March, (ed.), *Handbook of Organizations* (Chicago: Rand McNally), pp. 142–69.

Thompson, M. (1983), "The Permanent Employment System: Japan and Mexico," in "Proceedings of the International Industrial Relations Association Association: Sixth World Congress," Vol. 4, Kyoto, mimeo.

TUC (1984), *TUC Strategy* (London: Trades Union Congress, mimeo).

Weber, M. (1947), *The Theory of Social and Economic Organization* (Glencoe, Ill.: The Free Press).

Wedderburn, B. (1982), "Introduction: A 1912 Overture," in W. T. Lord Wedderburn of Charlton & Murphy *Labour Law and the Community: Perspectives for the 1980s* (London: Institute of Advanced Legal Studies, University of London).

Notes on Contributors

Bernard Carter was educated at Bradford University's Postgraduate School of Yugoslav Studies and has written widely on Yugoslav affairs ever since. Among his published work is *The Economy of Yugoslavia*, which Mr. Carter authored with Fred Singleton. He currently is actively engaged in industrial relations in Great Britain.

Tom Keenoy received his Bachelors degree from the University of Strathclyde and his doctorate from the University of Oxford. He presently serves as Lecturer in Industrial Relations at University College, Cardiff, Wales. His current and past research focuses upon the development of industrial relations theory as well as the management of employment relationships in socialist societies.

István Kemény received his PhD equivalent diploma in Political Economy, Philosophy and Pedagogy from Budapest University in 1950. He currently serves as a fellow of the Paris-based École des Hautes Etudes en Sciences Sociales. Prior to arriving in Paris in 1977, Dr. Kemény directed several national survey projects in Hungary. He is the author of well over a dozen academic articles as well as nine books, including *The World of the Csepel Iron and Metal Works, The Workers of Pest County, The Attitudes of Economic Leaders* and *The Gipsy Population in Hungary* (all in Hungarian) as well as a more recent monograph, *Ouvriers Hongois*, which appeared in France in 1985.

Craig R. Littler is Senior Lecturer at the School of Social and Industrial Association, Griffith University, Queensland. He is author of several works in the area of comparative industrial relations, including *The Development of the Labour Process in Capitalist Societies; Class at Work: the Design, Allocation and Control of Jobs* (with Graeme Salaman); *Management and Industry in China* (with Martin Lockett); and, *The Dynamics of Organizations* (with Gill Palmer). He also co-edited *The Experience of Work; Managerial Strategies and Industrial Relations* (with Howard Gospel); and *Industrial Relations and the Law in the 1980s* (with Patricia Fosh). Dr. Littler currently serves as editor of *The Pacific Journal of Labour and Management*.

Daniel N. Nelson is Professor of Political Science at the University of Kentucky. In 1975, he received his PhD in Political Science from The Johns Hopkins University. Dr. Nelson is the author of *Democratic Centralism,* and *Local Politics and Elite-Mass Relations in Communist Systems*. He also has served as editor of and contributor to *Communist Politics: A Reader; Soviet Allies; Communism and the Politics of Inequalities; Local Politics in Communist Countries; Romania in the 1980s;* and, *Communist Legislatures in Comparative Perspective*. His articles have appeared in *World Politics, Comparative Politics, Journal of Politics, Slavic Review, Soviet Studies, Problems of Communism* and elsewhere.

Gill Palmer is Principal Lecturer, Queensland Institute of Technology, Brisbane. She had published previously in the area of industrial relations, including two major works: *British Industrial Relations,* and *The Dynamics of Organization.*

Joseph L. Porket is a British scholar of Czech origin. He took his master's degree at the Prague School of Economics in 1949 and his doctorates at the Charles University in Prague in 1968 and at the University of London in 1973. He specializes in industrial relations, manpower problems, and social policy in Socialist countries. His articles have appeared in such journals as *The British Journal of Industrial Relations, Social Policy and Administration, The Slavonic and East European Review, Osteuropa-Wirtschaft, Aging and Society,* and *Survey.*

Alex Pravda was born in Prague but educated in England and received his doctorate from the University of Oxford. He is Lecturer in Politics at the University of Reading and has held visiting appointments at the University of Michigan and Stanford University. He is author of *Reform and Change in the Czechoslovak Political System, January—August 1968* and co-editor of *Czechoslovakia: The Party and the People*. A contributing author of five volumes on Soviet and East European politics dealing in particular with issues of labour and labor organizations he has also published numerous articles on labor and union-related questions in such journals as *Soviet Studies, Problems of Communism* and *The International Political Science Review*. He is currently completing a comparative study on workers and politics in communist systems.

Blair A. Ruble received his PhD in Political Science from the University of Toronto. He serves as Staff Associate at the Social Science Research Council in New York. Mr. Ruble is author of numerous articles in such journals as *The British Journal of Industrial Relations, Canadian Slavonic Papers, Knowledge, Osteuropa, Problems of Communism, The Russian Review*, and *The Wilson Quarterly*. His monograph *Soviet Trade Unions: Their Development during the 1970s* as well as the co-edited volume *Industrial Labor in the USSR*, which he prepared with Arcadius Kahan, are of direct interest to the readers of this volume. In addition, Mr. Ruble served as an American co-editor for *A Scholar's Guide to Humanities and Social Sciences in the Soviet Union*, a collaborative research project of the American Council of Learned Societies and the USSR Academy of Sciences. He currently is working on a study of urban governance in the city of Leningrad.

Marilyn Rueschemeyer is Assistant Professor of Sociology at the Rhode Island School of Design and adjunct Assistant Professor of Sociology at Brown University. She is affiliated with the Russian Research Center and the Center for European Studies at Harvard University, where she co-chairs a study group on the German Democratic Republic. In 1979 and 1982, Dr. Rueschemeyer was a Senior Associate Member of St. Antony's College, Oxford. She is the author of *Professional Work and Marriage: An East−West Comparison*, and, together with Igor Golomshtok and Janet Kennedy, co-authored *Soviet Emigre Artists: Life and Work in the USSR and The United States*.

C. Bradley Scharf is an Associate Professor of Political Science at Seattle University. He received his Ph.D. from Stanford University in 1974. His articles on comparative social policy as well as the politics of the German Democratic Republic have appeared in leading journals. Dr. Scharf is author of *Politics and Change in East Germany*.

Jeanne L. Wilson is an Assistant Professor of Political Science at Wheaton College in Norton, Massachusetts. Her doctoral dissertation at Indiana University as well as her current research interest focus upon Chinese industrial organization and labor policy.

Index